Lecture Notes in Computer Science 15999

Founding Editors

Gerhard Goos
Juris Hartmanis

AF167583

The series Lecture Notes in Computer Science (LNCS), including its subseries Lecture Notes in Artificial Intelligence (LNAI) and Lecture Notes in Bioinformatics (LNBI), has established itself as a medium for the publication of new developments in computer science and information technology research, teaching, and education.

LNCS enjoys close cooperation with the computer science R & D community, the series counts many renowned academics among its volume editors and paper authors, and collaborates with prestigious societies. Its mission is to serve this international community by providing an invaluable service, mainly focused on the publication of conference and workshop proceedings and postproceedings. LNCS commenced publication in 1973.

Florian Skopik · Vincent Naessens ·
Bjorn De Sutter
Editors

Availability, Reliability and Security

ARES 2025 EU Projects Symposium Workshops
Ghent, Belgium, August 11–14, 2025
Proceedings, Part II

 Springer

Editors
Florian Skopik ⓘ
Austrian Institute of Technology
Vienna, Austria

Vincent Naessens ⓘ
KU Leuven
Ghent, Belgium

Bjorn De Sutter ⓘ
Ghent University
Ghent, Belgium

ISSN 0302-9743   ISSN 1611-3349 (electronic)
Lecture Notes in Computer Science
ISBN 978-3-032-00646-2   ISBN 978-3-032-00644-8 (eBook)
https://doi.org/10.1007/978-3-032-00644-8

ARES EU Symposium Workshops 2025 Foreword

Alongside the main track of the 20th International Conference on Availability, Reliability and Security (ARES), the EU Projects Symposium hosted a total of nine workshops. These workshops collectively received 92 paper submissions, of which 41 were accepted for publication and presentation at ARES 2025. All submissions that were not desk-rejected underwent a rigorous double-blind peer-review process, with each receiving a minimum of three independent reviews by members of the respective technical program committees (TPCs). In cases where conflicts of interest with the workshop organizers arose, the ARES organizing committee took responsibility for assigning alternative reviewers and managing the final decision process to ensure impartiality and fairness.

As the chairs of the EU Symposium workshops, we are pleased to see how these workshops have been shaped into vibrant platforms for focused discussion and dynamic exchange, reflecting the breadth and depth of ongoing research in numerous EU-funded projects. The diversity of topics and the engagement of participants contribute meaningfully to the overarching goals of the ARES conference and highlight the importance of continued collaboration across disciplines and institutions.

We would like to take this opportunity to express our sincere gratitude to all the workshop organizers for their dedication and commitment—from proposal submission through to review coordination and final session delivery. Organizing a workshop is no small task, and your efforts have been essential to the success of this year's program. A special word of appreciation goes to the TPC members, who, often under significant time pressure, provided thoughtful, thorough, and constructive reviews. Your contributions—regardless of whether a paper was ultimately accepted or not—have helped authors improve their work and ensured that the proceedings uphold the high standards that the ARES community expects. Your efforts play a crucial role in maintaining the academic rigor and vitality of both the workshops and the wider ARES conference community.

August 2025

Florian Skopik
Vincent Naessens
Bjorn De Sutter

ARES EU Symposium Workshops 2025 Organization

General Chair

Bjorn De Sutter   Ghent University, Belgium

General Workshop Chair

Florian Skopik   Austrian Institute of Technology, Austria

Proceedings Chairs

Vincent Naessens   KU Leuven, Belgium
Michiel Willocx   KU Leuven, Belgium

Workshop Chairs

Aggeliki Panou	University of Piraeus, Greece
Aida Akbarzadeh	Norwegian University of Science and Technology, Norway
Apostolis Zarras	Foundation for Research & Technology, Greece
Aristeidis Farao	InQbit Innovations SRL, Romania
Christos Xenakis	University of Piraeus, Greece
Wissam Mallouli	Montimage, France
Edgaro Montes de Oca	Montimage, France
Gautam Srivastava	Brandon University, Canada
Georgios Kavallieratos	University of Oslo, Norway
Georgios Spathoulas	Norwegian University of Science and Technology, Norway
Giuseppe Bianchi	Consorzio Nazionale Interuniversitario per le Telecomunicazioni, Italy
Ilsun You	Kookmin University, South Korea
Jan Hajny	Brno University of Technology, Czech Republic
Jesús García Rodríguez	University of Murcia, Spain
Krzysztof Cabaj	Warsaw University of Technology, Poland
Lukas Malina	Brno University of Technology, Czech Republic

ETACS 2025 Preface

This volume is the proceedings of the 5th Workshop on Education, Training and Awareness in CyberSecurity (ETACS) that was held in conjunction with ARES 2025 in Ghent, Belgium in August 2025. ETACS seeks novel submissions from academia, government as well as industry contributing to cybersecurity education, training and awareness. The focus is on practical research into higher-education cybersecurity curricula, professional training, building of cyber ranges and their coalitions across Europe, methods to assess and raise awareness in cybersecurity, the implementation of systems, and lessons learned. Furthermore, the EU-wide agreement on the identification of skills necessary for cybersecurity work roles is one of the main interests of the workshop. The event aims to gather people from universities, professional training institutions, industry, government and EU agencies to discuss current problems and solutions for cybersecurity education and training.

The papers in this proceedings were selected by a peer review process, where each paper was reviewed by at least 3 reviewers in a double-blind review. A total of 15 reviewers were involved in the review process. We very much appreciate their contribution and commitment. All chairs and program committee members with conflicts of interest were excluded from the review process, including reviewer assignments, reviews and decisions. Chairs were not involved in the reviews. 14 papers were submitted to ETACS 2025 and 7 papers were accepted. All accepted papers had positive weighted average scores, thus suggested for acceptance by the review process.

The workshop is supported by the European Union under Grant Agreement No. 101087529 CHESS and the Ministry of the Interior of the Czech Republic under grant VJ03030003 under program IMPAKT 1. Note that views and opinions expressed are however those of the author(s) only and do not necessarily reflect those of the European Union or the European Research Executive Agency. Neither the European Union nor the granting authority can be held responsible for them.

May 2025

Jan Hajny
Giuseppe Bianchi
Pavel Loutocky
Rocco De Nicola
Sara Ricci

ETACS 2025 Organization

Workshop Chairs

Jan Hajny	Brno University of Technology, Czech Republic
Giuseppe Bianchi	Consorzio Nazionale Interuniversitario per le Telecomunicazioni, Italy
Pavel Loutocky	Masaryk University, Czech Republic
Rocco De Nicola	IMT School for Advanced Studies Lucca, Italy
Sara Ricci	Brno University of Technology, Czech Republic

Program Committee

Pedro Adao	Universidade de Lisboa, Portugal
Yianna Danidou	European University Cyprus, Cyprus
Petr Dzurenda	Brno University of Technology, Czechia
Letterio Galletta	IMT Lucca, Italy
Magdalena Glas	University of Regensburg, Germany
Frantisek Kasl	Masaryk University, Czechia
Imre Lendak	University of Novi Sad, RS & Eötvös Loránd University, Hungary
Olivier Levillain	Télécom SudParis, France
Francesco Mancini	CNIT/University of Rome "Tor Vergata"
Marc Ohm	University of Bonn & Fraunhofer FKIE, Germany
Edmundas Piesarskas	Lithuanian Cybercrime Center of Excellence for Training, Research & Education, Lithuania
Paolo Prinetto	Cybersecurity National Laboratory, Italy
Joseph Squillace	Pennsylvania State University, USA
Kendra Walther	University of Southern California, USA
Tanja Zseby	Vienna University of Technology, Austria

STAM 2025 Preface

Security testing and monitoring are essential disciplines for ensuring the resilience and reliability of distributed systems, which form the backbone of modern society. From telecommunication networks to cloud computing, industrial systems, smart communities, and the Internet of Things, these systems operate in increasingly open and interconnected environments. This openness, while enabling greater interoperation, also exposes systems to a range of vulnerabilities and malicious activities that must be addressed comprehensively.

The workshop focuses on frameworks, methodologies, and tools designed to enhance security in distributed environments. It explores how modeling misbehaviors and attacks deepens our understanding of malicious activities and contributes to their prevention. Discussions also center on the limitations of existing models and approaches, shedding light on potential advancements to overcome these challenges. A key theme of the workshop is addressing the complexity of security testing and monitoring in distributed systems. The dynamic nature of these systems, coupled with the integration of artificial intelligence, poses new challenges that demand innovative solutions. Participants examine how testing and monitoring strategies can adapt to these complexities to ensure system robustness and integrity. In addition to presenting scientific research, the workshop provides practical insights through interactive training activities. These activities offer participants the opportunity to engage with real-world security scenarios, apply advanced testing techniques, and gain hands-on experience with monitoring tools tailored for distributed systems. By fostering a collaborative environment, STAM 2025 advances the field of security testing and monitoring while equipping participants with the knowledge and skills to address the emerging threats of tomorrow's interconnected systems.

STAM 2025 brings together cybersecurity practitioners and researchers to exchange ideas and perspectives on challenges and solutions in the field. It welcomes novel contributions on models, methods, algorithms, and real-world applications. Topics of interest include risk assessment frameworks for complex systems; trust and privacy assessment in distributed and critical environments; techniques for modeling vulnerabilities, threats, and attacks; security testing and monitoring methods and tools; automation for testing and monitoring in distributed environments; evaluation of resilience and tolerance to attacks in critical systems; integration of CI/CD practices; AI and machine learning for cybersecurity; industrial experience reports; training activities to raise awareness; and practical demonstrations of tools and frameworks for securing distributed systems.

August 2025

Valentina Casola
Wissam Mallouli

STAM 2025 Organization

Workshop Chairs

Valentina Casola	University of Naples Federico II, Italy
Wissam Mallouli	Montimage, France

Program Committee

Valentina Casola	University of Naples Federico II, Italy
Ana Rosa Cavalli	Institut Polytechnique de Paris/Telecom SudParis, France
Alessandra De Benedictis	University of Naples Federico II, Italy
Nicolas Ferry	University Côte d'Azur, France
Gürkan Gür	Zurich University of Applied Sciences, Switzerland
Ole Höfener	Massive Dynamic Sweden, Sweden
Eider Iturbe	Tecnalia, Spain
Charalambos Klitis	EBOS Technologies, Cyprus
Wissam Mallouli	Montimage, France
Stefan Marksteiner	AVL List Gmbh, Austria
Edgardo Montes de Oca	Montimage, France
Phu Nguyen	SINTEF, Norway
Andrea Pferscher	University of Oslo, Norway
Panagiotis Grammatikis	University of Western Macedonia, Greece
Erkuden Rios	Tecnalia, Spain
Martin Schneider	Fraunhofer FOKUS, Germany
Cristina Seceleanu	Mälardalen University, Sweden
Hui Song	SINTEF, Norway
Dragos Truscan	Åbo Akademi University, Finland
Fatiha Zaidi	Université Paris-Sud, France

ENS 2025 Preface

It is our great pleasure to introduce research papers presented at the 8th International Workshop on Emerging Network Security (ENS 2025), co-located with the 20th International Conference on Availability, Reliability, and Security (ARES 2025). The conference was held in Ghent, Belgium during August 11–14, 2025.

The ENS 2025 workshop focused on the evolving field of network security for 5G, beyond 5G, and emerging 6G systems, addressing the challenges posed by increasingly complex and high-capacity communication networks. It aimed to bring together researchers, industry experts, and practitioners to explore secure architectures, protocols, and technologies that ensure privacy, trust, and data protection in advanced networks incorporating concepts like SDN, NFV, IoT, AI, and cloud computing. Building on the success of previous 5G-NS workshops, ENS 2025 also sought to foster collaboration across communities, particularly between the 5G and AI sectors, to fully realize the potential of next-generation communication infrastructures.

This year ENS received 10 submissions, of which 50% were accepted. Each paper was peer-reviewed by our experts from the Technical Program Committee (TPC) and, on average, received 3.5 reviews. This year, our TPC consisted of fifteen experts from eight countries around the world (China, France, Finland, Greece, Italy, Poland, the UK, and the USA). The whole review process was conducted using double-blind methodology, and assisted by five Workshop Chairs.

August 2025

Pascal Bisson
Krzysztof Cabaj
Wojciech Mazurczyk
Edgaro Montes de Oca
Ilsun You

ENS 2025 Organization

Workshop Chairs

Pascal Bisson	Thales, France
Krzysztof Cabaj	Warsaw University of Technology, Poland
Wojciech Mazurczyk	Warsaw University of Technology, Poland
Edgaro Montes de Oca	Montimage, France
Ilsun You	Kookmin University, South Korea

Program Committee

Chafika Benzaid	University of Oulu, Finland
Grzegorz Blinowski	Warsaw University of Technology, Poland
Daniele Bringhenti	Politecnico di Torino, Italy
Luca Caviglione	Institute for Applied Mathematics and Information Technologies CNR, Italy
Michał Choraś	ITTI Ltd, Poland
Gilles Guett	Institut Mines-Télécom Atlantique, France
Georgios Karopoulos	Joint Research Centre, Greece
Zbigniew Kotulski	Warsaw University of Technology, Poland
Sławomir Kukliński	Warsaw University of Technology, Poland
Amitabh Mishra	University of Delaware, USA
Paweł Rajba	University of Wroclaw, Poland
Leonardo Regano	Università degli Studi di Cagliari, Italy
Stavros Shiaeles	University of Portsmouth, UK
Jani Suomalainen	VTT Technical Research Centre of Finland, Finland
Hui Tian	National Huaqiao University, China

Contents – Part II

**Proceedings of the Eighth International Workshop on Emerging
Network Security (ENS 2025)**

Contents – Part I

Proceedings of the Sixth Workshop on Security, Privacy, and Identity Management in the Cloud (SECPID 2025)

Proceedings of the First International Workshop on Secure, Trustworthy, and Robust AI (STRAI 2025)

Proceedings of the Fifth International Workshop on Security and Privacy in Intelligent Infrastructures (SP2I 2025)

Proceedings of the Fifth Workshop on Education, Training and Awareness in Cybersecurity (ETACS 2025)

ETACS 2025 Preface

This volume is the proceedings of the 5th Workshop on Education, Training and Awareness in CyberSecurity (ETACS) that was held in conjunction with ARES 2025 in Ghent, Belgium in August 2025. ETACS seeks novel submissions from academia, government as well as industry contributing to cybersecurity education, training and awareness. The focus is on practical research into higher-education cybersecurity curricula, professional training, building of cyber ranges and their coalitions across Europe, methods to assess and raise awareness in cybersecurity, the implementation of systems, and lessons learned. Furthermore, the EU-wide agreement on the identification of skills necessary for cybersecurity work roles is one of the main interests of the workshop. The event aims to gather people from universities, professional training institutions, industry, government and EU agencies to discuss current problems and solutions for cybersecurity education and training.

The papers in this proceedings were selected by a peer review process, where each paper was reviewed by at least 3 reviewers in a double-blind review. A total of 15 reviewers were involved in the review process. We very much appreciate their contribution and commitment. All chairs and program committee members with conflicts of interest were excluded from the review process, including reviewer assignments, reviews and decisions. Chairs were not involved in the reviews. 14 papers were submitted to ETACS 2025 and 7 papers were accepted. All accepted papers had positive weighted average scores, thus suggested for acceptance by the review process.

The workshop is supported by the European Union under Grant Agreement No. 101087529 CHESS and the Ministry of the Interior of the Czech Republic under grant VJ03030003 under program IMPAKT 1. Note that views and opinions expressed are however those of the author(s) only and do not necessarily reflect those of the European Union or the European Research Executive Agency. Neither the European Union nor the granting authority can be held responsible for them.

May 2025

Jan Hajny
Giuseppe Bianchi
Pavel Loutocky
Rocco De Nicola
Sara Ricci

ETACS 2025 Organization

Workshop Chairs

Jan Hajny	Brno University of Technology, Czech Republic
Giuseppe Bianchi	Consorzio Nazionale Interuniversitario per le Telecomunicazioni, Italy
Pavel Loutocky	Masaryk University, Czech Republic
Rocco De Nicola	IMT School for Advanced Studies Lucca, Italy
Sara Ricci	Brno University of Technology, Czech Republic

Program Committee

Pedro Adao	Universidade de Lisboa, Portugal
Yianna Danidou	European University Cyprus, Cyprus
Petr Dzurenda	Brno University of Technology, Czechia
Letterio Galletta	IMT Lucca, Italy
Magdalena Glas	University of Regensburg, Germany
Frantisek Kasl	Masaryk University, Czechia
Imre Lendak	University of Novi Sad, RS & Eötvös Loránd University, Hungary
Olivier Levillain	Télécom SudParis, France
Francesco Mancini	CNIT/University of Rome "Tor Vergata"
Marc Ohm	University of Bonn & Fraunhofer FKIE, Germany
Edmundas Piesarskas	Lithuanian Cybercrime Center of Excellence for Training, Research & Education, Lithuania
Paolo Prinetto	Cybersecurity National Laboratory, Italy
Joseph Squillace	Pennsylvania State University, USA
Kendra Walther	University of Southern California, USA
Tanja Zseby	Vienna University of Technology, Austria

WalkthroughCyber: Teaching Cyber-Awareness in Montessori Middle Schools

Margherita Renieri[1]([✉]) [iD], Alessandra Renieri[2] [iD], and Letterio Galletta[1] [iD]

[1] IMT School for Advanced Studies Lucca, Lucca, Italy
{margherita.renieri,letterio.galletta}@imtlucca.it
[2] I. C. "Paolo Soprani", Castelfidardo, Italy
alessandra.renieri@icsoprani.edu.it

Abstract. Adolescents today are growing up in a hyper-connected digital environment, so it is essential to educate them on responsible technology use. While the importance of cyber-awareness education is widely recognized, there is a lack of effective teaching methodologies. This paper presents a pilot study aimed at designing a cyber-awareness teaching approach tailored to Montessori middle schools. The proposed methodology was implemented in a course delivered to two Italian classes. The course lasts approximately ten hours and is divided into six didactic units covering key cybersecurity topics. It combines participatory lectures that encourage active discussion with practical, game-based activities designed to enhance engagement and reinforce learning.

Keywords: Cybersecurity Education · Game-Based Learning · Gamification · Adolescent Education

1 Introduction

Over the last decades, the digital revolution has deeply transformed our society, habits, and values. The pervasiveness of the Internet is so widespread in our daily experience that the new concept of *onlife* [10] has been coined to denote an environment where the differences between real and virtual are blurred. This emerging notion of *onlife* changes the social rules that regulate privacy, personal freedom, and interpersonal relationships.

Adolescents are digital natives [28] because they have never known a world without the Internet and are growing up in a media-convergent environment [1]. This environment exposes them to both the opportunities and the risks of a hybrid digital-physical reality. To protect them from the negative effects, they must be educated to develop the awareness and critical thinking required to safely live their *onlife*.

Over the last few years, international lawmakers have focused on this topic, and remarkable progress has been made. In Italy, the law recognizes adolescents as a vulnerable social group whose education is crucial to growing responsible

F. Skopik et al. (Eds.): ARES 2025 Workshops, LNCS 15999, pp. 5–22, 2025.
https://doi.org/10.1007/978-3-032-00644-8_1

and active citizens. For this reason, *Law n.92/2019* [30] introduced the topic of *civic education* in schools of all levels with a particular emphasis on middle school. This is a cross-cutting topic that aims to teach society's basic social, economic, legal, civic, and environmental structures. The *Article 5* of the Law [30] is dedicated to the *digital citizenship education*. It points out that civic education must include a module on cyber-awareness to teach students the digital knowledge and skills required by a connected society, depending on their age and background. In particular, they must learn how to use digital technologies responsibly and appropriately, avoiding potential risks that can affect their physical and psychological well-being.

Although the Law [30] recognizes the importance of cyber-awareness as a subject, a methodological gap exists in teaching this subject properly in schools. This issue does not concern only Italy, but the international community of educators and technical experts considers devising an effective methodology for cyber-education in schools an open question [15,19,27,31]. This paper presents the results of a pilot study aimed at developing a didactic methodology for teaching cybersecurity awareness in middle schools, a demographic often underrepresented in existing initiatives. The training, delivered at the *Comprehensive Institute* (C.I.) *"Paolo Soprani" of Castelfidardo*, follows Montessori principles and consists of six units covering key cybersecurity topics. A qualified educator conducts the course and combines participatory lectures with hands-on, game-based activities to foster reflection and conceptual understanding. The assessments of pre- and post-questionnaires for students and families supported content customization and evaluation of the program's effectiveness.

Structure of the paper. Sect. 2 presents educational paradigms and methodologies, while Sect. 3 describes the participants, the learning environment, and the course structure, including topics, activities, and learning objectives. In Sect. 4, we present the results of the pre- and post-questionnaires answered by students and their families, assessing the effectiveness of our training. Section 5 positions our work within the existing literature, and Sect. 6 concludes the paper and outlines directions for future research.

2   Background

2.1   Education Paradigms

Over the last few years, the digital revolution has affected learning and pedagogical methodologies, producing a constant evolution of different education paradigms [12]. The first one, called Education 1.0, considers students as containers to be filled with knowledge provided by the teacher through frontal lectures. Education 2.0 diverges from the previous paradigm and introduces a *"student-centered"* view where students are allowed to acquire knowledge and skills by engaging in projects around problems they may face in the real world. Projects may involve the use of technological tools that have become relevant to the learning process. Education 3.0 puts forward the idea that students are the creators of their own knowledge and promote *"educational opportunities where social networking and social benefits outside the immediate scope of activity play a strong role"* [18]. This can be performed through Game-Based Learning methods that bring experiences of playing games into an educational context. One of these methods is *gamification* that introduces *"gaming mechanics to non-gaming contexts for raising levels of involvement and motivation."* [32]. An effective gamification activity is characterized by a strong narrative component, a good balance between the educational and gaming aspects, and the ability to transfer the acquired skills to the real world. Education 4.0 is the current evolution of the education paradigms that encourages students to learn in an immersive game-based context by using tools such as IoT, virtual reality, and augmented reality.

2.2   Montessori's Method

"Education is a natural process that child performs by himself making different experiences within the environment."

(M. Montessori) [23]

Dr. M. Montessori developed her method of education starting from a scientific observation of how children learn from their environment, often working with their hands, performing the same task repeatedly until they reach satisfaction. Thus, it is important to prepare the environment, develop appropriate *"sensorial materials"*, follow the child, and understand its potential.

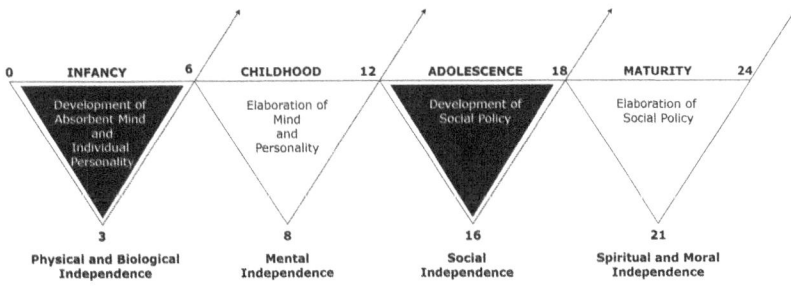

Fig. 1. Montessori's Four Planes of Development [14].

It is important to know that the development of a human being follows four planes or stages (see Fig. 1). During the first one (birth to 6 years), the child is considered to have an *"absorbent mind"* and brings to consciousness what was unconscious through movement. Children develop intelligent hands under the direction of their minds and then they *"create"* their language. In the second plane (6 to 12 years), the child has a *"reasoning mind"*, asking why, how, and when. This is the stage of *"imagination"* and of *"justice"*. The third plane (12 to 18 years), likewise the first one, is a time when knowledge is organized through experiences. Adolescents focus their idealistic interest in humanity and their vocation. The last plane (18 to 24 years) allows for the finalization of the development. We will focus our attention on the third plane. Adolescents need to find reference points, balancing adult expectations and behavior with their hormone expectations and behaviors, within the Society's structure. They need to work and act for their developmental plane, in order to create themselves. Cooperating with peers or adults allows them to understand the concept of human collaboration, but also the meaning of *"work"* and its importance. They need to work with their whole bodies, learning and practicing skills needed as adults. Very often, the actions are carried out as *"imitations"* of others; thus, we understand how important it is for adolescents to understand others' perceptions of their self-image. Adolescents acquire meta-cognition: they start to understand how they think and what others' perspectives are. For adolescents, this kind of communication is a way to express emotions, connect with others, test perspectives, and feel how much their voices are heard. Talking with peers and adults leads to self-awareness. Montessori wrote [24] that the best setting to meet all the needs of adolescents is a *"working farm"*, away from parents and cultural obstacles: the *"prepared environment"*, the structured program supports the free development of the individual personality and the experience of a genuine social organization creating a microcosm society. To design a Montessori curriculum for adolescents in an Italian public urban setting, we need to keep in mind all the adolescents' needs and fit them with the Ministry's required needs. First and foremost, implementation requires us to choose a place that accommodates the transmutation experienced by the adolescent from *"social infant"* to *"social man"*. Kahn [17] introduces the concept of *Pedagogy of Place*. Here, learning is experiential and knowledge is well-rounded (holistic). It should facilitate true and meaningful work, the ability to make free choices, and the ability to self-assess and self-determine peacefully. Disciplines are tools for development, but they are never the cause of fragmented knowledge: they must aggregate, offering a cosmic education. The teacher gives up their *"central, cathedratic power."* Instead, adolescents are placed in the center. The teacher is involved in organizing and observing the psychic and cultural life of adolescents. They must inspire with an early enthusiasm for learning and present culture in a meaningful and elevated way and they must develop and train the technique of freedom [25].

2.3 Technology in Montessori Education

The diffusion of *Information and Communication Technologies* (ICTs) has affected the main education methodology. The inclusive Montessori learning methods make them more open to innovation than the mainstream ones [20], but the effects of any variation to the base methodology should be empirically tested before being used with students. Taking into account the use of technological tools, Dr. M. Montessori understood that the introduction of *"mechanical aids will become a general necessity in the schools of the future. [...] However, I would like to underline that these aids will become not be sufficient to achieve the totality of education"* [22]. So, according to her, technology would become a supplementary learning tool. In this regard, Valle [35] points out that ICTs tools can be used for educational purposes but *"it is necessary to try and study them but above all to observe the use that children make of them. Only at this point, if the specific technology proves to be up to the task, we can use it in the same way as the other development materials"*. The same theory has been analyzed by MacDonald [21] that highlights that digital devices could be used as tools for *"the self-construction of knowledge and the search for knowledge in general"* from primary schools. Consequently, Eteokleous [6] introduces a new approach defined as *"learning with computers"* where students use technology to generate new meaning in constructivist or socio-constructivist ways.

3   *WalkthroughCyber*

WalkthroughCyber (WtC) is an initiative developed as part of the civic education program at the C.I. "Soprani", located in the province of Ancona (Italy). The initiative aims to develop students' technical competencies while encouraging mindful, responsible, and ethical engagement with digital technologies. Inspired by *place-based education*, it encourages family involvement through questionnaires and classroom discussions, linking digital culture with everyday life. Consistent with Montessori's idea of the *"prepared environment,"* the course offers structured materials to support student autonomy and guide teachers in facilitating exploratory, goal-oriented learning. The approach also incorporates game-based activities to encourage active participation and engagement.

3.1   Students and Learning Environment

The attendees of WtC are 7th and 8th-grade students from the C.I. "Soprani". The school is among twenty-four institutes authorized by the Italian Superior Council of Public Education through the *n. 237 M.D. (07/30/21)*, [5] to experiment with a Montessori-inspired secondary school model.

The 7th-grade class includes 26 students (21 girls, 5 boys), with three students diagnosed with learning disorders and one supported by a special education teacher. The 8th-grade class has 27 students (11 girls, 16 boys), including two with learning disorders and three with additional support. Students are aged between twelve and fourteen and are familiar with digital tools through previous experiences in coding, robotics, and ICT-related activities.

The learning environment follows Montessori principles. Each classroom is equipped with digital boards, tablets, and notebooks, integrated into daily learning.

3.2   Course Organization

The course consists of ten curricular hours across six units on networking and cybersecurity, designed in line with European Union Agency for Cybersecurity

(ENISA) guidelines [8]. It also draws on insights from the European Cybersecurity Month campaign [7], concerning key digital risks commonly faced by
teenagers. Each unit is delivered through a two-hour interactive session that
combines a focused theoretical introduction with practical, hands-on activities, promoting both engagement and experiential learning. The methodology
integrates *participatory frontal lessons* with student-centered strategies to foster engagement, critical thinking, and collaborative learning. Brainstorming sessions surfaced misconceptions and prior knowledge, encouraging open dialogue
about digital risks. The program was designed as an extended *"real-world task"*,[1]
promoting digital skills, network tool use, and autonomous information management. Typical activities were framed within the principles of digital ethics
and responsible behavior, while collaborative projects fostered peer learning and
actively promoted the dissemination of responsible digital practices throughout
the school community. Practical tasks were organized as group-based games and
active learning exercises, aimed at fostering collective awareness. Each group
produced artifacts documenting learning progress and enriched the course port-
folio. Although the course emphasized group work, it also respected individual
learning paths, consistent with Montessori's approach. Personal reflection and
self-evaluation moments were included to help students consolidate their knowledge and provide feedback on their learning experience.

3.3   Didactic Units Analysis

We provide an overview of each didactic unit, highlighting the knowledge and
skills acquired by students. All activities were conducted in Italian, students'
native language. Table 1 summarizes the theoretical and practical outcomes
across the units. Consistent with Montessori principles, students were also
encouraged to further explore these topics during their free-working time or
at home.[2]

   U1 - Network. The first unit introduced students to the fundamental concepts of computer networking, presenting how networks operate and the role of
protocols. The lesson was structured as a dialogic session and enhanced with
multimedia content such as a short educational video that traced the history of
the Internet. Students applied these concepts through two main activities: developing a timeline to map the key milestones in the evolution of computer networks
and performing an IP discovery exercise on their personal devices. These experiences supported their ability to extract and structure technical information,
encouraged reflection on technological developments, and helped bridge theoretical learning with practical, real-world application.

   U2 - Cryptography. The second unit focused on the principles of data security and the historical use of encryption. Students were introduced to two classical encryption methods: the Caesar Cipher and the Vigenère Table. Working in

---

[1] This task engages students in solving complex, practical problems by applying previously acquired knowledge and skills in real-life contexts.
[2] Each class schedule includes a designated amount of free-working time.

Table 1. Overview of the knowledge and abilities acquired after each unit.

Unit	Knowledge	Ability
U1 - Network	Basics of networking; how networks and protocols work	Retrieve technical info; configure personal devices
U2 - Cryptography	Fundamentals of cryptographic theory; cipher comparison	Encode/decode messages using a key
U3 - Online Services	Digital identity and privacy; secure cloud tool usage; online communication	Set up accounts; use Google Suite; manage email appropriately
U4 - Social Networks	Online self-presentation principles	Use platforms effectively; identify reliable sources
U5 - Cyber-risks	Vulnerabilities, threats, data protection, and defense strategies	Evaluate online content; manage personal data responsibly
U6 - Netiquette	Norms for appropriate digital interaction	Define online behavior rules

small groups, they created their encryption tables and applied them to decode secret messages. The main activity is decrypting messages that allowed students to simulate real-world cryptographic practices, enhancing their problem-solving skills and reinforcing their understanding of how basic algorithms can secure communication across historical and contemporary contexts.

U3 - Online Services. The third unit addressed the secure usage of online services. In a hands-on laboratory session using school tablets, students explored how to use online services via web browsers such as Gmail and Google Suite tools. The focus was not only on using these applications but also on managing sensitive data responsibly when navigating online. To consolidate this knowledge, each student composed emails, demonstrating the correct use of recipient fields (To, CC, BCC), subject lines, and message bodies for different audiences (e.g., friend, teacher, parent). This activity emphasized communication skills and helped students practice safe and proper digital correspondence.

U4 - Social Networks. The fourth unit examined the responsible use of social media applications. After reviewing topics covered in prior units (such as online safety, email use, and encryption), students were asked to create a digital product: an Instagram post, a short TikTok video, or a reel. This creative task allowed students to express their understanding in a familiar digital format, reflecting on ethical content creation and considering the implications of sharing information online. The activity encouraged awareness of digital footprints and audience-appropriate messaging.

U5 - Cyber-risks. In the fifth unit, students focused on recognizing and responding to online threats. They identified various cyber-risks through a collaborative brainstorming session, including phishing, malware, and social engineering. Each group was then assigned specific terms to define and illustrate through a *memory-style game of cyber-concepts*. This engaging activity supported the acquisition of technical vocabulary and equipped students with the skills to identify and respond to online threats, fostering awareness of digital self-protection.

U6 - Netiquette. The final unit addressed digital etiquette and community rules for online behavior. In a *circle-time*[3] discussion, students shared ideas about what it means to be respectful and safe online, both at school and at home. Using Google Docs collaboratively, each group contributed to drafting a shared *Decalogue* comprising ten best practices for digital behavior in the spirit of those on *cyber hygiene* by the ENISA [9]. The final document resulted from active negotiation and shared values, helping students solidify their understanding of responsible digital citizenship.

3.4   Post-Training Games

As a final assignment conducted months after the course, students collaboratively designed educational games on cybersecurity topics, allowing evaluation of long-term knowledge retention and real-world understanding. The games featured a cyberbullying-themed crossword puzzle, interactive role-play exercises simulating cyber attacks, and a cybersecurity board game modeled on Snakes and Ladders. The diversity of topics chosen for these games demonstrated that students had engaged with and internalized various aspects of the course content. The process of turning learned concepts into game mechanics demonstrated not only their comprehension but also their capacity to apply knowledge as a concrete skill. Those materials served as a tangible indicator of learning and can be used to raise awareness among their peers.

4   Assessment Results and Evidence

This section presents the assessment results, focusing on students' learning outcomes and their awareness of digital culture and online safety. Based on pre- and post-activity questionnaires for students and families, the evaluation aimed to measure the program's effectiveness. Involving families provided a broader view of the participants' digital environment and allowed for comparing cyber-awareness across generations. The questionnaire was designed to collect both personal and technical information and to assess knowledge changes throughout the training. The assessment addresses the following research questions:

RQ1: What are the natural sense and perception of cyber-risk of students?
RQ2: What is the family awareness of cyber-risks?
RQ3: Did participants share the cybersecurity knowledge and skills acquired during the course with their family?
RQ4: Did WalkthroughCyber improve participants' cyber-awareness, technical knowledge and skills?

---

[3] It is a structured strategy that fosters open dialogue, collaboration, and active student engagement in addressing shared concerns.

4.1 Pre-Activity Questionnaires Structure

The pre-activity questionnaires assessed digital habits, initial cybersecurity awareness, and general attitudes toward technology use at home and school. They are composed of the following sets of questions:

1. **Rating scale questions** (5 for students, 5 for families) to evaluate the level of digital knowledge. Examples: "*How many hours do you use your internet-connected device during the weekend?*" (students) and "*How many digital devices do you and your family use at home?*" (families).
2. **Yes/No questions** (2 for students, 5 for families) to identify participants' conditions and practices. Examples: "*Do you share your device with another family member?*" (students) and "*Have you set up any parental controls on the apps your child uses?*" (families)
3. **Open-ended questions** (1 for students, 2 for families) to gather opinions and beliefs. Example: "*Name three online risks you believe are the most common or harmful.*" (for both students and families).
4. **Multiple-choice questions** (2 for students, 1 for families) to collect detailed information on digital habits and views on cybersecurity education. Examples: "*Which social media platforms do you use regularly?*"(students) and "*In your opinion, who should be responsible for teaching children about cybersecurity?*"(families).

Below, we present the pre-activity questionnaire results, first focusing on students' responses, followed by their families' ones. Students reported using an average of 2.43 devices, with 83% sharing them with someone else, typically with an adult: 35.8% share devices with their parents, 30.2% with both parents and siblings, and 7.5% with siblings and other relatives, such as grandparents, aunts, and uncles.

Table 2. Students' perceptions of device and Internet use (5-point Likert scale): **TD** = Totally Disagree, **D** = Disagree, **N** = Neutral, **A** = Agree, **TA** = Totally Agree.

Perception	TD	D	N	A	TA
Fun	1.9%	17.0%	32.1%	35.8%	13.2%
Boredom	18.9%	50.9%	24.5%	5.7%	0%
Safety	5.7%	15.1%	49.1%	26.4%	3.8%
Self-confidence/Awareness	0%	13.2%	34.0%	24.5%	28.3%

Table 2 shows that students consider the Internet a positive experience where they can have fun without getting bored. According to them, the Internet is where they feel safe and feel good in a moderate way 30.2% and 52.8%,[4] respectively. They spend, on average, 1.59 hours per day surfing the Web for entertainment on weekdays and 2.07 hours on weekends. In addition, they claim to use

---

[4] These data represent the combined total of the A and TA responses. In this case, the values correspond to $(26.4 + 3.8)$ and $(24.5 + 28.3)$, respectively.

more than one social network, allowing them to face different social experiences on at least two different devices. In more detail, 94% of the students (50 out of 53) have a WhatsApp account, 55% use TikTok, 53% have an Instagram profile, 38% use Snapchat, and 34% have a BeReal account. Thus, they use different *virtual* places to meet each other using different technological tools.

Table 3. Families' perceptions of their child's use of devices and the Internet (5-point Likert scale): **TD** = Totally Disagree, **D** = Disagree, **N** = Neutral, **A** = Agree, **TA** = Totally Agree.

Perception	TD	D	N	A	TA
Calm	5.7%	5.7%	64.2%	22.6%	0%
Disagreement	9.4%	37.7%	41.5%	7.5%	1.9%
Concern/Fear	7.5%	13.2%	52.8%	20.8%	3.8%
Child's Confidence/Awareness	0%	3.8%	30.2%	49.1%	15.1%

Table 3 shows that 52.8% of families are neutral about concerns over their children's digital device use, while 24.6% express agreement or strong agreement. However, 64.2%report trusting their children's digital awareness.[5] However, the survey also reveals that families perceive a certain degree of insecurity regarding their children's online activities. To further explore the meaning of *risk* from the families' perspective, the survey included an open-ended linguistic question asking for synonyms of the term. Approximately half of the participants equated *risk* with *danger*, while the next most common answers were *fraud* (about 9.43%) and *crime* (about 5.7%).

Family answered that 62% impose some rules associated with responsible and secure online behavior. To verify children's awareness of these family rules, we ask students the same question. We find out that just 26% of them are aware of the presence of the family guidelines. This result highlights that adults should properly define their guidelines and clearly communicate them to their children to make them effective. Finally, families were asked to identify who should educate children about cybersecurity topics. About 51% of respondents considered the family primarily responsible for this role. In addition, our results show that adolescents and adults develop specific attitudes that make them vulnerable to different online safety threats.

Figure 2 illustrates the main threats identified by students and families in their responses to the open-ended question on the definition of *cyber-risk*. The results reveal differing perceptions between generations and a generally fragmented understanding of cybersecurity issues across both groups.

Among the 53 responses, students predominantly emphasized direct and visible threats such as *cyberbullying* (22 responses), *hacker attacks* (17), and *viruses* (15), with comparatively little focus on data-related risks. Families, on the other

---

[5] The percentages are computed as done in footnote 6.

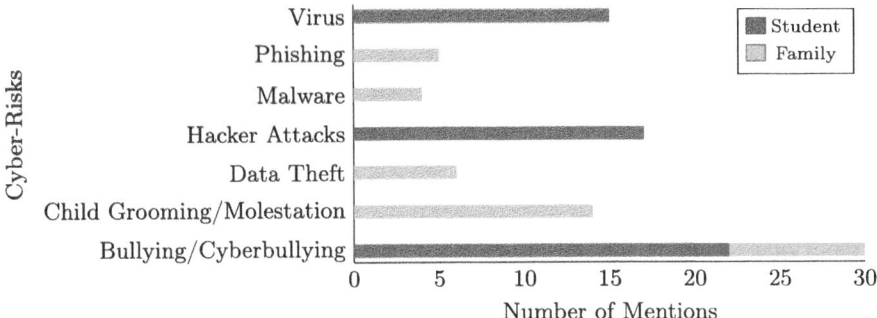

Fig. 2. Most common families' and students' replies to the *open question* regarding the most relevant cyber-risks.

hand, showed greater concern for privacy violations and child safety, most frequently mentioning *child grooming and molestation* (14), *bullying and cyberbullying* (9), and data-related threats including *data theft* (6), *phishing* (5), and *malware* (4). The gap observed in our sample may reflect generational differences in digital experience: adults often *"learned how to use email and social networks late in life,"* while adolescents grew up immersed in digital environments [26]. Although consistent with previous research [13,33,34], these findings are context-specific and offer a focused view of how generational factors may influence digital behavior and awareness.

Our pre-activity survey highlights that while both groups demonstrate a basic understanding of certain online threats, their awareness remains superficial. Students, though confident in their digital skills, often underestimate privacy-related risks and lack a clear sense of their *virtual identity*. Families, despite their concern, frequently lack effective tools or strategies to guide safe digital behavior at home. These findings emphasize the need for structured educational interventions to strengthen cybersecurity knowledge and bridge the generational divide in digital risk perception.

4.2   Post-Activity Questionnaires Structure

The post-activity questionnaires focused on evaluating the educational impact of the course on students and their families. They are structured into four main sections:

1. **Family Engagement and Behavior Change.** Includes 3 *open-ended* and 2 *yes/no questions* for families to assess whether students shared their learning at home and if it influenced family digital practices. Example: *"Did your child talk to you about the WtC project at home?"* (families).
2. **Cybersecurity Knowledge Assessment.** Comprises 11 questions for students and 9 for families, mainly *multiple-choice*, aimed at evaluating basic cybersecurity knowledge. Example: *"Which of the following is a valid IP address format?"* (for both students and families).

3. **Cognitive and Social Impact.** Uses *yes/no* and *multiple-choice questions* to explore the cognitive and social effects of the training on students and families. Examples: *"If you received an email requesting personal information, would you provide it?"* and *"Do you think having the same Decalogue at school and at home is effective?"* (for both students and families).
4. **Student Feedback on Engagement and Training Impact.** Collects students' reflections through 2 *5-point Likert scale questions* on curiosity and enjoyment, 2 *rating scale questions* to identify the most and least appreciated lessons, and 5 *open-ended questions*, including opinions on favorite activities and new concepts learned. Example: *"List three new concepts you learned during the course."* (students).

Below, we present the results of the post-activity questionnaires, focusing on key insights from the four main sections. The feedback highlights both the strengths and weaknesses of the project, confirming the overall positive impact of the experience on the students. Participants were asked to rate their levels of curiosity and enjoyment using a 5-point Likert scale. Around 81% of respondents selected A or TA when evaluating WtC as an engaging experience, while around 66% reported that they enjoyed the activities. These findings suggest that the course was an effective and enjoyable learning experience for students.

Table 3 summarizes the results of two additional open-ended questions in the questionnaire, which asked students to explain their choices regarding the most and least appreciated activities.

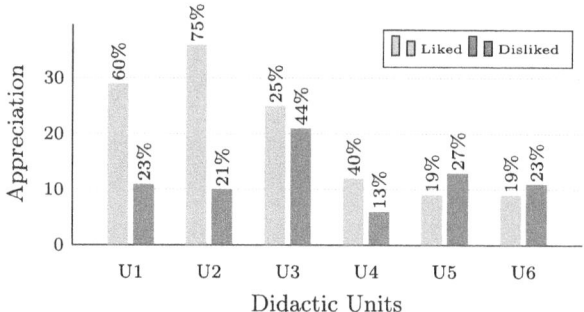

Fig. 3. Distribution of student preferences for the didactic units, as reported in the post-activity questionnaire.

U2 - Cryptography was the most appreciated unit (75%), with students favoring interactive, hands-on activities such as cryptography exercises, gamified tools, and group work. These tasks were described as engaging, enjoyable, and effective in linking theory to real-world skills. In contrast, **U3 - Online Services** was the least appreciated unit (44%), with feedback indicating that familiar tasks like email writing lacked engagement. Criticism focused more on the delivery method than the content itself, highlighting the importance of interactive approaches, effective time management, and attention to group dynamics (Fig. 3).

The training course engaged participants in practical activities designed to enhance their cyber-awareness. The post-activity questionnaire included questions to assess both students' understanding of the Decalogue and their acquisition of cybersecurity knowledge. The results of the technical questions from the post-activity questionnaire show that 78% of participants correctly identified the proper format of an IP address,[6] and around 68% successfully decrypted a message encoded with the Caesar cipher.[7] These outcomes confirm that participants acquired key technical knowledge and improved their understanding of core concepts. Over 58% of participants expressed interest in expanding the knowledge acquired during the course, particularly in areas such as cryptography, networking (including IP addressing), and cybersecurity (e.g., viruses and cyberattacks), subjects with which they were least familiar. To assess the impact of the course beyond the classroom, we also collected feedback from the students' families. Family involvement provided valuable insights into students' engagement and behavioral changes. Approximately 49% of families reported that their child shared information about the project, while only 36% observed changes in their child's digital habits. These findings suggest a positive, though partial, transfer of good practices, indicating that greater family involvement, such as participation in similar courses, could further strengthen these outcomes. The questionnaire also explored the cognitive and social impact of the course, focusing on the role of the Decalogue. About 58% of students considered the Decalogue essential for understanding appropriate online behavior, and 83% believed it should be explicitly written and shared in common spaces. Additionally, over 66% agreed that the same set of guidelines should apply both at school and at home. Overall, these results highlight that the course not only enhanced students' technical knowledge but also fostered awareness of responsible digital behavior. The participants recognized the value of clear guidelines and the importance of consistency across different environments, demonstrating an ability to internalize and apply these principles effectively.

4.3   Summary

Here, we discuss the outcomes of the questionnaires to evaluate the effectiveness of WtC in relation to the four research questions defined in Sect. 4.

***RQ1:** What are the natural sense and perception of cyber-risk of students?* Responses to the pre-activity questionnaires indicated that most students regard the Internet as a positive and entertaining environment. In general, they feel safe online and show moderate self-awareness when navigating the web. However, the open-ended responses indicated a limited understanding of specific cyber-risks. Terms like "*cyberbullying*", "*viruses*", and "*hacker attacks*" were among the most

---

[6] The question was: "*Which of the following is a valid IP address format?*".

[7] The question was: "*Decrypt, using the Caesar Cipher, the word JLXOLRFHVDUH.*".

cited, suggesting that commonly discussed threats largely shape their perception of risk. More technical issues, such as phishing, identity theft, or data protection, were rarely mentioned. This highlights the need for targeted and structured educational support.

RQ2: What is the family awareness of cyber-risks? Post-activity data show that 24.6% of families expressed concern about their children's online activities, while most considered their children reasonably aware of proper online behavior. Cyber-risks were mainly associated with terms like *"danger"*, *"fraud"*, and *"crime"*. Notably, although 62% of families reported setting internet use rules, only 26% of students were aware of them, pointing to a possible communication gap at home. This gap points to a communication breakdown that could limit the effectiveness of parental guidance. In addition, families appeared to prioritize protective measures, such as preventing inappropriate contact and securing personal data, instead of encouraging the development of technical skills and digital awareness.

RQ3: Did participants share the cybersecurity knowledge and skills acquired during the course with their family? Family questionnaire responses indicate that 49% of students shared what they learned in the project at home. While this is a promising outcome, only 36% of families observed a behavioral change in their child. These results suggest that while knowledge transmission between students and families occurred to some extent, its depth and impact were limited. One possible explanation is that students may lack the communicative tools to explain technical content effectively, or that families may not have been fully receptive to these insights. These findings emphasize the importance of more inclusive training sessions involving families.

RQ4: Did WalkthroughCyber improve participants' cyber-awareness, technical knowledge and skills? The post-activity questionnaire results suggest that *WalkthroughCyber* had a significant impact on students' awareness and knowledge of cybersecurity. Notably, most participants correctly answered technical questions regarding topics covered by the training. Our results demonstrate the effectiveness of hands-on, engaging learning activities in conveying technical knowledge. Significantly, after attending the course and learning what constitutes a cyber-crime, 22% of participants reported that they had previously been victims of one. This response suggests an increased ability to recognize cybercrime and a previously unacknowledged vulnerability. The training played a crucial role in helping students contextualize their past digital experiences within a framework of security and awareness. Furthermore, over 58% of participants wanted to deepen their understanding of topics such as cryptography, networking, and security, with which they had limited familiarity before the course. This demonstrates that the training not only conveyed information but also successfully fostered ongoing interest and curiosity. Developing a shared Decalogue in the final unit further reinforced concepts of digital responsibility in line with the cyber hygiene practices by ENISA [9]. The majority of participants believed the Decalogue should be communicated and supported using a consistent set of digital guidelines at school and home.

In conclusion, the results across the research questions support the value of structured, interactive cybersecurity education for middle school students. They highlight the critical role of family engagement in the learning process in fostering a more structured and lasting culture of digital awareness. Future developments of the project should consider additional strategies to engage families, extend technical content, and improve communication between students and their home environments.

5   Related Work

Currently, there are no systematic guidelines for teaching cybersecurity across all school levels. Several initiatives, often promoted by companies or universities, have proposed gamified approaches to enhance engagement, though most target either primary or high school students.

For younger audiences, projects like *Google's Interland* [29] and *Internet Hero* [2] are notable examples. The first is a serious game for children aged 7 to 12, addressing cyberbullying, phishing, and password security. The second, developed within the *Play the Net2* project, provides technical and social guidance for children aged 9 to 12 through a virtual environment that explores emails, malicious programs, social networks, and network connections.

WtC shares the goal of raising cyber-awareness but differs in methodology. Rather than relying solely on independent gaming experiences, our course integrates active frontal lectures inspired by Montessori's method with practical, game-based classroom activities under teacher supervision. This combination of guided learning and interactive exercises is central to our educational strategy.

For high school students, several programs have been launched to provide technical foundations and promote cybersecurity awareness, such as *Cybertrials* [19], *Young Cyber Security Academy* [4], *GenCyber* [16], and *Up to University* [11]. Among these, *GenCyber* is particularly structured, offering a one-week summer camp with game-based learning and post activity surveys to assess effectiveness. However, it focuses on introducing cybersecurity principles and encouraging STEM career paths.

The work by Chernova and Gavrilova [3] presents the closest approach to ours, proposing a middle school course focused on technical skills and safe online behavior. Nevertheless, our training course is distinguished by a more structured design, combining theoretical content with practical exercises in each unit, performed during regular school hours in a supervised environment.

Unlike many of these initiatives, which often lack teacher guidance and structured assessment, WtC emphasizes the balance between educational content and playful activities. Including pre- and post-questionnaires enables us to evaluate learning outcomes and reinforce the connection between knowledge acquisition and skill development.

6　Conclusion

In this paper, we presented the results of *WalkthroughCyber*, a pilot study aimed at designing a didactic approach for teaching cyber-awareness in middle school settings inspired by Montessori principles. The course consisted of ten curricular hours across six units on networking and cybersecurity, designed in line with European Union Agency for Cybersecurity (ENISA) guidelines [8], and taking into account insights from the European Cybersecurity Month campaign [7]. Each unit was delivered through a two-hour interactive session that combines theoretical and practical activities. The effectiveness of the proposed methodology was evaluated through pre- and post-activity questionnaires for students to assess their prior knowledge and their progress in computer science and cybersecurity concepts. Questionnaires were also supplied to families to measure their prior expertise on IT and cybersecurity and to report possible behavioral changes of their children.

Future developments will focus on adapting the activities to better support students with learning disorders and those assisted by support teachers, as well as examining the potential impact of gender on learning outcomes. In response to the evolution of hybrid learning environments (see Sect. 2), a virtual component (e.g. co-designed video game) will be introduced to enhance student engagement. Improvements to the questionnaire will aim to explore the inter-generational digital gap and foster broader involvement of families and teachers for a more comprehensive understanding of adolescents' cyber-awareness. Further lines of investigation include analyzing behavioral changes observed at home, with 36% of families reporting such changes after the course while also recognizing the limitations of parental perception in capturing students' private digital habits. Additional research will examine the relationship between device usage time and the presence of parental control tools, to distinguish between self-imposed and externally regulated limits. Other important directions involve evaluating the applicability of the course's recommendations in diverse socio-educational contexts and strengthening the place-based education approach by engaging local institutions in real-world learning experiences.

Acknowledgments. This work was supported by the project *"SEcurity and RIghts in the CyberSpace"* (SERICS), PE0000014 funded by the European Union - NextGenerationEU under the National Recovery and Resilience Plan M4C2 I1.3., CUP: D67G22000340001. The authors are grateful to the *C.I. "Soprani"* for carrying out the experimental activity and sharing the data.

References

1. Arnold, H., Livingstone, S.: Children and the Internet: Great Expectations, Challenging Realities. Polity (2009)
2. Bauer, G., Martinek, D., Kriglstein, S., Wallner, G., Wölfle, R.: Digital game-based learning with "Internet Hero": a game about the internet for children aged 9 12 years, pp. 148–161. New Academic Press (2017)

3. Chernova, E., Gavrilova, I.: Training teenagers to ensure their own cybersecurity. In: International Scientific Conference" Far East Con"(ISCFEC 2020), pp. 2926–2930. Atlantis Press (2020)
4. Curioni, A.: Young cyber security academy (2022). https://cybersecurity.leonardo.com/en/news-and-stories-detail/-/detail/leonardo-young-cyber-security-academy
5. of Education, M.: Ministerial decree (d.m) of 30 july 2021, n.237 (2021). https://www.miur.gov.it/documents/20182/5385739/Decreto+ministeriale+n.+237+del+30+luglio+2021.pdf/19528543-72c1-4c1b-c7db-4e52e1c2cbdc?version=1.0&t=1632132719086
6. Eteokleous, N.: Evaluating computer technology integration in a centralized school system. Comput. Educ. **51**(2), 669–686 (2008)
7. European Union Agency for Cybersecurity (ENISA): European cybersecurity month. https://cybersecuritymonth.eu/. Accessed 04 June 2025
8. European Union Agency for Cybersecurity (ENISA): European cybersecurity skills framework (ecsf) user manual. https://www.enisa.europa.eu/publications/european-cybersecurity-skills-framework-ecsf (2022). Accessed 04 June 2025
9. European Union Agency for Cybersecurity (ENISA): Cyber hygiene (2025). https://www.enisa.europa.eu/topics/cyber-hygiene
10. Floridi, L.: The Onlife Manifesto: Being Human in a Hyperconnected Era. Springer Nature (2015)
11. GARR, C.: Up2U Project (Italian Project) (2020). https://www.garr.it/it/comunita/scuola/progetti/up2u
12. Gerstein, J.: Moving from education 1.0 through education 2.0 towards education 3.0. In: Blaschke, M.L., Kenyon, M.C., Hase, D.S. (eds.) Experiences in Self-Determined Learning, chap. 7. CreateSpace Independent Publishing Platform (2014)
13. Halperin, R., Dror, Y.: Privacy and the digital generation gap: myth and reality. In: 9th Mediterranean Conference on Information Systems, MCIS 2015, Samos, Greece, October 2-5, 2015. Proceedings, p. 5. AISeL (2015). http://aisel.aisnet.org/mcis2015/5
14. International, A.M.: The child's development (2023). https://amiusa.org/families/childs-development/
15. Jerman Blažič, B., Jerman Blažič, A.: Cybersecurity skills among European high-school students: a new approach in the design of sustainable educational development in cybersecurity. Sustainability **14**(8), 4763 (2022)
16. Jin, G., Tu, M., Kim, T.H., Heffron, J., White, J.: Evaluation of game-based learning in cybersecurity education for high school students. J. Educ. Learn. (EduLearn) **12**, 150 (2018). https://doi.org/10.11591/edulearn.v12i1.7736
17. Kahn, D.: Pedagogy of place: using the prepared environment for the third plane. NAMTA J. **26**(3), 152–154 (2001)
18. Keats, D., Schmidt, J.P.: The genesis and emergence of education 3.0 in higher education and its potential for Africa. First monday **12**(3), 3–5 (2007)
19. Lab, C.N.: Cybertrials (2023). https://www.cybertrials.it/
20. Lillard, A.S.: Playful learning and Montessori education. Namta J. **38**(2), 137–174 (2013)
21. MacDonald, G.: Technology in the Montessori classroom: benefits, hazards and preparation for life. NAMTA J. **41**, 99–107 (2016)
22. Montessori, M.: Introduction on the Use of Mechanical Aids (1947)
23. Montessori, M.: La Scoperta del bambino. Garzanti (1950)
24. Montessori, M.: The erdkider: i fanciulli della terra. schema per una riforma della scuola secondaria. Vita dell'Infanzia (1957)

25. Montessori, M.: Il Metodo del bambino e la formazione dell'uomo. Scritti e documenti inediti e rari (2002)
26. Palfrey, J., Gasser, U.: Born Digital: Understanding the First Generation of Digital Natives. Basic Books Inc, USA (2008)
27. Pencheva, D., Hallett, J., Rashid, A.: Bringing cyber to school: integrating cybersecurity into secondary school education. IEEE Secur. Priv. **18**(2), 68–74 (2020). https://doi.org/10.1109/MSEC.2020.2969409
28. Prensky, M.: Digital natives, digital immigrants. on The Horizon **9** (2001)
29. Program), G.G.B.I.A.: Google s Interland (2018). https://beinternetawesome.withgoogle.com/en_us/interland
30. of the Republic, P.: Law of 20 August 2019, n.92 (2019). https://www.gazzettaufficiale.it/eli/id/2019/08/21/19G00105/sg
31. Richardson, M.D., Lemoine, P.A., Stephens, W.E., Waller, R.E.: Planning for cyber security in schools: the human factor. Educ. Plann. **27**(2), 23–39 (2020)
32. Scholefield, S., Shepherd, L.A.: Gamification techniques for raising cyber security awareness. In: HCI for Cybersecurity, Privacy and Trust: First International Conference, HCI-CPT 2019, Held as Part of the 21st HCI International Conference, HCII 2019, Orlando, USA, July 26–31, 2019, Proceedings 21, pp. 191–203. Springer (2019)
33. Steijn, W.M.P., Vedder, A.: Privacy concerns, dead or misunderstood? The perceptions of privacy amongst the young and old. Inf. Polity **20**(4), 299–311 (2015). https://doi.org/10.3233/IP-150374
34. Tsai, H.y.S., Jiang, M., Alhabash, S., LaRose, R., Rifon, N.J., Cotten, S.R.: Understanding online safety behaviors: a protection motivation theory perspective. Comput. & Secur. **59**, 138–150 (2016)
35. Valle, M.: La pedagogia montessori e le nuove tecnologie. Un'integrazione possibile (2017)

An Exploratory Study on Teaching Software Supply Chain Security Concepts to High School Students

Marc Ohm[1,2]([envelope]) [iD], Yannik Börgener[1] [iD], and Timo Pohl[1] [iD]

[1] University of Bonn, Bonn, Germany
{ohm,pohl}@cs.uni-bonn.de, s6ykboer@uni-bonn.de
[2] Fraunhofer FKIE, Bonn, Germany

Abstract. Software supply chain security is steadily gaining importance as more attacks on the software supply chain take place. Yet, it is uncommon that software supply chain security concepts are part of computer science curricula. This paper presents a two-day lecture series for high school students, employing engaging pedagogical methods like serious games to raise awareness of this attack vector. We evaluate competence gains and knowledge retention via competency tests, as well as the subjective impressions of students regarding lecture quality through evaluation forms. Our evaluation reveals that despite lacking prior knowledge, students were able to independently identify and explain key software supply chain security concepts and positively engaged with the serious game as a learning tool.

Keywords: Software Supply Chain · High School Education · Serious Game · Cybersecurity

1 Introduction

Modern software products commonly rely on a vast network of individual components as direct and transitive code dependencies, often numbering in the tens or hundreds, creating an extensive attack surface that demands dedicated monitoring and maintenance. Software supply chain security encompasses the protection of all "components, libraries, tools, and processes used to design, build, and publish a software artifact" [4]. It represents a critical challenge in contemporary cybersecurity, as the compromise of even a single software component can have far-reaching consequences, affecting millions of users across numerous organizations. The implications of inadequate security extend beyond individual applications, as evidenced by recent incidents such as the attacks on the XZ library, event-stream, and Ultralytics, demonstrating how vulnerabilities in seemingly minor components can propagate through entire digital infrastructures. The inherent complexity and scale of software supply chains present

F. Skopik et al. (Eds.): ARES 2025 Workshops, LNCS 15999, pp. 23–39, 2025.
https://doi.org/10.1007/978-3-032-00644-8_2

numerous potential infiltration points [9], with malicious manipulation of software components being a particularly prevalent and significant threat in the current software development landscape [11].

Given the profound impact of software supply chain security, it is crucial for computer scientists and programmers to possess awareness and at least a foundational understanding of this domain. However, despite its growing importance, this relatively specialized topic is often absent from early computer science education curricula. To address this gap, our research investigates the feasibility of introducing software supply chain security concepts to high school students. Drawing upon the demonstrated success of playful teaching methodologies like gamification [6,7] in conveying complex cybersecurity topics, we developed a two-day, 180-minute lecture series. This curriculum incorporates engaging methods, including serious games and evidence-based pedagogical approaches, to make intricate cybersecurity principles accessible and enjoyable for younger learners.

The effectiveness of our teaching approach was evaluated through two primary methods. First, we employed competency tests to objectively assess the students' initial comprehension of the taught concepts and their knowledge retention over several weeks. Second, we gathered student feedback to subjectively evaluate the engagement and perceived effectiveness of the chosen teaching methods.

The main contributions of this paper are as follows:

- A detailed description of a two-day, 180-minute lecture series on software supply chain security tailored for high school students.
- An objective evaluation of the students' acquired competencies and the retention of knowledge over time.
- A subjective assessment of the effectiveness and reception of playful teaching methods in the context of software supply chain security education.

The remainder of this paper is structured as follows: Sect. 2 provides a comprehensive description of the curriculum, the teaching methodologies, and the evaluation instruments employed in this study. Section 3 presents observations gathered during the lectures and analyzes the students' competence gains and their reception of the teaching methods. Finally, Sect. 4 offers a discussion of the findings, with Sect. 5 concluding the paper, offering key insights and future research directions.

2   Methodology

This section presents our approach to curriculum design and evaluation from two complementary perspectives: practical insights gained from the teacher's implementation and accompanying research aimed at validating its effectiveness. To evaluate the lecture design, we will analyze student performance on assessments administered after the curriculum delivery, aligning the results with the established learning objectives. Additionally, a feedback form will be utilized to gather student perspectives on the teaching methods employed.

From the teacher's viewpoint, a primary challenge is motivating students to engage with the subject, particularly given the niche nature of software supply chain security. To address this, the curriculum emphasizes the pervasive potential impact of software supply chain attacks through the extensive use of real-world examples and recent incidents. The teacher's overarching goal is to create a motivating and engaging learning experience, especially considering that this topic is not a mandatory component of the school's core curriculum and will not be included in the final examinations, which are dictated by state educational standards. To achieve this, the pedagogical design encourages students to independently discover core concepts, collaboratively share their knowledge, and apply their newly acquired competencies within a serious game framework [14].

The curriculum is structured as two 90-minute lectures. This timeframe is chosen to maintain student interest while allowing for comprehensive coverage of the intended learning outcomes. The outline for the curriculum is presented in Table 1. It incorporates extensive use of plenary discussions and small group activities to foster student collaboration and active learning. The designated knowledge level for this curriculum aligns with "upper secondary education" according to the International Standard Classification of Education (ISCED) [13], corresponding to the final years of high school.

Table 1. Phases of the lecture. The double line separates the first and second day.

Duration	Phase	Content	Arrangement
5 min	Introduction	Welcome and organizational stuff	Teacher's talk
10 min	Elaboration	Analog supply chain using the example of a cake	Plenary
5 min	Recapitulation	Categorize parts of supply chains	Plenary
15 min	Elaboration	Transition from analog to digital supply chains	Plenary
5 min	Recapitulation	Abstraction of the concept of supply chains	Plenary
10 min	Introduction	Introduction to security of supply chains using possible attacks	Plenary
5 min	Recapitulation	Presentation of the SLSA framework	Teacher's talk
15 min	Elaboration	Analysis of real world incidents	Small groups
15 min	Elaboration	Presentation of real world incidents and mapping to SLSA	Small groups
5 min	Closing		Plenary
5 min	Introduction	Welcome	Plenary
10 min	Recapitulation	Review of attack methods	Plenary
10 min	Introduction	Presentation of the serious game	Teacher's talk
40 min	Elaboration	Playing the serious game	Small groups
15 min	Recapitulation	Feedback to the game and open questions	Plenary
5 min	Closing		Plenary
5 min	Didactic buffer		

2.1   Learning Goals and Competences

The curriculum is designed to prioritize raising awareness of software supply chain security rather than focusing on an in-depth technical understanding, with the lecture series intentionally kept concise at 180 min. This decision is also necessitated by the school's requirement to cover the required core competencies before incorporating supplementary content, leaving little time at the end of the school year. As outlined in Table 2, the learning goals are developed based on Anderson's revision of Bloom's Taxonomy of Educational Objectives [1], with a primary focus on memorizing foundational features and examples, understanding key attack vectors, and applying the Supply-chain Levels for Software Artifacts (SLSA) framework[1].

Table 2. Learning goals and associated levels

Level	Goal
Remember	Name the basic characteristics of a supply chain
Remember	Name the basic characteristics of a software supply chain
Remember	Name the basic characteristics of software supply chain security
Understand	Describe the different attack vectors (threats) of the SLSA framework in their own words
Apply	Correctly assign the different attack vectors (threats) of the SLSA framework to the SLSA diagram
Remember	Name examples of attack vectors (threats)
Understand	Explain which properties a package must have in order to be suitable for a Dependency Confusion attack.

2.2   First Lecture/Introduction

The first lecture aims to introduce the concept of software supply chains and provide an initial understanding of associated attacks and potential disruptions. The session commences by soliciting students' prior knowledge of software supply chains and their intuitive understanding of the term. To facilitate familiarization with the topic, the method of Advance Organizer [2] is employed. This pedagogical approach utilizes a visual aid provided in advance to help students mentally structure new information and connect it to their existing knowledge and skills.

Following introductory remarks, students are tasked with individually depicting a traditional supply chain for a "cake". The objective of this exercise is to enable students to independently discover fundamental supply chain concepts such as producers, suppliers, and distribution using a familiar product. Subsequently, students are asked to transfer this understanding to the context of a

---

[1] https://slsa.dev.

software supply chain, with the Firefox web browser serving as a concrete, widely known open-source example.

After the individual work, the students' depictions of software supply chains are used as a basis for mapping these concepts to the SLSA framework's depiction of a software supply chain. SLSA is a security framework that outlines threats to software supply chains and provides a set of standards and controls to enhance integrity and secure software packages and infrastructure [12].

With a foundational understanding of the concept and scope of software supply chains established, the lecture transitions to introducing potential attacks and disturbances through a brief presentation. To further explore these issues, students are divided into groups of three to analyze recent, prominent incidents. We use the prominent example cases Codecov[2], SolarWinds[3], event-stream[4], CrowdStrike-related IT outages[5], and the attack technique Dependency Confusion[6]. These cases are selected for their comprehensive documentation and representativeness of common software supply chain vulnerabilities.

For each incident, the instructor provides the student groups with a custom worksheet containing relevant background information. The initial task for each group is to analyze their assigned case and describe it in their own words. Subsequently, the class is reorganized into mixed "expert" groups using the jigsaw method [8], with each group focusing on one specific incident. These expert groups collaboratively discussed their findings until a consensus was reached and a collective understanding of the case was formulated. Finally, each group presented their assigned incident and analysis to the rest of the class. Furthermore, these mixed expert groups were tasked with mapping the analyzed incidents to their corresponding points within the SLSA framework's depiction of a software supply chain and discussing potential preventative mechanisms.

The lecture concludes with a whole-class discussion of all analyzed incidents to address any remaining questions and to provide a comprehensive summary of the key takeaways from the session.

2.3   Second Lecture/Fostering Knowledge

The second lecture is designed to reinforce the knowledge acquired during the first session with a review part, followed by the application of the taught concepts in a serious game. Initially, the instructor conducts an interactive review of all key concepts from the first lecture, actively engaging students to promote knowledge retention. Subsequently, a serious game is introduced to allow students to explore the practical implications of attacks targeting the software supply chain. The

---

[2] https://about.codecov.io/apr-2021-post-mortem/.

[3] https://www.gao.gov/blog/solarwinds-cyberattack-demands-significant-federal-and-private-sector-response-infographic.

[4] https://snyk.io/de/blog/a-post-mortem-of-the-malicious-event-stream-backdoor/.

[5] https://www.cisa.gov/news-events/alerts/2024/07/19/widespread-it-outage-due-crowdstrike-update.

[6] https://owasp.org/www-project-top-10-ci-cd-security-risks/CICD-SEC-03-Dependency-Chain-Abuse.

term "serious games" refers to tools intentionally designed to be both entertaining and educational [3].

Inspired by "CIST: A Serious Game for Hardware Supply Chain" [5], which focuses on countermeasures, our game adopts a different perspective by placing players in the role of attackers aiming to infiltrate a corporate network. This shift in focus aligns with the first lecture's emphasis on vulnerabilities and threats within the software supply chain, as the existing curriculum does not cover countermeasures. Unlike the original game's random event structure, our version follows a structured progression towards a defined objective, guided by a digital companion providing narrative context. This educational tool serves as a practical application of the learned material, aiming to deepen understandin. Through gameplay, participants learn how seemingly isolated employee compromises can escalate to affect entire corporate networks and public perception, developing problem-solving skills and enhancing their awareness of social engineering attacks and network security.

The serious game comprises a playing field representing a corporate network, illustrated in Fig. 1, a set of game cards, and a digital companion that manages game progression. The game utilizes five categories of cards: information cards, malware cards, access rights cards, attack cards, and software supply chain attack cards. Except for the "access rights" card, each card can be used only once. Following is a summary of the card types. Details about each card can be found in the appendix.

Information cards Contain details about systems (e.g., operating system, dependencies) or individuals (e.g., employee names, social media handles) that can be leveraged for attacks.

Malware cards Enable players to deploy malware or prepare exploits, potentially in conjunction with software supply chain attacks.

Access rights Represent gained privileges within the network. Each system on the game board has an access rights indicator, initially set to "No Access". Acquiring access rights expands the player's available actions.

Attack Cards Represent attack patterns based on the MITRE ATT&CK framework [10], used to gather information or gain further access.

Software Supply Chain Attack Cards Provide five distinct attack vectors: Compromising the build process, creating a dependency confusion package, uploading a modified package, distributing malware, and compromising the source repository.

The game board initially appears collapsed which is intended to allow a gradual exploration of the IT landscape. It expands as players successfully infiltrate the network and gain knowledge of its structure. Access cards and software supply chain attack cards have designated spaces on the board, while standard attack and malware cards do not.

The game commences with players utilizing their knowledge of company employee names to search for online profiles. They encounter "Nelly Meyer", a cat influencer seeking a partnership with a smart cat gadget manufacturer and using the "SocialWatch" software for social media management. By impersonating the manufacturer and sending a spear phishing email, players successfully compromise Nelly's computer. From this initial foothold, they navigate laterally through the corporate network, identifying outdated and vulnerable software. The scenario culminates in the players compromising the build system, implanting malicious code, and ultimately using Nelly's social media account to promote the malicious package.

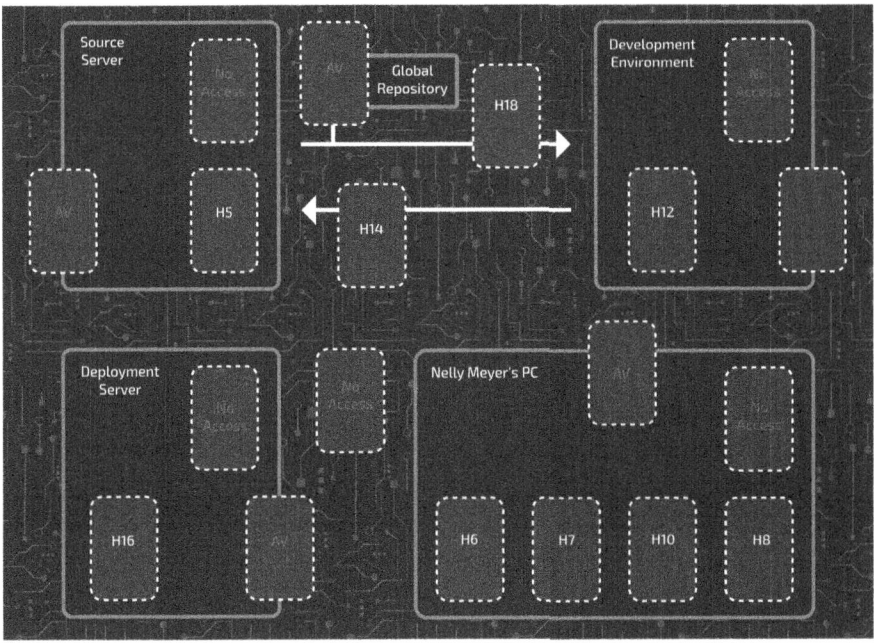

Fig. 1. The game board of our serious game. Translated to English from the original German version.

The digital companion, a web-based tool[7], orchestrates game progression and storytelling while displaying and allowing players to interact with their available playing cards. When players form valid card combinations representing successful actions, they advance in the game and unlock new narrative elements. The system provides hints for partially correct combinations and gathers feedback on incorrect attempts, contributing to game refinement. Furthermore, the companion acts as a quality control mechanism by displaying only currently playable cards, ensuring synchronization between the physical and digital components of the game.

---

[7] https://github.com/cybertier/software-supply-chain-serious-game.

2.4 Evaluation

To evaluate the effectiveness of the curriculum in achieving the defined learning goals, a written competency test is administered on two occasions. Students are given 15 min to complete the test independently, without assistance from teachers. The first test is conducted shortly after the completion of the lecture series, and the second test follows approximately one month later. This repeated assessment aims to determine the extent to which the competencies are fostered and to test if students are able to recall the learned content over time.

Both competency tests consist of seven tasks, as detailed in Table 3. Tasks 1 through 5 remain identical across both test administrations. However, tasks 6 and 7 incorporate A/B variants that are alternated between students to assess different levels of understanding. Specifically, students who receive variant A for a particular task in the first test are presented with variant B for the same task in the second test, and vice versa. The first task requires students to define a software supply chain and its components in their own words. Tasks 2 and 3 are multiple choice questions (true/false) assessing understanding of software supply chains and their security implications. Tasks 4 through 6 focus on the SLSA framework, requiring students to map threats to phases in the software supply chain, match threat names with their definitions, and associate the attacks discussed in the lecture with corresponding phases in the SLSA diagram.

Tasks 6 and 7 are designed to gauge the depth of understanding achieved by the students. Specifically, Task 6 (depicted in Fig. 3a) aimed to evaluate students' ability to connect theoretical concepts with practical examples. Variant A required students to map provided descriptions of software supply chain attacks to their corresponding attack vectors within the SLSA framework. In contrast, Variant B challenged students to generate relevant attack examples for given SLSA attack vectors, drawing upon examples discussed during the lessons. The results indicate that students encountered greater difficulty with Variant B, suggesting a less robust understanding of applying theoretical knowledge to specific scenarios.

To gather insights into the pedagogical approaches and the effectiveness of the serious game, student feedback is collected using a 4-point Likert scale.

3 Results

The proposed curriculum was evaluated in a German high school (Gymnasium) in North Rhine-Westphalia during December 2024 where computer science is an elective subject according to state regulations.

The two lectures, detailed in Sect. 2, were conducted in two consecutive weeks within an eleventh-grade computer science course. The first lecture had an attendance of 13 students, while the second lecture was attended by the entire class of 16 students.

The students are around 16 years old on average and have previous experience with computer science from an elective subject they took in previous years. The

Table 3. Tasks used for the competency tests.

Task	Type	Competency
1	free text	Students name the basic characteristics of a software supply chain
2	multiple choice	Name the basic characteristics of a software supply chain
3	multiple choice	Name the basic characteristics of software supply chain security
4	assignment	Correctly assign the different attack vectors of the SLSA framework to the diagram
5	assignment	Describe the various attack vectors of the SLSA framework in their own words
6A	assignment	Assign given attacks (name and description provided) on the software supply chain to the corresponding attack vectors of the SLSA framework
6B	assignment	Name suitable attacks for the given attack vectors of the SLSA framework
7A	multiple choice	indicate whether statements about dependency confusion are correct or incorrect
7B	free text	explain which properties a package must have in order to be suitable for a dependency confusion attack

curriculum for that elective subject up to the eleventh grade includes data structures, algorithms, formal languages, automata theory, information systems, and human and societal factors. Programming is something that students typically understand at a basic level, and they are able to write smaller programs.

According to the participating teacher, the students in this course were described as "strong performers", having completed the semester's learning objectives ahead of schedule. This allowed for the integration of our additional curriculum within the allocated timeframe.

3.1 Observations During the Lectures

Despite the students having no prior experience with software supply chains, initial engagement was high, with five out of fourteen students demonstrating an intuitive understanding of the potential scope of the topic and initiating a preliminary discussion. The instructor guided this enthusiasm by acknowledging their insights while emphasizing the complexity of defining a software supply chain, noting that even undergraduate computer science students often struggle with a precise definition. This approach aimed to manage expectations and ensure a foundational understanding before delving into more advanced concepts.

Provided with a general prompt and an image of a cake, students collaboratively brainstormed the constituent elements of its supply chain. Initially, their focus was on individual ingredients such as flour, milk, and eggs. Subsequently, they were prompted to categorize these individual items into broader, related components. Through ten minutes of collaborative effort, the students successfully developed a comprehensive supply chain model for the cake, identifying all key stages. While the students required minor guidance regarding the explicit inclusion of a recipe as a crucial element, the final model effectively integrated all student contributions and achieved the desired structural representation through facilitation by the study leader.

The collaboratively constructed analog supply chain was documented via photograph and subsequently projected for the class. This physical model served as a foundational structure for introducing the concept of a software supply chain. The instructor facilitated the transition by adapting the existing model, introducing new terminology relevant to software while visually differentiating the original components (represented in green) from the newly added software-specific elements (represented in blue). Through this process, the students independently arrived at the understanding that software is composed of interconnected software components. Remarkably, their independently generated model closely mirrored the structure of an established industry standard framework, the SLSA. This unexpected alignment sparked productive discussions regarding potential vulnerabilities and attack vectors within software systems.

Three students who missed the initial session were introduced to the taught concepts in the review session that took place in the beginning of the second day. This repetition served to reactivate prior knowledge for all students. Activity in the review session was dominated by two particularly engaged students at first, but participation broadened to include almost the entire class by its conclusion. The review proved to be a valuable pedagogical tool, effectively enabling absent students to integrate with the ongoing learning process.

Following this successful knowledge reactivation, the class transitioned to the serious game activity. The students' eagerness to begin playing resulted in some initial misunderstandings regarding the game rules and the utilization of the game plan. For the serious game activity, the students were divided into four small groups, each consisting of four members. Each group received game boards and cards and accessed digital instructions via a QR code linking to a companion website. The majority of student groups successfully completed the game, solving all presented puzzles and demonstrating a strong grasp of software supply chain security and broader cybersecurity concepts. However, some groups initially encountered difficulties due to ambiguities in the instructions and instances of missing game cards. These issues were addressed during the session, ensuring that all groups could successfully complete the game before proceeding to a competence assessment.

3.2 Gained Competences of Students

This section presents the evaluation of student competence acquisition based on the learning goals previously established. The analysis focuses exclusively on students who completed both instructional sessions and both assessment tests. Task 1 was excluded from the evaluation due to the high variability in the quality and length of free-text responses, which hindered quantitative analysis. Conversely, Task 2 aims to test the same competence as task 1 and was deemed more suitable for quantifying students' understanding of software supply chains as it utilizes closed questions.

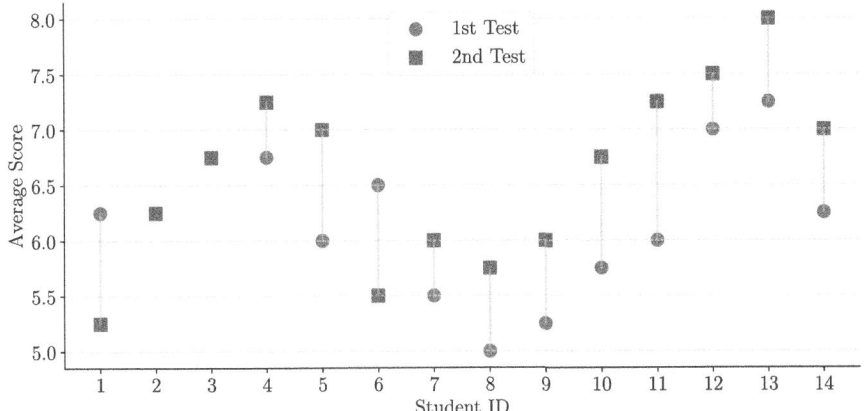

Fig. 2. Average performance per student in task 2–5. Red circles represent the first test and green squares the second iteration. (Color figure online)

Figure 2 illustrates the average performance of students in Tasks 2 through 5 across both assessments. Overall, the data indicates an improvement in student knowledge regarding software supply chains and their security. Notably, $10/14$ students achieved higher scores in the second test, administered three weeks after the first. This improvement suggests potential knowledge retention and/or active engagement with the topic following the initial introduction. The score remained identical for two students, and two more students demonstrated a decrease in performance from the first to the second test.

Tasks 6 and 7 employed an A/B testing approach to assess different levels of understanding among students. The distribution of scores for each variant within these tasks is detailed in Fig. 3.

A similar trend was observed in Task 7 (shown in Fig. 3b). Variant A presented students with true/false statements about dependency confusion, assessing their recognition of key concepts. Variant B, however, asked students to provide free-text answers, requiring them to define the necessary conditions for a package to be exploited in a dependency confusion attack, given a list of internal and external dependencies. The lower scores in Variant B suggest that students struggled with articulating the underlying principles of dependency confusion in their own words.

In conclusion, the findings indicate that students retain knowledge about software supply chains and their security over a short period of time. The overall improvement in performance between the two tests suggests that our teaching methods are effective in conveying the lecture content within the given timeframe and promoting knowledge retention. However, the disparities in performance between the A and B variants in Tasks 6 and 7 highlight areas where students may require further reinforcement in applying theoretical knowledge and generating concrete examples.

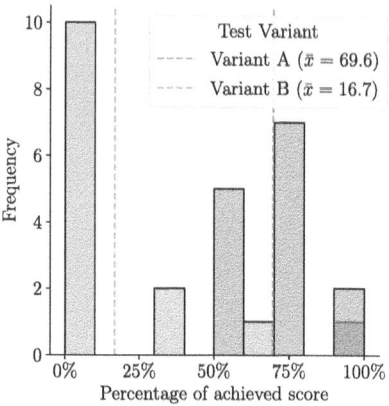 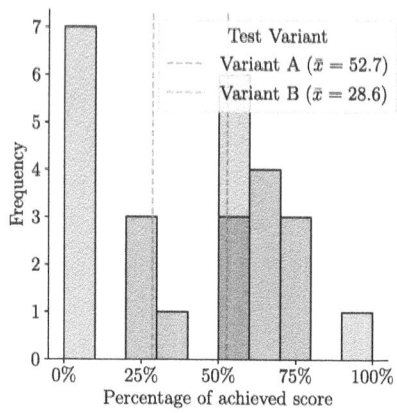

(a) Distribution of scores achieved for task 6 for variant A and B. Variant A asked to map given attacks to leveraged attack vectors while variant B required naming an example attacks for given attack vectors.

(b) Distribution of scores achieved for task 7 for variant A and variant B. Variant A is multiple choice (true/false) and Variant B asks for a free text answer.

Fig. 3. Average performance of students in task 6 and 7. Both features two variants to assess different levels of understanding.

3.3   Reception of Employed Methods

We conducted a subjective evaluation of our teaching method by distributing feedback forms to the students. The aggregated responses are visually represented in Fig. 4.

Prior to the lesson series, none of the participating students possessed knowledge of software supply chains. However, post-instruction, the vast majority of students reported finding the topic relevant. The initial lesson garnered positive feedback, with students specifically highlighting the clarity and interest of the presented case studies. Furthermore, the implemented format of alternating group work was particularly well-received by the students.

The serious game component of the teaching method elicited high levels of student motivation and concentration. Nevertheless, feedback indicated that four students found the game difficult to understand, although the specific reasons for this were not detailed in their responses. Despite the availability of a dedicated feedback button within the game, this feature was utilized only once. Given the limited sample size, statistically significant conclusions regarding the game's impact cannot be drawn. However, the majority of students reported that the game was motivating and engaging, with only one student expressing negative feedback. Overall, the evaluation of the serious game highlighted both positive student engagement and a specific area for improvement related to game comprehension.

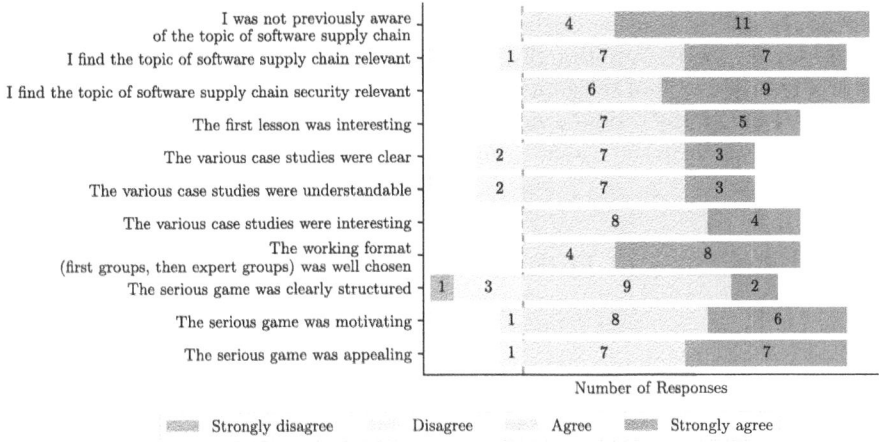

Fig. 4. Student answers from the feedback form. The 4-point Likert scale shows an overall positive feedback.

In summary, the students' overall perception of the lecture series was positive, indicating the effectiveness of the teaching methods employed while also identifying specific areas for future development.

4 Discussion

A competency test indicated that students developed a foundational understanding of the software supply chain and security, with most able to answer basic questions about the SLSA framework. However, the current curriculum primarily emphasizes potential attacks and lacks coverage of countermeasures. Expanding the curriculum to include these countermeasures would necessitate an extension of the lecture to at least three days.

The implementation of the lesson series, while covering all planned content within the allocated time, was considered ambitious. This was feasible due to the high-performing nature of the class, as noted by both the teaching staff and study leadership, and the students' consistent engagement without interruptions. For classes with varying academic strengths or in typical teaching environments, more time should be allocated. We recommend adding a single introductory lesson on supply chain basics, followed by a double period focusing on supply chain security with relevant case studies. The third unit, covering the serious game, can remain as is.

Students generally engaged well with the serious game, successfully integrating the physical game board with digital instructions. While minor technical issues like duplicate card usage occurred, teachers effectively managed these without causing significant student frustration. Nevertheless, feedback from the study leader and students suggests areas for improvement. The most prominent need is for clearer rules and timing, specifically regarding card placement and the possibility of using cards multiple times. More explicit explanations can address these points. Additionally, some students experienced confusion due to the progressive reveal of the game board, hindering their ability to gain an initial overview. Finally, the serious game could be enhanced by incorporating multiple difficulty levels to better cater to individual student knowledge and maintain engagement.

5   Conclusion and Future Work

This study provides initial evidence for the effectiveness of our newly developed lecture in fostering a basic understanding of software supply chain and security among students. The competency test results indicate that students successfully grasped foundational concepts, including familiarity with the SLSA framework. Furthermore, the implementation of the serious game was generally well-received, with students demonstrating an ability to integrate the physical and digital components of the learning activity.

Based on our observations and student feedback, several avenues for future research and development have been identified. Firstly, to enhance the generalizability of our findings, future studies should evaluate the lecture's effectiveness in more diverse educational settings, including courses with varying levels of academic performance. This will provide a more comprehensive understanding of the lecture's impact and identify potential areas for adaptation.

Secondly, the curriculum could be enhanced to provide a more complete picture of software supply chain security. While the current focus on attacks is valuable, the inclusion of countermeasures would offer students a more holistic understanding of the field. We propose expanding the lecture series to incorporate this aspect. Given the current time constraints, this would likely necessitate an increase in the allocated teaching time, potentially to three days. A revised structure could include an introductory single lesson on supply chain basics, followed by an extended double period dedicated to supply chain security, incorporating relevant case studies. The existing third unit focusing on the serious game would remain unchanged.

Finally, there are opportunities to refine the serious game to further enhance its pedagogical value. Based on study leader observations and student feedback, future iterations should prioritize clearer explanations of the game rules and timing, specifically regarding card placement and usage. Addressing the initial confusion caused by the progressive reveal of the game board by potentially offering an initial overview could also improve the student experience. Furthermore, to cater to a wider range of student knowledge levels and increase engagement, the development of multiple difficulty levels for the serious game should be explored. These improvements, focusing on clarity, accessibility, and adaptability, will contribute to a more effective and engaging learning experience for students.

Appendix

All game cards are categorized and listed below. The cards are not necessarily numbered in ascending order.

A.1.1 Software Supply Chain Attack

AV1 - Compromised Build Process: With access to a development environment, you can manipulate the build process to insert malicious code into the generated software.

AV2 - Dependency Confusion: Create a public package used as a dependency with the same name as an internal package but with a higher version number.

AV3 - Upload Modified Package: Create a modified version of the software with malware and replace the package on the deployment server.

AV4 - Distribute Malware: Distribute manipulated malware to end users via trusted distribution channels (e.g., social media) using social engineering techniques.

AV5 - Compromise Source Repo: Manipulate the source server so that your malicious code is already included in the software's source code.

A.1.2 Attack

A1 - Reconnaissance: Search publicly available information about the company's employees.

A2 - Buy Exploit: Purchase an exploit on the darknet for a victim's software. The exploit uses vulnerabilities to run malicious code on the computer, often hidden in programs, images, or PDFs without the victim's awareness.

A4 - Deliver Exploit via Social Engineering: Send a person an exploit-manipulated file and convince them to open it by making the content seem interesting to them.

A5 - Install Malware: Install malware on a system to which you have access.

A6 - Analyze System: Analyze a system to which you have access.

A7 - Embed Exploit in Software: Add an exploit to an existing piece of software.

A8 - Add and Upload Own Malware: Add your malicious code to the original program and upload it to the deployment server.

A9 - Reanalyze System: Reanalyze a system after your access rights have changed.

A.1.3 Information

H5 - OS of Source Server: Analysis of the production server showed that it runs the outdated Linux distribution Ubuntu 12.04. Since 2017, no updates have been released, and known exploits can take advantage of unpatched vulnerabilities.

H6 - Employee: Nelli Meyer: Nelli Meyer, a passionate cat lover, reviews cat-related products on Instagram. She's interested in trying out SmartCat's smart litter box but finds it too expensive. She has contacted the manufacturer for a collaboration and is awaiting a response.

H7 - Employee: Nelli Meyer: Nelli Meyer manages the company's social media channels and uses tools like "SocialWatch."

H12 - Source Code of Software: By analyzing the development environment, you've gained access to the source code and can now examine or modify it.

H14 - Build Process Information: During analysis of the development environment, you discovered that changes to the source code are uploaded to the source server and tested there. The code is compiled and executed on the server.

H17 - Company Employees Info: You have obtained a list with the names of some of the company's employees.

H18 - Software Dependencies: By analyzing the development environment, you identified the software's dependencies. These are retrieved using a package manager from both the source server and global repositories.

A.1.4 Malware

H1 - Computer Worm (Malware): This computer worm is commonly available for free on the clear web. It infects other computers in the network once access to one machine is gained and the network is insufficiently secured.

H3 - Exploit for Ubuntu 12.04: This exploit targets systems running Ubuntu 12.04. It can be executed directly or embedded in software to gain full access to the target system.

H10 - Exploit for SocialWatch: This exploit targets systems with SocialWatch installed. Once executed, it grants full access to the affected system.

H16 - Modified Software on Production Server: You have placed a modified version of the program on the production server, allowing customers to download it.

A.1.5 Access Rights

H8 - Access to Social Media Channels: Using Nelli Meyer's computer, you can access the company's social media accounts, publish posts, and contact customers directly.

H9 - Inside Company Network: By accessing Nelli Meyer's computer, you also gain access to the company's internal network.

H11 - Access to Development Environment: The worm has infected other computers in the company network, granting full access to a machine used for software development, including the development environment.

H13 - Read Access to Source Server: During analysis of the development environment, you obtained credentials to connect to the source server, though access is heavily restricted.

H15 - Full Access to Source Server: By using the exploit and test function of the source server, you now have full access to it.

H19 - Full Access to Deployment Server: By gaining full access to the source server, you retrieved login credentials for the deployment server.

H23 - Full Access: You have full access to Nelli Meyer's computer.

References

1. Anderson, L.W., Krathwohl, D.R.: A Taxonomy for Learning, Teaching, and Assessing: A Revision of Bloom's Taxonomy of Educational Objectives, complete Inc, Addison Wesley Longman (2001)
2. Ausubel, D.P.: The use of advance organizers in the learning and retention of meaningful verbal material. J. Educ. Psychol. **51**(5), 267 (1960)
3. Breuer, J., Bente, G.: Why so serious? On the relation of serious games and learning. J. Comput. Game Culture **4**, 7–24 (2010)
4. Geer, D., Tozer, B., Meyers, J.S.: For good measure: counting broken links: A quant s view of software supply chain security. USENIX Login **45**(4) (2020)
5. Hart, S., Halak, B., Sassone, V.: CIST: a serious game for hardware supply chain. Comput. Secur. **122**, 102912 (2022)
6. Jerman Blažič, B., Jerman Blažič, A.: Cybersecurity skills among European high-school students: a new approach in the design of sustainable educational development in cybersecurity. Sustainability **14**(8), 4763 (2022)
7. Jin, G., Tu, M., Kim, T.H., Heffron, J., White, J.: Game based cybersecurity training for high school students. In: Proceedings of the 49th ACM Technical Symposium on Computer Science Education, pp. 68–73 (2018)
8. Kilic, D.: The effect of the jigsaw technique on learning the concepts of the principles and methods of teaching. World Appl. Sci. J. **4**(1), 109–114 (2008)
9. Ladisa, P., Plate, H., Martinez, M., Barais, O., Ponta, S.E.: Risk explorer for software supply chains: understanding the attack surface of open-source based software development. In: Proceedings of the 2022 ACM Workshop on Software Supply Chain Offensive Research and Ecosystem Defenses, pp. 35–36 (2022)
10. MITRE Corporation: MITRE ATT&CK: Adversarial tactics, techniques, and common knowledge (2013). https://attack.mitre.org
11. Ohm, M., Plate, H., Sykosch, A., Meier, M.: Backstabber s knife collection: a review of open source software supply chain attacks. In: Detection of Intrusions and Malware, and Vulnerability Assessment: 17th International Conference, DIMVA 2020, Lisbon, Portugal, June 24–26, 2020, Proceedings 17, pp. 23–43. Springer (2020)
12. The Linux Foundation: Supply chain Levels for Software Artifacts (SLSA). https://slsa.dev/
13. Unesco: International standard classification of education (ISCED) 2011. UNESCO (2012)
14. Zhonggen, Y.: A meta-analysis of use of serious games in education over a decade. Int. J. Comput. Games Technol. **2019**(1), 4797032 (2019)

Challenges in Adapting an Industrial Training Course for Academia a Cybersecurity Risk Management Course Case Study

Stéphane Paul[1], Jamal El Hachem[2(⊠)], and Guy Gogniat[3]

[1] Thales cortAIx/Labs, 91120 Palaiseau, France
stephane.paul@thalesgroup.com
[2] Université Bretagne Sud, UMR CNRS 6074, IRISA, Vannes, France
jamal.el-hachem@univ-ubs.fr
[3] Université Bretagne Sud, UMR CNRS 6285, Lab-STICC, Lorient, France
guy.gogniat@univ-ubs.fr
https://master-cyberus.eu/

Abstract. Industry often requests training courses from academia, or encourages its employees to participate to workshops and conferences organized by academia. Conversely, academia occasionally delegates the teaching of some master courses to industrial experts. Although the selected industrial experts may be recognized trainers in their industrial domains, they will most certainly face a number of challenges related to the course adaptation to academia. This paper presents six challenges that industrial experts will need to cope with when adapting their courses from industry to academia. The challenges are illustrated using a cybersecurity risk management course that was adapted from an industrial training in a big size French company to an European Erasmus Mundus master degree in cybersecurity. The paper proposes a number of guideline solutions for each of those challenges, and assesses the solutions validity through feedback collected during three consecutive years from master 1 students. The student assessment challenge is highlighted as a key topic to be carefully addressed due to its novelty for an industry subject-matter expert, and due to its major impact on student engagement.

Keywords: Course adaptation methodology · Cross-feeding industry-academia · Cybersecurity risk management

1 Introduction

Academia is keen to invite experts from industry to provide students with hands-on experience on targeted subjects. On the other side, industry may allow some of its experts to teach in academia, with the aim of improving their relationship with academia, fostering partnerships for research projects, or establishing

F. Skopik et al. (Eds.): ARES 2025 Workshops, LNCS 15999, pp. 40–58, 2025.
https://doi.org/10.1007/978-3-032-00644-8_3

channels to recruit students as trainees, during their studies, or as professionals, as soon as they finish their courses. It is a win-win partnership, which is often at the initiative of individual teachers and industrial experts, rather than an organizational governance decision at corporate level. When an industrial engineer, who provides internal courses in his company, is asked to deliver a similar course to master students in academia, he needs to adapt his course. This paper reflects on a cybersecurity risk management course, which was built by Thales to train its own internal staff on the French EBIOS-Risk Manager method widely used for cybersecurity risk management [1], and which was later adapted to teach students in the University of South Brittany Cyberus programme. The transposition of the original course targeting industry engineers to a course targeting master 1 students is challenging and requires multiple adaptations. This paper presents a method to effectively manage a course adaptation and avoid training design errors. It outlines the key features of each educational context, presents the main challenges, solutions and lessons learnt from this industry to academia journey. It aims at helping all industrial engineers to adapt their internal training courses to the requirements and constraints of a master 1 or master 2 course in academia.

The remainder of the paper is structured as follows. Section 2 lists the challenges in adapting an industrial training course to an academic master course's requirements and constraints. Section 3 illustrates how these challenges were overcome on the specific case of a cybersecurity risk management course adaptation. Section 4 provides an in-depth analysis of the students' feedback, based on questionnaires, highlighting the improvements along three edition refinements, from 2022 to 2025. Finally, Sect. 5 concludes this paper by exploiting the lessons learnt to define a generic course adaptation guideline to help industrials in adapting their training courses to an academia context.

2   Challenges in Adapting an Industrial Training Course to a Master Degree Course in Academia

Several challenges confront an industrial trainer in adapting a technical course to academia. These challenges can be grouped in two categories:

- Adaptations to the audience [13], i.e., coping with the shift from active engineers in industry to master students at university. The adaptations to the audience have to carry out the following actions: revise the educational goals to target students, consider the lack of professional (organizational, procedural and technical) background, deal with the generation stereotypes, and cope with the lack of student expectations;
- Requirement from academia to formally and explicitly assess the students, through diverse assessment methods and instruments to evaluate the learning results [5], i.e. students participation, case/problem-solving tests, performance tests, final exam, etc.

2.1   Challenge N°1 Adapt the Educational Goals to Students

A good course is built with a targeted audience in mind, and its educational goals are set consistently for that audience to ensure that the students acquire fundamental competencies for productive and evolving careers [13]. Academia generally refers to its work as teaching, while industry is more concerned by training. Behind the vocabulary, there are major differences that suppose significant course adaptations when moving a course from industry to academia. Teaching and training are both essential processes in education and professional development, but they have distinct focuses and approaches. Training focuses on developing specific skills and competencies that are directly applicable to a particular job or task. Training has short-term goals, such as improving performance in a specific area or preparing employees for a new role or responsibility. Training is narrowly focused on specific tasks, procedures, or technologies relevant to a particular job or industry. It is often task-oriented, emphasizing practical application and hands-on experience. By contrast, teaching focuses on knowledge and understanding. It aims at imparting knowledge, developing critical thinking, and fostering a deep understanding of concepts and theories. Teaching has long-term goals, such as preparing students for future academic pursuits, careers, or personal growth. Teaching encourages independent thought, creativity, and the ability to apply knowledge in various contexts.

Thus, the first challenge can be worded as follows: adapt the educational goals, moving from a focused and specialized training course to a more open course.

2.2   Challenges Related to Differences in Professional Background

Adapting learning materials in higher education according to the student's needs and background is crucial. Suitable learning objects and material should be adjusted to fit participant's professional background [12]. However, master students lack professional background. By contrast, trainees in industry attending technical courses are generally senior engineers, with strong professional backgrounds and domain expertise. Newbies are the exception, as young industrial recruits are rarely sent to technical training courses. Young recruits rather attend social or organizational on-boarding courses, such as welcome conventions or quality management trainings, to build a professional network or gain awareness on organizational processes and procedures. In terms of professional background, it is necessary to distinguish between organizational and procedural background, and technical background. The differences in each of these backgrounds between engineers and students will require specific course adaptions.

Challenge n°2 - Cope with the Lack of Organizational and Procedural Professional Background. Learning should be adapted to learners characteristics such as knowledge and meta cognitive knowledge such as preference, behavior, profile, ability and interest [11]. However, master students usually lack organizational and procedural professional background, necessitating course adaptation. By organizational and procedural background, we mean knowledge about industrial processes and the general organization of an enterprise. This covers an understanding of roles and duties (i.e., who does what) and general best practices (i.e., how it is usually done in the given enterprise or discipline). This knowledge is very important when working on realistic case studies, as understanding the business case and how it is run is much more difficult for students than for senior engineers. Typically, system maintenance is something that is systematically overlooked by master students, whilst it is an immediate and key focus of attention for practiced engineers.

Thus, the second challenge can be worded as follows: adapt the difficulty and time allowance of tutorials, as students will face the difficulty of understanding the professional organizational and procedural context in addition to applying the newly learnt technical skills.

Challenge n°3 - Cope with the Lack of Practical Cybersecurity Technical Background. It is essential to raise awareness about potential cybersecurity risks and improve students practical skills for an effective cybersecurity teaching and learning [8]. Indeed, technical skills are central to prepare the next generation engineers and provide an interesting subset of the learning objective [10]. The European Cybersecurity Skills Framework (ECSF) introduced by the European Union Agency for Cybersecurity (ENISA) identified necessary competencies, knowledge, and skills required by cybersecurity professionals to guide cybersecurity courses and certifications [3].

In industry, we usually find two types of technical courses. Courses for beginners are the first type. For these courses, there are no prerequisites, so most of the attendees are without any technical background in the targeted domain; however, we often also find self-trained engineers, with months or even years of practice, but with no theoretical background. Advanced courses are the second type of courses. These courses target specialists or experts wanting to deepen or to extend their scope of knowledge. These trainees have strong technical backgrounds and hands-on experience in topics which are aligned or related to the course. By contrast, master students usually have theoretical background, due to their recent courses or personal reading, but they usually lack hands-on experience, and they lack discussing and confronting the foundations of their knowledge with colleagues and / or customers. Students think they know, whilst in fact many fundamental notions are still fuzzy in their minds. This is known as the Dunning-Kruger effect, a cognitive bias related to the overconfidence of people unskilled at a particular task [7]. This Dunning-Kruger effect has a direct detrimental outcome on the students' attention. If a brief reminder of the topic's fundamentals is proposed, students will immediately complain, loose attention, and disengage: they know it all; the course is bound to be boring!

Thus, the third challenge can be worded as follows: adapt the approach to avoid the Dunning-Kruger effect when providing a refresher course.

2.3 Challenge N°4 Deal with Generation Stereotypes

Student learning experience is complex. It is necessary to consider several pedagogical conditions when designing and implementing learning experiences [13]. As previously mentioned, there is generally a considerable difference between the age of trainees in industrial technical courses, and the age of students in master classes. Pushing just a little the caricature, it is not unusual to find industrial trainers that are younger than most of their course attendees. This is rarely the case in academia. Current master students are from the Z generation (i.e., post year 2000). Born in an ultra-connected world, this generation is the first to have grown up with smartphones and the Internet from birth. They have an expectation of immediacy. Their habit of obtaining information instantly can make them impatient and less able to focus on long-term tasks. Moreover, generation Z is accustomed to juggling between multiple tasks, and thus struggling to fully concentrate on a single activity. If PCs and mobile phones with internet connections are allowed during the courses, the temptations to multitask are numerous. Thus, the fourth challenge can be worded as follows: adapt the course rhythm to the habits of the Z generation.

2.4 Challenge N°5 Deal with the Lack of Attendance Expectations

Engineering leaders and instructors should adapt their pedagogical context to students' motivation and interest to make impactful contributions [6]. In industry, engineers attending a training will have carefully selected a particular course in a corporate catalog, discussed every detail of the course description with their hierarchical manager, and assessed its adequacy with their job training needs. Some will even contact the trainer or their training manager prior to their registration to ensure the course adequacy. In addition, subscription to the course can only be performed when the selection has been validated by the training committee. Consequently, industry engineers arrive to their selected training course with expectations, and they will severely judge the course if their expectations are not met. Thus, understanding and meeting the trainee expectations is an important part of industrial training. This will usually start by a round table during which the trainees present themselves, their job, their experience, and their expectations. The trainer usually asks questions to clarify some topics, or provides immediate feedback on the expectations with respect to the course outline. An expectation that cannot be met is better shun prior to starting the course. With a class of 18 trainees, allowing 2 min of time per trainee consumes over half-an-hour of time. If one adds a debriefing period at the end of the course to discuss how the expectations were met, this whole sequence consumes a significant period on a 1-day or 2-day course. By contrast, master students select a curriculum, not the individual courses that are part of the curriculum. With the exception of a few specialties, it is a take-it or leave-it choice for all the core subjects in the curriculum. Thus, the students usually attend their first core courses without much clue about what they are about to learn, or having given any thought about it prior to the course. This can be a problem, as learners'

expectations are at the basis of active learner engagement in a course.
Thus, the fifth challenge can be worded as follows: students must be provided with meaning before the course really starts.

2.5   Challenge N°6 Need to Formally Assess the Students

Industrial technical courses require that the trainer provides feedback to the trainees during the course. This is usually performed by orienting the trainees back on the right tracks during exercises or practicums, organizing debriefing sessions afterwards, and/or providing the correct answers at the end. Dealing with errors is part of the educational process. This feedback is common to all educational processes, whether industrial training or teaching in academia. However, in addition, academia requires that students be formally assessed, and provided with marks at the end of the course. Students assessment can be used as a learning tool to help teachers support the student's development [4]. The syllabus is often quite open as to how the students should be assessed, leaving some autonomy to the teacher on how he is to perform the assessment. Possible options include continuous assessment during the course, including attendance and level of participation in class, marked quizzes / exercises / case studies, final examination, marked homework (i.e., essays or projects), and oral defense. Moreover, all these options can be selected alone or in combination. They can also be organized for each student individually, or for small groups, or with a combination of individual and group work. This leaves a disturbingly high number of options for a trainer who does not usually need to formally assess his corporate colleagues. However, marking is not only a new obligation for an industrial trainer preparing to deliver an academic course. It is also a fundamental driver for students. The trainer must be aware of the impact of his marking protocol on the behavior of the students. Grades can hinder learning by having students develop strategies for grade optimization, rather than concentrate on the acquisition of lasting knowledge. When poorly used, grading can have an interfering effect on educational objectives. Indeed, grading is a source of strong emotions for the students. The prospect of receiving grades can generate stamina, or stress and anxiety [14]. Good grades can generate feelings of pride, satisfaction, and self-confidence. Conversely, low grades can cause disappointment, frustration, or sadness. These emotions may significantly influence the student's global perception of the course, overriding all other more objective criteria.
Thus, the sixth and last but not least challenge can be worded as follows: an assessment protocol must be designed so as to energize the students towards their learning goals, and not hinder the educational objectives of the course.

3   Proposed Solutions: a Cybersecurity Risk Management Course Case Study

In 2022, two cybersecurity risk management courses from Thales were fused and used as the baseline to build a new EBIOS-Risk Manager course for master 2 students at ESME Sudria (Ivry), and for master 1 students at University of South Brittany (UBS). This section first recalls the history of the creation of the two industrial risk management courses at Thales. It then details the way in which the six aforementioned challenges (see Sect. 2) were dealt with for the initial adaptations, as well as for subsequent adaptations, considering students' feedback. It is to be highlighted that this paper will reflect only on the lessons learnt from the master 1 training course, because the adapted course has been delivered for the past three years at UBS, and a final delivery is scheduled for next year. By contrast, the EBIOS-Risk Manager course at the engineering school was terminated after just 1 year (for reasons that are irrelevant here).

3.1   Historical Background of Risk Management Trainings at Thales

The first cybersecurity risk management course was designed and delivered at Thales early 2016. At the time, due to the rise of threats in the cyberspace, more and more commercial projects were starting to have cybersecurity requirements. Thus, a 1-day risk management course was created, targeting essentially Engineering Delivery Managers (EDMs), Architects (ARCs), Design and Product-Line Authorities (DAs, PLAs), Integration, Verification, Validation and Qualification (IVVQ) managers. The goal was to allow these generalists to perform simple risk assessments, allowing them to understand the cybersecurity needs of their systems, and to secure their systems at the right level, in line with the needs. The goal was also to allow them to interface with cybersecurity experts for more cybersecurity-critical projects, understand their jargon and their main tasks, to allow for an efficient and fruitful cooperation between engineering generalists and cybersecurity experts. It had no prerequisites in terms of cybersecurity knowledge. The course has been delivered since then, and is still being delivered, with a major update in 2019, after ANSSI published a new version of its method, now called EBIOS-Risk Manager.

In parallel, in 2019, a new training kit (in French only) for the EBIOS-Risk Manager method was proposed by ANSSI to train cybersecurity experts to the new version of the method. This kit was rapidly adapted by Thales to create a 2-day internal training course for its own cybersecurity experts. This course has been delivered since then, and is still being actively delivered. So, in 2022, when Cyberus and ESME-Sudria requested a cybersecurity risk management course from Thales, the company was actually delivering two different courses internally: a 1-day risk management course targeted at generalists (i.e., SEMs, ARCs, DAs, PLAs and IVVQ managers), and a 2-day risk management course targeted at cybersecurity experts. These two courses were fused and used as a baseline to build a new EBIOS-Risk Manager course for master 2 students and master 1 students. This section details how these two courses were adapted with respect to the six challenges listed in the previous section.

3.2   Solution N°1 Adapting the Educational Goals to Students

Our first challenge relates to adapting the course's educational goals, moving from a focused and specialized training for engineers, to a more open and generic course for students.

As mentioned above, Thales initially had two risk management courses: one was designed to target generalists (i.e., SEMs, ARCs, DAs, PLAs and IVVQ managers), whilst the second was designed to target specifically cybersecurity experts. These two courses make no sense outside of Thales, because they are built by and for Thales. They typically make continuous reference to Chorus 2.0, Thales' engineering baseline, which is not publicly accessible. In practice, this means that the risk management activities are not taught as standalone activities that must be performed just to comply with the selected risk management method. On the contrary, the risk management activities are positioned in their rightful place in the company's engineering processes, which are known and followed by all system, software and hardware engineers in their day-to-day jobs. The training was built with a full understanding of the attendees' day-to-day tasks. The additional cybersecurity work that is requested from them is fully compatible and suited to their job and target objectives. These courses cannot be delivered as-is to master students. New educational goals must be defined, and the course adapted.

Solution: The industrial course should not be transformed in a pure academic teaching course to suit the master students. Academia would not request an industrial to deliver a theoretical course that they could provide by themselves. Even if it is never explicitly stated in the request, academia expects from industry that the education be practical, full of real-live examples and anecdotes, and feedback on what works in specific and complex circumstances. Thus, the course for students must be adapted to be more theoretical and open than the fined-tuned training for in-house engineers, but it must remain grounded on real-live studies, and illustrated by industrial successes and failures.

3.3   Solution N°2 Coping with the Lack of Organizational and Procedural Professional Background

As stated above, academia expects from industry realistic examples and case studies. However, working on a realistic case study requires a good understanding of organizations and procedures. The cybersecurity risk management tasks come as an overlay to understanding the organization, procedures, and possibly, also the domain, e.g., satellites, ships, industrial control systems, civilian or military, etc. What may appear as obvious to practiced engineers, will appear as strange and new to students.

Solution: Students must be given significantly more time to execute the case studies compared to senior engineers, irrespective of their cybersecurity skills.

However, it is dangerous for time-keeping reasons to announce long case study sequences. If the allocated time for Thales trainees is 30 min, the idea is also to specify 30 min of time for the master students, in order to keep them focused on the task, and also to provide them with an idea of the time that they should take to do the job when they are learned. Nevertheless, it must be clear in the trainer's schedule that multiple extensions will be eventually granted: "Have you finished? No? Ok, let's have 15 min more... but now, please focus on so and so to keep moving!" With successive extension grants, the total case study tutorial might last 1 h or even more... but the students must believe they were granted a favor, to keep them focused. Granting more time for exercises and tutorials will make up for the essential of the time extension between the industrial training course and the academic adaptation. Overall, a 12h industrial course will become a 16h academic course, for the same fundamental content. The increase in the number of learners, typically 18 in industrial training courses, and above 40 in academic conditions, may also account for time extension, as attention must be given to all students and / or working groups. However, this time extension will remain marginal compared to the time extensions due to the students' lack of organizational and procedural background.

3.4   Solution N°3 Coping with the Dunning-Kruger Effect Related to Cybersecurity Technical Background

Performing cybersecurity risk management requires a solid understand of key concepts, such as the three cybersecurity criteria (i.e., confidentiality, integrity and availability), threats and vulnerabilities, security controls, including cryptography, architecture design principles and patterns, etc. Master 2 students, and in a lesser measure master 1 students, will usually claim having knowledge about all those. When asked if a refresher course is required, the students will usually reject the proposal. However, discovering later that students have misconceptions (see real-life example of student misconception below), or at best fuzzy conceptions, of these concepts will jeopardize the whole risk management course. It is needed to overcome the Dunning-Kruger effect, so that students allocated their full attention to the refresher course.

Question: Define information availability.
Student answer (misconception): Information is available when in can be found on internet.
Expected answer: Property of information when it is accessible and usable upon demand by an authorized entity.

Solution: There are several strategies to avoid the Dunning-Kruger cognitive bias. We chose to work on self-awareness. The goal is to push students to recognize their own limitations and strengths. This is performed by giving students a small test asking the students to define the confidentiality, integrity and availability security criteria, provide examples of security measures contributing towards those criteria, as well as other simple questions about vulnerabilities, threats, risks, and ways to assess them. Students are given 10 min to answer 13 simple questions with very short answers, i.e., no more than 3 lines per answer.

The French saying *Whatever is well conceived is clearly said, And the words to say it flow with ease* [2] takes all its meaning here. During this exercise, students realise that the task is more complex than it seemed at first. The notions seemed clear, but strangely, the students cannot find the right words to state them. When the refresher course is proposed after the exercise, the class is eager to find the right answers.

3.5 Solution N°4 Dealing with Generation Stereotypes

The French EBIOS-Risk Manager method is structured in five workshops. In our training course, each workshop is covered by iterating lectures, quizzes, simple exercises, and hands-on case studies. Based on previous teaching experience, we know that senior engineers in industry can easily cope with up to 45 min of lecture before moving to hands-on exercises. By contrast, we start losing the attention of a significant number of master students when the lecture sequences last more than 15 min.

Solution: Adapt the course to enforce shorter iteration loops between lectures, quizzes, and exercises. The ever-changing rhythm keeps students focused.

3.6 Solution N°5 Dealing with the Lack of Attendance Expectations

Expectations and attention are closely intertwined. Expectations guide the allocation of attentional resources, influence what we perceive and how we respond to our environment, and play a crucial role in cognitive processes, including learning. We will not discuss here the usual course design practices to keep attendance attention that are common to all contexts, industry and academia alike. We will focus just on the difference outlined in the previous section, i.e., the lack of student expectations when attending our risk management course (cf. Challenge n°5). This lack of initial expectation adds difficulty in keeping students engaged compared to engineers who have carefully selected their choice of course.

Solution: Expectations can shape attentional resources in multiple ways. For our risk management course, we chose to work on goal-directed behaviour, tainted by a bit of emotional influence. The former rests upon the fact that our expectations often stem from our goals and intentions, i.e., our attention is directed towards information that is relevant to achieving these goals. The latter rests upon the fact that our expectations are influenced by our emotional states. Positive emotions can broaden the scope of attention. This is performed by giving students an oversight of our own work, and what could be the typical day-to-day work of a risk manager. Most students, especially master 1 students, do not yet have a clear idea of the job they want to perform. Making our own job appealing naturally brings interest in the risk management topic.

3.7 Solution N°6 Formally and Explicitly Assessing the Students

Risk management is intrinsically a collaborative activity. We believed from the start that the essential part of the student marks should be based on group work, with groups of 3 to 5 students. This mark should then be fine-tuned with some individual marks, to compensate the somehow unfair homogeneity of group marks. Based on previous teaching experience in academia, we knew that home-work poorly reflects the individual competencies of students. Indeed, students that are organized in trios and who regularly receive group homework are known to distribute the subjects between themselves, each student specializing in and working on one subject on behalf of the whole trio. With this approach, a student can receive top marks without having ever studied a subject.

Initial Solution: For the first year of the master programme courses, we decided for a combination of three marks: (i) continuous individual assessment during the course, through quizzes and exercises, accounting for 30%; (ii) contin-uous group assessment during the course, through complex case study tutorials, accounting for 50%; and (iii) group oral defence on different topics related to risk management, accounting for 20%. For the latter, the students were asked to select one subject among a list, including for example, international catalogs of cybersecurity controls, the evolution of the concept of risk through the ages, or privacy versus cybersecurity. Depending on the subject complexity, the group size could vary from 2 to 10 students. All students were asked to present some part of their common work. This first approach turned out to be very unpopular among the students, and with reason. Indeed, 80% of the total mark were related to continuous assessment during the course. Students claimed that they were in a learning curve, and that their marks poorly reflected their understanding of risk management after the course's end. This assessment protocol negated that errors are part of learning; it did not take into account the learning resulting from debriefings, feedback and corrections. Additionally, it did not account for revi-sion homework. Moreover, the group oral defense proved inadequate to correctly assess the students. During the defense, it was very clear that some students had taken up the group coordination role, and most of the preparation work, whilst others were barely understanding what they were talking about. However, we had promised a group mark, and we kept to it, even if it was clearly unfair. For the following years, we therefore decided for an alternate assessment protocol.

Revised Solution: For the last two years, we have been proposing a full risk assessment case study as an examination performed, two or three weeks after the end of the course, in groups of three to four students (18 points), complemented by a small individual question (2 points). For the third year, the protocol was further improved by running the second year's subject as a mock exam at the end of the course. This protocol has proved more effective in correctly evaluating the students, and has shown better acceptance by the students. However, the unfairness of group notation remains. For the fourth and last year of teaching, we are considering increasing slightly the weight of the individual work by contrast to the group work.

3.8   Summary

In summary, to suit academia requirements, our industrial course underwent six major modifications:

1. Because academia expects more than teaching from an industrial expert delivering the course, the trainer leveraged storytelling techniques to illustrate the otherwise theoretical concepts. The amount of storytelling was progressively increased over the years; in addition, at the end of year 3, a mock exam was held, which exemplified a full risk management case study.
2. Due to their lack of professional background, students were allowed significantly more time for exercises and case study tutorials. During year 1, students were allowed more time than engineers, but with a predefined time limit for each exercise and tutorial in order to fit the course in the allocated number of hours. Starting from year 2, students were granted as much time as they actually needed. On year 3 this implied an additional 1h30, which was granted on the spot by the master degree administration.
3. Because students only have theoretical cybersecurity knowledge, starting from year 2, students were given a small unmarked test at the beginning of the course to increase their self-awareness and avoid the Dunning-Kruger cognitive bias.
4. Due to their belonging to the Z generation, students were provided with much shorter iterations between lectures, quizzes, exercises and case study tutorials, typically with lectures lasting less than 15 min. The quizzes were introduced starting from year 2. In addition, starting from year 2, the exercises and tutorials remained identical, but were not marked anymore; this resulted in lecture / practice iterations, rather than lecture / assessment iterations.
5. Due to their absence of expectations when first attending the course, the students were given meaning for the subject. Starting from year 2, this was particularly exercised by explaining the everyday job of a Governance, Risk and Compliance (GRC) manager.
6. A marking protocol was defined and shared with the students prior to the course. However, during year 1, the choice of continuous marking proved counter-productive. Starting from year 2, the assessment protocol was simplified to consist essentially in a final examination performed as a group of three to four students.

4   Supporting Data: an Analysis of Students' Feedback

After each course, we collected student feedback. Hot takes were collected by the teacher directly and orally during the last session. This was performed before the oral defense (the first year), and before the final exam (the following years).

Cold takes were collected in written form, using a questionnaire, after the oral defense or final exam. This section analyses the cold takes. Hot takes were too unstructured to be systematically analysed.

4.1   The Master Degree Feedback Questionnaire

The master degree feedback questionnaire comprises ten topics:

- Topic 1 - Course planning and organization: this topic deals with the availability, content, clarity and relevance of the syllabus.
- Topic 2 - The methods: this topic deals with the teaching efficacy.
- Topic 3 - Course materials and resources.
- Topic 4 - Teaching: this topic deals with the course content in terms of pace, clarity, illustration, freshness, as well as in relation to other courses.
- Topic 5 - Assessment: this topic deals with the provided information and adequacy of the way students are assessed.
- Topic 6 - Distance learning specifics: not applicable.
- Topic 7 - Pedagogical follow-up (for distance learning): not applicable.
- Topic 8 - The course as a whole: this topic deals with students' self-improvement assessment, and satisfaction.
- Topic 9 - Strengths.
- Topic 10 - Aspects needing improvement.

The questions of the eight first topics are rated on a 4-levels Likert scale [9], i.e., agree, somewhat agree, somewhat disagree, and disagree. The number of questions for each of these eight topics ranges from 2 to 14. The last two topics comprise only one open question and are free text. It is noteworthy that topic 5 as a whole is directly related to our Challenge n°6. The mapping of the other topics to our challenges is more complex. This does not come as a surprise, because the questionnaire was established by the university independently from, and prior to this study and paper.

Table 1. Average number of students and respondents per year

	Year 2022–23	Year 2023–24	Year 2024–25
Number of class students	23	26	43
Number of questionnaire respondents	23	21	26
Percentage of respondents	100%	81%	60%

Table 1 shows the number of students, and the number of cold takes collected for each of the past three years.

Table 2 shows the average Likert scores per topic for each of the past three years. A clear improvement of the ratings can be seen between the first and the second year, followed by some stabilizing the last year. Overall, this clearly shows

Table 2. Average Likert scores per relevant topics and per year (from 1 to 4, the smaller the better)

Topic	Year 2022–23	Year 2023–24	Year 2024–25
1 - Course planning and organization	1.60	1.18	1.25
2 - The methods	2.20	1.24	1.26
3 - Course materials and resources	1.73	1.33	1.25
4 âĂŞ Teaching	2.03	1.41	1.40
5 âĂŞ Assessment	2.46	1.50	1.41
8 - The course as a whole	2.45	1.50	1.30

that lessons were learnt from the first year, and that the course was significantly improved. The following analyses how the questionnaire topics relate to our challenges, how they highlight the positive effects of our solutions, but also the shortcomings remaining to be solved before the fourth and last year of teaching.

4.2   Analysis of Feedback Questionnaires

Challenge n°1, i.e., adapting the educational goals to students, by leveraging storytelling techniques to illustrate the otherwise theoretical concepts, can be mapped to three questions of *The Methods* and *Teaching* topics. The individual ratings for these three questions are provided in Table 3. The figures show a continuous improvement over the years. As such, increased storytelling seems to have allowed accomplishing our first challenge. For the third year, we attribute the small improvement to the mock examination, which grounded the course in a real case study.

Table 3. Likert scores for Challenge n°1 relevant questions

Questions	Year 2022–23	Year 2023–24	Year 2024–25
Links are made between theoretical concepts and their practical application [The Methods]	1.8	1.2	1.2
The examples help better understand the subject [Teaching]	2.0	1.3	1.2
There are sufficient illustrations [Teaching]	1.8	1.5	1.3

This assessment is confirmed by the free text responses of topic 9 in the questionnaire. Over the three years, most responses mention the examples, the practical sessions, the real-live scenarios, the workshops, and case studies delivered by a real professional as the key strengths of the course.

Challenge n°2, i.e., coping with the lack of organizational and procedural professional background by allowing significantly more time for exercises and case study tutorials can be mapped to two individual questions from the *Teaching* and

Table 4. Likert scores for Challenge n°2 relevant questions

Questions	Year 2022–23	Year 2023–24	Year 2024–25
The course is adequately paced [Teaching]	2.8	1.8	1.8
The time frame for completing the assignments or exams is appropriate [Assessment]	2.9	1.7	1.7

Assessment topics. The individual ratings for these two questions are provided in Table 4.

The figures show a significant improvement between the first and second year, followed by a plateau. We attribute the Year 2 improvement to the allowance granted to the students to take as much time as they need to perform their assignments, without any predefined deadline. However, the Year 2 and Year 3 plateau remains quite high. Part of the reasons for this poor rating is related to the teacher's logistics constraints. Indeed, the teacher lives near Paris, whilst the course is delivered in Lorient. To reduce the travel and lodging costs, the approximately 20h of teaching are delivered within $3\frac{1}{2}$ consecutive days. This results in an extremely dense programme. For the 2023–25 years, this issue is clearly visible in the answers to the topic 10 question related to shortcomings. The near totality of the comments relate to timing and pace. For the fourth and last year, we are considering delivering the course with a weekend in the middle. This should allow the students to breathe a little bit without expanding too much the teacher's travel costs. Other related improvements are discussed below, in relation to Challenge n°6.

Challenge n°3, i.e., coping with the lack of practical cybersecurity technical background can be mapped to one question of the *Teaching* topic: *The course content is not repetitive with other courses*. The rating for this question dropped from 1.7 during the first year to a stable 1.2 for the two following years. Since the content of this course and the content of the other courses were not changed, we believe that the change of student perception is essentially related to the small unmarked test at the beginning of the course. This test increased student self-awareness, and avoided the Dunning-Kruger cognitive bias. As such, this challenge has been adequately met.

Challenge n°4, i.e., dealing with the generation Z stereotype, is difficult to map to any specific question. Thus, the most appropriate mapping may be *The course as a whole* topic. Table 2 shows a major improvement between the first and second years. We attribute this improvement to the additional quizzes and to the fact that the exercises and tutorials were not marked anymore. Thus, even if the exercises and tutorials remained identical, this resulted in lecture / practice iterations, rather than lecture / assessment iterations.

Challenge n°5, i.e., dealing with the lack of attendance expectations, is highly related to engagement, and can be mapped to three questions from *The Methods* topics. The individual ratings for these three questions are provided in Table 5. The figures show a significant improvement between the first and second year, followed by a small rise. We attribute the major improvement to the time taken to explain the actual job of a Governance, Risk and Compliance (GRC) manager, and making the job sound appealing. The small raise during the third year is probably related to the lesser time allowance to that end, with the side effect that a few students requested job details during the course breaks.

Table 5. Likert scores for Challenge n°5 relevant questions

Questions	Year 2022–23	Year 2023–24	Year 2024–25
The activities offered during the course engage you (questions)	1.8	1.0	1.2
The group in your room is dynamic and willing to participate in activities, or answer questions	1.9	1.1	1.2
The teaching methods encourage you to reflect on covered topics	2.5	1.2	1.3

Challenge n°6 is directly related to questionnaire topic 5 as a whole. This is a key topic for students. Indeed, it can be seen in Table 2 that, over the three years, the rating of *The course as a whole* is nearly identical to the rating of the *Assessment* topic. The dramatic improvement between the first and second year (i.e., from 2.46 to 1.50) is undoubtedly related to the change of marking protocol, with the shift from continuous assessment (and oral defense) to a final exam protocol. This can be clearly seen in the first year's free text responses of topic 10 in the questionnaire. Most of the responses mention assessment as the main shortcoming, resulting in student demotivation and overall not beginner-friendly course. A detailed analysis of the individual questions for the 2024–25 year shows that the worst ratings in this *Assessment* topic (i.e., respectively 1.7 and 1.5) are given to the following questions: *The time frame for completing the assignments or exams is appropriate*, and, *The level of difficulty of the material is appropriate*. Considering that the examination is a complete risk management study on a real anonymized industrial use-case, these questions also relate to our Challenge n°2, i.e., coping with the lack of organizational and procedural professional background, and the need to allow more time to students compared to practiced engineers. Even if the ratings of those questions have significantly improved compared to the first year (i.e., respectively 2.9 and 2.6) there is room for further improvement. The examination lasting 4 h, it seems highly unpractical to increase its duration. For the fourth and final year, we are thus considering a reduction of the difficulty of the exam, which should also have a positive side effect on the perceived time allowance to complete the assignment.

5   Lessons Learnt and Methodological Guidelines

Figure 1 shows the general context in which industry has a subject-matter expert regularly running a course and a request from academia to deliver that course to

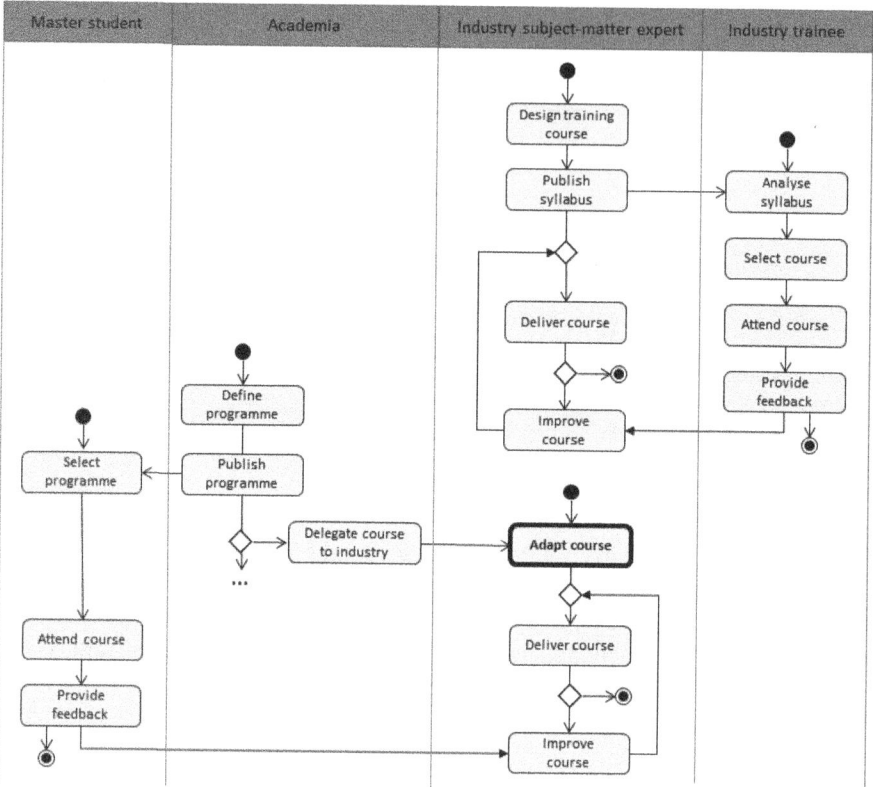

Fig. 1. Academia delegating a course to industry - general context

master students. Within this process, the **Adapt course** activity is highlighted as the focus of this paper. Based on the adaptation of a risk management course from Thales to Cyberus, we have short-listed a number of challenges that the industrial expert will need to cope with when adapting his course from industry to academia. Figure 2 shows that we have grouped these challenges in two categories:

- Adaptations to the audience;
- Definition of a protocol to formally and explicitly assess the students.

The former is probably the easiest to deal with, as a good industrial trainer will necessarily be used to define educational goals adapted to the targeted audience, consider the audience's background, both in terms of organizational / procedural, and technical backgrounds, as well as cope with their specifics in terms of rhythm or (lack of) expectations.

By contrast, assessment is a completely new topic for most industry internal trainers. Setting up the wrong assessment protocol can definitively degrade the overall student appreciation and engagement for a course, irrespectively of the

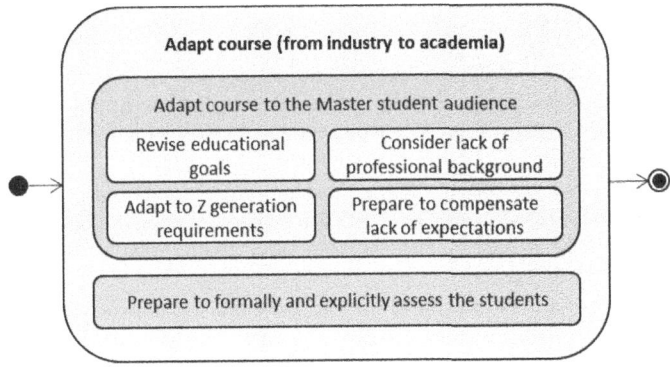

Fig. 2. Key challenges when adapting an industrial course for academia

course quality. As such, assessment is probably the most important challenge that the industrial expert will have to cope with. We do recommend that sufficient time is allocated to elaborate the adequate assessment protocol, in line with the academia's assessment requirements.

References

1. ANSSI: EBIOS Risk Manager, French National Security Agency (2019). https:// cyber.gouv.fr/en/publications/ebios-risk-manager-method
2. Boileau, N.: L'art po tique (chant i), po sie fran aise. https://www.poesie-francaise. fr/nicolas-boileau/poeme-l-art-poetique-chant-I.php
3. Briones Delgado, A., Ricci, S., Chatzopoulou, A., Cegan, J., Dzurenda, P., Koutoudis, I.: Enhancing cybersecurity education in Europe: the REWIRE s course selection methodology. In: Proceedings of the 18th International Conference on Availability, Reliability and Security (2023). https://doi.org/10.1145/3600160. 3605091
4. Broekkamp, H., Van Hout-Wolters, B.: Students adaptation of study strategies when preparing for classroom tests. Educ. Psychol. Rev. **19**(4), 401–428 (2007). https://doi.org/10.1007/s10648-006-9025-0
5. Ibarra-Sáiz, M., Rodríguez, G., Lukas-Mujika, J.F., Santos-Berrondo, A.: Methods and instruments to assess learning outcomes in master's degrees. analysis of teachers perception of their evaluative practice. Educación XX1 **26**, 21–45 (2023)
6. Kem, D.: Personalised and adaptive learning: Emerging learning platforms in the era of digital and smart learning. Int. J. Soc. Sci. Hum. Res. **05**(02) (2022). https:// doi.org/10.47191/ijsshr/v5-i2-02
7. Kruger, J., Dunning, D.: Unskilled and unaware of itâĂŕ: how difficulties in recognizing one's own incompetence lead to inflated self-assessments (1999). https:// doi.org/10.1037/0022-3514.77.6.1121
8. Lazarov, W., Stodulka, T., Schafeitel-Tähtinen, T., Helenius, M., Martinasek, Z.: Interactive environment for effective cybersecurity teaching and learning. In: Proceedings of the 18th International Conference on Availability, Reliability and Security. ARES '23 (2023). https://doi.org/10.1145/3600160.3605007

9. Likert, R.: A technique for the measurement of attitudes. Archives of Psychology (1932)
10. MacDonald, L., et al.: Aligning learning objectives and approaches in global engineering graduate programs: review and recommendations by an interdisciplinary working group. Develop. Eng. **7**, 100095 (2022). https://doi.org/10.1016/j.deveng.2022.100095
11. Martin, F., Chen, Y., Moore, R.L., Westine, C.D.: Systematic review of adaptive learning research designs, context, strategies, and technologies from 2009 to 2018. Educ. Tech. Research Dev. **68**(4), 1903–1929 (2020). https://doi.org/10.1007/s11423-020-09793-2
12. Thalmann, S.: Adaptation criteria for the personalised delivery of learning materials: A multi-stage empirical investigation. Austr. J. Educ. Technol. **30**(1) (2014)
13. Wood, R., Shirazi, S.: A systematic review of audience response systems for teaching and learning in higher education: the student experience. Computers & Education **153**, 103896 (2020)
14. Yerkes, R., Dodson, J.: The relation of strength of stimulus to rapidity of habit-formation. J. Comp. Neurol. Psychol. **5**(18) (1908). https://doi.org/10.1002/CNE.920180503

Psychological and Behavioral Aspects and System Dynamics: Insights from Exercises Using a Cyber Range

José Manuel Castillo[1]($\boxtimes$) ⓘ, Nicolas Louveton[1] ⓘ, and Marc Parenthoen[2] ⓘ

[1] CeRCA, CNRS UMR 7295, Université de Poitiers, Université François-Rabelais de Tours, Poitiers, France
{jose.manuel.castillo.pimentel,
nicolas.louveton}@univ-poitiers.fr
[2] XLIM, CNRS UMR 7252, Université de Poitiers, Poitiers, France
marc.parenthoen@univ-poitiers.fr

Abstract. In recent years, the popularity of cyber exercises has significantly increased, positioning them as essential activities for the development of technical skills related to the detection, mitigation, and response to cyber incidents. However, to date, most of these procedures have focused primarily on building technical competencies and have been designed exclusively for expert cybersecurity audiences, neglecting their potential application in training novice and non-technical teams. This paper aims to address these gaps by presenting an overview of cyber exercises oriented toward the development of both strategic and technical competencies for cyber crisis management. By considering the evaluation of psychological variables such as mental workload, situational awareness, and presence as well as behavioral indicators, this article offers a critical reflection on the design and content of such exercises.

Keywords: Cyber Ranges · Mental Workload · Situation Awareness · Presence

1 Introduction

Jean Monnet, one of the founding fathers of the European Union, once stated that "*people only accept change when they are faced with necessity and only recognize necessity during crises*", implying that change often does not arise from initiative, but rather from a lack of alternatives. This reflection applies directly to the field of cybersecurity, where many organizations only act once the risk has become a tangible threat. As Lazarov et al. [1] point out, *no one is immune to cyberattacks*; that is, from government organizations to small businesses, all are exposed to a wide range of cyber risks that can compromise the security of their information systems and, consequently, disrupt their operations.

Training in preventing, mitigating, and managing cyber incidents has become essential for both public and private organizations. Among the most prominent training modalities are *cyber exercises*. These are conducted in simulated environments that enable the training and assessment of cybersecurity capabilities, including incident response and the enhancement of situational awareness [2]. They have become a widely accepted and consolidated means of strengthening problem-solving skills among technical personnel [3].

Cyber Ranges (CR) are regarded as key immersive platforms for conducting training sessions in the cybersecurity field. Over the past fifteen years, these platforms have seen notable expansion for developing technical skills and strengthening organizational resilience and preparedness against threats and attacks [4]. Through their isolated infrastructures connecting virtual machines as they could be in the real world, cyber ranges offer a safe and legal environment where individuals can train in handling cyberattacks [5].

This work aims to present the results of the initial experiments conducted for the development of RéSISTeCC, a Framework that uses a cyber range as an immersive platform to train employees from small public institutions and small businesses in the management of cyber crises. To achieve this, the article is organized as follows: Sect. 2 briefly presents the objective and purpose of RéSISTeCC, including its setup for the initial experiments. Section 3 outlines the characteristics of the participants and the exercise scenario. Section 4 synthesizes the psychological measures used and the results obtained. Section 5 briefly describes the provisional performance measures employed during these experiments. Finally, Sect. 6 discusses the progress made so far in developing this type of exercise, proposing an analysis of both the content and the structure of such exercises.

2 RéSISTeCC Framework

Specifically, the RéSISTeCC Framework aims to train personnel from small local authorities and small socioeconomic entities to effectively manage cyber crises [6]. To achieve this, it relies on using a Cyber Range as an immersive learning platform that fosters interaction between learners, the information system, and facilitators, while enabling the development of learning scenarios tailored to the specific characteristics of these organizations [7].

As mentioned in the introduction of this article, CRs are sophisticated environments designed to replicate an information system within an isolated setting. They are composed of virtual machines hosting systems, applications, and data, all interconnected to form a network infrastructure that mirrors the complexity of a real-world information system. In this context, CRs offer a secure environment for the practical acquisition of cybersecurity skills, allowing cyberattacks to be conducted without risk [8, 9].

Conventionally, CRs have been designed to train expert audiences or technical teams specializing in cybersecurity. Their most common use in the literature involves training two teams composed of cybersecurity professionals: typically, a conventional CR configuration involves establishing a red team, simulating hacking activities, and a blue team, responsible for defending the system. These two teams are supervised by facilitators forming the white team, in charge of the pedagogical management of the exercise and of adapting stimuli based on team responses. Additional teams may include the green team (ensuring the operational functioning of the cyber range), the yellow team (representing legitimate users), the orange team (responsible for strategic decision-making), and the purple team (handling crisis communication) [8, 9]. These roles are flexible, and individuals may simultaneously belong to multiple teams.

Concerning the RéSISTeCC framework, following the terminology proposed by Yamin et al.[9], the training is primarily aimed at the orange team (strategical), the purple team (in charge of the communication), and blue team (technical incident response), while the facilitators operate across the white (pedagogical guidance), red (attack simulation), yellow (business operations), and green (technical maintenance) teams.

2.1 RéSISTeCC Cyber Range Characteristics

Regarding the configuration of the RéSISTeCC Cyber Range, for the initial exercises, the generic replica of an information system was used, designated as "LOREM". The information (e.g., product or service lists, databases, tools, topology) was adapted to meet the specific needs of each target company (see Fig. 1).

The infrastructure simulated by the cyber range was divided into a local area network (LAN) on the left side of the firewall and an extended network (emulating a minimal Internet WAN network) on the right side. The local network included an LDAP (Lightweight Directory Access Protocol) server, a data server with a database and shared files, a backup server, an ERP (Enterprise Resource Planning), a CRM (Customer Relationship Management) and a set of virtual servers for hosting specific functionalities, as well as a set of workstation terminals. The specific functionalities servers could host, for example, civil status software, industrial control system or development environments, based on the entity's core activities. The firewall also acted as a gateway to the extranet. The extended network was peopled by a DNS (Domain Name System) server, the company's outsourced email server, its website, various cloud-hosted services, and, of course, the hackers' machines.

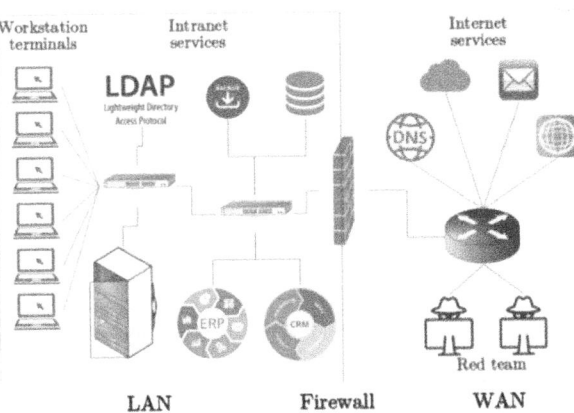

Fig. 1. LOREM's generic simulated information system infrastructure for cyber crisis exercises with small socio-economic entities.

Participants had access to all the virtual machines in the local network from their workstations using SSH, RDP or HTTPS protocols and could also use various services in the extended network. They could ask the facilitators to modify network wire connections, VLANs and switches within the LAN firewall rules included, or to publish a message on the website, for example, as they would with their IT service providers. To simplify data populating and to reduce exercise costs, we have distinguished two ways for addressing individuation: specific data with generic software and specific functionality without data. Shared data about human resources, planning, suppliers, customers, finances were handled by the same open-source software *Dolibarr*. These data were specific to four main sectors of activity: local authority, public institution, industry and service, while servers hosting functionalities acted as empty shells without data implementation. Thus, a scenario can technically address integrity, availability and confidentiality with all the finesse of the observable data, as well as the availability of a critical service.

3 Study Design

3.1 Participants

Throughout 2024, various experimental exercises were conducted involving different Crisis Units from different organizations, such as local councils and small and medium-sized enterprises (SMEs) from the Nouvelle-Aquitaine region. Each Crisis Unit always comprised participants from only one organisation.

Participants were recruited by employers' associations, chambers of commerce, local authority technical agencies, regional e-health support groups as well as directly via the University of Poitiers, through its relationship network. Their level of expertise in managing cyber-origin crises was relatively low, which resulted in a lack of internal procedures for managing these types of incidents. No Crisis Unit had previously participated in this type of simulation or exercise.

The participation of organisations' Crisis Units was voluntary, but we did not interfere in the collective decision process of organisations. Before the exercise, some people felt surprised to be involved in the crisis unit of a cyber crisis. Exercises were conducted during the participants' working hours.

Different representatives from each Crisis Unit participated in a preliminary interview with the pedagogical leaders of the exercise. This preliminary interview aimed to gather information about various aspects of the participating organizations, such as the nature of their activities, their critical or essential activities, the IT and digital tools used in their daily operations, and their perceived level of vulnerability, among other aspects of their structure.

The results of these preliminary interviews served to contextualize the exercise scenario and design the different stimuli composing it. For instance, in the case of companies, the scenario focused on the theft of patent-related and intellectual property information concerning various products. In contrast, in the case of municipalities, it was centered on the theft of identity information of the community's child population. Participants were informed about the types of data collected throughout the exercise (behavioural, image rights, verbalization, etc.) and assured that their participation would remain anonymous. Table 1 presents the composition of each Crisis Unit.

Table 1. Participants Characteristics

Crisis Unit	Type of Structure	Main Activity	CU Composition
C1	Startup Incubator	Tech and business consulting	4 Employees
C2	Public institution	Municipality	5 Employees
C3	Very small business	IT services	2 Employees
C4	SME	IT services	5 Employees
C5	SME	Furniture production	4 Employees
C6	SME	Cosmetics production	6 Employees
C7	Startup Incubator	Tech and business consulting	4 Employees
C8	SME	accounting and legal service	7 Employees

3.2 Scenario and Exercise Setup

As Limousin [10] stated, a pedagogical scenario defines the execution environment, the narrative, the learning objectives, and the overall structure of the training. A scenario is the chronological progression of events (i.e., stimuli injections) which occur during the exercise. These stimuli can represent events and disruptions that participants must face when managing a crisis; they can also be used to guide participants toward completing specific tasks [10, 11]. In our case, the scenario script focused on the theft of critical information for the structures. In this way, the fictional hackers posted a link on a fictional social network (representing X - Twitter), directing participants to a website that displayed part of the stolen data. The hackers aimed to sell the database via Telegram on a fictitious dark website.

The facilitators supervised the development of the scenario and injected the stimuli. They consisted mainly of two types: *Structuring Stimuli*, meaning stimuli that guided participants to complete specific tasks within the scenario, or *Saturating Stimuli*, which aimed to distract them from specific tasks or generate tension among the participants. The facilitators played various roles, such as company colleagues, police officers, journalists, clients, parents (in the case of public entities), and hackers. The participants and the facilitators communicated via email, SMS, or phone.

Before starting the exercise, the participants of each Crisis Unit underwent a brief introduction phase led by the facilitators, during which the objectives of the exercise, the simulation rules, access procedures, and available materials were explained. Additionally, a 15-min period was allocated for the participants to get to know the information system (CR appropriation phase). During this time, stimuli was injected to facilitate adaptation, such as drafting emails, consulting databases, and managing calls from clients or suppliers. A pedagogical break was also scheduled in the middle of the exercise to understand the decisions made by the participants during the first part of the exercise and identify the difficulties they encountered. At the end of the simulation, participants went through a debriefing session (after-action review) to share their impressions of the simulation with the animators. This session also served to reinforce the pedagogical objectives of the simulation.

The exercise was divided into three main phases. The first phase was the *identification of the cyber-attack*, that was focused on anomaly detection and included the following tasks: identifying internal and external anomalies, identifying compromised data and the attacker's intentions. The second phase involved *the activation and establishment of the crisis unit* while isolating the compromised information system and taking first defense countermeasures. This phase included tasks such as ensuring that the fundamental crisis management roles were properly assigned (leader, coordinator, crisis secretary), and defining the frequency of situation updates within the crisis unit. The third phase centered on *planning a crisis response and characterizing the extent of the cyberattack* with evidence. Notably, participants were required to complete the following tasks: notifying at least one relevant authority, filing a report with the authorities, initiating a discussion on how to organize work in both the short and medium term during a crisis, designing a cyber crisis communication strategy, defining communication channels to be used during a cyber crisis among others. Figure 2 illustrates the procedure during the scenarios.

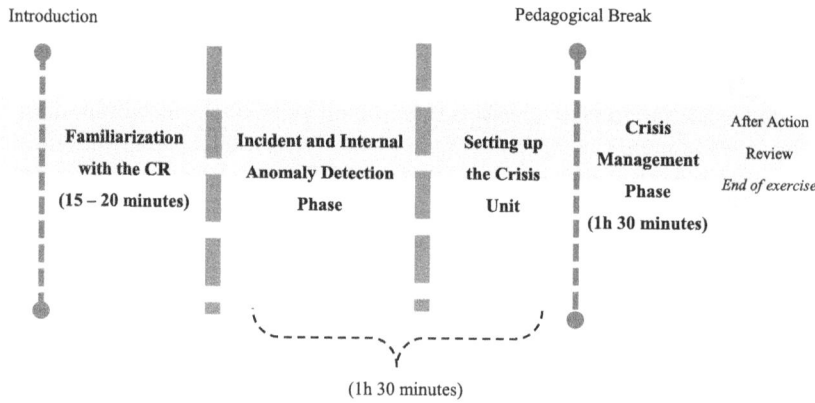

Fig. 2. Graphical representation of the RESISTECC exercise outlining its main phases.

The physical configuration consisted of grouping the participants into one room and the facilitators into another. Each participant was assigned a laptop which displayed one workstation terminal of the cyber range. A few mobile phones were provided for communication with facilitators. A conference camera filmed the participants, allowing facilitators to observe them through real-time film projection. The facilitators supervised participants' actions and dialogues in real time to regulate events and inject stimuli. They could influence the system within the cyber range from attackers' computers or from the cyber range HMI, acting as providers or employees, by making phone calls or by physically entering the participants' crisis room.

4 Psychological Aspects

For this first cluster of experimental exercises, the initial psychological variables assessed were three: Mental workload, Situation Awareness and Presence. In this section, a brief definition of these variables will be presented, along with the justification for their evaluation and a brief description of the results obtained for each of them.

The different questionnaires used can be found at the following link (https://osf.io/RESISTECC).

4.1 Mental Workload

Stramler [12] defines mental workload as any measure of mental effort required to perform a task. Mental workload (MWL) is a widely used variable in ergonomics due to its usefulness in the design of complex systems and in the evaluation of workstations, since it allows for an assessment of the task in the operator's internal state. The interest in evaluating this dimension lies in its ability to understand the perceived level of cognitive effort experienced by participants during the exercise. Thus, having visibility into this effort will allow us to design scenarios and learning objectives tailored to the participants' level of experience.

The French version of the NASA TLX [13] was used to evaluate this variable. This instrument is easy to apply and assesses participants' mental, physical, and temporal demands. It also evaluates the participants' perceived effort, workload, and frustration concerning the task performed. In its short version, mental workload is obtained from the average of all these subcomponents. Figure 3 presents the results of the Mental Workload of each participant from each Crisis Unit.

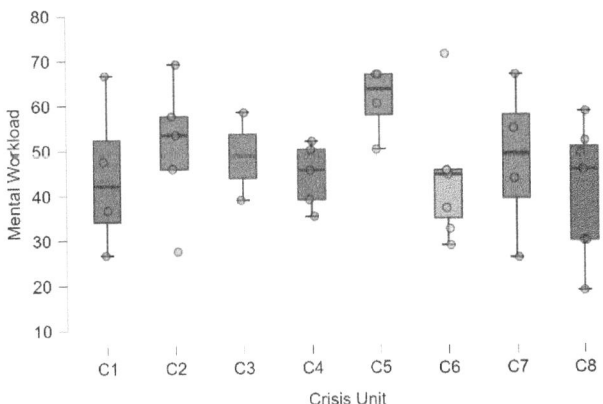

Fig. 3. Results of Mental Workload

From Fig. 3, it can be observed that the levels of MWL differ across each Crisis Unit, from a global perspective, meaning that when looking at the average reached by each Crisis Unit, mental workload ranges from 40.34 to 60.87. The Crisis Unit 5 (C5) presents the highest average (m = 60.87), indicating that this unit experienced a significantly higher mental workload than the others. In contrast, Crisis Unit 8 (C8) shows the lowest average (m = 40.34), suggesting a lower mental workload relative to the other units. Regarding the analysis of standard deviations, it is observed that Crisis Unit 7 (SD = 17.31) and Crisis Unit 1 (SD = 17.12) present the most considerable standard deviations, indicating significant heterogeneity in mental workload within these groups (with some individuals experiencing high mental workload while others felt lower workload), suggesting greater variability in crisis management within these units. Finally, Crisis Unit 4 (C4) has a standard deviation of 7.12, and Crisis Unit 5 (C5) has one of 7.87. These standard deviations are lower than those of the other units, suggesting a more homogeneous mental workload. These differences indicate that the perceived difficulty of the scenario varies across the crisis units, regardless of their composition. This, in turn, reflects differences in group dynamics during crisis management. Additionally, when examining the results of each participant, no trend is observed that MWL increases based on strategic or technical position, or according to greater responsibility during crisis management. At this stage, no definitive conclusions can be drawn; for the moment, all crisis units have positioned themselves at a moderate level of mental workload.

4.2 Situation Awareness

The second variable assessed was Situation Awareness (SA), which is the real-time understanding an operator has of events and conditions within a complex system, integrating these elements into a coherent framework [14]. This cognitive process is influenced by several factors, including the quantity of available information, familiarity with the system, situational requirements (e.g., complexity), and the operator's cognitive resources, such as alertness, concentration and available mental capacity [15]. Our interest in evaluating this variable aligns with what was proposed by Nemeth [16], namely that a successful crisis response relies on a well-founded understanding of the work domain and on how operators perceive and overcome obstacles to achieve their goals.

The evaluation of this variable was carried out using the SART instrument developed by Taylor [15], which assesses three dimensions: Demand, Supply (available resources), and Understanding on a Likert scale. Taylor's model proposes that the operator's level of understanding is conditioned by the interaction between the operator's supplies and the context demands. Because the original questionnaire is in English, we performed a direct translation of the items comprising the scale. Figure 4 presents the results of SA for each participant and each crisis unit.

According to the results, it is observed that Crisis Unit 5 (C5) had the lowest average score (m = 4.15), indicating that its participants experienced greater difficulty in maintaining good SA. This suggests that they perceived lower demands (such as instability or the complexity of the situation) than participants in other units. Conversely, Crisis Units 1 (m = 5.88) and 8 (m = 5.68) recorded the highest averages, reflecting better situation awareness. Regarding variability, Crisis Unit 8 exhibited the lowest standard deviation (0.81), suggesting a stronger consensus regarding SA among its members. In contrast, Crisis Units 3 (2.59) and 2 (2.32) had the highest standard deviations, indicating

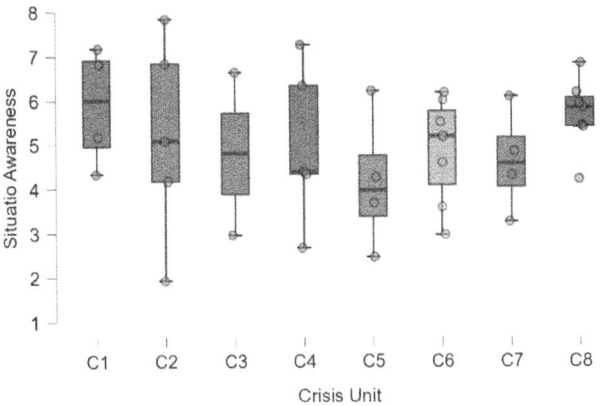

Fig. 4. Results of Situation Awareness

highly divergent perceptions within these groups: some participants felt very aware of the situation, while others perceived much lower levels of awareness.

Regarding the relationship between these results and those of MWL, it is observed that units with a higher mental workload tend to exhibit lower situational awareness, as illustrated by the results of Crisis Unit 5 and 2. Conversely, units with a lower mental workload show higher situational awareness, as for Crisis Units 8 and 6. These findings suggest that a high cognitive load may hinder SA perception. At the individual level, the data suggest that the level of responsibility (i.e., hierarchy in decision-making) appears to be associated with better SA. However, further analyses or more data are necessary to explore the relationship between these two variables and the link between hierarchical position within a crisis units and situational awareness.

4.3 Presence

The last psychological variable measured was the state of presence. According to Witmer and Singer [17], Presence is defined as the subjective experience of being in each environment, resulting from an individual's level of immersion and engagement. It is closely linked to the state of immersion. The evaluation of this state is particularly relevant in the context of cyber range training, because it promotes an experiential approach by encouraging active participation and teamwork [18]. In other words, an increase in participants' sense of presence is considered essential for learning, as it strengthens both emotional and cognitive connections with the training content while fostering reactions to stimuli like those observed in real-world contexts [19, 20].

This psychological variable was assessed using the Presence Questionnaire [21]. This questionnaire was adapted to the characteristics of the cyber range, and only three subdimensions were retained: realism, the possibility to act, and the possibility to examine.

Figure 5 presents the results for the subdimension *Possibility to act*. It can be observed that in this dimension, the scores ranged relatively constantly across the different units, with scores around 4. This subdimension is related to participants' ability to generate actions, the perception of control over the situation, the interaction with the simulation environment, and the capability of producing anticipatory response actions. In this way, Crisis Units 5 and 6 show the lowest mean scores; however, Crisis Unit 5 exhibits greater variability (SD = 0.79) compared to Crisis Unit 6. Crisis Unit 2, on the other hand, achieved the highest mean score for the possibility to act (m = 4.40). Furthermore, Crisis Unit 2 (SD = 1.28) and Crisis Unit 7 (SD = 1.29) show high variability, suggesting that participants' responses within these groups were highly dispersed.

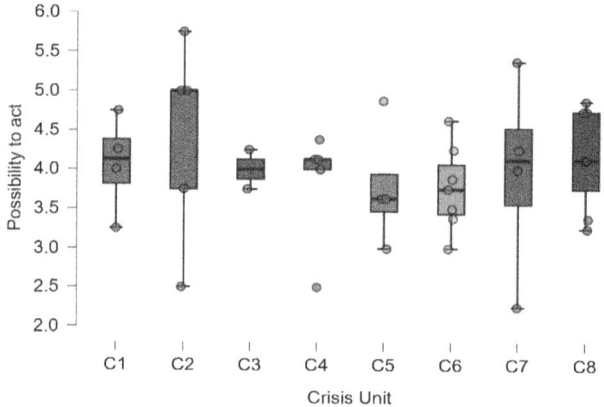

Fig. 5. Results of the subdimension of presence, Possibility to act

The second subdimension was *Realism*, which refers to the participants' perception of how faithfully the simulator reflects real life, for example, whether their decisions or interactions during the simulation correspond to how they would act in real life. According to the results, Crisis Unit 1 presents the highest mean (5.86), indicating that this unit perceived the exercise as more realistic than the others. Conversely, Crisis Unit 8 has the lowest mean (3.95), suggesting that this group found the exercise less realistic. In terms of variability, Crisis Units 2 (1.17), 4 (1.07), and 5 (1.04) have the highest standard deviations, indicating highly divergent opinions about the realism within these groups. This suggests that some participants found the simulation realistic while others did not. In contrast, Crisis Unit 3 has the lowest standard deviation, which indicates a homogeneous perception of realism within this group, meaning there was a consensus among its members. Since the results differ from one unit to another, in this state, it is not possible to conclude the overall level of realism of the cyber exercise (Fig. 6).

The last subdimension of presence is the possibility to examine (see Fig. 7). Crisis Unit 8 (mean = 3.43) obtained the lowest mean score, indicating a reduced perceived ability to explore the crisis. In contrast, Crisis Unit 2 (mean = 4.40) achieved the highest mean score, closely followed by Crisis Unit 1 (4.38) and Unit 4 (4.35), which perceived a greater opportunity to examine the situation. Regarding variability, Crisis Unit 8 (1.46) exhibited the highest standard deviation, suggesting a considerable diversity of opinions regarding the possibility of examining the crisis within this group. This case is particularly noteworthy, as Crisis Unit 8 obtained the lowest mean and showed the greater dispersion, indicating that while some participants found it challenging to

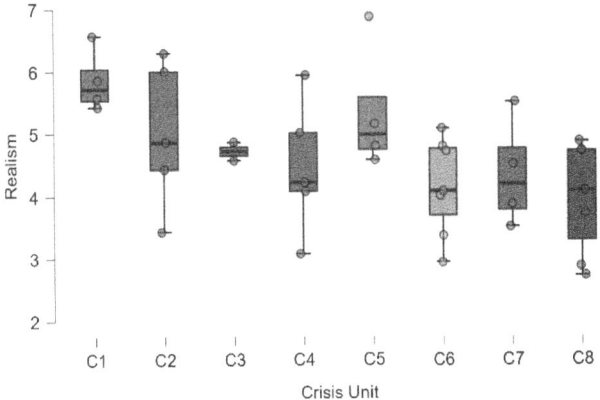

Fig. 6. Results of subdimension of presence, Realism

examine the situation, others did not. Finally, Unit Crisis 3 (0.18) displayed the lowest standard deviation, reflecting a high level of agreement among participants regarding their perception.

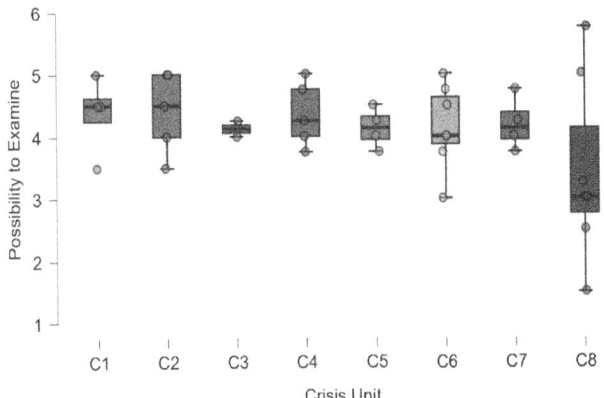

Fig. 7. Results of subdimension of presence, Possibility to examine

Up to this point, it is difficult to clearly understand the levels of presence during the exercise. The differences observed between the various Units appear to result from a combination of technical, human, and contextual factors.

5 Behavioral Aspects

5.1 Familiarization with Cyber Range

During the initial phase of the exercise, the familiarization with the cyber range was not entirely smooth; that is, various problems emerged consistently across the different crisis units. The difficulties encountered during this first stage were generally related to login issues and challenges in retaining user information and passwords, which may be associated with an overload of information.

An initial degree of difficulty was also observed in using digital tools (such as email or applications). Furthermore, some participants faced significant challenges in identifying relevant information (e.g., within the database) and, in some cases, in getting familiar with the operating system. Additionally, it was noted that certain technical staff members were unfamiliar with the system's architecture. Most of these issues were resolved by the technical team responsible for managing the cyber range during the first minutes of the exercise. These aspects highlight the complexity of calibrating the cyber range for this type of training.

Two important aspects emerge from this first part and warrant further discussion. First, the *physical proximity* of participants played a critical role in their getting familiar with the cyber range, as cooperation among participants facilitated adaptation to its use. Collaborative work and communication gradually increased as the exercise progressed. Second, a certain level of *mistrust* or *heightened vigilance* was observed among participants at the beginning of the exercise, particularly in response to the initial stimuli introduced by the facilitators. The initial interaction between participants and these stimuli appeared prudent. Several factors may explain this reaction: on the one hand, the bias associated with being evaluated during the exercise, and on the other hand, the nature of the stimuli themselves, which consisted of emails and telephone calls.

5.2 Exploring First Performance Measures

Each phase of the exercise included key actions related to managing a cyber-originated crisis. In Phase 1, which involved identifying internal and external anomalies, stolen data, and the attacker's intentions, the crisis units generally succeeded in detecting and communicating about internal and external anomalies (all unit crises achieved this action). However, not all Crisis Units identified the compromised data: only half of the Crisis Units (C2, C4, C5, C7) completed this task, reflecting a difficulty in accurately assessing the extent of the breach. Despite this, most Crisis Units could recognize the attacker's intentions, with only Crisis Unit 6 failing to do so.

In Phase 2, which required the activation of the crisis unit and the assignment of key crisis management roles, overall performance was lower. Only Crisis Units 1 and 8 managed to activate the crisis management device and allocate fundamental roles (leader, coordinator, secretary). No Crisis Unit successfully defined the frequency of situation updates. This general difficulty in structuring the response was later evident during task execution and decision-making. Two main factors could explain this challenge: first, a bias due to the participants already being assembled at the beginning of the exercise, possibly reducing the perceived necessity to activate the crisis unit formally; second, the crisis might not have been perceived as sufficiently critical to trigger an immediate and structured activation process.

Phase 3 focused on crisis management actions such as internal and external communication planning, notification to authorities, technical response activities (e.g., checking backups, firewall status, server disconnection), organizing work schedules, and prioritizing critical activities. Results show that all Crisis Units successfully notified at least one competent authority, demonstrating a solid understanding of regulatory obligations.

However, only five of the Crisis Units (C3, C4, C5, C6, C7, C8) managed to correctly handle technical response actions like verifying the integrity of backups or discussing the need to disconnect servers. Communication strategy development was partially successful, with Crisis Units 2 and 5 struggling. It was also observed that the prioritization of administrative and operational activities was particularly challenging, with only Crisis Units 5, 7, and 8 achieving this step, highlighting an overall difficulty in distinguishing and managing critical business functions under crisis conditions. This can reflect the difficulty for participants in representing the temporality of the crisis to themselves.

6 Discussion

In spite of the dispersion of data, the synthesis of psychological variables reveals a slight trend observable through the mean values obtained by each group. Regarding mental workload, most groups experienced a moderate workload level (except C5, which exhibited a higher level). This indicates that the difficulty of the exercise may not have been excessively high, allowing future exercises to incorporate more saturating (stress-inducing) stimuli to increase the perceived difficulty. However, these stimuli must not generate excessive stress in participants, as our descriptive results indicate that high levels of mental workload may negatively impact participants' situational awareness.

Concerning Presence levels, the dimension with the highest score was Realism, whereas the Possibility to act and the Possibility to examine showed moderate to low levels. These results can be interpreted considering behavioral observations. As previously mentioned, participants encountered various difficulties in becoming familiar with the cyber range, which may have negatively influenced the Possibility to act and the Possibility to examine dimensions. In contrast, the high Realism scores show that exercise's design and the perceived consequences of a cyber-attack on the organizational structure positively influenced this dimension, suggesting conceptual fidelity to the crisis scenario rather than to the technical properties of the simulator (cyber range). This initial set of exercises was conducted within an experimental framework. At this stage, further data and evidence are required to draw firm conclusions regarding the psychological variables. More research is necessary to draw clearer conclusions from this type of study; however, the results obtained offer pathways for future investigation.

This paper has outlined the interactive process of building crisis management exercises using a cyber range. Many challenges can be identified that need to be overcome. These challenges will be classified into two aspects: the content, that is, the substance of the training, and the form, in other words, the elements that must be implemented to achieve successful training.

6.1 Considerations Regarding Exercise Content

As mentioned at the beginning of this article, the objective of ReSISTeCC is to establish itself as an immersive platform for acquiring knowledge in cyber crisis management through experiential learning and participant collaboration. Crisis management involves accurate assessment and understanding of the situation and the development of appropriate responses tailored to each stage of the crisis and the specific context in which it unfolds.

It is well known that the effectiveness of crisis management largely depends on the type of internal procedures (inherent to the organizational structure) and the experience and knowledge of the participants. Nevertheless, based on the observations gathered during the experimental exercises conducted in 2024, it is possible to outline a preliminary framework of the pedagogical objectives underlying this type of simulation. These objectives can be grouped into four main categories: (i) Cyber incident management, (ii) Constitution and operation of a Crisis Unit, (iii) Ability to make strategic decisions during a cyber crisis, and (iv) the development of both internal and external communication strategies. Each pedagogical objective should be composed of a series of intermediate objectives, which must be operationalized into measurable actions that allow for an objective evaluation of the exercise. Breaking down these pedagogical objectives into intermediate goals would help guide learning and actions in a more progressive and structured manner.

The first pedagogical objective concerns cyber incident management, which primarily targets technical teams. This overarching objective can be broken down into intermediate goals, such as the identification of anomalies and cyber-related incidents, that is, whether participants can detect one or more anomalies or dysfunctions within their operational systems, and whether the technical team can gather further information related to these anomalies. This objective would also include the ability to communicate the situation clearly and in a structured manner to strategic teams.

The second pedagogical objective is the rational and evidence-based establishment of a crisis unit. This refers to the participants' ability to activate an internal crisis unit after assessing the technical facts and evaluating the severity of the incident through various indicators, thereby shifting into a degraded response mode. Intermediate objectives in this area include the distribution of roles and responsibilities among team members, defining an operational perimeter, and establishing a coordination rhythm (e.g., situation updates).

The third pedagogical objective focuses on leadership and strategic decision-making throughout the crisis management process. This involves organizing and developing a work plan for the continuity of the organization's operations in the short, medium, and long term. It also includes anticipating future challenges, such as formulating hypotheses regarding the evolution of the incident and potential changes in the situation.

The fourth pedagogical objective, as its title indicates, is related to managing internal and external communication. In other words, this objective focuses on assessing whether participants define, establish, and implement an internal and external communication strategy throughout the development of the cyber crisis.

Once the pedagogical objectives have been defined, the second point is the establishment of metrics for evaluating, on the one hand, the performance of the crisis units during the exercise, and on the other hand, the knowledge retained during the exercise.

Regarding the first point, the evaluation of performance, it is necessary to create an observation matrix based on the pedagogical objectives and their respective intermediate goals, which must be translated into specific behaviors. This classification will thus facilitate the creation of stimuli aligned with the achievement of each intermediate objective, and consequently, with the fulfillment of the pedagogical objectives. Table 2 presents an example of the matrix.

Table 2. Example of the Behavior Observation Matrix for Competency Development

Phase	Pedagogical Objective	Intermediate goal	Observable Actions
1	Cyber Incident Management	Understanding and Qualification of Incident	Participants determine which activities or workstations are affected by the cyber-originated incident
			Participants identify the characteristics of the affected data
			Participants estimate the timing of the occurrence of the attack or incident
2	Constitution and operation of a Crisis Unit	Activation of the internal crisis Unit	Depending on the severity of the incident, the participants decide to activate the internal crisis management unit

The main challenge lies in the *reliability* and *validity* of the instrument; therefore, such a matrix must be validated by cybersecurity and crisis management experts, who should be external to the ReSISTeCC development team. The expert review plays a key role in this process, ensuring that the instrument adequately covers the pedagogical objectives. This process involves gathering a group of experts in cybersecurity, crisis management, and organizational behavior, who will evaluate the questions and metrics of the instrument to ensure they are relevant, clear, and aligned with existing best practices and theories in the field. The recommendations and adjustments from this review will help refine the matrix, ensuring that it effectively measures the key variables related to performance and reactions to cyber incidents.

Regarding the second point, that is the retention of knowledge acquired during the crisis exercise, it is deemed pertinent to administer a knowledge test to participants at the beginning, at the end of the exercise, and within a period ranging from 3 to 6 months after the exercise is completed. The test should be linked to the pedagogical objectives of the exercise, and this practice can help establish the actual effectiveness of the training, as it allows for the establishment of a baseline of the participants' knowledge in crisis management.

6.2 Consideration Regarding Exercise Form

To ensure the effective transmission of pedagogical objectives, that is, to facilitate meaningful learning, several aspects of the ReSISTeCC are being considered for inclusion or enhancement. The following section outlines the proposed changes, which will be evaluated in future experimental studies.

The first aspect to be improved is the exercise setup to achieve the pedagogical objectives. This will involve extending the duration of the exercise from 3.5 to 7 h and dividing it into two distinct phases: The first phase will include the participation of the technical teams from the organizations, during which Pedagogical Objective 1 (cyber incident management) will be assessed. This phase aims to evaluate the teams' responsiveness and understanding of cyber incidents. The second phase will focus on the strategic teams, who will receive the situational analysis produced by the technical teams during the first phase of the exercise. This phase will also allow for the assessment of the remaining pedagogical objectives.

The second aspect to be improved concerns eliminating unnecessary elements, both in the configuration of the cyber range and in the introduction of stimuli. In this regard, drawing inspiration from the narrative principle known as *Chekhov's gun* is relevant, which posits that every element introduced in a scenario must serve a purpose within the unfolding narrative. Accordingly, all stimuli, tools, and informational cues presented during the exercise (mails, alerts, or databases) should be meaningfully integrated into the progression of the scenario. This approach ensures narrative coherence and reinforces learning by avoiding superfluous elements that may distract participants or dilute the pedagogical focus.

The third aspect to be integrated into the ReSISTeCC exercise format is the creation of visual stimuli. Until now, only messages, social media posts, and phone calls have been used to structure and cognitively saturate participants. It is now considered relevant to incorporate additional types of stimuli, specifically visual ones, such as videos and images, to more effectively represent various events within the scenario and enhance participants' immersion.

To facilitate communication among members of the different cells, as well as to improve the visibility and handling of the generic information system, it is considered relevant to introduce a functional view for both participants as a pedagogical tool and facilitators as companions. This functional view would establish relationships between the core information system assets (e.g., LDAP, Firewall, Data Base server, ERP, CRM, Backup, Web server, Email server…) and the workstation-level assets (e.g., scheduling/time management tools, website, emailing, etc.). By defining specific states for each asset, such as 'active', 'compromised', 'under maintenance', or 'disconnected', the system can provide real-time feedback to users about the status of critical infrastructure. Additionally, the functional view would allow for dynamic transitions between these states based on system events (e.g., a security breach, maintenance update, or network failure), ensuring that the information flow between teams is consistent and responsive. While state values are assumptions for participants in their view, they are facts for facilitators' view; therefore, they should help the dynamic adaptation of the strategic scenario coherently with technical actions.

7   Conclusion

Training through cyber ranges mobilizes a considerable amount of technical and human resources, as to ensure effective training, practitioners must be involved in planning, design, execution, and evaluation [22]. In other words, building a CR platform is a complex and challenging process due to the comprehensive design and construction of the simulated or emulated environment [1]. In our case, the main challenges lie in the design of a scenario and the calibration of a cyber range tailored to the training of non-expert teams in crisis management. This work has highlighted various technical and human factors that must be considered. Further research is needed to test and refine the structural components of the cyber range itself. Continuing the study of these variables will contribute to the development of more relevant simulation scenarios that foster learning, ultimately supporting small communities and socio-economic entities in preparing to face increasingly complex situations; in other words, helping them confront the challenges of a world that is becoming increasingly insecure with each passing day.

References

1. Lazarov, W., Stodulka, T., Schafeitel-Tähtinen, T., Helenius, M., Martinasek, Z.: Interactive environment for effective cybersecurity teaching and learning. In: Proceedings of the 18th International Conference on Availability, Reliability and Security (ARES 2023), pp. 1–9. Association for Computing Machinery, New York (2023). https://doi.org/10.1145/3600160.360500

2. Pfaller, T., Skopik, F., Reuter, L., Leitner, M.: Data collection in cyber exercises through monitoring points: observing, steering, and scoring. In: International Conference on Information Systems Security and Privacy, pp. 355–366. Science and Technology Publications, Lda (2025). https://doi.org/10.5220/0013309900003899

3. Skopik, F., Leitner, M.: Preparing for national cyber crises using non-linear cyber exercises. In: Proceedings of the 18th International Conference on Privacy, Security and Trust (PST 2021), pp. 1–15. IEEE (2021). https://doi.org/10.1109/PST52912.2021.9647795

4. Leitner, M., et al.: Enabling exercises, education and research with a comprehensive cyber range. J. Wirel. Mob. Netw. Ubiquitous Comput. Dependable Appl. **12**, 37–61 (2021). https://doi.org/10.22667/JOWUA.2021.12.31.037

5. Glas, M., Pernul, G.: Cyber ranges: five use cases for improving cybersecurity skills development in organizations. IEEE Secur. Priv. Mag. 1–10 (2025)

6. Parenthoen, M.: RéSISTeCC: Résilience par simulation immersive Stratégique et technique de Crise cyber. In: Proceedings of the conference "Recherche et de l'Enseignement de la Sécurité des Systèmes d'Information (RESSI 2023), pp. 1–4. Neuvy-sur-Barangeon, France (2023)

7. Castillo, J.M., Louveton, N., Parenthoen, M.: Immersive training in cyber crisis management: the case of the RESISTECC project. In: Proceedings of IHM 2024, Paris, France (2024)

8. Russo, E., Costa, G., Armando, A.: Building next generation cyber ranges with CRACK. Comput. Secur. **95** (2020). https://doi.org/10.1016/j.cose.2020.101837

9. Yamin, M.M., Katt, B., Gkioulos, V.: Cyber ranges and security testbeds: scenarios, functions, tools and architecture (2020). https://doi.org/10.1016/j.cose.2019.101636

10. Limousin, P.: Contribution à la scénarisation pédagogique d'exercices de crise (PhD thesis). École Nationale Supérieure des Mines de Saint-Étienne, Saint-Étienne (2017)

11. Tena-Chollet, F.: Élaboration d'un environnement semi-virtuel de formation à la gestion stratégique de crise, basé sur la simulation multi-agents (PhD thesis). École Nationale Supérieure des Mines de Saint-Étienne, Saint-Étienne (2012)

12. Stramler, J.H.: The dictionary for human factors/ergonomics. CRC Press (1993)

13. Cegarra, J., Morgado, N.: Étude des propriétés de la version francophone du NASA-TLX. In: EPIQUE 2009: 5ème Colloque de Psychologie Ergonomique, pp. 233–239 (2009)

14. Adams, M.J., Tenney, Y.J., Pew, R.W.: Situation awareness and the cognitive management of complex systems. Hum. Factors 37(1), 85–104 (1995)
15. Taylor, R.M.: Experiential measures: performance-based self-ratings of situational awareness. In: Garland, D.J., Endsley, M.R. (eds.) Experimental Analysis and Measurement of Situation Awareness. Embry-Riddle Aeronautical University Press, Daytona Beach, FL, USA (1995)
16. Nemeth, C., Wears, R.L., Patel, S., Rosen, G., Cook, R.: Resilience is not control: healthcare, crisis management, and ICT. Cogn. Technol. Work 13, 189–202 (2011). https://doi.org/10. 1007/s10111-011-0174-7
17. Witmer, B.G., Singer, M.J.: Measuring presence in virtual environments: a presence questionnaire. Presence Teleoper. Virtual Environ. 7(3), 225–240 (1998)
18. Petridou, E., Sparf, J., Hemmingsson, O., Pihl, K.: Immersive simulation and experimental design in risk and crisis management: implications for learning. J. Contingencies Crisis Manag. 31, 1009–1017 (2023). https://doi.org/10.1111/1468-5973.12464
19. Cummings, J.J., Bailenson, J.N.: How immersive is enough? A meta-analysis of the effect of immersive technology on user presence. Media Psychol. 19, 272–309 (2016). https://doi.org/ 10.1080/15213269.2015.1015740
20. Kuhail, M.A., Elsayary, A., Farooq, S., Alghamdi, A.: Exploring Immersive Learning Experiences: A Survey (2022). https://doi.org/10.3390/informatics9040075
21. Robilliard, G., Bouchard, S., Renaud, P., Cournoyer, L.: Validation canadienne-française de deux mesures importantes en réalité virtuelle: l'Immersive Tendencies Questionnaire et le Presence Questionnaire. Poster presented at the 25th Annual Conference of the Société Québécoise pour la Recherche en Psychologie (SQRP), Trois-Rivières, Canada, 1–3 November (2002)
22. Ahmad, A.: A cyber exercise post assessment framework: in Malaysia perspectives (PhD thesis) University of Glasgow, Glasgow (2016)

Cybersecurity Micro-credentials and Career Path Design: The Digital4Security Good Practices

Sara Ricci[1]([📧])(ⓘ), Petr Dzurenda[1](ⓘ), Carmel Somers[2](ⓘ),
Horacio González-Vélez[3](ⓘ), and Lisa Janine Moravek[1]

[1] Brno University of Technology, Brno, Czechia
{ricci,dzurenda,moraveklisa}@vut.cz
[2] Digital Technology Skills, Dublin, Ireland
carmel.somers@digitaltechnologyskills.ie
[3] Cloud Competency Centre, National College of Ireland, Dublin, Ireland
horacio@ncirl.ie

Abstract. Cybersecurity is critical to safeguarding digital economies, yet the sector faces a significant expert shortage. Addressing this gap requires scalable and flexible education to upskill both specialists and nonspecialists. This paper introduces a novel, good-practice methodology for the design of micro-credentials and an AI-driven career path planning solution, both aligned with the European Cybersecurity Skills Framework (ECSF). The primary objective is to support the scalable development of standardized, ECSF-aligned cybersecurity micro-credentials that address evolving labour market needs and facilitate personalized career progression. The proposed approach is validated through the Digital4Security case study, where 17 ECSF-aligned micro-credentials were developed and analyzed. Additionally, a dedicated open-source web application, the Cybersecurity Career Path Designer, supports personalized pathway planning for users by matching existing skills to ECSF profiles. This work demonstrates a practical and scalable framework for aligning education with cybersecurity market needs.

Keywords: Micro-credentials · Career Path · ECSF Framework · Cybersecurity Education · Methodology

1 Introduction

Cybersecurity is critical to protecting governments, businesses, and individuals, especially as digital technologies become central to modern economies. The COVID-19 pandemic intensified the reliance on digital platforms, thereby increasing exposure to cyber threats [15]. Despite a record number of 5.5 million professionals in the field, the global cybersecurity workforce faces a 4.7 million shortfall, with Europe alone lacking more than 392,000 experts [10].

ⓒ The Author(s) 2025
F. Skopik et al. (Eds.): ARES 2025 Workshops, LNCS 15999, pp. 77–95, 2025.
https://doi.org/10.1007/978-3-032-00644-8_5

Public sector institutions, such as governments and central banks, face particular difficulty in attracting skilled talent compared to private industries such as finance [13]. The European Network and Information Security Agency (ENISA) has repeatedly highlighted not only the scarcity of professionals, but also the urgent need for continuous and up-to-date training in the legal, technical, and policy domains [7,13]. Addressing this talent gap requires flexible and scalable education to up-skill both specialists and the broader population.

Our pan-European survey [19] conducted between December 2023 and January 2024, as part of the DIGITAL4Security initiative, yielded 190 valid responses from cybersecurity professionals in 14 EU member states. Among the various insights garnered, a notable finding pertains to program delivery preferences: 24% of respondents expressed a preference for modular learning formats that award micro-credentials. This preference underscores the growing demand for flexible, skills-focused, and stackable educational offerings that allow learners to gain recognition for discrete areas of expertise. This inclination aligns with broader trends in higher education, where micro-credentials are increasingly recognised as viable pathways for rapid upskilling and continuous professional development. Recent research highlights that micro-credentials offer learners short, practical, and up-to-date courses tailored to specific career paths, thereby enhancing employability and meeting the dynamic needs of the workforce [21]. Furthermore, the potential of micro-credentials to revolutionize higher education by providing modular, competency-based learning opportunities that are responsive to technological advancements and stakeholder expectations has also been cited [1].

1.1 Contributions and Paper Organisation

This paper contributes to advancing cybersecurity education by proposing a novel, good-practice methodology for the design of micro-credentials and an AI-driven solution for career path planning, both aligned with the European Cybersecurity Skills Framework (ECSF). The primary objective is to support the scalable development of standardised, ECSF-aligned cybersecurity micro-credentials that address evolving labour market needs and facilitate personalised career progression. This investigation is guided by the following research questions (RQs):

(RQ1) *How can effective micro-credentials be designed to align with ECSF roles while ensuring quality, modularity, and relevance?*
(RQ2) *How can AI and optimization techniques be applied to support micro-credential labelling and career path development in cybersecurity?*
(RQ3) *How can a usable, practical tool be developed to assist learners in exploring and planning cybersecurity career paths using micro-credentials?*

The rest of the article is organised as follows. Section 2 reviews the current state of micro-credentials in the EU. Section 3 outlines the foundational components of our approach, including the ECSF and the AI and optimisation techniques employed. Section 4 presents our micro-credential development methodology, addressing RQ1 by detailing the mapping of learning outcomes to ECSF profiles and the quality evaluation process. Section 5 introduces the career path development methodology, addressing RQ2 through AI-driven labelling, ECSF-based profile matching, and ILP-based optimization. Section 6 describes the CCPD tool, supporting RQ3, while Sect. 7 illustrates its application through a case study based on Digital4Security micro-credentials. The final section provides concluding remarks and outlines potential next steps.

2   The European Micro-credentials Landscape

Micro-credentials have emerged as significant policy and educational innovation in Europe, responding to the increasing demand for flexible, accessible, and modular learning pathways. This demand is driven by the convergence of several factors, including digital and green transitions, demographic change, global economic changes, and the aftermath of the COVID-19 pandemic. In this context, the EU has taken strategic steps to formalise a common European approach to micro-credentials, as evidenced by the Council Recommendation of June 2022 [17] and the preceding 2021 proposal [16] of the European Commission. These instruments provide a structured framework for the development, implementation, recognition, and quality assurance of micro-credentials across Member States, sectors, and institutional providers. The core rationale behind micro-credentials lies in their potential to support lifelong learning and enhance employability. They offer a flexible, learner-centred modality for acquiring specific skills and competences without the need to commit to long, full-degree programmes. According to the Council Recommendation 2022 [17]:

> *"Micro-credentials are defined as documented statements of learning outcomes that result from a small volume of learning, assessed against transparent criteria and underpinned by quality assurance. Crucially, they are designed to be portable, shareable and, where appropriate, stackable, that is, capable of being combined into larger credentials or qualifications depending on national and institutional frameworks."*

The Recommendation proposes a standardised set of descriptors and principles to ensure comparability and mutual recognition across borders. These include the title of the micro-credential, issuing body, learning outcomes, notional workload, preferably expressed in European Credit Transfer System (ECTS), assessment methods, quality assurance processes, and the level and type of learning achieved and linked, where applicable, to the European Qualifications Framework (EQF). Such standards are vital for transparency, facilitating recognition across Member States and between education and labour market systems. The landscape of micro-credentials in Europe is heterogeneous. Some countries, such as Ireland, France, and the Netherlands, have begun integrating micro-credentials into their national qualifications frameworks. Ireland's National Framework of Qualifications has initiated pilots to incorporate micro-credentials within formal and non-formal learning systems [18]. In France, the development of "certificats de compétences" and their integration into the "Répertoire Spécifique" serves a similar purpose [22]. Meanwhile, Dutch higher education institutions have explored micro-credentials through stackable modules within Bachelor's and Master's programmes, often supported by the SURF platform and national funding initiatives [11]. At the institutional level, alliances of European universities under the Erasmus+ programme have launched a key pilot project for transnational micro-credential schemes. These alliances serve as testbeds for cross-border recognition and interoperability [9].

In terms of application, micro-credentials offer several benefits. They support personalised learning by allowing people to acquire competencies at their own pace and according to their specific goals. They enable rapid response to labour market demands by providing focused training in areas of emerging need. For employers, micro-credentials facilitate targeted workforce development and can serve as tools for human resource management, particularly in sectors undergoing transformation. For education providers, they open new avenues for participation with adult learners, professionals, and non-traditional student populations. Despite these advantages, there are considerable challenges. One of the primary issues is the lack of harmonised quality assurance across different types of providers. While higher education institutions typically operate within established accreditation systems, non-formal providers such as private companies or civil society organisations may lack formal mechanisms for quality control. Recognition is another area of concern. Although the European approach proposes a common definition and standards, the degree to which Member States adopt and implement these measures remains variable. In particular, questions remain about the stackability of micro-credentials and the authority of different providers to issue them.

The integration of micro-credentials into employment and active labour market policies also holds promise. Training linked to micro-credentials can be included in recognised programmes supported by individual learning accounts or public employment services. They can be used to address skills bottlenecks in specific sectors or regions and to support transitions between employment statuses, including for self-employed and platform workers. The Council Recommendation explicitly suggests their use in fulfilling mandatory training requirements and supporting re-entry into the labour market for long-term unemployed or low-qualified individuals. To fully realise the potential of micro-credentials, the Commission has committed to several supportive measures. These include developing quality assurance guidelines, adapting existing tools such as the ECTS user guide, enhancing interoperability through the Europass platform, and promoting research and dialogue among stakeholders. Furthermore, EU funding mechanisms, particularly Erasmus+ and the European Social Fund Plus (ESF+), provide financial support for pilot projects, capacity building, and implementation activities.

3   Key Components of Cybersecurity Skill Development

In this section, we describe the key components of our cybersecurity skill development. Specifically, Sect. 3.1 introduces the ECSF framework, Sect. 3.2 looks at the REWIRE project and its relevant outputs on automated curriculum design, and Sect. 3.3 presents the Digital4Security project and its skill needs analysis which is the basement of our micro-credential design methodology.

3.1   European Cybersecurity Skills Framework

The European Cybersecurity Skills Framework (ECSF) [6] is a practical tool developed by ENISA and its ad-hoc working group to support the identification and articulation of tasks, competencies, skills, and knowledge relevant to cybersecurity roles in Europe. It aims to provide a standardised reference for roles, competencies, skills, and knowledge within the cybersecurity domain, supporting skills recognition and the structured development of cybersecurity training programs. The ECSF framework categorises the cybersecurity workforce into 12 distinct profiles, each analysed in terms of key tasks, required skills, and knowledge areas. In total, the framework identifies 84 key skills and 69 key knowledge areas, offering a comprehensive taxonomy to guide academic curricula and training content. The 12 ECSF profiles include: Chief Information Security Officer (CISO), Cyber Incident Responder, Cyber Legal, Policy & Compliance Officer, Cyber Threat Intelligence Specialist, Cybersecurity Architect, Cybersecurity Auditor, Cybersecurity Educator, Cybersecurity Implementer, Cybersecurity Researcher, Cybersecurity Risk Manager, Digital Forensics Investigator, and Penetration Tester.

3.2   REWIRE Skills Grouping and Cybersecurity Profiler

The REWIRE Cybersecurity Profiler (CSProfiler) [4] Web application tool supports the development of curriculum aligned with the ECSF through six steps: collection of data from academic sources, AI-assisted course labelling for the alignment of the ECSF, manual refinement, and presentation of results based on user-defined profiles. A central challenge in using the ECSF framework is the diverse phrasing of its 84 skills and 69 knowledge areas in 12 professional profiles. To improve clarity, REWIRE introduced a grouping method that clusters similar skills and knowledge areas into 31 coherent categories. These clusters were initially derived from the NIST NICE competencies [23], adapted to the European context, and validated by cybersecurity experts. The grouping improves the usability of the ECSF, facilitates clearer links between roles and competencies, and reveals possible gaps in the current ECSF structure that could inform future updates. We refer to [3] for more details.

To automate skill identification in course descriptions, REWIRE employed an AI-based labelling methodology using a Recurrent Neural Network (RNN) with Long Short-Term Memory (LSTM) architecture [2]. Trained on 937 manually labelled cybersecurity job ads, the model predicts relevant skills with consistency across academic and industry datasets. This enables cross-domain skill mapping and supports curriculum alignment with labour market demands. The approach reduces manual workload, improves scalability, and ensures a feedback loop for continuous curriculum refinement. After training, the model labels each course description with the appropriate cybersecurity skill groups and, consequently, maps the proposed curriculum to the coverage of the ECSF profiles.

To determine the optimal combinations of curriculum courses to achieve the desired ECSF profile, REWIRE used an Integer Linear Programming (ILP) [14] method, specifically 0–1 ILP, since the decision variables (i.e. whether to select a course or not) are binary in nature. This algorithm identifies the best combination of courses based on user-defined input conditions, such as the number of years of the study programme, the maximum number of courses per semester, the total number of ECTS credits, and the desired ECSF profiles to be covered by the curriculum.

3.3 Digital4Security Mission and Skills Needs Analysis

Digital4Security is a ground-breaking pan-European master's programme aimed at addressing the escalating challenges posed by cybersecurity threats and data privacy concerns across all industries. This four-year initiative has received support from a Consortium comprising 31 partners spanning 14 countries. The consortium aims to design a European Master's Program in Cybersecurity Management & Data Sovereignty. The goal is to equip European businesses, particularly SMEs, with the critical skills needed to prevent and respond to cybersecurity threats, ensuring a secure digital future for all.

As an initial step, the Digital4Security project conducted a survey [19] between December 2023 and January 2024, collecting 190 valid responses from cybersecurity professionals across 14 EU member states. Aligned with the ECSF, the survey aimed to identify priority knowledge areas and competencies to ensure alignment with evolving cybersecurity threats. The results confirmed a strong foundation of established skills, while also highlighting the growing importance of communication, creativity, technical proficiency, and integrity. The survey design focused on seven key ECSF role profiles (i.e., CISO, Cyber Threat Intelligence Specialist, Cybersecurity Educator, Digital Forensics Investigator, Cybersecurity Auditor, Risk Manager, and Cyber Legal, Policy & Compliance Officer) to gather role-specific insights. It also explored expectations for the master's programme and addressed concerns from organisations managing sensitive data or operating smart technologies, where targeted cybersecurity threats are more prevalent.

4   Micro-credentials Development Methodology

We propose a novel methodology for micro-credential development that strengthens the connection between academia and industry. Specifically, micro-credential Learning Outcomes (LOs) and lecture content serve as detailed descriptors, offering a structured framework for articulating the skills and knowledge that students are expected to acquire. The proposed methodology consists of three steps:

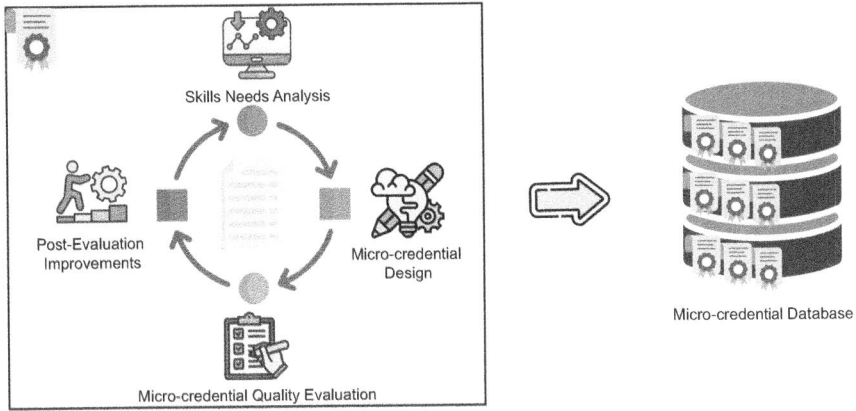

Fig. 1. Micro-credentials Development Methodology.

(1) a skills needs analysis focused on current market demands in the cybersecurity field, with particular emphasis on ECSF role profiles; (2) a micro-credential design strategy informed by the skills analysis and aligned with the existing Digital4Security Master's programme in Cybersecurity Management & Data Sovereignty; and (3) a micro-credential quality evaluation that reflects market needs and ECSF profiles. The proposed methodology is depicted in Fig. 1

From an educational design perspective, integrating micro-credentials into the Digital4Security programme offers several strategic advantages. It aligns with contemporary pedagogical trends that emphasise modularization, personalization, and lifelong learning. In addition, it reflects the increasing importance of competency-based education in fields such as cybersecurity, where professionals must continuously adapt to emerging threats, regulatory requirements, and technological innovations. Additionally, micro-credentials provide an avenue for recognizing prior learning and professional experience, thus enhancing the inclusivity and accessibility of the programme.

Considering these findings and scholarly perspectives, the inclusion of micro-credential pathways in the Digital4Security curriculum represents a pedagogically informed response to the increasing demand for flexibility in higher education. This approach supports the development of modular and adaptable programme structures that can better accommodate the varied learning needs and professional contexts of cybersecurity practitioners across Europe.

4.1   Skills Needs Analysis

Having proven relevant for funded European projects that focus on digital skills [20], needs analyses identify the level of skills and training requirements in a given team or organisation. For the Digital4Security project, in designing the survey each step was carefully planned and executed, starting by setting a clear objective to guide the creation of focused and relevant questions. The survey was structured logically, with questions phrased using plain English principles, encompassing a variety of formats including multiple-choice and open-ended responses. The survey was designed to be concise (the average was 11 min to complete), in anticipation of a higher completion rate, and was optimised for mobile devices to facilitate accessibility. Prior to the survey's launch, a pilot test was conducted to address any potential issues. The utmost importance was placed on maintaining respondents' privacy and anonymity. Clear instructions and an explanatory introduction were provided at the outset. Effective distribution strategies were employed, and a detailed plan for data analysis was defined. The survey questions aimed to:

1. identify the *first and second most in-demand cybersecurity roles* within respondents' organizations to inform the design of relevant micro-credential content;
2. determine the *three most important skills* required for cybersecurity professionals;
3. assess the *key knowledge areas and skills* necessary for cybersecurity management roles.

These questions were carefully selected to ensure the survey captures actionable insights directly linked to curriculum development. By identifying the most in-demand cybersecurity roles, we aim to align micro-credential content with real organisational needs, thereby enhancing employability and relevance. Determining key skills and knowledge areas for general and management-specific roles allows us to design content that supports both up-skilling and role-specific professional development. Given the Master's programme's emphasis on cybersecurity management, this focus ensures that the micro-credentials reflect the competencies required for leadership positions in the field.

4.2   Micro-credential Design

Our micro-credential design strategy is informed by the skills needs analysis and the existing Digital4Security master's programme in Cybersecurity Management & Data Sovereignty. This approach incorporates the following good-practice strategies:

- **Need:** Micro-credentials must address current market demands.
  Response: We selected components from the proposed master's programme that correspond to the most in-demand skills. Notably, the master's programme was itself developed based on the skills needs analysis. By further selecting cybersecurity topics that reflect emerging trends, we strengthen our alignment with labour market demands.
- **Need:** Micro-credentials should follow a standardised methodology to ensure scalability and broad adoption.
  Response: Our micro-credentials are aligned with the ECSF role profiles, and each credential includes a clear mapping to the relevant ECSF profile. This enables learners to target the skills required for specific roles.

- **Need:** Micro-credentials must support modularity, personalization, and upskilling pathways.
  Response: Each master's module is designed to carry 5 or 10 ECTS. To enhance flexibility and personalization, these modules are divided into smaller, topic-oriented micro-credentials tailored to learners' specific needs.
- **Need:** Micro-credentials should respond to company demands and promote understanding between industry and education sectors.
  Response: Industry partners are actively involved in content development, design and evaluation. In particular, their direct participation in teaching ensures the delivery of practice-oriented and industry-relevant education.

4.3 Micro-credential Quality Evaluation

The methodological approach to evaluating micro-credentials offered as part of a master's programme in Digital4Security involves a number of stages. The target learners for this programme are non-technical but digitally aware individuals seeking to enhance their professional competence in the domain of cybersecurity and digital risk. The methodology supports a structured evaluation of the micro-credential curriculum to ensure academic rigour, industry relevance, and alignment with the ECSF. Each section of the methodology corresponds to a specific evaluative action to ensure complete validation of the curriculum.

1. **Alignment of Learning Outcomes with Lesson Content:** A mapping matrix cross-references Learning Outcomes (LOs) with lesson titles and descriptions to verify alignment [12]. Lessons not clearly supporting LOs are flagged, and revisions are proposed where gaps are found.
2. **Application of Bloom's Taxonomy at Master's Level:** LOs are analysed for alignment with EQF Level 7 using Bloom's Taxonomy. Action verbs are categorised by cognitive domain to confirm expectations of specialised knowledge, critical thinking, and independent judgement [8].
3. **Content Accessibility for Non-Technical, Digitally Aware Learners:** Lesson structure and language are reviewed for accessibility. Technical jargon and assumed prior knowledge are identified, and recommendations ensure clarity and inclusivity for digitally literate but non-technical learners.
4. **Relevance to Industry Roles:** Content is mapped to industry roles using frameworks and job taxonomies. This identifies relevant professional profiles (e.g., DPO, Risk Analyst) and demonstrates alignment with practical applications [5].
5. **Mapping to ECSF Role Profiles:** LOs and content are cross-referenced with ECSF competencies to identify aligned roles (e.g., Policy Professional, Risk Manager). Gaps in knowledge or skills are documented for future development.
6. **Evaluation of Content Flow, Quality, and Coverage:** The sequence and coherence of content are evaluated through LOs and module descriptors. The analysis checks for logical progression, topic integration, and redundancy or omission.

7. **Identification of Content Gaps via ECSF Alignment:** Gaps in ECSF-related knowledge or skills are identified through re-analysis. Recommendations focus on enhancing applied content to better prepare learners for ECSF-aligned roles.

Through the application of this multi-dimensional evaluation methodology, curriculum developers and academic coordinators can ensure that micro-credentials in Digital4Security are pedagogically sound, appropriately challenging, accessible to the target learner, and aligned with the strategic goals of cybersecurity workforce development. The results of each evaluation phase contribute to a comprehensive report, supporting iterative improvement and the design of evidence-based curriculum.

4.4   Post-Evaluation Improvements

Following the evaluation, the micro-credential owner conducted an internal review of the assessment findings and implemented targeted improvements. These included refining learning outcomes to ensure full alignment with lesson content, adjusting assessment methods to better reflect Level 7 cognitive demands, and enhancing content accessibility for nontechnical learners. In addition, further examples and applied components were integrated to address the gaps identified in relation to the ECSF role profiles.

5   Career Path Development Methodology

We propose an AI-driven methodology for the development of cybersecurity career pathways, aligning individual learner profiles with the ECSF framework. The approach integrates Curriculum Vitae (CV) analysis, skill extraction, and optimised pathways selection to bridge the gap between personal career goals and industry requirements. Learner CVs serve as structured representations of an individual's professional background, skills, education, and work experience,

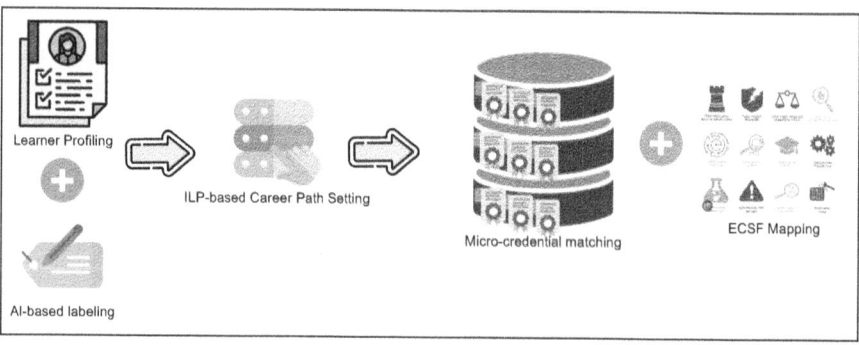

Fig. 2. Career Path Development Methodology.

offering a personalised snapshot of their current capabilities. In our approach, CVs are processed using an RNN-based algorithm trained on ECSF-aligned job advertisements to extract and classify relevant cybersecurity skill groups. This AI-driven labelling enables the translation of unstructured CV text into standardised ECSF terminology, facilitating accurate skill profile. The labelled data provides a robust foundation for comparing individual competencies with target role requirements, thereby supporting personalised career path optimisation and informed micro-credential recommendations. The proposed methodology is shown in Fig. 2 and consists of the following three steps:

- **Learner Profiling:** The data used for learner profiling and career path analysis were extracted from individual CVs. A CV is typically prepared by the learner and outlines their academic background, work experience, certifications, and acquired skills. These documents serve as key input for career planning and competency assessment. They provide a structured overview of a learner's current qualifications and professional development trajectory, making them suitable for AI-based skill extraction and role matching.
- **AI-based Labelling:** CVs are processed using AI techniques to extract and classify skills and competencies, aligned with the ECSF terminology. This generates structured profiles that reflect each individual's current capabilities and areas for growth. Our application employs an RNN to extract cybersecurity skills from textual input. Sentences are tokenised, converted into integer sequences, and analysed by the RNN to classify relevant skill. The model is trained on a labelled dataset of 937 cybersecurity job advertisements, with ground truths manually annotated. Using the same model for both job ads and micro-credential descriptions offers the following benefits: 1) consistent skill identification across datasets, 2) alignment between job market demands and academic content, 3) dynamic career path updates based on evolving industry trends. Once trained, the model processes each micro-credential description automatically generating associated skill groups.
- **ILP-based Career Path Setting:** An ILP model filters and selects optimal career paths based on ECSF-defined role requirements. The model ensures logical progression and role relevance tailored to the learner's background. The ILP algorithm is configured to match micro-credentials to the selected ECSF profiles, ensuring that all skill groups included in the profile but not yet acquired by the learner are covered by the selected combination of micro-credentials. The user can specify the minimum and maximum number of micro-credentials they are willing to undertake, and the algorithm will return the best possible match based on these constraints.
- **Micro-credential Matching and ECSF Mapping:** Based on the optimised path, the appropriate micro-credentials are matched to the skills gaps of the learner. This step ensures that the recommended learning is coherent, compliant with the ECSF and responsive to the demands of the labour market.

This methodology enables scalable, personalised career planning and better aligns academic training with industry demand in cybersecurity.

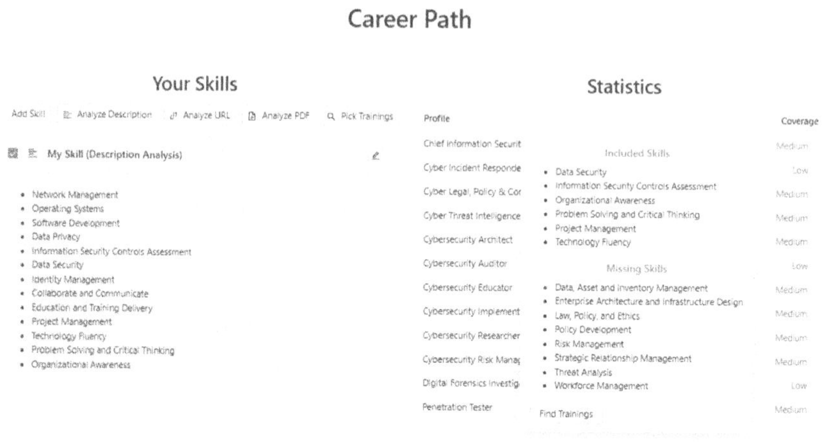

Career Path

Fig. 3. Cybersecurity Career Path Designer: Learner Profiling and ECSF mapping.

6   Cybersecurity Career Path Designer: Purpose, Targeted Users, and Usability

The Cybersecurity Career Path Designer (CCPD) is an open-source, freely available, dynamic web application that serves as a comprehensive tool for designing and analysing your own professional career path in the cybersecurity domain. The source codes are available on the GitLab repository[1]. Building on the foundation of the REWIRE CyberSecurity Profiler (CSProfiler) [4], it expands its capabilities by allowing dynamic analysis of individuals' skills and knowledge and mapping them into specific ECSF profiles. Users can define their own cybersecurity skills profile in several ways: 1) direct entry, 2) text description analysis (e.g., a short description of their own skills), 3) URL analysis (e.g., a description of the content of a field of study, course, or training), 4) PDF analysis (e.g. a CV), and finally, 5) the option to insert a completed course from a database of available courses. CCPD maps these users' skills to specific cybersecurity roles defined by ECSF profiles, identifies recommended micro-credentials for these roles, and allows users to design their own career path to achieve the desired roles.

The CCPD tool fully integrates the AI-driven cybersecurity career path development concept. The tool is divided into two main sections, see Fig. 3: 1) the left section (Your Skills) allows users to define their own skills and 2) the right section (Statistics) provides the statistical analysis and compliance of the professional profile with ECSF profiles. When users add skills, they can choose from several options, i.e. add a skill, analyse description/URL/ PDF, or simply select an existing course from the available ones. They will have to enter different data depending on the selected option, e.g. name of the skill group or link to

---

[1] https://gitlab.com/brno-axe/D4Sec/cybersecurity-career-paths.

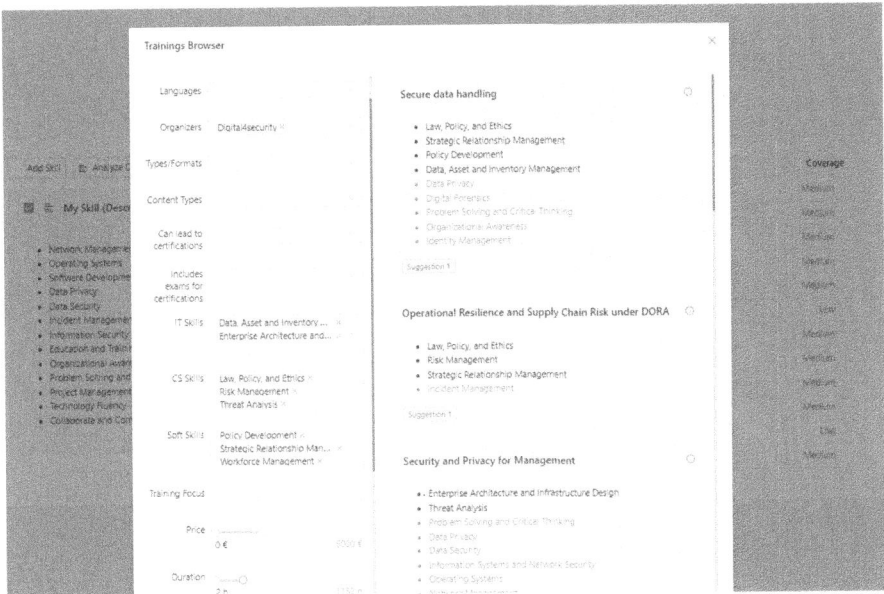

Fig. 4. Cybersecurity Career Path Designer: micro-credentials filtering depending on the ECSF selected and learner knowledges.

the data source for analysis. Users can correct the analysis results by adding or removing skills. The corresponding ECSF profiles and their level of compliance with the user's professional profile will then be displayed in the right section. The user then has the option of selecting the ECSF profile that is to be selected. This is where the ILP algorithm plays a key role. The user first clicks on'Find Training' as shown in Fig. 3. Based on the analysis of the skills provided, the algorithm will determine the skill groups to which the micro-credentials relate and, based on the set filter, it will suggest the optimal combination of available micro-credentials, see Fig. 4. Note that filtering allows one to display available courses based on your own preferences such as countries, languages, organisers, types/formats, and content types. If necessary, users can also filter the courses based on the required skills that the courses must contain. Finally, the user can choose the ILP algorithm strategy to ensure that the most suitable combination of micro-credentials is found by setting requirements for 1) total price and 2) duration, 3) displaying the maximum number of proposals, and 4) setting the maximum number of micro-credentials per proposal. After evaluating the user's conditions with the ILP algorithm, the user can then see the recommended combinations of these micro-credentials (i.e., labelled Suggestion 1, Suggestion 2, etc.). Black text fonts of the available skills within the micro-credentials description indicates skills that the user already possesses, while grey text indicates the user's missing skills. It is also worth mentioning that the ILP algorithm can be set to prioritise courses that are close to the user. This is selected using

Micro-credential Quality Evaluation											
Module	ECTS	Micro-credential	Micro-ECTS	Industry	CISO	Legal	Risk Man	Educator	Threat Sp.	Auditor	Non-Tech
Cybersecurity Law & Data Sovereignty	5	Cybersecurity Law	3		Partial fit	Ideal fit	Strong fit				Partial fit
		Secure data handling	2		Partial fit	Ideal fit	Strong fit	Partial fit		Partial fit	Strong fit
Risk Management of Cyber-Physical Systems	5	Risk Management of Cyber-Physical Systems	5	✓ Yes	Strong fit	Strong fit	Strong fit				Partial fit
Cybersecurity in Industry - Security of OT and Cyber-Physical Systems	5	Cybersecurity in Industry - Security of OT and Cyber-Physical Systems	5	✓ Yes			Ideal fit	Partial fit		Strong fit	Partial fit
Law, Compliance, Governance, Policy, and Ethics	10	Law, Compliance, Governance, Policy, and Ethics	5		Strong fit	Strong fit				Partial fit	Partial fit
Cybersecurity Education & Training Delivery I	5	Cybersecurity Teaching	3	✓ Yes				Ideal fit			Strong Fit
		Cyber Range Scenario Design	3	✓ Yes				Ideal fit	Partial fit		Partial fit
Cybersecurity Economics & Supply Chain	5	DORA Compliance and ICT Risk Management Operational Resilience and Supply Chain Risk under DORA	3					Ideal fit		Strong fit	Strong fit
			2			Strong fit	Strong fit			Partial fit	Partial fit
Business Resilience, Incident Management and Threat Response	10	Business Resilience, Incident Management and Threat Response	5		Strong fit		Partial fit		Partial fit		Partial fit
Communication Design for Cybersecurity	5	Communication Design for Cybersecurity	5			Strong fit	Strong fit	Strong fit			Strong fit
Cybersecurity Culture, Strategy & Leadership	10	Cybersecurity Culture and Landscape	5	✓ Yes	Strong fit	Strong fit	Strong fit	Partial fit			Partial fit
		Cybersecurity Strategy and Leadership	5	✓ Yes							
CISO and Crisis Communication	5	CISO and Crisis Communication	5	✓ Yes	Ideal fit	Partial fit	Strong fit	Partial fit			Strong fit
Enterprise Architecture, Infrastructure Design and Cloud Computing	10	Enterprise Architecture, Infrastructure Design and Cloud Computing	6		Partial fit			Partial fit			Partial fit
AI & Emerging Topics in Cybersecurity	10	Trends in Cybersecurity	3	✓ Yes	Partial fit	Partial fit	Strong fit	Partial fit		Partial fit	Partial fit
Technological Foundations for CS & Security Controls	10	Security and Privacy for Managementng	2	✓ Yes		Partial fit	Partial fit	Partial fit		Partial fit	Strong fit

Fig. 5. Quality Evaluation of proposed micro-credentials with respective moudules.

the'Training Focus', where the user selects which of the IT, cybersecurity, and soft skills areas is closest to him/her.

7   Case Study

In this section, we apply both the proposed micro-credential design and career path methodologies to the Digital4Security case study. Specifically, Sect. 7.1 presents the micro-credential design process, following the methodology described in Sect. 4, whereas Sect. 7.2 illustrates a career path design using the Cybersecurity Career Path Designer tool described in Sect. 6.

7.1   Micro-credential Design and Quality Evaluation

Following the skills needs analysis and the proposed methodology, 17 micro-credentials have been designed. Figure 5 presents a summary of the quality evaluation conducted on 17 proposed micro-credentials across 13 master's level modules. The figure displays the module titles with their corresponding ECTS credits, the aligned micro-credentials with assigned ECTS, and the degree of alignment with relevant ECSF role profiles (specified as either ideal, strong, or partial fit). Additionally, it indicates whether each micro-credential is designed for a non-technical audience. It is important to note that the table does not capture the full scope of the evaluation; a more detailed example of the assessment process is provided below for the "Cybersecurity teaching" micro-credential. Specifically, following the seven methodological steps outlined in Sect. 4:

| | Micro-credential Quality Evaluation | | | | | | | |
LOs	Learning Outcome Description	Bloom Level	Adult Education & Lesson Planning	Cybersecurity Education Methods	SME Needs & Crisis Communication	Practical Cybersecurity for SMEs	Collaborative & Interactive Tools	Creating Interactive Media Content
1	Critically evaluate methodologies and materials for cybersecurity education	5	1	1			1	
2	Appraise students' needs to plan and carry out training.	5 & 3		1	1	1	1	
3	Create new teaching material using modern technologies	6			1	1		1
4	Analyse adult learners' needs and design lesson plans	4 & 6	1					
5	Evaluate education methods and develop teaching strategies	6 & 5		1			1	
6	Create interactivity and engagement	6		1			1	
7	Design multimedia content for cybersecurity education	6				1	1	1
8	Propose training around cybersecurity incidents for SMEs	3 & 6			1			
9	Support SMEs in live incident communication	3			1			
10	Design and implement awareness training using tools	6 & 3					1	1
11	Plan course structure, create lesson plans, learn soft skills	6 & 2	1					

Fig. 6. Bloom's level classification table for each Learning Outcome.

1. **Alignment of Learning Outcomes with Lesson Content:** Lessons were marked with a '1' where alignment was evident or empty where it was lacking, as shown in Fig. 6. This process ensured that each LO was addressed appropriately, with gaps and redundancies noted for revision.

2. **Application of Bloom's Taxonomy at Master's Level:** The action verbs within the LOs were analysed and classified according to Bloom's Taxonomy. The learning outcomes align strongly with Bloom's taxonomy, especially in the higher-order cognitive domains of Analyse, Evaluate, and Create.

3. **Assessment of Content Accessibility for a Non-Technical but Digitally Aware Learner:** Thematic analysis of lesson titles such as "Cybersecurity Teaching Methods (Games, Simulations)" and "SME Needs & Crisis Communication" confirmed a conceptual (rather than technical) focus. The use of accessible language and the absence of technical jargon supported the suitability of the content for non-specialist learners.

4. **Relevance of Content to Industry Roles:** A structured mapping was performed to identify roles supported by the micro-credential. Five relevant industry roles were identified: Education & Training, SMEs (Small and Medium Enterprises) Cybersecurity Awareness & Comms, Corporate Learning & Development, Public Sector / NGOs, Technology & Cyber Consulting Firms . These were derived through thematic analysis and cross-referencing with job role databases (e.g., ESCO, LinkedIn).

5. **Mapping to ECSF Role Profiles:** The content was mapped to ENISA's ECSF, confirming directly aligned with the Cybersecurity Educator.

6. **Evaluation of Content Flow, Quality, and Coverage:** The lesson sequence was reviewed to assess the coherence and progression of the topics. The quality of the content was validated by checking for clarity, consistency, and precision.

7. **Identification of Content Gaps Based on ECSF Alignment:** Additional insights were drawn from learner personas and peer programme comparisons, highlighting the need to integrate behaviour change frameworks such as COM-B or Fogg behaviour model to help educators design training that sticks.

7.2   Career Path Design

As a first step, the 17 designed micro-credentials were uploaded to the database using a standardised template containing key parameters (e.g. duration, ECTS, cost). Cybersecurity skills were automatically extracted using the AI-driven algorithm. The tool can be used to analyze ECSF coverage across the 17 designed micro-credentials. The proposed micro-credentials collectively support mainly the ECSF profiles: CISO, Cyber Incident Responder, Cyber Legal, Policy & Compliance Officer, Cybersecurity Educator, Cybersecurity Risk Manager, and Digital Forensic Investigator.

Figure 3 shows an example were a technical CV was uploaded and analysed. The user's extracted skills are shown on the left, while the right panel displays owned and missing skills for each ECSF profile, along with an overall coverage assessment (low, medium, high). This functionality helps learners identify the profiles that best align with their background. Based on this, the system recommends suitable courses as shown Fig. 4. In addition, the tool can offer strategic guidance for users with no previous cybersecurity experience by generating career pathways. For instance, we requested tailored pathways for three ECSF profiles, each limited to a maximum of four micro-credentials:

– **CISO Pathway:** Secure Data Handling + Cybersecurity Strategy and Leadership + Security and Privacy for Management;
– **Cyber Legal, Policy & Compliance Officer Pathway:** Cybersecurity Law + Cybersecurity in Industry;
– **Cybersecurity Educator Pathway:** Cybersecurity Teaching + Cybersecurity Culture and Landscape + Enterprise Architecture, Infrastructure Design and Cloud Computing.

8   Conclusions

This article presents a novel, good-practice methodology for the design of micro-credentials and an AI-driven solution for career path planning, leveraging the ECSF to align education with current market needs in cybersecurity. The proposed methodology ensures that micro-credentials not only address relevant ECSF skill groups but are also accessible to a wide range of learners, including nontechnical yet digitally literate individuals. In the AI-driven career path planning approach, learner CVs serve as input data for profiling, enabling targeted upskilling by identifying existing competencies and recommending optimal learning pathways based on ECSF role requirements and individual goals.

The application of this methodology in the Digital4Security case study demonstrates its feasibility and potential impact. Seventeen ECSF-aligned micro-credentials were developed and assessed, collectively covering a broad spectrum of cybersecurity roles. The system further supports strategic guidance for users with limited cybersecurity experience, providing coherent, ECSF-aligned learning pathways tailored to specific professional profiles.

Acknowledgements. This work was supported by the project DIGITAL4Security: A European Masters Programme in Cybersecurity Management & Data Sovereignty (URL: https://digital4security.eu), funded by the European Commission under the DIGITAL programme (call: DIGITAL-2022-SKILLS-03-SPECIALISED-EDU, grant no. 101123430, Feb 2024âĂŞJan 2028), and by the Ministry of the Interior of the Czech Republic under grant VJ03030003, within the IMPAKT 1 programme.

References

1. Ahsan, K., Akbar, S., Kam, B., Abdulrahman, M.D.A.: Implementation of micro-credentials in higher education: a systematic literature review. Educ. Inf. Technol. **28**(10), 13505–13540 (2023)
2. Berg, S., et al.: Ilastik: interactive machine learning for (bio) image analysis. Nat. Methods **16**(12), 1226–1232 (2019)
3. Dzurenda, P., Ricci, S.: R3.4.1 mapping the framework to existing courses and schemes (2022). https://rewireproject.eu/deliverables/
4. Dzurenda, P., Ricci, S., Sikora, M., Stejskal, M., Lendák, I., Adao, P.: Enhancing cybersecurity curriculum development: AI-driven mapping and optimization techniques. In: ARES'24: 19th International Conference on Availability. Reliability and Security, pp. 1–10. ACM, Vienna (2024)
5. Eibl, G., Jungbauer, C., Litvyak, O., Volkl, P., Luidold, C.: Proactive curriculum for cyber security education: a model of micro-credentials and active blended learning. In: CEEeGov '24: Central and Eastern European EDem and EGov Days 2024, pp. 234– 239. ACM, Budapest (2024)
6. ENISA: European cybersecurity skills framework role profiles (2022). https://www.enisa.europa.eu/publications/european-cybersecurity-skills-framework-role-profiles
7. ENISA: Communication on the cybersecurity skills academy (2023). https://digital-strategy.ec.europa.eu/en/library/communication-cybersecurity-skills-academy
8. Grm, S.P., Bjørnåvold, J., Rusu, A.: Analysis and overview of NQF level descriptors in European countries. cedefop research paper. no 66. Cedefop-European Centre for the Development of Vocational Training (2018)
9. Grumbinait?, I., Colus, F., Carvajal, H.B.: Report on the outcomes and transformational potential of the European Universities initiative. Report ISBN 978-92-68-20047-6, European Commission, Directorate-General for Education, Youth, Sport and Culture, Luxembourg (2025). available at: https://www.vleva.eu/storage/1337/Report-European-Universities-Initiative.pdf (Accessed: 7/May/25)
10. ICS2: Cybersecurity workforce study (2024). https://www.isc2.org/Insights/2024/10/ISC2-2024-Cybersecurity-Workforce-Study

11. Kerver, B., Riksen, D.: Whitepaper on open badges and micro-credentials. whitepaper, SURFnet, Utrecht (2016). available at: https://www.surf.nl/files/2019-06/Whitepaper-on-open-badges-en-micro-credentials.pdf. Accessed 7 May 25
12. Lam, B.H., Tsui, K.T.: Curriculum mapping as deliberation-examining the alignment of subject learning outcomes and course curricula. Stud. High. Educ. **41**(8), 1371–1388 (2016)
13. Nurse, J.R., Adamos, K., Grammatopoulos, A., Di Franco, F.: Addressing the eu cybersecurity skills shortage and gap through higher education. European Union Agency for Cybersecurity (ENISA) Report (2021)
14. Papadimitriou, C.H., Steiglitz, K.: Combinatorial optimization: algorithms and complexity. Courier Corporation (1998)
15. Pipikaite, A., Bueermann, G., Joshi, A., Jurgens, J.: Global cybersecurity outlook 2022. In: Geneva: World Economic Forum (2022)
16. Publications Office of the European Union: Proposal for a COUNCIL RECOMMENDATION on a European approach to micro-credentials for lifelong learning and employability. EUR-Lex **Document SWD(2021) 367 final**(COM(2021) 770 final), pp. 1–21 (2021), available at: https://eur-lex.europa.eu/legal-content/EN/TXT/?uri=celex:52021DC0770 (Accessed: 7/May/25)
17. Publications Office of the European Union: COUNCIL RECOMMENDATION of 16 June 2022 on a European approach to micro-credentials for lifelong learning and employability. EUR-Lex **Document 32022H0627(02)**(2022/C 243/02), 1–16 (2022). available at: https://eur-lex.europa.eu/legal-content/EN/TXT/?uri=oj:JOC_2022_243_R_0002. Accessed 7 May 25
18. Quality and Qualifications Ireland: A Brief Guide to the Irish National Framework of Qualifications (NFQ). Report Version 1.0, QQI, Ireland (2024). available at: https://www.qqi.ie/sites/default/files/2024-08/a-brief-guide-to-the-irish-national-framework-of-qualifications-nfq.pdf. Accessed 7 May 25
19. Somers, C.: D2.1 market needs analysis (2024). https://www.digital4security.eu/project-resources/
20. Somers, C., et al.: Systematic needs analysis of advanced digital skills for postgraduate computing education: the digital4business case. In: AIED 2024. CCIS, vol. 2150, pp. 179–191. Springer, Recife (2024)
21. Varadarajan, S., Koh, J.H.L., Daniel, B.K.: A systematic review of the opportunities and challenges of micro-credentials for multiple stakeholders: learners, employers, higher education institutions and government. Int. J. Educ. Technol. High. Educ. **20**(1), 13 (2023)
22. Werquin, P.: Case study France: Microcredentials for labour market education and training. First look at mapping microcredentials in European labour-market-related education, training and learning: take-up, characteristics and functions. Report, CEDEFOP, Thessaloniki (2023). available at: https://www.cedefop.europa.eu/files/france_microcredentials_mapping.pdf. Accessed 7 May 25
23. Wetzel, K.: Nice Framework Competencies: Assessing Learners for Cybersecurity Work. Tech. rep, National Institute of Standards and Technology (2021)

EDURange Cloud: On Demand Cybersecurity Sandboxes Through Kubernetes

Ryder Selikow[1]([✉])[iD], Jens Mache[1][iD], Jack Cook[2][iD], Joseph Granville[2][iD], Richard Weiss[2][iD], and Hsiao-An Wang[3][iD]

[1] Lewis and Clark College, Portland, OR 9719, USA
{ryderselikow,jmache}@lclark.edu
[2] The Evergreen State College, Olympia, WA, USA
cookjackc@gmail.com, jwgranville@gmail.com, weissr@evergreen.edu
[3] Northeastern University, Boston, MA, USA
hs.wang@northeastern.edu

Abstract. This paper describes EDURange Cloud, a cybersecurity education platform and framework powered by Kubernetes. The novelty of this approach is that it modularizes common internal components such as a Web server, FTP server, or database so that one can pick and choose the ones that are needed and scale the resources as desired to support the demand of the classroom exercise. It allows us to solve the problems that everyone faces when they build and run hands-on cybersecurity exercises in a classroom. Most often, we have greater needs for scalability, modularity, and ease of use.

This framework allows instructors to efficiently design, modify and host their own cybersecurity exercises and competitions. The benefits of how we use Kubernetes include enhanced modularity through isolated instances, cost-effective scaling that adjusts resources based on demand, and the agility to deploy or update challenges rapidly.

This approach addresses several critical problems. For example, it minimizes the instructor's workload in class and enables independent challenge-pod resets for troubleshooting student problems. Additionally, some of the cybersecurity content may not tolerate resource sharing as it results in conflicts. The modularization and replication of containers mitigates that conflict by allocating independent replicas to each student which enables them to explore possible actions that could negatively impact other students, e.g. modifying a shared database. Furthermore, Kubernetes offers students a full GUI desktop in EDURange WebOS to interact without having to worry about local virtual machine (VM) deployment. It also offers instructors the ability to design and deploy more complex learning scenarios that may involve diverse components including both the GUI and the terminal interface, as well as flexibility of resource management and load balancing by limiting data bandwidth demands. Lastly, this framework is an infrastructure for reproducible educational research, enabling scalable studies on student behavior, assessment design, and pedagogical interventions in cybersecurity instruction.

© The Author(s), under exclusive license to Springer Nature Switzerland AG 2025
F. Skopik et al. (Eds.): ARES 2025 Workshops, LNCS 15999, pp. 96–112, 2025.
https://doi.org/10.1007/978-3-032-00644-8_6

Keywords: Cybersecurity Education · Kubernetes · Modularity · Cyber Range · Gamification · Capture the Flag · Red/ Blue Teaming

1   Motivation

The platform was developed in direct response to the demands of cybersecurity education. The goal was to provide students with the real-world skills required to understand cybersecurity and counter complex and evolving threats. As cybersecurity continues to expand in scope and urgency, it is essential to integrate hands-on, scenario-based learning in a way that is flexible, scalable, and easy for both student and instructor. Cloud computing and Kubernetes in particular provide a mechanism for achieving these goals.

One of the challenges in hosting cybersecurity exercises in the cloud is using resources efficiently without compromising the learning experience. Containers have helped reduce virtualization overhead by allowing multiple environments to share the same operating system. In some cases, it is even possible for multiple students to share a single container. However, this approach breaks down when students need to modify shared resources, as their actions can interfere with each other and lead to unexpected errors.

For example, consider our SQL injection exercises, where students interact with a backend SQL database through a sample web application. In traditional shared setups, if one student modifies or deletes a critical table, such as removing a table required for the challenge, it can disrupt the experience for the entire class and require the instructor to intervene and reset the shared instance manually. Kubernetes addresses this issue by providing each student with an isolated environment. This ensures that students can experiment freely, even in ways that might break the system, without affecting anyone else. If something goes wrong, either the student or the instructor can reset the individual instance in real time, restoring it to a clean state without disrupting others. This ability to recover quickly from mistakes supports deeper exploration and reduces the instructor's workload during live sessions.

This need for isolation, flexibility, and ease of recovery in technical exercises directly informed the design of our solution. The platform addresses this gap by offering a fully interactive browser-based learning experience that combines scalable infrastructure, isolated environments, and engaging content. Drawing from research highlighting the efficacy of gamified, practice-oriented instruction, the platform is built to support Capture the Flag (CTF) exercises, penetration testing simulations, and other critical cybersecurity skills. By approaching platform design as both an engineering and educational research problem, we aim to lower barriers to access, improve consistency across learning environments, and enable new kinds of empirical insight into cybersecurity education practices.

2   Design Philosophy

One of the foundational principles of EDURange Cloud is the elimination of local host requirements. This creates an even playing field for all students. With

EDURange Cloud, every student accesses a fully containerized and consistent environment via a simple URL, enabling immediate immersion without the need for software installation or compatibility debugging.

Underpinning this ease of use is a Kubernetes-powered backend that automates the provisioning, scaling, and managing challenges and system components. Each student receives an issolated environment, configured based on the specific learning objectives of the challenge, ensuring fairness and reducing friction (Fig. 1).

3   Classroom Tests

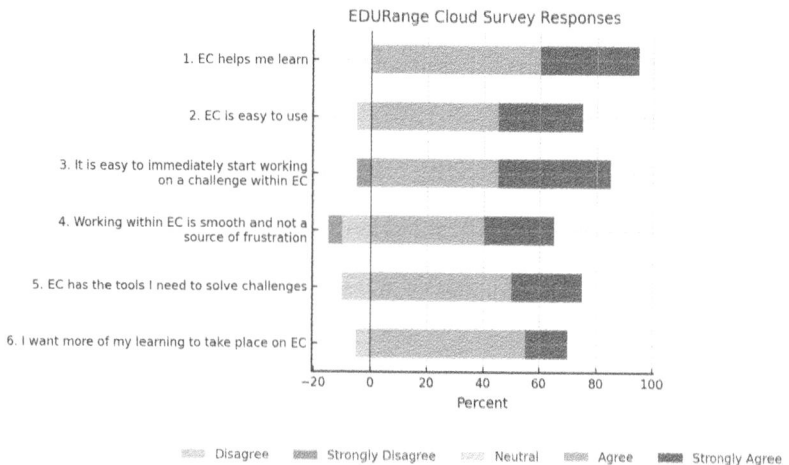

Fig. 1. Classroom Survey. 19 student responses to key usability and learning experience questions about the EDURange Cloud platform, measured using a 5-point Likert scale. Most participants reported positive experiences, with high levels of agreement across all dimensions.

As the development of EduRange Cloud continued, we wanted to engage in a few proof-of-concept experiments with the varying types of challenges that the platform can support. The hands-on exercises were used in a class called "Networks and Web Development" at a small liberal arts college. The prerequisite was Computer Science 2. The students were a mix of sophomores, juniors, and seniors. We engaged in three classroom deployments, on different days with SQL injection labs, metasploit labs, and privilege escalation and content modification lab exercises. respectively. At the end of the class period, we conducted an optional survey to collect student feedback about their learning experience in the one-hour-long class periods throughout the three days. Overall, the students provided the following comments related to the user experience of the platform and the educational contents:

- Good user interface, snappy.
- It was fun to get to try out queries on my own.
- Very clean and well done, You can feel all the time that went into this project. Until it crashed and quickly restarted, it was running perfectly.
- I enjoyed the ability to work with the terminal and potentially malicious payloads without having to worry about destroying my computer.
- I think the overall concept is terrific, and I like how clean the UI is, the instructions were clear, and hints are available whenever I get stuck.
- Maybe it would be nice to make full use of the window size; I now noticed the "open in new tab" button, which I haven't tried.
- Noticed some problems with lag but you were able to find that bug. Would have also liked a bit more instruction, eventually found it in the files, but would like it to be a bit clearer.

4   Technical Architecture

At its core, the platform leverages Kubernetes to dynamically orchestrate per-user challenge instances that are consistent, isolated, and tailored to specific learning objectives. These environments are provisioned on-demand and encapsulate a full user experience–from launching challenges and interacting with tools to submitting results and tearing down resources.

The architecture is composed of modular components that handle both user-facing workflows and backend infrastructure. This includes the EDURange WebOS desktop environment, the Remote Terminal system, and a suite of backend services such as the Instance Manager, Database Controller, and plugin framework. Together, these components enable instructors to deliver customized, reproducible challenges at scale without needing deep infrastructure expertise (Fig. 2).

4.1   User Flow and Experience

The user experience of our platform has been carefully designed to embody EDURange Cloud's core philosophy: eliminating local setup friction while ensuring a consistent, high-quality learning environment. From a student's perspective, EDURange Cloud offers a seamless, structured workflow that prioritizes ease of use, immersion, and pedagogical effectiveness. After authenticating through GitHub OAuth, students are directed to a personalized dashboard. This design choice was made to avoid storing user passwords on the platform. From the dashboard, students can join instructor-led class group by entering access codes. Students are able to interact with the challenges in the class group asynchronously, supporting self-paced learning. Launching a challenge triggers the deployment of a fully isolated Kubernetes pod tailored to the scenario, such as a WebOS desktop, remote-terminal, vulnerable web server, and other configured components.

Within EDURange WebOS, students interact with applications relevant to the challenge such as terminals, browsers, and various other cybersecurity tools

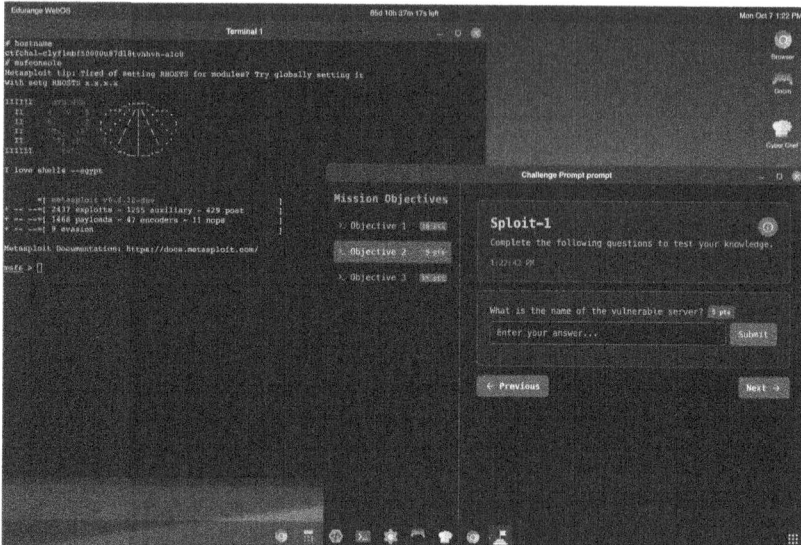

Fig. 2. EDURange WebOS Interface with Cybersecurity Tooling. Metasploit running within the EDURange WebOS browser environment, demonstrating access to real-world cybersecurity tools through the browser-based desktop system.

mirroring real-world cybersecurity workflows. Their progress is tracked in real time, with activity logs and competition scores updating automatically. Upon completion, results are updated on the dashboard, and the environment is automatically torn down to free resources, ensuring a streamlined and efficient user experience. This architecture reflects the core design goal of EDURange Cloud: enabling students to immediately engage with hands-on cybersecurity learning without the friction of local software setup or configuration inconsistencies.

4.2   Platform Deployment and Installation

Recognizing the importance of accessibility and ease of use for educational tools, the EDURange Cloud Platform Installer was intentionally developed to minimize deployment complexity when setting up the platform on a new Kubernetes cluster. Built with Electron and React, the installer integrates user-friendly interactive interfaces while maintaining stringent security protocols through a deliberate separation of UI and system-level operations. It supports both bare-metal and cloud-managed Kubernetes clusters, offering flexibility across diverse infrastructure environments. The installer can preserve progress between steps, enabling error recovery and incremental configuration–features highly valued by instructors who may not have extensive infrastructure expertise. As a result, the system aims to allow educators to manage complex installations with minimal technical intervention.

4.3   Database Design and Connection Management

At the core of EDURange Cloud's reliability and performance is its carefully designed database architecture, which serves as the backbone of user identity, challenge tracking, and platform coordination. The platform uses PostgreSQL managed via Prisma ORM, providing an efficient, intuitive interface for complex data relationships among users, challenges, and activities. This database directly supports the Instance Manager by storing life-cycle states, enables the Activity Logger to maintain real-time audit trails, and provides WebOS with live challenge progress updates.

To optimize performance without compromising transactional integrity, we implemented PgBouncer transaction pooling to efficiently manage database connections for most platform services. However, recognizing critical components such as the Database Controller require continuous and precise database interactions, direct connections were deliberately employed to ensure transactional consistency and robust reliability. This hybrid connection management strategy allows EDURange Cloud to perform reliably under significant and varying workloads typical of educational environments. The database infrastructure leverages Kubernetes' Horizontal Pod Autoscalers (HPAs) to dynamically scale both the connection pooling layer and database replicas based on demand. During high-traffic periods, such as when multiple classes simultaneously launch challenges, the connection pool automatically expands to handle the increased connection volume. Similarly, read replicas scale horizontally to distribute query load while maintaining a consistent primary database for write operations. This architecture ensures that database performance remains responsive even during usage spikes, a critical requirement for educational environments where entire classrooms may begin exercises simultaneously.

4.4   Challenge Architecture and Execution Environment

Kubernetes pods are a central part of EDURange Cloud's hands-on learning experience. These self-contained, modular environments are built to replicate realistic cybersecurity scenarios. Each pod is orchestrated by Kubernetes and provisioned dynamically for individual users, ensuring secure, isolated instances that mirror real-world conditions. This architecture enables students to engage directly with practical challenges ranging from network penetration testing to vulnerability demonstration and system administration-related learning scenarios, all within environments tailored to specific learning objectives (Fig. 3).

4.5   Component Architecture

WebOS Desktop Environment: At a technical level, EDURange WebOS is a React-based application that simulates a desktop operating system entirely within the browser. It implements a dynamic application registry that loads challenge-specific tools at runtime based on the Challenge Definition File. This

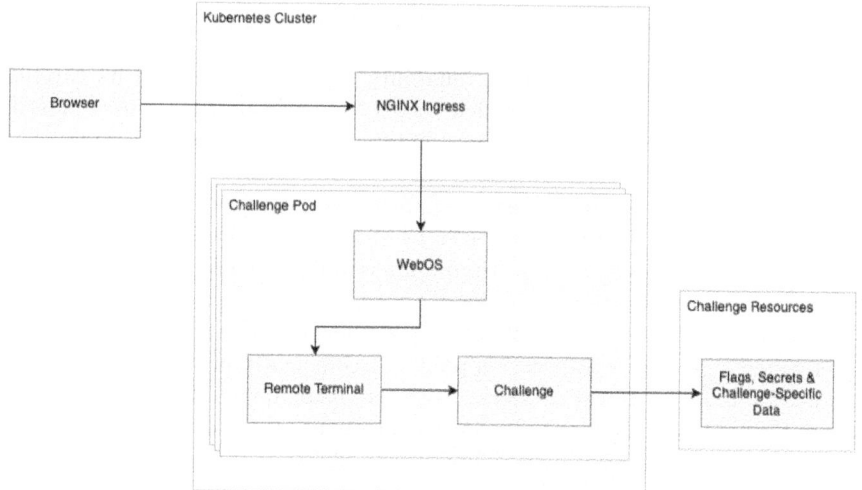

Fig. 3. Kubernetes-Orchestrated Challenge Pod Architecture. Challenge pod structure in EDURange Cloud showing containerized isolation between WebOS, Remote Terminal, and challenge-specific containers, supporting modular customization and security.

architecture enables each challenge to present a tailored set of applications without requiring modifications to the core system. The separation between the shell components (taskbar, window management, notifications) and the challenge specific applications allows for rapid development of new educational tools while maintaining a consistent user experience. When a student launches a challenge, WebOS initializes with only the applications specified in the CDF, which might include terminals, browsers, specialized security tools, or instructional materials. Each application follows a standardized API for window management, file access, and inter-application communication. This standardization ensures that instructors can easily create new applications or modify existing ones without understanding the entire system architecture (Fig. 4).

Additionally, the browser-based implementation enables EDURange WebOS to run seamlessly on low-powered devices like Chromebooks or tablets, making the platform accessible to institutions with limited hardware resources, a critical advantage for schools with budget constraints. The elimination of client-side software requirements beyond a modern web browser also simplifies deployment across diverse educational settings and reduces IT support burdens. Furthermore, the WebOS integrates directly with the platform's activity logging system, enabling detailed tracking of student interactions for assessment purposes. By implementing the user interface as a Web application rather than a remote desktop connection, EDURange Cloud delivers on its promise of accessible, consistent, and performance-optimized cybersecurity education without sacrificing functionality or educational value.

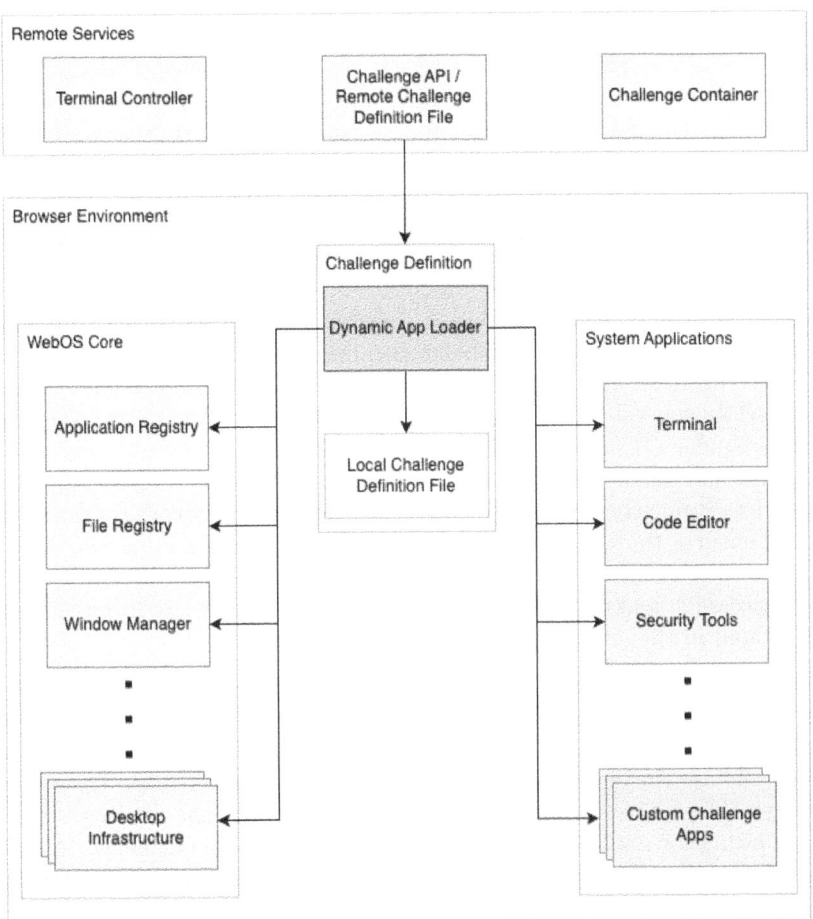

Fig. 4. WebOS Architecture and Dynamic Application Loading System. This diagram illustrates EDURange WebOS's modular architecture where the Application Registry serves as the central hub that processes the Challenge Definition File and coordinates with the core system components. The Dynamic App Loader instantiates only required applications, maintaining separation between persistent infrastructure and challenge-specific tools while enabling communication with remote services.

Remote-Terminal Interface: The EDURange Remote Terminal is a sophisticated browser-based terminal system that enables students to interact securely and responsively with challenge environments from within WebOS. Originally implemented using WebSockets, the terminal was re-architected after observing that many corporate and educational networks block or degrade WebSocket traffic. To address this, the current design employs a hybrid model: Server-Sent Events (SSE) for server-to-client streaming and HTTP POST requests for client-to-server input, both operating over standard HTTPS to ensure broad compatibility across restrictive network environments. This shift introduced new challenges, most notably a surge in TCP requests overwhelming the Kubernetes ingress controller, particularly under high-usage scenarios. To resolve this, we engineered an adaptive batching system that dramatically reduces overhead while preserving responsiveness. Output data is batched using multiple criteria–including buffer size, time delay, terminal control sequences, and user activity level–before being sent to the client. This ensures that large outputs like logs or command results don't flood the network, while interactive applications like Vim remain responsive.

The frontend, built with xterm.js, mirrors this efficiency with an intelligent input batching system that balances immediacy and throughput. Critical keystrokes (like ESC or Ctrl+C) bypass the buffer to maintain UX fluidity in text editors, while general input is grouped into tightly timed batches to minimize request frequency. Combined with WebGL-accelerated rendering, font scaling, and connection diagnostics, the frontend delivers a robust, user-friendly terminal interface inside the browser. By adapting to variable network conditions, the terminal ensures that students, regardless of their geographic location or institutional connectivity, can meaningfully participate in challenges, reinforcing our goal of accessible and equitable cybersecurity education. An additional diagram can be found in the appendix describing this system.

Challenge Application Containers: The challenge application container primarily consists of two modularized components, the Challenge Type Definitions (CTDs) and the Challenge Definition Files (CDFs). Challenge Type Definitions (CTDs), dictate the configuration, services, and application stack for each challenge type. The CTDs act as blueprints that ensure consistent challenge behavior while allowing for extensive customization and expansion. Challenge Definition Files (CDFs) instantiate these templates with concrete metadata, application settings, scoring objectives, hints, resources, and deployment parameters. The Instance Manager uses this metadata to orchestrate deployments, the WebOS uses it to load apps and themes, and the Activity Logger relies on it to track objective completions and student actions. This separation of type and instance allows for high re-usability and rapid development of new challenges with minimal effort. This separation also allows sharing of challenges across platforms.

This approach offers several key advantages over traditional virtualization. The system achieves reduced bandwidth requirements, as only the relevant application data is transferred rather than an entire desktop video stream. Students experience near-native responsiveness for most applications, eliminating the frustration of laggy interfaces commonly encountered with remote desktop solutions. The consistent interface across all challenge types reduces cognitive load as students move between different exercises, allowing them to focus on learning cybersecurity concepts rather than adapting to new environments.

Instance Manager: The Instance Manager serves as the central orchestration engine of EDURange Cloud, acting as the interface between user intent and infrastructure execution. It consumes deployment requests from the dashboard, queries the Challenge Registry for CDF and CTD definitions, interacts with the database to track deployment state, and provisions challenge environments via Kubernetes APIs. This tightly coordinated flow ensures consistency across the platform, from what the student sees in the dashboard to what is instantiated on the cluster. Its integration with other EDURange Cloud components is seamless: the Dashboard submits requests and receives live deployment status; the Monitoring Service captures metrics and health indicators; the Activity Logger tracks deployment histories, access patterns, and administrative actions. The Instance Manager also connects to the Challenge Registry to fetch and validate templates and images, supporting versioning and customization workflows. Designed for resilience, the Instance Manager supports retry logic, dead-letter queues for failed deployments, state persistence, and geographic redundancy. It includes performance optimizations such as pre-fetching container layers, parallelized provisioning, and predictive scaling based on course schedules and historical usage patterns (Fig. 5).

5   Discussions

5.1   Scalability and Resource Management

Scalability is a core strength of EDURange Cloud, enabling the platform to support a wide range of use cases, from individual classroom exercises to student competitions of all sizes, without requiring manual reconfiguration. This scalability is achieved through Kubernetes-native mechanisms such as autoscaling, resource isolation, and dynamic provisioning. The core infrastructure components of EDURange Cloud, including the Instance Manager, Remote Terminal backend service, PostgreSQL database, certificate manager, and monitoring services, are deployed as persistent, horizontally scalable microservices. These components are equipped with Kubernetes Horizontal Pod Autoscalers (HPAs), which automatically increase or decrease the number of pod replicas based on CPU and memory utilization. This ensures that infrastructure services remain performant under varying loads while minimizing over-provisioning during idle periods.

Challenge pods, by contrast, are ephemeral and user-specific. They are not managed via HPAs but instead instantiated dynamically by the Instance Manager when a student launches a challenge. Each challenge pod includes its own dedicated WebOS container and, if required by the challenge type, a Remote Terminal container, ensuring full isolation and flexibility across concurrent sessions. Kubernetes schedules these pods based on resource requests and limits defined in the Challenge Type Definitions (CTDs), optimizing for node usage and performance. To handle spikes in demand, EDURange Cloud utilizes Kubernetes Cluster Autoscaler, which can automatically provision additional worker nodes to accommodate incoming challenge pod deployments. This means the platform can elastically expand infrastructure capacity in response to real-time usage patterns, then scale down once demand subsides–enabling cost-effective operation at any scale. This dynamic scaling model not only ensures system resilience but

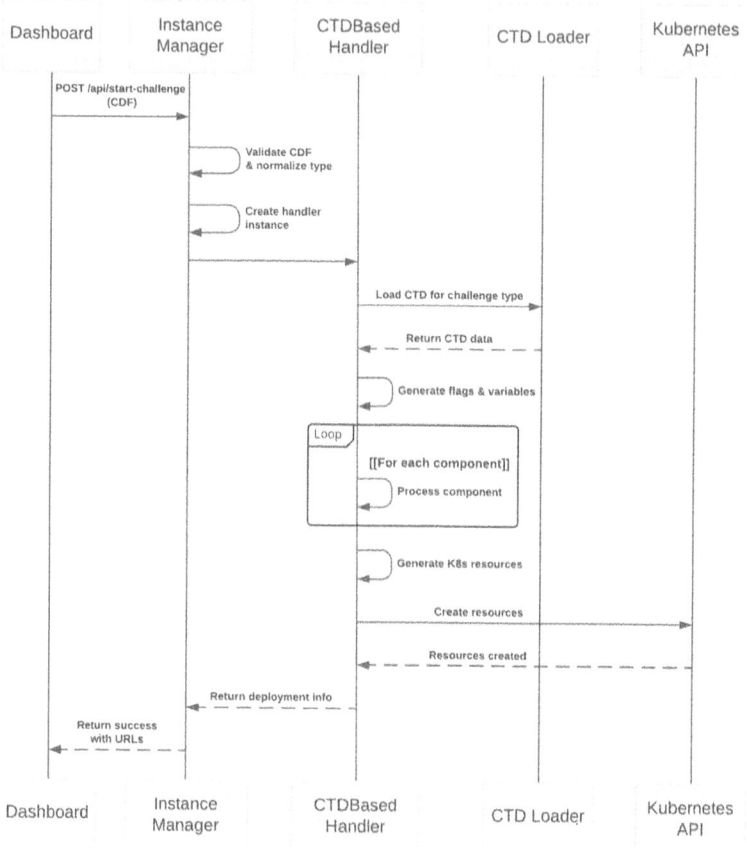

Fig. 5. Challenge Deployment Sequence in EDURange Cloud. The diagram illustrates the automated flow from challenge request to deployment. The Instance Manager processes a Challenge Definition File (CDF), loads the appropriate Challenge Type Definition (CTD), generates security parameters, and creates the necessary Kubernetes resources, enabling consistent yet customizable learning environments without requiring infrastructure expertise.

aligns with our broader mission of making advanced cybersecurity training accessible to institutions of all sizes–without demanding high levels of infrastructure expertise or cost.

5.2 Platform Modularity

Modularity is at the heart of EDURange Cloud's architecture, enabling extensibility, maintainability, and customizability across every layer of the platform. This approach empowers both platform developers and instructors to rapidly adapt EDURange Cloud to diverse pedagogical goals without requiring core system modifications. EDURange Cloud separates challenge logic into two levels: Challenge Type Definitions (CTDs) define the general structure and requirements of a class of challenges, including container composition, permissions, and system behavior for that challenge type. Challenge Definition Files (CDFs) instantiate specific exercises based on CTDs and determine the WebOS app set and other challenge specific parameters. CDFs contain YAML-formatted metadata, app settings, objective scoring, hints, resources, and deployment parameters. This division allows instructors to reuse a CTD to create dozens of unique challenges without re-engineering their environments, and allows CTDs to evolve independently of specific content.

EDURange WebOS is itself modular, built with a dynamic application registry that loads challenge-specific tools at runtime. Apps such as the browser, terminal, file viewer, or custom security utilities are defined per challenge and loaded based on the challenge's CDF. Developers can create their own apps using the WebOS plugin API, which provides standardized access to filesystem, networking, notifications, and more. Beyond the WebOS, the platform as a whole includes a robust system plugin architecture that enables server-side extensibility. Monitoring Plugins provide activity tracking, time analysis, and learning analytics. Security Plugins enhance non-repudiation, detect suspicious behavior, and alert instructors. Assessment Plugins allow for automated grading, rubrics, and reporting integration. Communication Plugins support student-instructor interaction, team collaboration, and peer discussion. Each plugin integrates through well-defined event hooks or API layers, allowing developers to augment or intercept challenge behavior without touching the platform core logic.

5.3   Challenge Types and Configurations

To support a wide range of educational goals, EDURange Cloud offers multiple challenge types, each defined by a distinct container architecture and pedagogical focus. These challenge pods are composed of varying combinations of tools, services, and configurations depending on the skills being taught. The platform currently supports four primary challenge types: system administration walkthrough, network-based system enumeration and penetration testing, vulnerability demonstration and exploitation, and collaborative red versus blue team, each targeting a specific area of cybersecurity instruction. Many additional challenge types are currently in development, and thanks to the use of modular Challenge Type Definitions (CTDs), instructors and developers can easily design and deploy custom challenge types tailored to their own learning objectives.

System Administration Challenges: Drawing from the inspiration of the collegiate cyber defense competition [National CCDC(2025)], these challenges aim to provide students with a real-world system configuration experience to mitigate potential system configurations and vulnerabilities resulting from user errors. These scenarios provide students access to a complete operating system environment via the Remote Terminal, and we attempt to simulate real-world infrastructures with pre-installed tools, vulnerable services, and configurable network settings, allowing students to understand how to properly deploy and maintain pre-installed services while also understanding how these services may potentially misused by a threat actor. They are ideal for teaching command-line navigation, system security practices, system security hygiene, including disabling unused ports, identifying suspicious and uncommon ports being used, and system hardening that may include firewall rule creation, enforcing password complexity requirements, enforcing periodic password changes, and disabling guest access.

Vulnerability Demonstration and Exploitation: These challenges focus on demonstrating common web vulnerabilities such as SQL injection, XSS, CSRF, weak KBA questions leading to password reset attacks, server-side validation failures, and broken authentication. We also have some system-based vulnerabilities, such as EternalBlue, EternalRomance, Dirty Pipe, and token impersonation, which introduce students to vulnerability-driven privilege escalation. In these scenarios, students will interact with vulnerable web applications or systems through the WebOS browser and remote terminal to explore the vulnerability, learn more about the nature of the vulnerabilities, how to exploit the vulnerabilities, and how to patch the vulnerability to mitigate the potential threat in an interactive and guided manner. This challenge enables students to learn about commonly exploited system vulnerabilities, allowing them to gain practical experience with vulnerabilities they may encounter in real-world applications and systems. Kubernetes is beneficial for this particular type of exercise as it offers individualized containers for each students, such that students wouldn't be altering the same system simultaneously, which may hinder the learning experiences. The scalability offered by the EDURange Cloud is something that traditional EDURange couldn't offer without management overheads. Kubernetes and containerization also make the resetting of scenarios simple and allow the students to reset their scenarios when needed freely. We also address the existing concern and issue where the instructor may be required to troubleshoot the scenario live if students mistakenly perform an unintentional exploit such as dropping a table in a SQL injection scenario.

Network-Based System Enumeration and Penetration Testing: These scenarios are deployed using a multi-container, multi-network setup to ensure that individual systems are deployed with vulnerabilities on the same or different networks, allowing students to compromise and root along the way, eventually leading to the students to practice lateral movement and compromise the active directory domain controller that resides in the internal network which may be separate from the machines deployed and configured in ways that are openly accessible to the public. We aim to use these containers to teach students the procedures of penetration testing in a Capture The Flag fashion, where each of the vulnerabilities they exploit will yield a flag demonstrating their understanding of the vulnerability. Each container associated with these scenarios will be deployed with an initial compromise vector and a privilege escalation path, as well as credential and secret files scattered around the system that will lead the students into other existing containers. Some boxes will also be equipped with intentionally misleading clues to make the challenges more interesting to the students. We desire to use this configuration to teach students the critical skills of network reconnaissance, directory exploration, creation of reverse shells, vulnerability exploitation, privilege escalation, network lateral movement, and proper documentation. Kubernetes will contribute towards the stability of these containers as it offers load balancing and will direct users towards different replicas of the machines, we elected Kubernetes as the underlying architecture knowing that it is possible that students would try all possible attack vectors that may include a denial of service attack or resource-intensive brute forcing, which could result in the target machine becoming slow, unresponsive, or unavailable.

Collaborative Red Versus Blue Team Challenges: These scenarios aim to provide students with real-time system defense experiences. We use a dual-container setup with distinct "attack" and "defend" machine configurations, where students will be issued an operational defender machine that is either a Linux or Windows machine that is pre-built with system misconfiguration and active backdoor processes or programs that allow the attacker to access the machine through RDP or SSH remotely, the student will then be playing the role of the defender or system administrator that is tasked with hardening the machine within the time limit such that they can leverage the indicators of compromises and engage in practices of system hardening. We foresee these scenarios to be used in class with a time limit, where the professor will continuously interact with the instances issued to the students to give them hints about system configurations that need to be changed, such as weak credentials for users, usage of suspicious ports, and updating ingress firewall rules under a time crunch. Students will learn to use programs and system internals, such as Process Monitor, Event Viewer, Windows Defender, Windows Management Instrumentation, netstat, ps, strace, AppArmor, among other tools. Alternatively, students can function as a red teamer, where they will learn about the usage of Metasploit and other offensive tools they can leverage to attack the blue team machines. We want to use this scenario to encourage student usage and learning of blue team tooling while providing students with real-time incident response experiences. In contrast, the red team box would give the students the expertise to properly employ persistence and utilize evasion tactics to simulate real-world attack scenarios. With the help of Kubernetes and the modular deployment architecture combined with Docker containerization, the instructor can easily scale the deployment to teach the class blue team practices for Windows, Linux, and red team practices without worrying about redundancy and load balancing, the flexibility provided by the architecture is capable of offering team engagements where we may have multiple members on a red team that are simultaneously attacking the blue team machine from various vectors such as remote connection, remote code execution exploits, reverse shell based command injection while a group of blue team members are tasked with simultaneously hardening multiple machines on the network to mimic the configuration in real-world organization. We will elaborate more about this possibility and plan in the discussion section.

5.4 Costs and Benefits

To make EDURange Cloud accessible to a wider range of users, we continue refining the EDURange Installer to support non-technical educators through a fully guided setup process. Also in aid of accessibility, EDURange Cloud is much more affordable than previous iterations of the project. In the past, EDURange had been hosted centrally on a single server, which would cost about $70 USD per month if ran 24/7. EDURange Cloud has a floor cost of about $40 USD per month, though this cost would potentially increase as user numbers grow into the hundreds.

6 Related Work

[Nelson and Shoshitaishvili(2024)] lists projects that address the challenge of providing students with access to a learning environment that enables them to work on hands-on challenge problems and experiment with cybersecurity concepts. Unlike similar platforms, such as DOJO [Nelson and Shoshitaishvili(2024)], EDURange Cloud leverages a Kubernetes architectural model. Many other projects use a model where students need to download pre-configured virtual machines, such as Seedlabs [Du(2015)] and Labtainers [Irvine et al.(2017)], which introduce additional overhead. Other platforms, such as Deterlab [Mirkovic and Benzel(2012)], attempt to leverage physical hardware, which creates limits for student capacity. Straying from previous designs [Moule et al.(2021)], EDURange Cloud provides each student with their own isolated, containerized environment.

7 Future Work

EDURange Cloud has already been deployed in classroom settings, though significant opportunities remain to expand its capabilities and improve its usability. Future development will focus on both advancing the platform's technical features and deepening its educational impact.

We are designing more complex and innovative challenges that utilize inter-pod connectivity and communication features, including more advanced red-blue team scenarios, where we scale the team sizes and deploy various blue team machines configured with different misconfigurations, long-form simulations, and web of trust key signings, showcasing cryptography key signing and exchange practices in the real world. This would be an interesting scenario to build as we continue to work to increase the diversity of the challenges that we offer through EduRange Cloud. To support learners, we plan to integrate AI-powered hints that adapt to student behavior in real time. We also explore more cost-effective deployment strategies, such as container pooling and dynamic teardown policies, to optimize performance in high-usage environments.

Instructor-facing tools are another priority. We are extending the metrics system to provide deeper insights into student performance and engagement through customizable dashboards and analytics plugins. At the same time, improvements to the plugin framework will allow the community to develop and share their own tools, enabling broader customization without modifying the core system.

Looking ahead, EDURange Cloud has the potential to serve as a powerful platform for cybersecurity education research. Its modular, instrumented, and scalable design makes it well-suited for collecting meaningful data on student behavior, evaluating instructional strategies, and exploring the impact of different pedagogical approaches in realistic, hands-on environments. As adoption grows, it can support broader studies in learning science and help shape the future of cybersecurity instruction.

8   Conclusions

EDURange Cloud represents a significant advancement in scalable, modular cybersecurity education. By leveraging Kubernetes and container-based architecture, the platform enables instructors to deploy hands-on, individualized training environments with minimal infrastructure burden. Its browser-native WebOS interface, adaptive Remote Terminal system, and modular plugin framework create a cohesive ecosystem that lowers barriers to entry while supporting a wide range of pedagogical goals.

Beyond its technical capabilities, EDURange Cloud is designed to address foundational challenges in cybersecurity instruction: eliminating setup friction, ensuring per-student isolation, and enabling reusable, customizable challenge environments. These affordances not only improve the instructional experience but also create new opportunities for educational research. We view EDURange Cloud not only as a deployable platform, but as foundational infrastructure for reproducible educational research. It enables scalable studies of student behavior, assessment design, and pedagogical interventions in cybersecurity instruction. As cybersecurity education continues to evolve, EDURange Cloud provides a flexible, research-informed foundation for delivering impactful, hands-on learning at scale.

Acknowledgments. This material is based upon work supported by the National Science Foundation under Grant No. 2216485 and 2216492.

EDURange Cloud is free and open source. For source code, documentation, and ongoing development updates, please visit: https://edurange.cloud

References

Du, W.: SEED labs: using hands-on lab exercises for computer security education (abstract only). In: Proceedings of the 46th ACM Technical Symposium on Computer Science Education, Kansas City, Missouri, USA, *(SIGCSE '15)*. Association for Computing Machinery, New York, NY, USA, 704 (2015). https://doi.org/10.1145/2676723.2678290

Irvine, C.E., Thompson, M.F., McCarrin, M., Khosalim, J.: Live lesson: labtainers: a docker-based Framework for Cybersecurity Labs. In: 2017 USENIX Workshop on Advances in Security Education (ASE 17). USENIX Association, Vancouver, BC (2017). https://www.usenix.org/conference/ase17/workshop-program/presentation/irvine

Mirkovic, J., Benzel, T.: Teaching cybersecurity with DeterLab. *IEEE Secur. Priv.* **10**, 73–76 (2012)

Moule, P., Tsirigotis, G., Triantafyllopoulou, D.: CourseLabs: a collaborative container-based framework for hands-on security education. In: *2021 USENIX Conference on USENIX Annual Technical Conference* (USA). USENIX Association, 693 705 (2021)

National CCDC. 2025. National Collegiate Cyber Defense Competition. https://www.nationalccdc.org/. Accessed 08 May 2025

Nelson, C., Shoshitaishvili, Y.: DOJO: applied cybersecurity education in the browser. In: Proceedings of the 55th ACM Technical Symposium on Computer Science Education V. 1, (Portland, OR, USA) *(seriesSIGCSE 2024)*. Association for Computing Machinery, New York, NY, USA, pp. 930–936 (2024). https://doi.org/10.1145/3626252.3630836

Selikow, R., Berol, N., Cook, J., Weiss, R., Mache, R.: Developing a modular cloud-based kubernetes powered framework for scalable cybersecurity education. In: *Proceedings of the 2024 on ACM Virtual Global Computing Education Conference V. 2* (Virtual Event, NC, USA) *(SIGCSE Virtual 2024)*. Association for Computing Machinery, New York, NY, USA, pp. 325–326 (2024). https://doi.org/10.1145/3649409.3691088

Enhancing Cybersecurity Curriculum Development Through European Cybersecurity Framework and Transformer Models

Marko Zivanovic[1]([✉]), Imre Lendák[2,3], and Ranko Popovic[1]

[1] Faculty of Technical Science, Novi Sad, Serbia
zivanovic.m@gmail.com

[2] Data Science and Engineering Department, Faculty of Informatics, Eötvös Loránd University, Budapest, Hungary
lendak@staff.elte.hu, lendak@uns.ac.rs

[3] Department of Power Engineering and Applied Software Engineering, Faculty of Technical Science, Novi Sad, Serbia

Abstract. This work-in-progress paper introduces the Cybersecurity Curriculum Similarity and Coverage Analysis Method (CSCAM), an AI-based tool designed to evaluate the alignment of academic cybersecurity programs with the European Cybersecurity Skills Framework (ECSF). By applying transformer-based language models, CSCAM converts curricular content and ECSF role descriptions into semantic embeddings, enabling precise sentence-level similarity comparisons. The methodology supports a quantitative assessment of curriculum coverage across defined cybersecurity roles. A case study involving multiple European academic programs and job market data demonstrates CSCAM's ability to identify gaps between educational offerings and industry demands. The analysis reveals varied coverage across ECSF roles. By incorporating job advertisement data, CSCAM generates targeted recommendations to improve curriculum alignment. Additionally, the study underscores the importance of considering remote work trends in curriculum planning. CSCAM provides a scalable, data-driven tool to support curriculum development and ensure responsiveness to the evolving cybersecurity workforce landscape.

Keywords: Cybersecurity Education · Curriculum Optimization · Cybersecurity Skills Framework · Machine Learning

1 Introduction

As digitalization advances throughout the world today multiple new trends and technologies achieve greater importance such as smart grids [1], quantum computing [2], and artificial intelligence [3]. The expanding reliance on digital technology in everyday life produces vast amounts of sensitive data shared globally which necessitates continuous advancement in digital services and persistent user education. The COVID-19 pandemic led to increased dependence on digital tools because remote work became vital

© The Author(s), under exclusive license to Springer Nature Switzerland AG 2025
F. Skopik et al. (Eds.): ARES 2025 Workshops, LNCS 15999, pp. 113–129, 2025.
https://doi.org/10.1007/978-3-032-00644-8_7

for business continuity throughout lockdown periods. The digital transformation led to organizations and individuals facing previously unknown cybersecurity threats [4]. An effective implementation of cybersecurity requires a workforce that is highly trained and educated because it plays an essential role in preserving digital environments. Even though sustainable digital growth depends heavily on cybersecurity which faces rising demand there remains a worldwide lack of skilled cybersecurity experts. Numerous European organizations [5, 6] alongside multiple projects [7–10] have pointed out the workforce gap as a key element affecting cybersecurity education challenges.

Multiple elements contribute to the current cybersecurity workforce shortage. The diverse and multidisciplinary nature of the knowledge required presents challenges in identifying cybersecurity professionals capable of meeting all the combined requirements [12]. The rapidly evolving landscape of cybersecurity presents a significant challenge in designing an appropriate curriculum. Academic institutions must adhere to government regulations regarding curriculum updates to ensure alignment with industry demands. In many European countries, study programs are accredited for periods ranging from 4 to 7 years [11]. These regulations, combined with the broad and evolving nature of industry needs, make it difficult to keep curricula current with the latest skills frameworks and industry requirements. Regional reports, such as Bloomberg Adria 2023 [13], indicate that only 8% of organizations are able to fill entry-level cybersecurity positions within one month, primarily due to the diverse knowledge base required. This, in turn, creates a chain effect impacting the recruitment and staffing of more senior positions. The increasing trend of digitalization across various industries [14] amplifies the demand for cybersecurity experts; however, the number of graduates produced by universities is insufficient to meet the growing needs of the industrial sector.

Extensive collaboration between academic institutions and industry could serve as a mitigation strategy for several of the factors mentioned above. Despite the global cybersecurity workforce reaching an estimated 5.5 million professionals, a persistent shortage of 4.4 million workers remains, with Europe experiencing a 12.8% increase in the gap of cybersecurity professionals compared to the previous year (International Information System Security Certification Consortium (ISC2), 2024 [13]). Furthermore, 67% of respondents reported a staffing shortage in the current year. This paper examines curricula from multiple regions of Europe, job advertisements, and frameworks to propose curriculum developments that could contribute to reducing the workforce gap.

This paper supports cybersecurity education by proposing a dynamic approach to curriculum development that responds to the evolving needs and trends of the industry. The primary objective of this article is to foster greater collaboration between academic institutions and industry, using The European Cybersecurity Skills Framework (ECSF) [15] as a reference point for cybersecurity education. The key contributions of this work are outlined as follows:

- A novel methodology that combines machine learning with the ECSF to assess and improve the alignment of academic curricula with cybersecurity roles.
- We further develop this approach to provide recommendations for aligning job ads with academic curricula based on specific ECSF roles.
- Based on these findings, this paper proposes a set of guidelines for cybersecurity curricula that can be dynamically adjusted in accordance with the recommendations.

The remainder of this paper is organized as follows: Sect. 2 offers a review of noteworthy literature on cybersecurity education and workforce training. Section 3 introduces a novel and dynamic approach to cybersecurity curriculum development, incorporating machine learning transformer models, job advertisements, and the ECSF [15] as a reference cybersecurity framework. Section 4 presents the case study and evaluation results. Section 5 concludes with implications and directions for future research.

2 Related Works

This section reviews the literature on curriculum development, guided by referent curriculum or cyber security frameworks. Additionally, we highlight recent research on cybersecurity curriculum development that leverages artificial intelligence (AI) and is supported by publicly accessible web applications with clear focus on workforce gap.

The Joint Task Force (JTF) was formed in September 2015 by multiple leading computing organizations such as the Association for Computing Machinery (ACM), IEEE Computer Society (IEEE-CS), the Association for Information Systems Special Interest Group on Information Security and Privacy (AIS SIGSEC), and the International Federation for Information Processing Technical Committee on Information Security Education (IFIP WG 11.8). A JTF was established to develop full cybersecurity educational guidelines that would enable the creation of new academic programs alongside related educational activities. The JTF released Curriculum Guidelines for Post-Secondary Degree Programs in Cybersecurity (CSEC2017) in the year 2017. CSEC2017 categorizes fundamental cybersecurity concepts into eight knowledge areas which contain several knowledge units. Every unit presents a set of topics with straightforward and succinct curricular description.

In 2019, D. Burley et al. examined the alignment of CSEC2017 content with specific professional requirements, highlighting the significance for academic institutions to integrate curricular recommendations with industry needs [17]. The proposed methodology creates a connection between the learning outcomes of CSEC2017 and the essential knowledge, skills, and abilities required for particular job roles, structured into three phases: selecting positions, identifying knowledge areas, and aligning position requirements with learning outcomes. D. Burley et al. implemented this approach within the Boeing, providing clear roadmaps for the company's job families.

A. Nadeem presented a crosscutting concept based on CSEC2017, driven by three key stakeholders: the course instructor, the security expert, and the students [18]. Once a course topic is selected, the security expert further develops the lecture, designs hands-on assignments, and creates exam questions. A collaborative approach based on CSEC2017 is introduced in [19], where selected CSEC2017 Knowledge Areas (KAs) are taught through partnerships with government agencies and capstone projects.

The European Agency for Cybersecurity (ENISA) introduced the European Cybersecurity Skills Framework (ECSF) to the public in 2022. This framework advances ENISA's mission to create a skilled cybersecurity workforce and establishes uniform standards for job roles and required competencies within the cybersecurity field. The ECSF divides cybersecurity roles into twelve specific profiles which include comprehensive information about their mission objectives and primary duties as well as the necessary skills and knowledge. The framework intends to create uniform language standards for cybersecurity professionals across Europe.

Rathod et al. examine the ECSF as a solution for skilling, upskilling, and reskilling within the cybersecurity sector [20]. Through two case studies, the paper argues that the ECSF offers a shared language and framework for the development of cybersecurity skills and competencies. Hajny et al. demonstrates how the ECSF can guide cybersecurity curriculum development [21]. The curriculum design process is further supported by a web application and an innovative method for course evaluation and quantitative analysis, based on the European Credit Transfer and Accumulation System (ECTS) credits.

The application of text mining and keyword extraction was explored by Takayuki Sekiya et al. to advance the definition of Knowledge Areas (KAs) introduced in CS2013, using a set of keywords associated with each KA [22]. Semi-supervised Latent Dirichlet Allocation (ssLDA) was employed to map topics to corresponding KAs. In [23], the Term Frequency-Inverse Document Frequency (TF-IDF) algorithm was utilized for keyword extraction, quantifying the degree of topic alignment between a set of guidelines and actual course content to assess their level of association.

The Brno University of Technology [24] employs the SPARTA [25] cybersecurity skills framework in its approach. Initially, the content of 89 existing study programs globally was analyzed, followed by the collection of recommendations from prominent institutions both within and outside the EU. Finally, a comprehensive survey was conducted. The proposed methodology seeks to address the gap between the demand for cybersecurity professionals and the supply of expertise in alignment with industry and societal needs. The European Union has established the Cybersecurity Strategy for the Digital Decade [8] to enhance cybersecurity awareness. A Political, Economic, Social, Technological, Legal, and Environmental (PESTLE) analysis was employed in [26] to examine the factors influencing cybersecurity education across Europe. Additionally, an analysis of data from the Cybersecurity Higher Education Database (CyberHEAD) [27], maintained by the European Union Agency for Cybersecurity (ENISA), provides an overview of the current state of cybersecurity skills supply within the European Union, as discussed in [24].

As identified by previous research, addressing the latest cybersecurity frameworks, reference curricula, and cybersecurity standards is essential for developing curricula that meet the ever-growing demands of the industry. In response, the authors propose a novel and dynamic approach to cybersecurity curriculum development that leverages machine learning transformer models, job advertisements, and the ECSF to foster collaboration between academic institutions and industry.

3   Methodology

The methodology employed in this study is based on the transformer model, contextual text similarity [28], and a referent cybersecurity framework. Both the curriculum and the referent cybersecurity framework can be represented as sets of sentences or textual data. By comparing the sentences from the referent cybersecurity framework with those in the curriculum, we can assess the similarity between the two sets. The proposed cybersecurity curriculum analysis method (CSCAM), illustrated in Fig. 1, is founded on this approach.

Before proceeding with the analysis of the curricula, the referent cybersecurity curriculum must be preprocessed. Each cybersecurity framework consists of sections and their corresponding descriptions. In the initial preprocessing step, each section description is segmented into an array of sentences. While raw text is suitable for word-based similarity algorithms, such as TF-IDF [29], semantic sentence similarity requires the use of vectorized data known as embeddings [30]. Embeddings allow the conversion of text into vectors that capture the underlying semantic meaning, thereby facilitating tasks like text similarity by providing a meaningful numerical representation of the text. The transformer model is employed to convert text into these semantic embeddings. Once all section descriptions of the referent cybersecurity framework are converted into arrays of embeddings, the CSCAM is ready to perform the curriculum analysis.

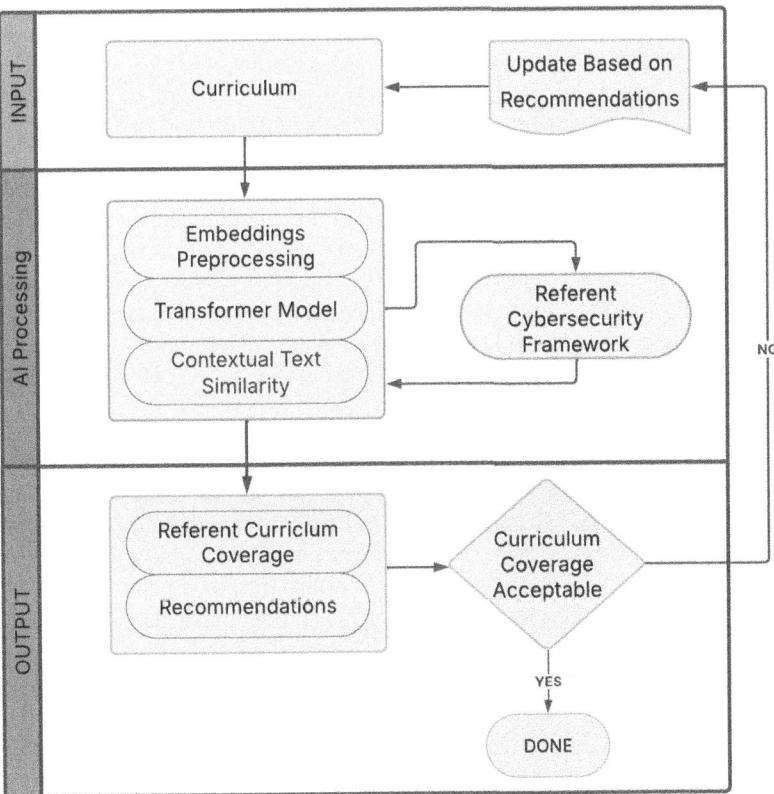

Fig. 1. Curriculum Analysis Methodology

The first step involves providing the curriculum in its raw form as input. The curriculum is expected to be submitted either as a text document, CSV or a PDF file. The provided curriculum will then be preprocessed, applying the same steps as those used for the referent cybersecurity framework, to convert the text into an array of embeddings.

At this stage, we proceed with the contextual sentence similarity analysis. The CSCAM compares each referent cybersecurity framework section description embedding (RCSSDE) with the embeddings of the curriculum sentences (CSEs) to identify the CSE that most closely matches the current RCSSDE. The referent curriculum coverage is then represented as an array of the coverage for each referent cybersecurity framework section.

$$C(section) = \sum_{section\ 0..n} CSCAM(RCSSDE, CSEs)$$

CSCAM is capable of providing actionable insights in the form of curriculum improvement recommendations. After analyzing the coverage results of each section, CSCAM can identify topics whose inclusion would lead to the greatest increase in section coverage with minimal changes to the overall curriculum. In most European countries, the accreditation period for academic institutions spans 4 to 7 years [11], and changes to the curriculum are often limited following accreditation.

$$overall\ curriculum\ change = \sum \Delta(C(section))$$

If the calculated coverage is deemed insufficient, an optional step involves updating the curriculum based on CSCAM's recommendations. After implementing these updates, the entire process should be repeated to assess the impact of the changes.

The following section demonstrates a case study of CSCAM's application using the ECSF as the referent framework. Additionally, by collecting curriculum data over several years, we can assess the impact of ECSF on the curriculum.

4   Case Study

The case study begins with a definition of the data that has been collected and analyzed. Initially, we apply CSCAM to map curricula to ECSF roles and assess their significance within the curricula. Subsequently, we map cybersecurity jobs within country of curricula to ECSF and compare with curricula coverage results. Based on findings from previous two steps, CSCAM provides recommendations for further curricula development.

4.1   Data Collected

The case study focuses on five curricula collected from different EU regions. Curricula are mainly collected from ENISA's Cybersecurity Higher Education Database (CYBER-HEAD) [31], university web sites and web archives. The cybersecurity jobs ads within the curricula countries are collected via LinkedIn platform [32]. Table 1 illustrates the data collected for the purpose of this case study.

4.2   Experiment with Curricula

The initial phase of this experiment involves verifying the format of the collected data and performing preliminary text preprocessing. Each curriculum is stored in a CSV file

Table 1. Data Collected

Country	University	Source of Curriculum	Source of Jobs
Czech Republic	Masaryk University Faculty of Informatics	University website	LinkedIn
Croatia	University of Zagreb Faculty of Electrical Engineering and Computing	University website	LinkedIn
Romania	Technical University Cluj-Napoca	University website	LinkedIn
Belgium	KU Leuven	University website	LinkedIn
Sweden	KTH Royal Institute of Technology Stockholm	University website	LinkedIn

comprising the following columns: university, year, curriculum, syllabus, ECTS, and description_raw. This structure serves as the sole valid input format for the CSCAM. The full curriculum content is included in the description_raw column, reflecting the unprocessed textual data as published on the respective institutional websites. Certain elements of human-readable formatting, such as bullet points ending in commas, may introduce ambiguities or excessively long sentences, and therefore require cleaning prior to further analysis.

After verifying the data format and completing the initial text preprocessing, the next step involves transforming the curriculum descriptions into discrete sentences. Each syllabus description, extracted from the description_raw column, is parsed and segmented into individual sentences using transformer-based language models [28, 32]. In addition to sentence segmentation, these models also generate sentence embeddings, which are later utilized for computing semantic similarity scores.

In this study, the ECSF is adopted as the reference framework. To assess semantic similarity between the ECSF and academic curricula, the same preprocessing steps are applied to the ECSF data. Each ECSF role is defined by multiple attributes, including: role name, alternative titles, summary statement, mission, deliverables, main tasks, key skills, key knowledge, and e-competences. For the purposes of this experiment, only the role name, key skills, and key knowledge attributes are considered. Accordingly, for each ECSF role, two sets of sentences and their corresponding embeddings are generated—one for key skills and another for key knowledge.

With all necessary data structures in place, the final step involves calculating sentence similarity scores. For each skill and knowledge statement associated with an ECSF role, the most semantically similar sentence is identified within the set of syllabus-derived sentences. A skill or knowledge element is considered covered only if at least one corresponding curriculum sentence achieves a similarity score above the CSCAM-configured threshold (set to 0.51 in this case study). Skills and knowledge elements yielding maximum similarity scores below this threshold are excluded from the overall coverage assessment. The resulting role-based coverage of ECSF by the curricula is visualized in the accompanying Fig. 2.

Senior-level ECSF roles, such as Chief Information Security Officer and Cybersecurity Architect, are comprehensively addressed across all analyzed curricula. The KTH Royal Institute of Technology further extends its coverage to include less senior positions, such as Cybersecurity Implementer and Cybersecurity Educator. In contrast, more specialized roles—namely, Cyber Incident Responder and Cybersecurity Auditor—exhibit comparatively lower levels of coverage. A detailed comparison of ECSF role coverage across institutions is presented in Fig. 3.

This experiment successfully established a mapping between academic curricula and ECSF-defined roles, enabling the quantification of role-specific coverage. However, a more nuanced understanding of the relevance and significance of each ECSF role could be achieved by cross-referencing these roles with the requirements observed in local cyber security job postings. This comparative analysis is explored in the following chapter.

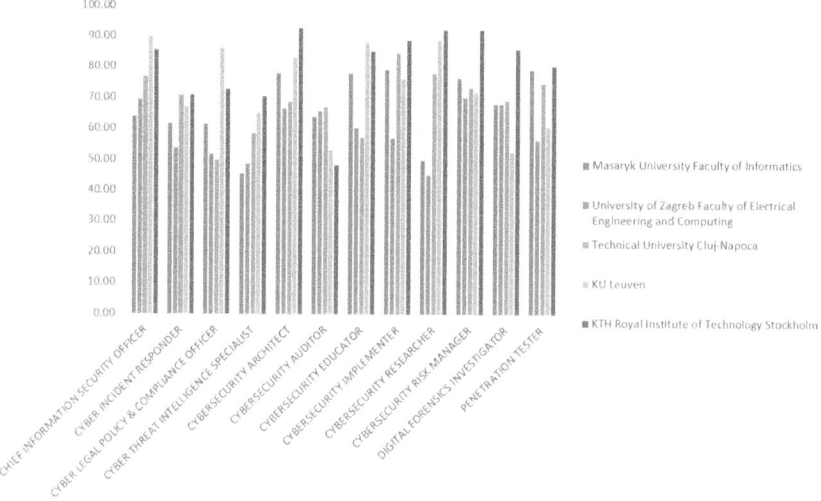

Fig. 2. Curricula ECSF roles coverage

4.3 Experiment with Job Ads

In parallel with the academic curricula, local cybersecurity job advertisements were also collected to assess industry demands and their alignment with educational offerings. This experiment aims to evaluate ECSF role coverage within the job market by analyzing relevant job postings. By comparing the ECSF role coverage between curricula and job advertisements, it becomes possible to identify alignment gaps and formulate recommendations for curriculum enhancement.

The mapping of job advertisements to ECSF roles follows a procedure analogous to that used for academic curricula. The collected job postings are stored in a CSV format compatible with the CSCAM system. Each file contains job advertisements from

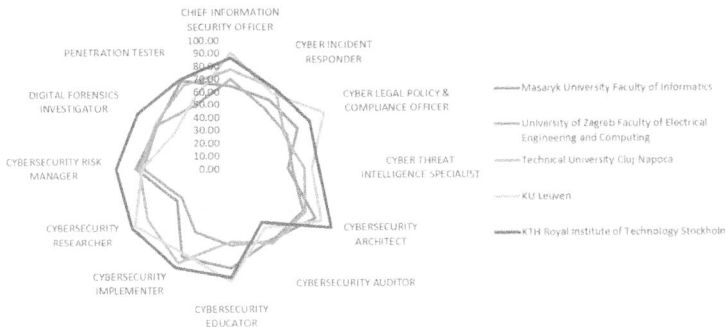

Fig. 3. Curricula ECSF roles coverage comparison

a specific country, and each individual job posting is treated analogously to a curriculum syllabus entry. The raw text from each ad undergoes preprocessing to ensure consistency and suitability for analysis. Once the data is formatted appropriately, sentence similarity computations and ECSF role coverage analyses are performed.

By comparing ECSF role coverage across academic curricula and corresponding job advertisements, gaps in coverage can be systematically identified, providing actionable insights for improving academic program alignment with industry needs. Figures 4, 5, 6, 7 and 8 illustrate this comparison for Masaryk University of Technology, University of Zagreb, Technical University of Cluj-Napoca, KU Leuven, and KTH Royal Institute of Technology, respectively.

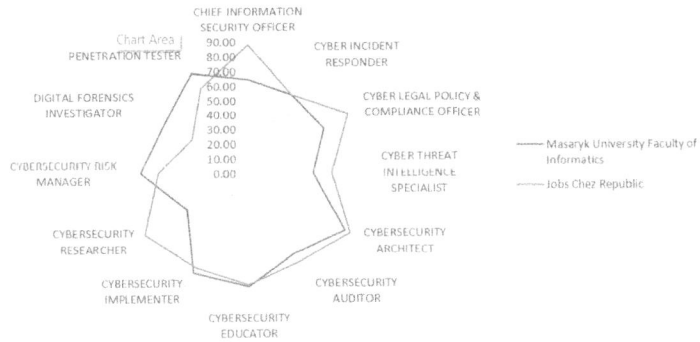

Fig. 4. Curriculum and Job Ads comparison Masaryk University of Technology

KTH Royal Institute of Technology leads with the smallest average curriculum-to-job requirements gap followed by KU Leuven and Masaryk University. The analysis demonstrates that their educational programs match well with current job market requirements represented by job ads.

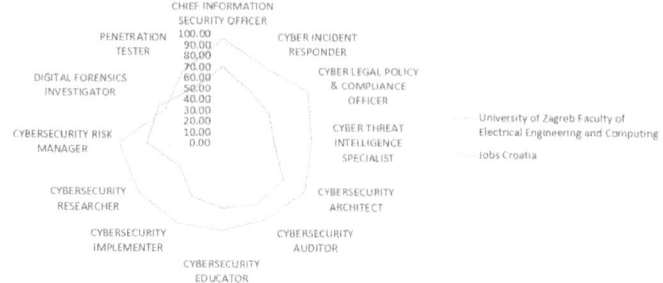

Fig. 5. Curriculum and Job Ads comparison University of Zagreb

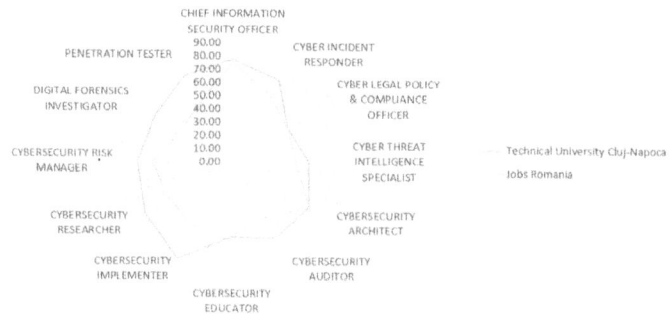

Fig. 6. Curriculum and Job Ads comparison Technical University Cluj-Napoca

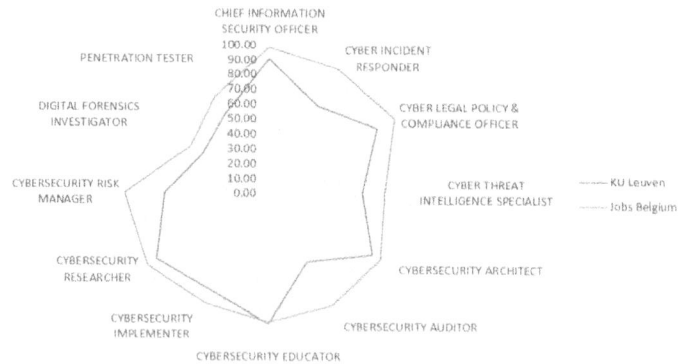

Fig. 7. Curriculum and Job Ads comparison KU Leuven

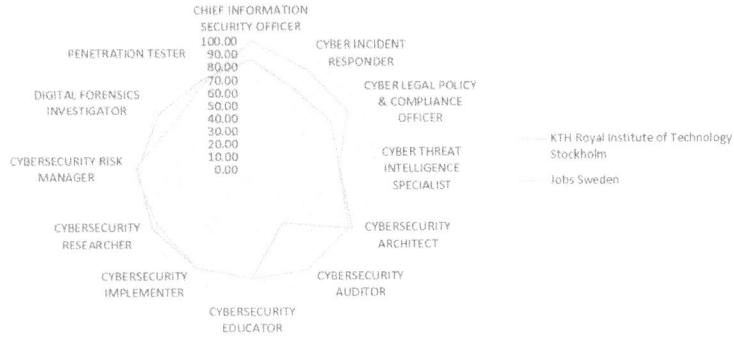

Fig. 8. Curriculum and job ads comparison KTH Royal Institute of Technology

The University of Zagreb and the Technical University of Cluj-Napoca exhibit greater inconsistencies between their curricula and job market requirements. The most significant skill gap exists in entry-level cybersecurity jobs such as Penetration Tester and Cybersecurity Implementer with specialized roles like Cyber Legal Policy and Compliance Officer also showing substantial discrepancies.

Table 2 presents specific recommendations to update the University of Zagreb's curriculum for better alignment with European Cybersecurity Skills Framework (ECSF) roles that lack sufficient coverage. By adopting these recommendations, the academic training can better meet the required competencies of the local cybersecurity job market.

4.4 Discussion

KTH Royal Institute of Technology and KU Leuven show successful alignment while universities such as the University of Zagreb and the Technical University of Cluj-Napoca display gaps that need improvement especially with their entry-level and specialized cybersecurity positions.

In addition to providing role-specific recommendations, CSCAM enables in-depth analysis of academic curricula for each ECSF role. Although the curriculum of KTH Royal Institute of Technology generally aligns well with job market demands, a gap remains concerning the Cybersecurity Auditor role as defined in the ECSF framework. The advanced CSCAM analytics offer detailed insights into how each syllabus addresses this specific role, along with targeted recommendations for enhancing the associated skills and knowledge. These insights can support curriculum adjustments aimed at narrowing the gap between academic preparation and industry requirements, as identified through job advertisements. Table 3 presents the detailed CSCAM analysis for the Cybersecurity Auditor role in relation to the KTH Royal Institute of Technology curriculum.

In our case study, we have compared the curricula solely with local job advertisements. However, in the context of the rapidly evolving cybersecurity landscape, remote work is increasingly common, and in some cases, even preferred. Figure 9 provides further insights into this trend. Job advertisements in Sweden and Belgium exhibit considerable similarity, while the curriculum of Technical University Cluj-Napoca demonstrates

Table 2. Recommendations for University of Zagreb curriculum

Role	Recommendations (improves skill(s)):
Cyber incident responder	Work on operating systems, servers, clouds and relevant infrastructures Collect, analyse and correlate cyber threat information originating from multiple sources improve following knowledge: Computer networks security Computer systems vulnerabilities
Cyber legal Policy & compliance officer	Lead the development of appropriate cybersecurity and privacy policies and procedures that complement the business needs and legal requirements; further ensure its acceptance, comprehension and implementation and communicate it between the involved parties Carry out working-life practices of the data protection and privacy issues involved in the implementation of the organizational processes, finance and business strategy improve following knowledge: Cybersecurity standards, methodologies and frameworks Cybersecurity related laws, regulations and legislations
Cyber threat intelligence specialist	Collect, analyse and correlate cyber threat information originating from multiple sources Automate threat intelligence management procedures improve following knowledge: Computer networks security Operating systems security
Cybersecurity auditor	Audit with integrity, being impartial and independent Analyse business processes, assess and review software or hardware security, as well as technical and organisational controls improve following knowledge: Auditing standards, methodologies and frameworks Cybersecurity standards, methodologies and frameworks

(continued)

Table 2. (*continued*)

Role	Recommendations (improves skill(s)):
Cybersecurity educator	Provide training towards cybersecurity and data protection professional certifications Design, develop and deliver learning programmes to cover cybersecurity needs improve following knowledge: Cybersecurity education and training standards, methodologies and frameworks Cybersecurity standards, methodologies and frameworks
Cybersecurity implementer	Integrate cybersecurity solutions to the organisation's infrastructure Assess the security and performance of solutions improve following knowledge: Computer networks security Secure development lifecycle
Cybersecurity researcher	Contributes towards cutting-edge cybersecurity business ideas, services and solutions Identify cross-sectoral cybersecurity achievements and apply them in a different context or propose innovative approaches and solutions improve following knowledge: Cybersecurity standards, methodologies and frameworks Legal, regulatory and legislative requirements on releasing or using cybersecurity related technologies

a smaller gap when compared to job ads in these countries, as opposed to local job ads. Similarly, the curriculum at the University of Zagreb aligns well with job advertisements in Romania. A more granular analysis at the level of specific ECSF roles reveals additional opportunities. Despite the local gap, the curriculum of the University of Zagreb aligns well with job advertisements for the role of Digital Forensics Investigator in both Croatia and Sweden—surpassing even the curriculum of KTH Royal Institute of Technology in Stockholm in this regard. Conversely, the KTH curriculum demonstrates strong alignment with job advertisements in Croatia for several roles, including Cybersecurity Educator, Cybersecurity Researcher, Cybersecurity Risk Manager, and Chief Information Security Officer. These findings suggest that the local gap in Croatia for certain ECSF-targeted roles could potentially be addressed through remote education offerings from KTH Royal Institute of Technology. Figure 10 illustrates potential international collaboration analysis.

These findings suggest that remote work opportunities could play a significant role in bridging the local gap, highlighting potential for cross-border employment and international collaboration.

Table 3. Cybersecurity Auditor role analysis

Curriculum	KTH Royal Institute of Technology Stockholm
Role	CYBERSECURITY AUDITOR
Total Coverage	48.44%
Coverage per Syllabus	DD2497 Project course in System Security: 12.5% DD2391 Cybersecurity Overview: 12.5% DD2510 Cybersecurity in a Socio-Technical Context: 12.5% EP2790 Security Analysis of Large-Scale Computer Systems: 7.81% EP2780 Digital forensics and incident response: 3.12%
Skills Coverage	46.88%
Skills per Syllabus	DD2497 Project course in System Security: 25.0% EP2790 Security Analysis of Large-Scale Computer Systems: 15.62% EP2780 Digital forensics and incident response: 6.25%
Skills Recommendations	Decompose and analyze systems to identify weaknesses and ineffective controls Organize and work in a systematic and deterministic way based on evidence
Knowledge Coverage	50%
Knowledge per Syllabus	DD2391 Cybersecurity Overview: 25.0% DD2510 Cybersecurity in a Socio-Technical Context: 25.0%
Knowledge Recommendations	Cybersecurity standards, methodologies and frameworks Cybersecurity controls and solutions

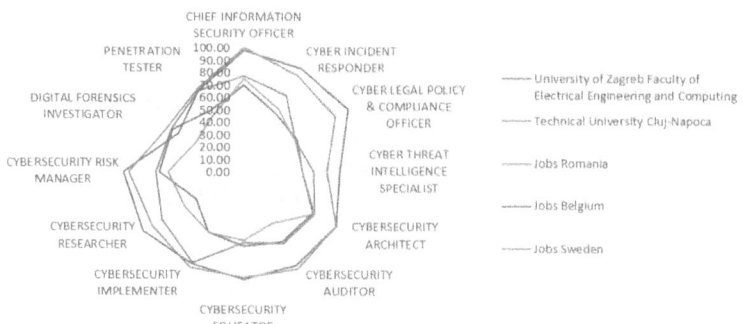

Fig. 9. Remote work analysis

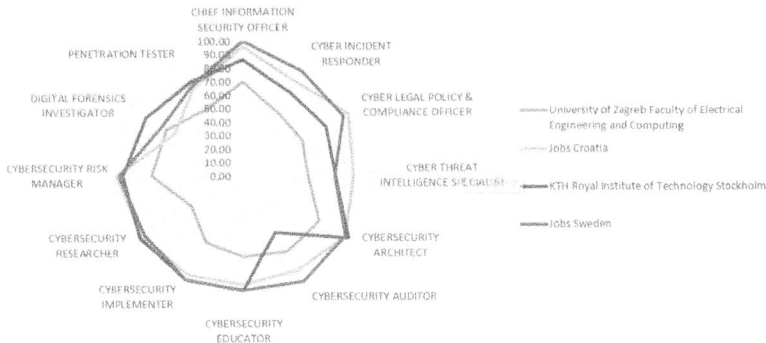

Fig. 10. International collaboration analysis

5 Conclusion

This paper presents a novel approach for evaluating and enhancing cybersecurity curricula using the Curriculum Similarity and Coverage Analysis Method (CSCAM) grounded in transformer-based semantic similarity and aligned them with the European Cybersecurity Skills Framework (ECSF). Through the application of CSCAM, we demonstrate how academic programs can be quantitatively assessed for their alignment with the ECSF cybersecurity role definitions and industry needs identified through cybersecurity job ads.

Our case study, encompassing curricula from five European universities and cybersecurity job postings from corresponding regions, revealed both strengths and gaps in existing academic offerings. The comparative analysis of curricula and job advertisements provided actionable insights and concrete recommendations for curriculum development. These included targeted improvements in specific knowledge and skill domains, as well as course-level adjustments. Importantly, CSCAM's analytics also accounted for emerging trends such as remote work, suggested that some academic programs may be more compatible with job markets beyond their local context, further reinforcing the value of cross-border alignment in cybersecurity education.

Future work will focus on integrating newer, more advanced transformer models to further improve semantic similarity analysis. Additionally, efforts will be directed toward increasing the automation of the similarity calculation process and developing a publicly available, open-source web application.

Acknowledgments. The following funding source is gratefully acknowledged by the authors Project no. TKP2021-NVA-29 is supported by the Ministry of Culture and Innovation of Hungary from the National Research, Development, and Innovation Fund, financed under the TKP2021-NVA funding scheme.

References

1. Annaswamy, A., Amin, M.: Smart Grid Research: Control Systems - IEEE Vision for Smart Grid Controls: 2030 and Beyond. IEEE (2013)
2. Faruk, J., Tahora, S., Tasnim, M., Shahriar, H., Sakib, N.: A review of quantum cybersecurity: threats, risks and opportunities. In: ICAIC (2022)
3. Nikolskaia, K., Naumov, V.: The relationship between cybersecurity and artificial intelligence. In: IT&QM&IS (2021)
4. Pipikaite, A., Bueermann, G., Joshi, A., Jurgens, J.: Global cybersecurity outlook 2022. In: Geneva: World Economic Forum (2022)
5. Cybersecurity skills development in the EU. ENISA (2019). https://www.enisa.europa.eu/publications/the-status-of-cyber-security-education-in-the-european-union. Accessed 10 May 2025
6. ECSO gaps in European cyber education and professional training. https://ecs-org.eu/. Accessed 10 May 2025
7. Assessing the courses for cybersecurity professionals already developed by CONCORDIA partners. https://www.concordia-h2020.eu/. Accessed 10 May 2025
8. SPARTA deliverables. https://www.sparta.eu/deliverables/. Accessed 10 May 2025
9. D6.3: Design of education and professional framework CyberSec4Europe, Brussels, Brussels, Rep. Call H2020-SU-ICT-03-2018 (2021)
10. REWIRE: Cybersecurity skills alliance—A new vision for Europe. https://rewireproject.eu/. Accessed 14 May 2024
11. Europe council decision 765/2008, setting out the requirements for accreditation and market surveillance relating to the marketing of products and repealing Regulation (EEC) No 339/93
12. Mogoane, S., Kabanda, S.: The relationship between cybersecurity and artificial intelligence. In: ICICIS (2019)
13. Bloomberg Adria Cybersecurity Workforce. https://rs.bloombergadria.com/tehnologija/digitalizacija/55963/sajber-napadi-ko-nas-u-srbiji-stiti-od-njih-i-zasto-toliko-kadrova-fali/news/?utm_source=linker&utm_medium=sw&utm_campaign=bloombergrs&utm_content=ad17. Accessed 10 May 2025
14. 2024 ISC2 Cybersecurity Workforce Study. https://www.isc2.org/Insights/2024/10/ISC2-2024-Cybersecurity-Workforce-Study. Accessed 10 May 2025
15. ENISA European Cybersecurity Skills Framework2022. https://www.enisa.europa.eu/publications/european-cybersecurity-skills-framework-role-profiles/@@download/fullReport. Accessed 10 May 2025
16. JTF. Curriculum Guidelines for Post-Secondary Degree Programs in Cybersecurity (2017). https://cybered.hosting.acm.org/wp-content/uploads/2018/02/newcover_csec2017.pdf. Accessed 10 May 2025
17. Burley, D., Lewis Jr, A.: Cybersecurity curricula 2017 and Boeing: linking curricular guidance to professional practice. IEEE Computer Community, pp. 29–37 (2019)
18. Nadeem, A.: Cybersecurity as a crosscutting concept across an undergrad computer science curriculum: an experience report. In: SIGCSE (2024)
19. Gonzalez, V., Perez, O., Romero, R.: Collaboration program to disseminate cybersecurity in the ECE curriculum. IEEE (2022)
20. Rathod, P., Polemi, N., Lehto, M., Kioski, K., Wessels, J., Lugo, R.: Leveraging the European cybersecurity skills framework (ECSF) in EU innovation projects: workforce development through skilling, upskilling, and reskilling. In: EDUCON (2024)
21. Hajny, J., Sikora, M., Adamos, K., Franco, F.: Curricula designer with enhanced ECSF analysis. In: ARES (2023)

22. Computer Science Curricula 2013, Association for Computing Machinery (ACM) IEEE Computer Society. https://www.acm.org/binaries/content/assets/education/cs2013_web_final.pdf. Accessed 10 May 2025

23. Matsuda, Y.: Curriculum analysis of computer science departments by simplified, supervised LDA. J. Inf. Process. (2018)

24. Hajny, J., Ricci, S., Piesarskas, E., Levillain, O., Galletta, L., De Nicola, R.: Framework, tools and good practices for cybersecurity curricula. IEEE Access (2021)

25. The EU's Cybersecurity Strategy for the Digital Decade. https://eur-lex.europa.eu/legal-content/EN/TXT/PDF/?uri=CELEX:52020JC0018. Accessed 07 Feb 2024

26. Ricci, S., et al.: Understanding cybersecurity education gaps in Europe. IEEE Trans. Educ. (2024)

27. Adamos, K., Di Franco, F., Grammatopoulos, A.: An analysis of European union cybersecurity higher education programs through the crowd-sourced database CyberHEAD. IEEE Secur. Priv. (2023)

28. Devlin, J., Chang, M.W., Lee, K., Toutanova, K.: BERT: pretraining of deep bidirectional transformers for language understanding. In: NAACL HLT (2019)

29. Mishra, A., Vishwarakama, S.: Analysis of TF-IDF model and its variant for document retrieval. In: IEEE CICN (2015)

30. Sitikhu, P., Pahi, K., Thapa, P., Shakya, S.: A comparison of semantic similarity methods for maximum human interpretability. In: IEEE AITB (2019)

31. Cyber security academic programs database. https://www.enisa.europa.eu/topics/education/cyberhead. Accessed 10 May 2025

32. LinkedIn job ads search engine. https://www.linkedin.com/jobs/search. Accessed 10 May 2025

33. Yin, C., Zhang, Z.: A study of sentence similarity based on the all-minilml6-v2 model with "same semantics, different structure" after fine tuning. In: ICIAAI (2024)

Proceedings of the Fifth International Workshop on Security Testing and Monitoring (STAM 2025)

STAM 2025 Preface

Security testing and monitoring are essential disciplines for ensuring the resilience and reliability of distributed systems, which form the backbone of modern society. From telecommunication networks to cloud computing, industrial systems, smart communities, and the Internet of Things, these systems operate in increasingly open and interconnected environments. This openness, while enabling greater interoperation, also exposes systems to a range of vulnerabilities and malicious activities that must be addressed comprehensively.

The workshop focuses on frameworks, methodologies, and tools designed to enhance security in distributed environments. It explores how modeling misbehaviors and attacks deepens our understanding of malicious activities and contributes to their prevention. Discussions also center on the limitations of existing models and approaches, shedding light on potential advancements to overcome these challenges. A key theme of the workshop is addressing the complexity of security testing and monitoring in distributed systems. The dynamic nature of these systems, coupled with the integration of artificial intelligence, poses new challenges that demand innovative solutions. Participants examine how testing and monitoring strategies can adapt to these complexities to ensure system robustness and integrity. In addition to presenting scientific research, the workshop provides practical insights through interactive training activities. These activities offer participants the opportunity to engage with real-world security scenarios, apply advanced testing techniques, and gain hands-on experience with monitoring tools tailored for distributed systems. By fostering a collaborative environment, STAM 2025 advances the field of security testing and monitoring while equipping participants with the knowledge and skills to address the emerging threats of tomorrow's interconnected systems.

STAM 2025 brings together cybersecurity practitioners and researchers to exchange ideas and perspectives on challenges and solutions in the field. It welcomes novel contributions on models, methods, algorithms, and real-world applications. Topics of interest include risk assessment frameworks for complex systems; trust and privacy assessment in distributed and critical environments; techniques for modeling vulnerabilities, threats, and attacks; security testing and monitoring methods and tools; automation for testing and monitoring in distributed environments; evaluation of resilience and tolerance to attacks in critical systems; integration of CI/CD practices; AI and machine learning for cybersecurity; industrial experience reports; training activities to raise awareness; and practical demonstrations of tools and frameworks for securing distributed systems.

August 2025

Valentina Casola
Wissam Mallouli

STAM 2025 Organization

Workshop Chairs

Valentina Casola — University of Naples Federico II, Italy
Wissam Mallouli — Montimage, France

Program Committee

Valentina Casola	University of Naples Federico II, Italy
Ana Rosa Cavalli	Institut Polytechnique de Paris/Telecom SudParis, France
Alessandra De Benedictis	University of Naples Federico II, Italy
Nicolas Ferry	University Côte d'Azur, France
Gürkan Gür	Zurich University of Applied Sciences, Switzerland
Ole Höfener	Massive Dynamic Sweden, Sweden
Eider Iturbe	Tecnalia, Spain
Charalambos Klitis	EBOS Technologies, Cyprus
Wissam Mallouli	Montimage, France
Stefan Marksteiner	AVL List Gmbh, Austria
Edgardo Montes de Oca	Montimage, France
Phu Nguyen	SINTEF, Norway
Andrea Pferscher	University of Oslo, Norway
Panagiotis Grammatikis	University of Western Macedonia, Greece
Erkuden Rios	Tecnalia, Spain
Martin Schneider	Fraunhofer FOKUS, Germany
Cristina Seceleanu	Mälardalen University, Sweden
Hui Song	SINTEF, Norway
Dragos Truscan	Åbo Akademi University, Finland
Fatiha Zaidi	Université Paris-Sud, France

Evaluating Large Language Models for Vulnerability Detection Under Realistic Conditions

Vincenzo Carletti, Pasquale Foggia, Carlo Mazzocca, Giuseppe Parrella$^{(\boxtimes)}$, and Mario Vento

Department of Computer Engineering, Electrical Engineering and Applied Mathematics, University of Salerno, Via Giovanni Paolo II, 132, 84084 Fisciano, SA, Italy
{vcarletti,pfoggia,cmazzocca,gparrella,mvento}@unisa.it

Abstract. Vulnerability Detection (VD) in source code is a critical task for ensuring the security of software systems, particularly in C/C++ languages, which are extensively adopted in safety-critical applications. The recent widespread adoption of Large Language Models (LLMs) for software engineering tasks has led to specialized open-source Code-LLMs, tailored to handle programming languages and code-specific challenges. Although these models have achieved promising results for VD through prompt engineering and fine-tuning strategies, existing studies often evaluate them in unrealistic settings, where test data comes from a similar distribution of training data. In this work, we present a comprehensive evaluation of open-source Code-LLMs for VD in C/C++ code, employing both prompt engineering and fine-tuning approaches. We introduce a novel benchmark dataset composed exclusively of functions extracted from real-world, production-level open-source projects, with the aim to conduct a more realistic analysis. Our results highlight the limitations of current Code-LLMs for VD when evaluated under a realistic setup, emphasizing the need for more robust and generalizable solutions for secure software development.

Keywords: Vulnerability Detection · Large Language Model · Software Security

1 Introduction

Software vulnerabilities are among the most critical concerns in today's digital world, as ongoing digitalization continues to reshape traditional services and applications [5]. This evolution amplifies the potential impact of such vulnerabilities when exploited by attackers to compromise systems and networks. According to the National Vulnerabilities Database (NVD) [25], more than 40.000 Common Vulnerability Exposures (CVEs) have been registered in 2024, with an increase of 38% from 2023. Among these, 34% are classified with a *High* or *Critical* severity according to the Common Vulnerability Scoring System (CVSS).

F. Skopik et al. (Eds.): ARES 2025 Workshops, LNCS 15999, pp. 135–152, 2025.
https://doi.org/10.1007/978-3-032-00644-8_8

A software vulnerability can be seen as a flaw (typically during design or implementation phase) in a piece of software that can be exploited by a malicious user to carry out an attack. While any programming language can lead to vulnerabilities, languages such as C and C++ pose greater security risks, as their design allows direct memory manipulation without built-in safety checks. These languages remain prevalent in critical systems, such as network device firmware and operating systems, and are still associated with many of the most common CVEs [24].

Vulnerability Detection is usually performed by domain experts, who leverage *static* [3,19,33,34] or *dynamic* [21,26] tools for program analysis. Static tools analyze the source code without executing it, when using dynamic tools, the program runs in controlled environment to detect malicious behavior. Both static and dynamic analysis tools are based on hand-crafted rules, devised by domain experts, and may need careful tuning to balance missed detections and false positives.

To overcome these limitations and enable the tools to generalize to previously undiscovered vulnerabilities (so-called *zero-day*), different approaches based on Machine Learning (ML) and Deep Learning (DL) techniques have been proposed. Such methods reduce the reliance on domain experts, who are primarily involved during data preparation and validation, as their effectiveness greatly depends on the data quality, quantity, and the chosen training strategy. DL approaches have shown to be more effective and accurate as well as potentially capable to generalize on new unseen kinds of vulnerabilities [8]. Different types of DL methods have been proposed for the task of vulnerability detection, such as Natural Language Processing (NLP)-based approaches [16,40], and Graph Neural Network (GNN)-based approaches [6,36,39].

Recently, Large Language Models (LLMs)-based methods have capitalized on the extensive pre-training of these models on large-scale datasets to effectively address downstream tasks involving source code [38]. In general, pre-trained LLMs can be leveraged for a variety of downstream tasks across different domains either using *fine-tuning* on task-specific datasets or through *prompt engineering* techniques, which allow for task adaptation without requiring further model training. In the context of source code, LLMs have been successfully applied to tasks such as code completion, code generation, and documentation generation [18]. These specialized models are commonly referred to as Code-LLMs. Consequently, several code-LLM-powered tools have emerged in the market (e.g., GitHub Copilot [14]), and many open-source Code-LLMs pre-trained on code-related tasks have been released [37]. LLM-based solutions for VD have also been proposed, employing both prompt engineering techniques and fine-tuning strategies. These approaches have explored the use of both open-source and commercial Code-LLMs to enhance VD.

In this context, several studies have highlighted the limitations of current state-of-the-art datasets and benchmarks used for VD, noting the presence of noisy labels, duplicated samples, and imbalanced data [2,6,12,15]. Moreover, many existing evaluations of ML and DL systems for VD have relied on test data drawn from the same distribution as the training data. This does not allow robustness and generalizability to be achieved. These systems should be assessed in a *realistic* setting, where the model is required to analyze unseen code originating from projects that were not part of the training phase. As a consequence, the training data itself should consist of code extracted from real software projects to capture realistic vulnerability patterns. Instead, several existing state-of-the-art datasets also include synthetic samples, which may introduce biases and do not accurately reflect the types of vulnerabilities encountered in practical scenarios.

In this work, we present a comprehensive evaluation of the capabilities of open-source Code-LLMs for VD, analyzing both *prompt engineering* and *fine-tuning* techniques. The prompt engineering phase explores three different prompting strategies: *zero-shot, few-shot,* and *Chain of Thought* (CoT). In the zero-shot setting, the model is asked to classify a given code snippet as vulnerable or not without being provided with any prior examples. In the few-shot setting, the model receives a limited number of labeled examples of known vulnerabilities before making a prediction. The CoT setting extends the zero-shot approach by incorporating intermediate reasoning steps, guiding the model through a structured rationale before reaching a final classification. In the fine-tuning phase, a subset of the model parameters is trained to adapt the model specifically for the VD task. The dataset used for training and evaluation is constructed by aggregating and refining multiple state-of-the-art datasets and open-source projects, thereby enabling a comprehensive assessment across a broad range of vulnerability types collected from diverse real-world projects over time. We focus specifically on VD in C/C++ methods, given the critical relevance of detecting such vulnerabilities in real-world safety-critical applications. To ensure a fair and realistic evaluation, we introduce a novel test set designed to benchmark VD systems. This dataset includes real vulnerability sampled from relevant recent open-source software projects. Our experimental results show that, when evaluated under realistic conditions (akin to those faced by security analysts using static analysis tools on unseen code) LLMs face significant challenges in achieving a favorable trade-off between false positives and false negatives.

Contributions. The main contributions of this work are as follows:

- We conduct a comprehensive evaluation of open-source Code-LLMs for detecting vulnerabilities in C/C++ source code. Our analysis also assess the effectiveness of these models using both prompt engineering and fine-tuning approaches.
- We evaluate the models in a realistic experimental setting, where training and validation are performed on a combination of state-of-the-art datasets, and testing is conducted on a newly introduced benchmark composed of real-world C/C++ code samples collected from open-source projects.
- We release our novel introduced test dataset to the research community to foster reproducibility and further investigation[1].

---

[1] https://anonymous.4open.science/r/code_analysis-cftb/README.md.

Organization. The remainder of this paper is organized as follows. Section 2 discusses relevant background and related work. Section 3 presents our novel introduced test dataset. Section 4 describes the experimental framework adopted in this study, while Sect. 5 reports and analyzes the experimental results. Finally, Sect. 6 concludes the paper and outlines directions for future work.

2 Background and Related Work

A vulnerability refers to a weakness within a software component, such as an error in the design or implementation of code that may enable a security threat. To standardize communication among security professionals, known weaknesses are catalogued in the community-maintained Common Weakness Enumeration (CWE), which assigns each weakness a unique identifier and detailed description. Furthermore, the CVE Program maintains a registry of publicly disclosed vulnerabilities, accessible through various platforms, such as the NVD [25].

VD as a machine learning task can be approached in different ways depending on the desired outcome. It is typically formulated as a binary classification problem when the objective is to determine whether a code fragment contains a vulnerability. If the goal is to identify the specific underlying weakness (e.g., by reporting its CWE identifier), the problem becomes a multi-label classification task. In the following, we review the background on LLM and most recent approaches that leverage Code-LLMs for VD.

LLMs. The term LLM was introduced in literature to distinguish language models based on their parameter size. Albeit there are no consensus on the number of parameters required to be considered as *"large"*, large size pre-trained language model are usually referred to LLM [38]. According to several taxonomies [12,38], LLMs can be divided into three categories based on their architectures by identifying two essential components: the *encoder*, which is responsible for processing and understanding the input sequence by capturing contextual information, and the *decoder*, which is tasked with generating output sequences, either by predicting the next token or by producing a transformed representation of the input. Based on these two components, we can define the following three categories:

- **Encoder-only LLMs:** These models, such as BERT [10], are designed primarily for understanding tasks. They process the entire input simultaneously to produce contextualized representations of the input tokens. This architecture is well-suited for classification, sequence labeling, and other discriminative tasks.
- **Encoder-Decoder LLMs:** Also known as sequence-to-sequence models, such as T5 [27], these architectures employ an encoder to read and understand the input sequence and a decoder to generate the output sequence. This structure is particularly effective for tasks like translation, summarization, and question answering.
- **Decoder-only LLMs:** These models, including GPT series [1], CodeLlama [28] and StarCoder [22], use only a decoder stack, typically with causal

attention to predict the next token in a sequence. They are optimized for generative tasks such as text completion, code generation, and dialogue systems.

With the term Code-LLM we refer to LLMs specifically trained for source-code related task.

Code-LLMs for Vulnerability Detection. Code-LLMs are generally not directly trained for VD, but are generally adapted to perform VD through two main techniques: *(i)* prompt engineering, without any additional training steps; and *(ii)* fine-tuning, where Code-LLMs are trained to adapt them for the VD task.

Regarding prompt engineering approaches, several studies have investigated the performance of LLMs on the VD task under various prompt strategies [4,12,20,31,32]. These investigations rely predominantly on proprietary LLMs, such as GPT-4 [1], which have been the primary models used in this line of research [38]. As a result, current analyses are largely influenced by the capabilities and limitations of closed-source models, limiting reproducibility and further experimentation by the research community. Furthermore, some recent work shows how these models have been able to perform well on VD on synthetic datasets only [20], but not in a real-world scenario [11]. For prompt formulation, existing studies adopt several structures, and there is currently no consensus on a universally optimal prompting strategy for the VD task [38].

Several studies have proposed methods that leverage state-of-the-art labeled datasets to adapt Code-LLMs for the VD task. Fine-tuning techniques can significantly improve the performance of Code-LLMs in this context [9,23, 29,30]. Additionally, more sophisticated fine-tuning strategies have also been explored [38]. Although fine-tuned models generally outperform those relying solely on prompt engineering techniques, it is essential to evaluate their effectiveness under *realistic* conditions; using test data drawn from projects that are distinct from those used during training and validation. Recent studies indicate that LLMs tend to underperform in the VD task when assessed in such rigorous and realistic settings [12]. Additionally, the absence of a standardized benchmark for evaluating these models constitutes a significant gap in the current literature [12,38].

In this scenario, our work provides a comprehensive evaluation of open-source Code-LLMs under realistic conditions, addressing a critical gap in the current literature. To this end, we introduce a novel test set composed of functions extracted from real-world, production-level open-source projects, enabling a more rigorous and meaningful assessment of model performance in practical scenarios. Unlike prior studies that primarily rely on proprietary LLMs, our evaluation focuses on openly available models, which allows us to assess their behavior under both prompt engineering and fine-tuning approaches. This dual perspective offers a more complete and transparent understanding of model capabilities for the VD task—an analysis that is often not feasible with closed-source models due to their limited accessibility and customization.

3   Our Benchmark: MVFSC Test Dataset

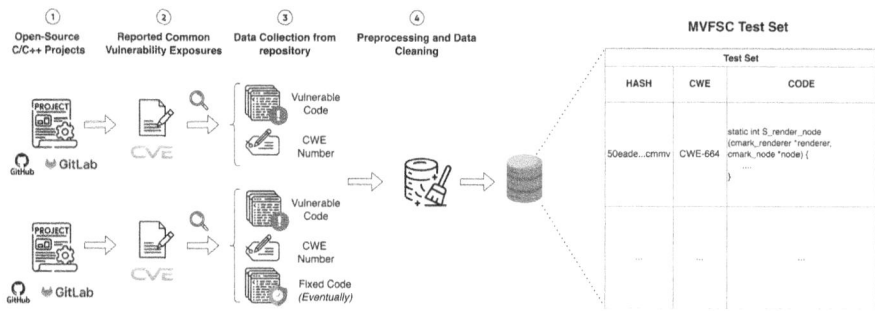

Fig. 1. Pipeline for the creation of the test set introduced in this work. The process includes: *(1)* selection of real-world C/C++ open-source projects; *(2)* retrieval of reported vulnerabilities through CVE records; *(3)* data cleaning and preprocessing to ensure consistency and remove duplicates or non-informative elements; and *(4)* collection and structuring of the corresponding vulnerable and non-vulnerable code samples.

In this section, we describe the procedure adopted for the construction of the novel test dataset introduced in this work: the MIVIA Vulnerable Function Source Code (MVFSC) test dataset.

Test data collection procedure. As previously mentioned, the test set was created through a manual process, which constitutes a significant contribution to the state of the art. The construction of the test set was carried out in four main phases, as illustrated in Fig. 1:

1. **Selection of open-source Projects.** A preliminary analysis was conducted to identify a diverse set of real-world open-source projects written in C and C++. The selection aimed to cover a wide range of application domains and codebases of varying complexity and size.
2. **Identification of reported vulnerabilities.** For each selected project, publicly disclosed vulnerabilities were retrieved using trusted databases such as CVE Details and the NVD maintained by NIST. Each vulnerability was then mapped to its corresponding CWE category.
3. **Preprocessing and Data Cleaning.** Before being organized into the final dataset, all collected samples underwent a series of preprocessing operations. A deduplication process was first applied to ensure that each entry was unique and representative, thereby preventing biases in the evaluation. This was achieved by computing a hash for each code snippet and removing duplicates accordingly. Furthermore, a cleaning step was performed to improve the effectiveness of the tokenization process: line breaks, newline feeds, tabs, and redundant spaces were removed, while ensuring the preservation of the original syntax and semantics.

Table 1. Distribution of Common Weakness Enumerations (CWEs) in the proposed test set. The table summarizes the most frequent vulnerability types identified in the collected code samples, based on their CWE classification.

CWE ID	Description	Occurrences
CWE-119	Improper Restriction of Operations within the Bounds of a Memory Buffer	95
CWE-787	Out-of-bounds Write	81
CWE-125	Out-of-bounds Read	68
CWE-754	Improper Check for Unusual or Exceptional Conditions	60
CWE-691	Insufficient Control Flow Management	37
CWE-190	Integer Overflow or Wraparound	34
CWE-664	Improper Control of a Resource Through its Lifetime	31
CWE-617	Reachable Assertion	22
CWE-707	Improper Initialization	17
CWE-369	Divide by Zero	13
Others	Other types of vulnerabilities not individually listed	29

4. **Collection and Organization of Code Samples.** Finally, the cleaned and validated code snippets were organized into a structured dataset. Each entry includes the source code, the associated CWE, the project of origin, a unique identifier, and a binary vulnerability label–classified as vulnerable (1) or non-vulnerable (0)—based on prior knowledge and manual inspection. When available, both vulnerable and fixed versions of each sample were included to facilitate accurate evaluation.

Dataset characteristics. Our test dataset consists of 972 functions extracted from real-world, production-level software projects. Of these functions, 487 are labeled as vulnerable, while the remaining 485 are identified as non-vulnerable, ensuring a balanced distribution. The dataset encompasses 10 distinct CWEs, thereby covering a broad spectrum of vulnerability types. These include, among others, improper memory handling (`CWE-119`), out-of-bounds write (`CWE-787`), and out-of-bounds read (`CWE-125`), as detailed in Table 1. All functions were sourced from publicly available open-source projects, such as *Cmark-gfm*, *Eclipse*, *ffmpeg*, *libarchive*, *OpenSSH*, *Qt*, *Redis*, *TensorFlow*, and *wireshark*, ensuring the relevance of the dataset to real-world development contexts. This diverse and representative collection of samples provides a robust foundation for assessing VD systems.

4 Experimental Framework

In this section, we present the experimental framework adopted for validating open-source Code-LLMs on the VD task. We provide a detailed description of the datasets used, including their structure, purpose, and preparation process. Additionally, we outline the evaluation methodology, which consists of an initial prompt engineering testing phase followed by a fine-tuning phase.

Table 2. Composition of the dataset used for training, validation, and test in our experiments. Each column corresponds to a dataset. The rows report the number of functions used for training, validation, and testing, respectively. "✗" indicates that the dataset was not used for that specific phase.

Scope Dataset	DiverseVul [7]	BigVul [13]	Devign [39]	Debian	Chrome	PrimeVUL [12]	MVFSC
Train	236,382	126,369	20,162	16,413	3,996	✗	✗
Validation	26,189	14,068	2,232	1,885	440	✗	✗
Test	✗	✗	✗	✗	✗	882	972

4.1 Dataset

In this section, we provide a detailed description of the datasets used for training, validating and testing our models.

The training and validation datasets used in this work are constructed by combining multiple state-of-the-art publicly available vulnerability datasets: DiverseVul [7], BigVul [13], and Devign [39], alongside additional functions extracted from widely-used open-source software projects such as Chrome and Debian. This composition ensures a heterogeneous and representative sample of real-world code, facilitating robust model training and validation. In this context, each sample in the dataset corresponds to a single C/C++ function, which is analyzed individually to determine whether it contains a vulnerability or not. To ensure data quality and prevent biases during model training, a data deduplication process was applied to identify and remove duplicate entries. Furthermore, samples with conflicting labels across different datasets were discarded to maintain consistency. Additionally, code comments and extraneous characters were stripped from the functions, as such elements could introduce noise and can negatively affect the training phase of ML and DL models. The training set consists of 403,322 samples, of which 32,943 are labeled as vulnerable and 370,279 as non-vulnerable. The validation set includes 44,814 samples, comprising 3,554 vulnerable and 41,260 non-vulnerable functions. The detailed distribution of functions across the training and validation sets for each dataset is reported in Table 2.

To test our models in a realistic scenario, we employ two different test sets, which contains code sampled from different projects with respect to those included during training and validation phases. The first dataset used is MVFSC, introduced in this work and previously detailed in Sect. 3. The second test dataset used is PrimeVUL [12], which consist of 441 paired functions (each vulnerable function is paired with its corresponding fix), which is introduced to evaluate the ability of LLMs to identify vulnerable functions and their fixes within textually similar context.

In this setting, we simulate a realistic scenario in which the samples included in the test set originate from software projects distinct from those used in the training set. Although these projects may have been partially involved during

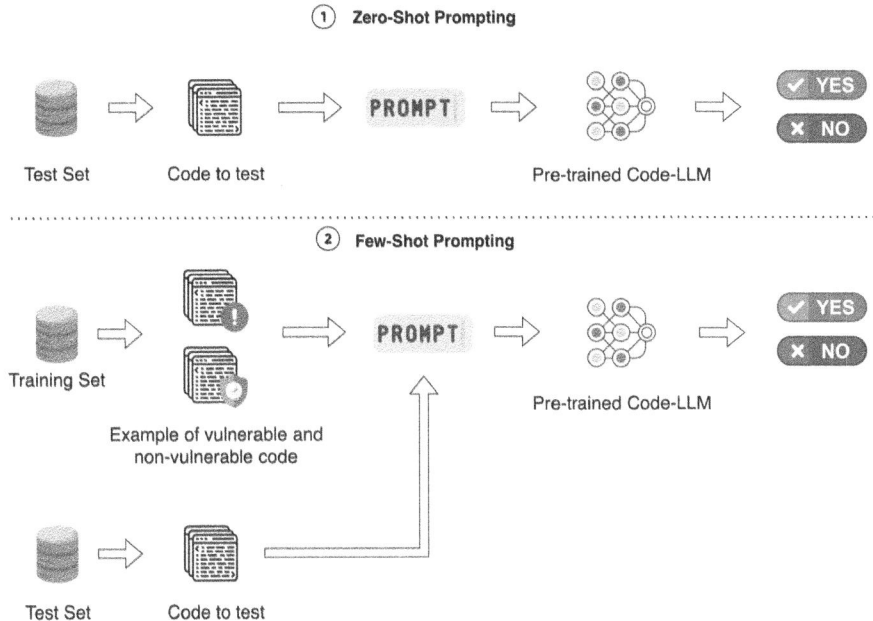

Fig. 2. Graphical illustration of zero-shot and few-shot prompting procedures used in this work.

the pre-training phase of the employed Code-LLMs, they were associated with different code-related tasks. This setup allows us to effectively assess the generalization capabilities of Code-LLMs specifically fine-tuned for VD task.

4.2   Experimental Setup

In this section, we explain both the open-source Code-LLMs tested in this work and the evaluation framework used to evaluate them for the VD task.

Code Large-Language Models. As introduced above, in this work, we focus on the evaluation of open-source Code-LLMs for VD task. Specifically, we employ CodeLlama [28] and StarCoder [22] with 7 billion of parameters, two state-of-the-art models known for their effectiveness in code understanding and generation. The choice of models with 7 billion parameters reflects a deliberate balance between performance and computational feasibility, considering the significant resource demands associated with training and fine-tuning large-scale models.

Zero-Shot, Few-Shot, and Chain Of Thoughts Prompting. In this work, we performed zero-shot, few-shot and CoT prompting to assess the performance of the open-source Code-LLMs without any additional fine-tuning. As shown in Fig. 2, the zero-shot phase involved providing the models with a prompt containing a question along with the code to analyze. The prompt structure (see Fig. 3) follows existing literature [35] and is designed to enable the model to evaluate the vulnerability of a function without any prior examples. In the few-shot phase, we provided the model with a set of example functions (both vulnerable and non-vulnerable) sourced from the training set used for model evaluation. This approach reflects a realistic scenario, where the prompt includes code from different codebases compared to the ones in the test set. These examples were used to guide the model in making more accurate predictions and improving its performance in classifying unseen functions. Additionally, we conducted experiments using the CoT prompting technique. This approach was tested because zero-shot and few-shot learning alone may be insufficient in some cases, particularly for complex tasks that require logical progression. By breaking the task into logical steps, CoT helps reduce false positives and false negatives, providing

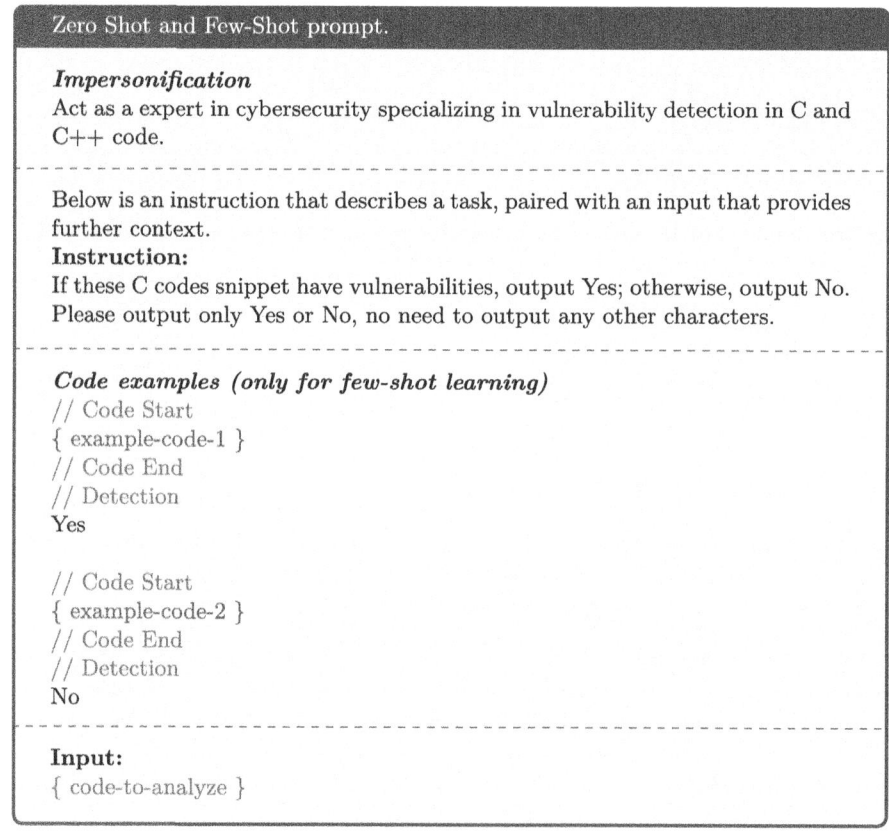

Fig. 3. Example of prompt used for zero-shot and few-shot learning. In case of zero-shot learning, the code examples are not provided to the model. The code example in blue are sampled from the training set, while code to analyze refers to function of the test set. The same prompt structure (without code examples) is used during fine-tuning phase. (Color figure online)

a more structured approach for the model to reason through the problem. A graphical example of prompt structure used for CoT can be found in Fig. 4.

During the prompting phase, a temperature value of 0.01 was selected. The temperature is a hyperparameter that influences the model's response variability. A low temperature ensures that the model's responses are more deterministic and less creative, enhancing the reproducibility of the results. This value was chosen to support the goal of obtaining consistent and reliable results for VD, while also minimizing the risk of hallucinations.

Chain of Thought prompt.

Impersonification
Act as a expert in cybersecurity specializing in vulnerability detection in C and C++ code.

- -

Classify the following C/C++ function:
{ code-to-analyze }

Please indicate your analysis result with one of options :

1. YES : A potential security vulnerability detected.
2. NO: No security vulnerability.

Let s think step-by-step in 3 steps:
 – Step 1: Identify the inputs and outputs of the function (1 sentence).
 – Step 2: Analyze briefly the operations performed on the inputs and focus on unusual practice. (1-3 sentences)
 – Step 3: Conclude with a concise response following showed rules (1 sentence).

Fig. 4. Example of prompt structure used for CoT in this work.

Model Fine-Tuning. The fine-tuning phase of this work focused on adapting the CodeLlama model using the Low-Rank Adaptation (LoRA) technique [17], a parameter-efficient method for fine-tuning. LoRA specifically targets the attention layers of the model, leaving the rest of the model frozen, thereby reducing the number of trainable parameters. With this method, only 0.12% of the model's parameters were trainable. The fine-tuning process used a training batch size of 48, a validation batch size of 64, and a context length of 512 tokens. It consisted of 3 epochs, with gradient accumulation steps set to 4, and a learning rate of $1e-4$, accompanied by a gamma of 0.85 for learning rate decay. The prompt employed during the fine-tuning phase to generate the dataset from the source code in the training and validation sets follows the same structure as shown in Fig. 2 (excluding the examples of vulnerable and non-vulnerable code). This configuration ensured efficient fine-tuning, balancing computational resources while optimizing the model for vulnerability detection tasks.

In this work, we adopt two distinct configurations of the CodeLlama architecture: a *classification module* and a *generation module*. These modules are positioned downstream of the standard transformer backbone of the model, which remains unchanged in both configurations. The classification module is specifically designed to determine whether a given code function is vulnerable or not. To this end, we frame the problem as a sequence-level classification task and employ a classification loss function that evaluates the probability associated with the final token of the output, comparing it to the correct label. This approach diverges from the conventional next-token prediction objective of language models, which may be suboptimal for classification tasks as it does not explicitly encourage correct sequence-level predictions. To further enhance performance, particularly in class imbalance and challenging samples, we utilize the focal loss [29] during training. This loss function increases the model's focus on harder examples and reduces the influence of easier or over-represented cases, thereby improving classification accuracy.

The *generation module* is employed for tasks that require the model to produce textual outputs, such as code generation. In this configuration, the model is fine-tuned using the standard next-token prediction objective, which aligns with the generative pretraining paradigm of language models. Unlike the classification setting, this module is not concerned with sequence-level categorization but rather with producing coherent and contextually appropriate continuations of the input sequence.

5   Experimental Results

In this section, we report the experimental results obtained by using the experimental framework described in Sect. 4.

Evaluation Metrics. Before proceeding with the result analysis, we present the evaluation metrics adopted in this study and clarify the classification terminology employed. Understanding the definitions of false positives and false negatives is essential for correctly interpreting the performance outcomes.

The evaluation relies on commonly used metrics, namely *Accuracy* (Eq. 1), *Precision* (Eq. 2), *Recall* (Eq. 3), *F1-Score* (Eq. 4), and *False Positive Rate* (FPR, Eq. 5). These metrics are computed based on the outcomes of the classification task, which include:

- *True Positives* (TP): vulnerable samples correctly classified as vulnerable;
- *True Negatives* (TN): non-vulnerable samples correctly classified as non-vulnerable;
- *False Positives* (FP): non-vulnerable samples incorrectly classified as vulnerable;
- *False Negatives* (FN): vulnerable samples incorrectly classified as non-vulnerable.

Accuracy quantifies the overall correctness of the model, defined as the proportion of correctly classified samples out of the total. *Precision* measures the proportion of true positive predictions among all positive predictions, indicating the system's ability to avoid false alarms. *Recall* expresses the proportion of actual positive samples that are correctly identified, thus reflecting the model's sensitivity. The *F1-Score* represents the harmonic mean of Precision and Recall, providing a balanced metric especially in the presence of class imbalance. Finally, the *False Positive Rate* (FPR) quantifies the proportion of negative instances incorrectly classified as positive, highlighting the tendency of the system to produce false alarms.

The formal definitions of the metrics are provided below:

$$\text{Accuracy} = \frac{TP + TN}{TP + TN + FP + FN} \tag{1}$$

$$\text{Precision} = \frac{TP}{TP + FP} \tag{2}$$

$$\text{Recall} = \frac{TP}{TP + FN} \tag{3}$$

$$\text{F1-Score} = 2 \cdot \frac{\text{Precision} \cdot \text{Recall}}{\text{Precision} + \text{Recall}} \tag{4}$$

$$\text{FPR} = \frac{FP}{FP + TN} \tag{5}$$

Zero-Shot, Few-Shot and CoT Prompting. The results reported in Table 3 highlight several important trends regarding the effectiveness of different prompting strategies when applied to open-source Code-LLMs for the task of VD. First, the inclusion of the impersonification component appears to influence the performance in a non-uniform manner, depending on the prompting strategy and model in use. Few-shot prompting exhibits a significant variance in outcomes, suggesting that the quality and representativeness of the examples provided in the prompt may substantially affect the model's ability to generalize. Interestingly, when combined with impersonification, few-shot prompting generally demonstrates increased stability and performance across different metrics, which may indicate that added contextual cues contribute positively to model alignment with the task. Finally, the application of CoT prompting in combination with impersonification leads to further improvements, particularly in recall and F1 metrics, suggesting that guiding the model through intermediate reasoning steps can enhance its detection capabilities. However, such gains may come at the cost of reduced performance in complementary aspects, such as precision or FPR.

In summary, although prompting strategies that include explicit examples (few-shot) or reasoning guidance (CoT) tend to improve model performance compared to zero-shot approaches, the overall results underscore the limitations of relying solely on prompting to address VD in realistic settings. The persistent challenges (e.g., high FPR, inconsistent behavior across different models, limited

Table 3. Evaluation metrics for StarCoder and CodeLlama across different prompting strategies on the test set. The column **Imp.** indicates whether the impersonification component is included (✓) or not (✗). Arrows (↑ or ↓) next to each metric denote the direction of improvement.

Strategy	Imp.	Model	F1-score ↑	Recall ↑	Precision ↑	Accuracy ↑	FPR ↓
Zero-shot	✗	StarCoder	0.58	0.70	0.49	0.48	0.74
		CodeLlama	0.33	0.25	0.50	0.50	0.25
	✓	StarCoder	0.51	0.48	**0.54**	**0.54**	0.41
		CodeLlama	0.55	0.61	0.51	0.51	0.60
Few-shot	✗	StarCoder	0.20	0.13	0.47	0.49	**0.15**
		CodeLlama	0.42	0.36	0.49	0.49	0.38
	✓	StarCoder	0.54	0.60	0.49	0.49	0.62
		CodeLlama	0.61	0.76	0.51	0.52	0.73
CoT	✓	CodeLlama	**0.63**	**0.88**	0.49	0.48	0.92

generalization) suggest that prompting alone is insufficient to ensure robust and reliable performance.

Model Finetuning. The evaluation results for CodeLlama fine-tuned on the VD task demonstrate noticeable improvements when compared to the models that were not fine-tuned. As we can see from Table 4, the classification module outperforms the generation module across both the validation and test sets, showing that fine-tuning enhances the model's ability to make precise and accurate predictions.

On the validation set, the fine-tuned classification model performs well across all metrics, indicating that the model is effectively generalizing to the validation data. The generation module, while still performing decently, shows lower scores compared to the classification model, particularly in terms of Precision and F1-score, suggesting that it is less effective at providing highly accurate outputs for the VD task.

On the MVFSC test set, however, the classification module shows a notable decrease in performance, with F1-score dropping to 0.53, Recall to 0.57, and Precision to 0.50. This indicates that the model faces difficulties in generalizing to unseen data in more rigorous and realistic scenarios, with the FPR increasing to 0.58. The generation module experiences an even more significant drop, with the F1-score falling to 0.14, and both Recall and Precision also showing a sharp decline. This highlights that the generation module struggles considerably when exposed to unseen data in real-world situations, pointing to potential limitations in its generalization capabilities.

To have a more comprehensive evaluation, we have also used PrimeVUL [12] as an additional test set for assess the performance of the fine-tuned models. In this case, the challenges of generalization become even more evident. For the classification module, the performance is notably lower than on the validation

Table 4. Evaluation metrics for CodeLlama fine-tuned for VD task on validation and test sets (classification and generation modules). Bold values indicate the best results for each dataset.

Dataset	Module	F1-score ↑	Recall ↑	Precision ↑	Accuracy ↑	FPR ↓
Validation	Classification	**0.86**	**0.92**	**0.81**	**0.91**	**0.11**
	Generation	0.71	0.78	0.66	0.85	0.16
MVFSC Test	Classification	**0.53**	**0.57**	**0.50**	**0.50**	0.58
	Generation	0.14	0.08	0.47	0.49	**0.09**
PrimeVUL [12]	Classification	**0.37**	**0.30**	**0.49**	**0.48**	0.33
	Generation	0.20	0.12	0.49	0.49	**0.13**

and test sets, with a F1-score of 0.37, Recall of 0.30, and Precision of 0.49. This further demonstrates the difficulty of the model in adapting to a new, real-world dataset that differs from the training set. The generation module performs even worse on PrimeVUL, with a F1-score of 0.20 and a very low Recall of 0.12, indicating that it struggles significantly with generalizing to this new data. These results suggest that even with fine-tuning, these models face substantial challenges in generalizing to new datasets, highlighting the need for further optimization to improve their robustness in real-world applications.

6 Conclusion

This work presents a comprehensive and realistic evaluation of open-source code-LLMs for VD in C/C++ source code. Our analysis covers several prompting strategies (including Zero-shot, Few-shot, and CoT) as well as fine-tuning phases, to assess model performance both before and after adaptation to the VD task. To ensure the validity of our findings, we introduce a new test dataset composed of functions extracted from real-world open-source projects. The experimental results reveal that current models face considerable challenges in delivering satisfactory performance under realistic settings. These findings underscore the importance of further research to improve the practical applicability of Code-LLMs in real-world security scenarios.

References

1. Achiam, J., et al.: GPT-4 technical report. arXiv preprint arXiv:2303.08774 (2023)
2. Akhoundali, J., Nouri, S.R., Rietveld, K., Gadyatskaya, O.: Morefixes: A large-scale dataset of CVE fix commits mined through enhanced repository discovery. In: Proceedings of the 20th International Conference on Predictive Models and Data Analytics in Software Engineering, pp. 42–51 (2024)

3. Arteau, P.: Spotbugs. SpotBugs (2025). https://spotbugs.github.io. Accessed 22 April 2025

4. Capuano, N., Carletti, V., Foggia, P., Parrella, G., Vento, M.: Leveraging open-source LLMs for zero-shot vulnerability detection: a comparative analysis. In: Barolli, L. (ed.) Advanced Information Networking and Applications, pp. 13–25. Springer Nature Switzerland, Cham (2025)

5. Casola, V., De Benedictis, A., Mazzocca, C., Orbinato, V.: Secure software development and testing: a model-based methodology. Comput. Secur. **137**, 103639 (2024)

6. Chakraborty, S., Krishna, R., Ding, Y., Ray, B.: Deep learning based vulnerability detection: are we there yet? IEEE Trans. Software Eng. **48**(9), 3280–3296 (2021)

7. Chen, Y., Ding, Z., Alowain, L., Chen, X., Wagner, D.: DiverseVul: a new vulnerable source code dataset for deep learning based vulnerability detection. In: Proceedings of the 26th International Symposium on Research in Attacks, Intrusions and Defenses, p. 654 668. RAID '23, Association for Computing Machinery, New York, NY, USA (2023)

8. Croft, R., Newlands, D., Chen, Z.: An empirical study of rule-based and learning-based approaches for static application security testing. In: Association for Computing Machinery, pp. 1–12. New York, NY, USA (2021)

9. Croft, R., Babar, M.A., Kholoosi, M.M.: Data quality for software vulnerability datasets. In: 2023 IEEE/ACM 45th International Conference on Software Engineering (ICSE), pp. 121–133. IEEE (2023)

10. Devlin, J., Chang, M., Lee, K., Toutanova, K.: BERT: pre-training of deep bidirectional transformers for language understanding (2018). https://arxiv.org/abs/1810.04805

11. Ding, Y., et al.: VELVET: a noVel Ensemble learning approach to automatically locate VulnErable sTatements. In: 2022 IEEE International Conference on Software Analysis, Evolution and Reengineering (SANER), pp. 959–970 (2022)

12. Ding, Y., et al.: Vulnerability detection with code language models: how far are we? . In: 2025 IEEE/ACM 47th International Conference on Software Engineering (ICSE), pp. 469–481. IEEE Computer Society, Los Alamitos, CA, USA (2025). https://doi.org/10.1109/ICSE55347.2025.00038 , https://doi.org/10.1109/ICSE55347.2025.00038

13. Fan, J., Li, Y., Wang, S., Nguyen, T.N.: A c/c++ code vulnerability dataset with code changes and cve summaries. In: 2020 IEEE/ACM 17th International Conference on Mining Software Repositories (MSR), pp. 508–512 (2020). https://doi.org/10.1145/3379597.3387501

14. GitHub: GitHub copilot (2025). https://github.com/copilot. Accessed 16 April 2025

15. Guo, Y., Bettaieb, S.: An investigation of quality issues in vulnerability detection datasets. In: 2023 IEEE European Symposium on Security and Privacy Workshops (EuroS&PW), pp. 29–33 (2023). https://doi.org/10.1109/EuroSPW59978.2023.00008

16. Hanif, H., Maffeis, S.: VulBERTa: simplified source code pre-training for vulnerability detection. In: Proceedings of the International Joint Conference on Neural Networks (2022)

17. Hu, E..J., et al.: LoRa: low-rank adaptation of large language models. ICLR **1**(2), 3 (2022)

18. Jiang, J., Wang, F., Shen, J., Kim, S., Kim, S.: A survey on large language models for code generation. arXiv preprint arXiv:2406.00515 (2024)

19. Kamiya, T., Kusumoto, S., Inoue, K.: CCFinder: a multilinguistic token-based code clone detection system for large scale source code. IEEE Trans. Software Eng. **28**(7), 654–670 (2002)

20. Khare, A., Dutta, S., Li, Z., Solko-Breslin, A., Alur, R., Naik, M.: Understanding the effectiveness of large language models in detecting security vulnerabilities. arXiv preprint arXiv:2311.16169 (2023)

21. LDRA: LDRA software quality, software testing, software standards (2025). https://ldra.com/. Accessed 22 April 2025

22. Li, R., et al.: StarCoder: may the source be with you!. arXiv preprint arXiv:2305.06161 (2023)

23. Li, Z., et al.: On the effectiveness of function-level vulnerability detectors for inter-procedural vulnerabilities. In: Proceedings of the IEEE/ACM 46th International Conference on Software Engineering, pp. 1–12 (2024)

24. MITRE Corporation: CWE 2024 Top 25 Most Dangerous Software Weaknesses (2025). https://cwe.mitre.org/top25/archive/2024/2024_kev_list.html. Accessed April 16 2025

25. National Institute of Standards and Technology (NIST): Common Vulnerabilities and Exposures (CVE). https://nvd.nist.gov/. Accessed April 16 2025

26. Nethercote, N., Seward, J.: Valgrind: a framework for heavyweight dynamic binary instrumentation. SIGPLAN Not. **42**(6), 89 100 (2007). https://doi.org/10.1145/1273442.1250746, https://doi.org/10.1145/1273442.1250746

27. Raffel, C., et al.: Exploring the limits of transfer learning with a unified text-to-text transformer. J. Mach. Learn. Res. **21**(140), 1–67 (2020)

28. Roziere, B., et al.: Code Llama: open foundation models for code. arXiv preprint arXiv:2308.12950 (2023)

29. Shestov, A., et al.: Finetuning large language models for vulnerability detection. IEEE Access **13**, 38889–38900 (2025)

30. Steenhoek, B., Rahman, M.M., Jiles, R., Le, W.: An empirical study of deep learning models for vulnerability detection. In: 2023 IEEE/ACM 45th International Conference on Software Engineering (ICSE), pp. 2237–2248. IEEE (2023)

31. Sun, Y., et al.: LLM4Vuln: a unified evaluation framework for decoupling and enhancing LLMs' vulnerability reasoning. arXiv preprint arXiv:2401.16185 (2024)

32. Ullah, S., Han, M., Pujar, S., Pearce, H., Coskun, A., Stringhini, G.: Can large language models identify and reason about security vulnerabilities? Not yet. arXiv preprint arXiv:2312.12575 (2023)

33. Wheeler, D.A.: Flawfinder. DWheeler (2009). https://www.dwheeler.com/flawfinder/. Accessed 22 April 2025

34. Woo, S., Kim, S., Lee, H., Oh, H.: VUDDY: a scalable approach for vulnerable code clone discovery. In: IEEE Symposium on Security and Privacy (SP), pp. 595–614. IEEE, San Jose, CA, USA (2017)

35. Yin, X., Ni, C., Wang, S.: Multitask-based evaluation of open-source LLM on software vulnerability. IEEE Trans. Softw. Eng. **50** (2024)

36. Zeng, C., Zhou, B., Dong, H., Wu, H., Xie, P., Guan, Z.: A general source code vulnerability detection method via ensemble of graph neural networks. In: Yang, H., Lu, R. (eds.) Frontiers in Cyber Security, pp. 560–574. Springer Nature Singapore, Singapore (2024)

37. Zhang, Z., et al.: Unifying the perspectives of NLP and software engineering: a survey on language models for code. Trans. Mach. Learn. Res. (2024). https://openreview.net/forum?id=hkNnGqZnpa

38. Zhou, X., Cao, S., Sun, X., Lo, D.: Large language model for vulnerability detection and repair: literature review and the road ahead. ACM Trans. Softw. Eng. Methodol. (2024)
39. Zhou, Y., Liu, S., Siow, J., Du, X., Liu, Y.: Devign: effective vulnerability identification by learning comprehensive program semantics via graph neural networks. In: Advances in Neural Information Processing Systems, pp. 10197–10207 (2019)
40. Zou, D., Wang, S., Xu, S., Li, Z., Jin, H.: VulDeePecker: a deep learning-based system for multiclass vulnerability detection. IEEE Trans. Dependable Secure Comput. **18**(5), 2224–2236 (2021)

LLMs in Security Testing and Monitoring: An Initial Study

Luong Nguyen$^{(\boxtimes)}$, Manh-Dung Nguyen , Anh Hao Bui ,
Ana Rosa Cavalli , and Edgardo Montes de Oca

Montimage EURL, 37 rue Bobillot, 75013 Paris, France
luong.nguyen@montimage.eu

Abstract. Cyber threats are becoming increasingly complex, causing
traditional security systems to struggle in keeping up and highlighting
the need for advanced solutions. Large Language Models (LLMs), such
as OpenAI's ChatGPT and Meta AI's LLaMA, have shown great potential to transform cybersecurity workflows with their abilities in natural
language understanding, pattern recognition, and automated reasoning.
These models are particularly promising for tasks like network monitoring, threat detection, and security alert triage. However, challenges
related to the reliability of outputs, adversarial risks, and ethical concerns
must be addressed. This paper presents a comprehensive survey of LLM-
based approaches for security testing and evaluates three open-access
LLMs, including Mistral-7B, Qwen3-8B, and Llama3.1-8B, demonstrating their ability to enhance security alert analysis. Our findings suggest
that LLMs can improve alert clarity and usability, making them more
accessible to non-experts while providing valuable insights for developers.

Keywords: Large Language Model · Cybersecurity · Advanced
Threats · Cyberdefense · Testing and Monitoring

1 Introduction

As cyber threats grow increasingly complex and frequent, the demand for intelligent, adaptable, and user-friendly security testing tools has become more pressing. Traditional rule-based systems and signature-based detection mechanisms
often struggle to keep up with rapidly evolving attack vectors. Recently, Large
Language Models (LLMs) have emerged as powerful tools that can transform
cybersecurity workflows. Their capabilities in natural language understanding,
pattern recognition, and automated reasoning offer exciting possibilities for
enhancing security processes [17]. Several LLMs, such as OpenAI's ChatGPT
and Meta AI's LLaMA, have gained widespread popularity due to their ability to analyze, summarize, and generate human-readable content from complex
technical data. This makes them particularly promising for network monitoring, threat detection, and alert triage, which are critical components of modern
security testing pipelines.

© The Author(s), under exclusive license to Springer Nature Switzerland AG 2025
F. Skopik et al. (Eds.): ARES 2025 Workshops, LNCS 15999, pp. 153–166, 2025.
https://doi.org/10.1007/978-3-032-00644-8_9

The intersection of LLMs and cybersecurity has sparked renewed interest within the cybersecurity community [8, 25]. Several tools now leverage LLMs to enhance security testing and monitoring. For example, OpenAI's GPT-3 and ChatGPT are used to assist in threat intelligence and vulnerability assessments by analyzing cybersecurity reports and identifying patterns. For instance, IBM's Watson for Cyber Security automates the analysis of unstructured data to generate actionable insights, and SIEM systems like Splunk use LLMs for log analysis and threat detection. Recently, ChatAFL [18] leverages pre-trained LLMs to perform grammar-aware mutations and predict the next input when fuzzing protocols to produce more effective inputs. These tools showcase the potential of LLMs to improve cybersecurity operations in different areas.

Challenges. Integrating LLMs into security testing and monitoring workflows presents several challenges. One key issue is ensuring the reliability and trustworthiness of LLM-generated outputs. Biases in training data can lead to inaccurate conclusions, potentially resulting in false positives or false negatives in security assessments. The interpretability of LLM-generated insights is another significant concern. Understanding the rationale behind their decisions is crucial for effective security responses, but the "black-box" nature of these models can limit their usefulness in real-world applications.

Additionally, the complexity of security alerts generated by monitoring systems such as Suricata [4] and Zeek [5] poses another challenge. While these alerts are rich in technical detail, they can be difficult for non-experts to understand, reducing their effectiveness in environments lacking experienced security analysts. To improve clarity and actionability, LLMs could enhance alert interpretation and usability, but this requires a deep understanding of their capabilities, limitations, and their integration into security workflows. Furthermore, concerns about adversarial manipulation, reliability, and ethical implications must be addressed to ensure the secure, reliable, and responsible use of LLMs in cybersecurity.

Proposal. In this paper, we provide a comprehensive exploration of the applications of LLMs in cybersecurity, with a specific focus on security testing and monitoring. We aim to address existing challenges by first presenting a thorough survey of LLM-based approaches in cybersecurity testing, particularly emphasizing network monitoring and threat detection. We examine how recent advances in LLMs have been utilized to automate security tasks and explore their potential to improve the quality and usability of security alerts. Building on this foundation, we propose a concrete use case to demonstrate the application of LLMs in security alert analysis. Through a comparative evaluation of three state-of-the-art open-access models, including Mistral-7B, Qwen3-8B, and Llama3.1-8B, we showcase their effectiveness in assessing and explaining security alerts across key evaluation criteria, including accuracy, clarity, completeness, actionability, and false positive assessment. Our findings aim to offer valuable guidance for both users and developers of security monitoring tools. For users, LLM-generated analyses can enhance understanding and response to alerts, making security tools more accessible to non-experts. For developers, insights derived from LLM evaluations can inform improvements in alert quality, user experience, and overall system performance.

Contributions. Our contributions are as follows.

- We present a comprehensive survey of LLM-based approaches in cybersecurity testing, with a focus on network monitoring and threat detection.
- We conduct a comparative evaluation of three state-of-the-art open-access LLMs Mistral-7B, Qwen3-8B, and Llama3.1-8B, demonstrating their effectiveness in security alert analysis across key evaluation criteria.

The rest of this paper is organized as follows. Section 2 provides background on Large Language Models and their relevance to cybersecurity. Section 3 presents a survey of LLM-based approaches in security testing. Section 4 focuses on how LLMs are employed for network monitoring and threat detection. Section 5 presents a concrete use case of LLM-based security alert analysis through a comparative evaluation of three open-access LLMs for analyzing alerts produced by popular security monitoring tools. Finally, Sect. 6 concludes the paper and discusses future work.

2   Background

The background of LLMs [20] in cybersecurity intertwines the evolution of language models with the growing importance of cyberdefense and the escalating threats of cyberattacks. LLMs, or Large Language Models, have progressively evolved from early pattern recognition chatbots like Eliza in the 1960s [10] to sophisticated transformer-based models like GPT-3 [16] and beyond.

Natural Language Processing (NLP) has been the backbone of LLM development, with significant milestones such as the introduction of long short-term memories (LSTMs) and the Stanford CoreNLP suite, which provided a suite of algorithms for intricate NLP tasks [23]. However, it was the advent of transformer architecture that truly revolutionized the field, paving the way for the development of highly effective LLMs.

Transformer-based models, exemplified by T5 [15] and GPT-3, marked a breakthrough in NLP and unleashed a wave of innovation in LLM development. These models applied language modeling techniques in pre-trained LLMs, enabling them to handle a wide range of tasks by altering spans with a single mask. The sheer size and complexity of models like GPT-3, with its 175 billion parameters, demonstrated the unprecedented capabilities of LLMs in understanding and generating human-like text.

As LLM technology advanced, specialized models tailored for specific domains emerged. Models like Xuan Yuan 2.0 [31], designed for financial chat applications, and HuaTuo [30], focusing on medical knowledge, showcased the versatility of LLMs in addressing industry-specific needs. Fine-tuning LLMs became increasingly common, allowing organizations to customize models to meet their unique requirements and improve business functions.

However, alongside their tremendous potential, LLMs also posed challenges in terms of deployment and security. The high costs associated with running and training LLMs, coupled with extensive hardware requirements, limited their widespread utilization. Moreover, concerns regarding the safety and ethical implications of LLMs prompted researchers to explore techniques such as parameter tuning, knowledge distillation, and retrieving support evidence from external knowledge bases to enhance the effectiveness and reliability of LLM deployment.

In the realm of cybersecurity, the application of LLMs holds immense promise for both defense and offense [19]. The exponential growth of scientific literature related to LLMs reflects their proven efficacy across various functions, including cybersecurity. While previous studies have explored the safety aspects of LLMs, the focus has shifted towards understanding their role in cyberdefense and cyberattack scenarios [8].

In conclusion, the evolution of LLMs has been intertwined with the advancements in NLP and the growing demands of various industries, including cybersecurity. As LLM technology continues to mature, its application in cybersecurity is poised to play a pivotal role in defending against evolving threats and mitigating the risks posed by cyberattacks.

3   LLMs for Security Testing

Security testing plays a pivotal role in safeguarding digital assets and infrastructure against cyber threats. It encompasses a range of methodologies aimed at identifying vulnerabilities, assessing risks, and ensuring the robustness of systems and applications in the face of evolving security challenges. Traditional security testing methods often struggle to keep pace with the dynamic threat landscape and the increasing complexity of modern software and systems. Manual testing processes can be time-consuming, resource-intensive, and prone to human error. Moreover, the rapid deployment of new technologies and the proliferation of interconnected devices exacerbate the challenges of identifying and mitigating security vulnerabilities effectively.

3.1   LLM Capabilities in Security Contexts

LLMs are transforming security testing by automating complex tasks such as code analysis, log inspection, and vulnerability detection. Their ability to understand and generate natural language, code, and structured data makes them well-suited for identifying weaknesses across diverse system components. LLMs also enable adaptive security testing frameworks that can evolve in response to emerging threats. Furthermore, LLMs offer significant potential in augmenting both offensive and defensive cybersecurity operations by providing intelligent reasoning and automation capabilities across a wide range of testing scenarios.

More specifically, LLMs contribute to security testing in several key ways. They can automate code and configuration analysis by interpreting source code, scripts, and configuration files to identify common security flaws such as hard-coded secrets, insecure function usage, and policy misconfigurations. Their natural language understanding and generation capabilities enable them to process unstructured text–including logs, alerts, and documentation–for tasks such as threat detection, vulnerability reporting, and incident summarization. For instance, studies such as [26] have applied LLMs to web content filtering, improving URL classification accuracy. LLMs also support reasoning and decision-making by assisting analysts in interpreting attack scenarios, generating threat models, and recommending remediation steps based on contextual information. As an example, [29] demonstrated the use of LLMs in generating honeywords to deceive attackers. Additionally, LLMs can create synthetic payloads, test cases, and malicious inputs through prompt-based fuzzing [18], helping to uncover vulnerabilities in applications, APIs, or protocols. Finally, pretrained on extensive technical corpora, LLMs serve as knowledge-rich assistants, capable of integrating and enriching information throughout both manual and automated security testing workflows.

In security contexts, these capabilities enable LLMs to act as versatile tools for both offensive and defensive tasks. They can assist penetration testers in crafting exploits or suggest improvements to security controls during audits. Moreover, their capacity to interpret heterogeneous data formats (e.g., logs, source code, CVEs, threat intel reports) makes them highly valuable in environments that require cross-domain reasoning. However, it is important to note that while LLMs excel at pattern recognition and language generation, they are not inherently trustworthy or deterministic. Their outputs can vary depending on prompts, and they may occasionally hallucinate or suggest insecure

3.2   LLM-Based Tools for Security Testing

In recent years, there has been a proliferation of tools harnessing the power of LLMs for security and penetration testing. These tools leverage advanced natural language processing and deep learning techniques to automate various aspects of the security testing workflow, including vulnerability identification, threat detection, and report generation. Several notable LLM-based tools used for security testing are listed below:

- PENTESTGPT [11]: PENTESTGPT is an automated penetration testing system driven by LLMs. Developed by Deng et al., this tool facilitates complex tasks such as question answering, summarization, and reasoning in penetration testing scenarios. PENTESTGPT comprises three self-interacting modules - reasoning, generation, and parsing - which collaborate to tackle penetration testing challenges effectively.

- VulDetect [22]: VulDetect is a transformer-based vulnerability detection framework that utilizes GPT-2, a Large Language Model, to detect anomalies in system logs. Fine-tuned on datasets containing vulnerable and non-vulnerable code, VulDetect demonstrates high efficiency in real-time vulnerability detection, making it a valuable asset in security testing arsenals.
- CyBERT [7]: CyBERT unveils a classifier for detecting cybersecurity feature claims, employing fine-tuning techniques on pre-trained BERT language models. Developed specifically for industrial control systems (ICS) device documentation, CyBERT aggregates reports to identify conflicting feature claims and enhance security testing in critical infrastructure environments.
- SecurityLLM [13]: Developed by Ferrag et al., SecurityLLM is a system designed for precise threat detection and data privacy. This framework utilizes Fixed-Length Language Encoding (FLLE) and Byte-level Byte-Pair Encoder (BBPE) Tokenizer to process text traffic data, enabling accurate identification of various cyber threats in IoT environments.
- SecureFalcon [12]: SecureFalcon is an LLM-based cybersecurity reasoning system focused on detecting software flaws. Fine-tuned with a dataset of C code instances, SecureFalcon employs binary classification techniques to distinguish between vulnerable and non-vulnerable patterns, thereby enhancing security testing outcomes.
- CySecBERT [9]: A variant of CyBERT, CySecBERT is a word embedding model based on BERT architecture. Developed by Bayer et al., CySecBERT is trained on diverse cybersecurity tasks, including malware detection, alert aggregation, and phishing website detection, showcasing its versatility in security testing applications.
- Generative-AI for Red Team Scenarios [14]: Garvey et al. explore the viability of using Generative-AI, including LLMs, to improve the development of Red Team scenarios in organizations. By constructing narratives based on input prompts, LLMs facilitate the creation of plausible and complex attack scenarios, enhancing creativity and imagination in security testing exercises.

These tools exemplify the diverse applications of LLMs in security testing, ranging from vulnerability detection and threat identification to scenario development and reasoning in penetration testing scenarios. Incorporating these tools into security testing workflows can significantly enhance the efficiency and effectiveness of cybersecurity assessments, empowering organizations to better defend against emerging threats and vulnerabilities.

4   LLMs for Monitoring and Detection

Effective monitoring and detection are critical components of cybersecurity strategies, enabling organizations to identify and respond to security incidents in real time. In today's dynamic threat landscape, rapid adaptation to evolving threats is essential, highlighting the need for intelligent and automated monitoring solutions. Traditional approaches, such as rule-based or signature-based detection, often struggle to keep pace with sophisticated and fast-moving cyber threats. Key challenges include the inability to detect zero-day attacks, high false positive rates, limited scalability, and the difficulty of analyzing large volumes of data in real time. Moreover, legacy systems frequently lack the agility to counter the constantly evolving tactics of cyber adversaries. LLMs, powered by advanced natural language processing, offer promising new capabilities to enhance monitoring and detection in cybersecurity.

4.1 LLMs for Real-Time Monitoring and Anomaly Detection

Large Language Models (LLMs) offer advanced natural language understanding capabilities that can significantly enhance real-time monitoring and anomaly detection in cybersecurity. By processing and correlating vast volumes of structured and unstructured data, such as network logs, system events, and threat intelligence feeds, LLMs can identify anomalous patterns and extract actionable insights with greater accuracy and contextual relevance. Unlike traditional rule-based or statistical anomaly detection systems, LLMs excel at interpreting semantics and intent, enabling the identification of subtle deviations from baseline behavior that may signal emerging threats [28]. Their adaptability and capacity for unsupervised learning make LLMs well-suited for environments where threats evolve rapidly and labeled data is scarce.

4.2 Enhancing Threat Intelligence with LLM-Powered Monitoring

LLMs have the potential to transform threat intelligence by enabling real-time extraction and synthesis of information from diverse textual sources. By analyzing data from open-source intelligence (OSINT), dark web forums, incident reports, and threat advisories, LLMs can uncover emerging attack trends, threat actor tactics, and indicators of compromise (IOCs) [17]. These models can automate the generation of intelligence summaries and enrich threat databases, thereby improving situational awareness and supporting more proactive threat mitigation. Furthermore, their multilingual and cross-domain capabilities allow for broader coverage of global threat landscapes, enhancing both strategic and operational cybersecurity efforts.

4.3 Tools Implementing LLMs for Monitoring and Detection

In recent years, there has been a proliferation of tools harnessing the power of Large Language Models (LLMs) for monitoring and detection in cybersecurity. These tools leverage advanced natural language processing capabilities and deep learning algorithms to automate various aspects of monitoring and detection workflows, from anomaly detection to threat intelligence analysis. Below is a curated list of notable tools implementing LLMs for monitoring and detection:

– CyBERT [7] and CySecBERT [9]: These tools are generic enough to be also used for monitoring and detection. They unveil a classifier for detecting cybersecurity anomlies on pre-trained BERT language models.

- HuntGPT [6]: HuntGPT is an innovative framework designed for cyber threat hunting and intelligence gathering, leveraging the power of natural language processing to sift through vast amounts of textual data for potential security risks. Its application extends to anomaly detection, identifying patterns indicative of cyber attacks, and proactive defense strategies.
- KARTAL [24]: KARTAL is a fine-tuned Language Model developed for detecting vulnerabilities in web applications. Employing a detector component controlled by prompts generated from a fuzzer component, KARTAL dynamically adapts to various scenarios, making it effective in identifying broken access control rules and other logical vulnerabilities.
- VisionGPT [27]: VisionGPT is a monitoring and detection platform that leverages LLMs to analyze security logs, identify suspicious patterns, and generate actionable alerts for Safe Visual Navigation

While LLMs offer significant potential for improving monitoring and detection capabilities in cybersecurity, their implementation poses several challenges and considerations. These include the need for robust training data, model interpretability, scalability, and the risk of adversarial attacks targeting LLM-based detection systems. Additionally, organizations must carefully evaluate the privacy and ethical implications of deploying LLMs for monitoring and detection purposes, ensuring compliance with regulatory requirements and ethical guidelines. By addressing these challenges and considerations, organizations can harness the full potential of LLMs to enhance their cybersecurity posture and effectively defend against evolving threats.

5   Use Case: LLM-Based Security Alert Analysis

Security monitoring systems generate numerous alerts that require expert analysis to determine severity, impact, and appropriate responses. Traditional rule-based systems often produce high false positive rates and lack contextual understanding. We demonstrate how LLMs can enhance security alert analysis through a comparative evaluation of three state-of-the-art open-access models: Mistral-7B, Qwen3-8B, and Llama3.1-8B.

5.1   Evaluation Framework and Methodology

We developed a security agent that leverages LLMs to analyze and evaluate security alerts from multiple sources. The system processes alerts from three widely used security monitoring tools: (i) Montimage Monitoring Tool (MMT) [2], a flexible network monitoring framework that captures and analyzes traffic in real-time using protocol-specific models; (ii) Snort [3], a signature-based intrusion detection and prevention system (IDS/IPS) known for its efficiency in detecting known threats; and (iii) Suricata [4], an advanced IDS/IPS and network security monitoring engine that supports multi-threading and deep packet inspection for high-performance traffic analysis.

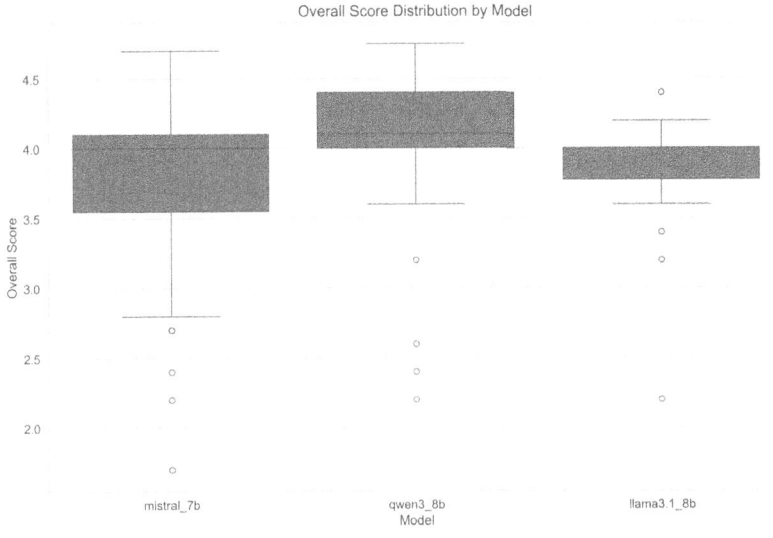

Fig. 1. Distribution of overall scores for each model.

The evaluation framework consists of three main components: Alert Ingestion, LLM-based Analysis and Quality Evaluation. The Alert Ingestion module is responsible for collecting and normalizing alerts from various security tools, ensuring consistent input for downstream processing. The LLM-based Analysis component processes these alerts using multiple large language models to generate comprehensive analyses, including explanations, severity assessments, impact evaluations, confidence scores, false positive likelihoods, mitigation recommendations, and relevant references. Finally, the Quality Evaluation module assesses the quality of the LLM-generated analyses based on five key criteria: accuracy, clarity, actionability, completeness, and false positive assessment.

To summarize, we evaluated three LLMs using a dataset of 144 security alerts, comprising 24 MMT, 45 Snort, 45 Suricata, and 30 Suricata-CSV alerts.

5.2 Evaluation Results and Analysis

Results. Our comparative analysis revealed significant differences in how each LLM performed in security alert analysis, as shown in Fig. 1. Qwen3-8B demonstrated the strongest overall performance (average score: 4.08/5), particularly excelling in completeness (4.50/5) and clarity (4.46/5). Llama3.1-8B showed balanced performance (average score: 3.85/5) with exceptional clarity (4.65/5), while Mistral-7B had the lowest overall score (3.72/5) but still provided valuable analysis. Figure 2 illustrates the analysis of model performance by alert type. Snort alerts were generally handled most effectively across all models (average score: 4.00/5), while Suricata alerts presented the greatest challenge (average

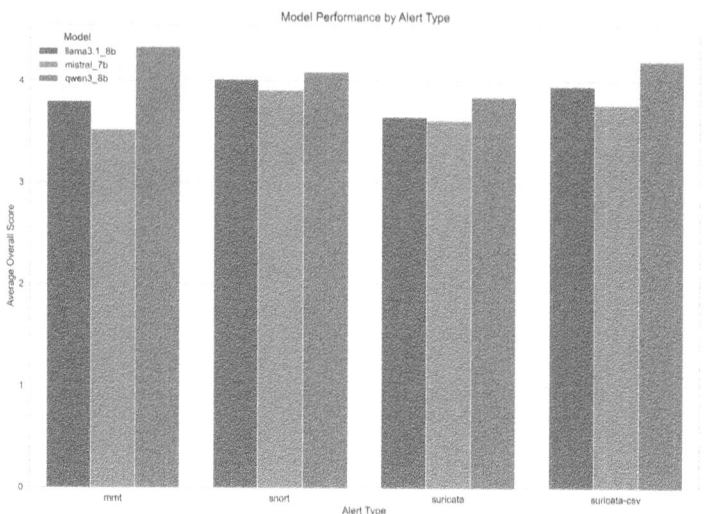

Fig. 2. Comparison of model performance across different alert types.

score: 3.70/5). Notably, Qwen3-8B showed exceptional performance with MMT alerts (4.33/5), demonstrating its ability to interpret complex network traffic patterns. Figure 3 displays the breakdown of performance by evaluation criterion. All models achieved their highest scores in clarity (average: 4.50/5), underscoring the ability of LLMs to convey complex security concepts in a clear and understandable manner. False positive assessment was consistently the weakest area (2.88/5), highlighting the challenge of determining alert legitimacy without additional context.

Analysis. Our evaluation yielded several important insights. First, in terms of contextual understanding, LLMs outperform traditional rule-based systems by interpreting security alerts within broader threat landscapes. They can connect alerts to known attack patterns and offer richer, more informative analyses. For instance, when analyzing an SSH brute force attack, Qwen3-8B achieved a high score of 4.75/5 by identifying specific IP addresses involved, suggesting concrete mitigation steps (including command-line examples), and referencing relevant CVEs and MITRE ATT&CK techniques. Second, model selection plays a critical role, as different LLMs exhibit varying strengths across alert types. The performance gap observed in MMT alert analysis (Qwen3-8B scoring 4.33/5 compared to Mistral-7B's 3.52/5) suggests that security operations centers may benefit from a multi-model strategy tailored to specific alert sources. Third, while all models demonstrated strengths in clarity and explanation, they struggled with false positive assessment, highlighting the need for additional environmental context to enhance detection accuracy. Finally, LLMs showed promise in generating actionable intelligence, often including specific, implementable mitigation steps

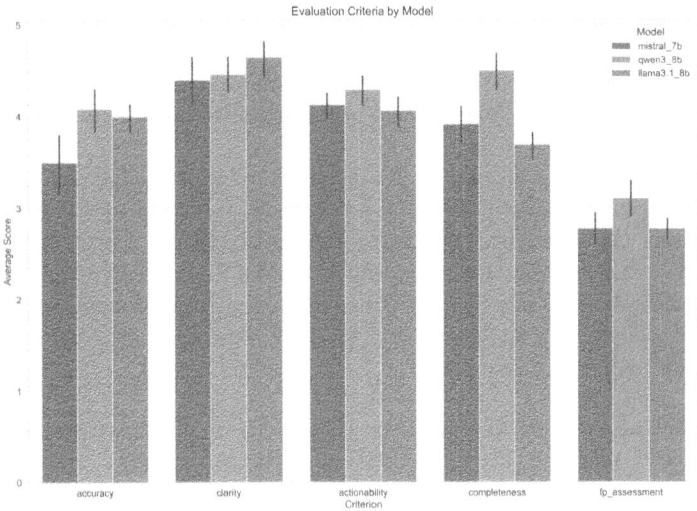

Fig. 3. Comparison of model performance across different evaluation criteria.

that can accelerate incident response and enhance security posture. Notably, a positive correlation between accuracy and completeness (correlation coefficient: 0.68) suggests that more thorough analyses tend to be more accurate as well.

Future Directions. While our results demonstrate the significant potential of LLMs in enhancing security alert analysis, several challenges remain. Future work should focus on implementing feedback mechanisms that enable security analysts to improve future analyses, enhancing models with organization-specific context to better assess false positives, developing ensemble approaches that leverage the strengths of different models based on alert type, and optimizing inference speed to ensure effective deployment in time-sensitive security operations environments.

This use case demonstrates that LLMs can serve as valuable assistants to security analysts, helping to reduce alert fatigue, improve response times, and enhance the overall effectiveness of security operations. The comparative analysis highlights the importance of model selection and evaluation frameworks in security applications, paving the way for more intelligent and contextually aware security monitoring systems.

6   Conclusion and Future Work

In this paper, we explore the applications of LLMs in cybersecurity testing and monitoring, focusing on their role, challenges, and opportunities. We present a survey of LLMs, discuss their use in security testing, particularly for network monitoring and detection, and demonstrate how LLMs can enhance security alert analysis through a comparative evaluation of three open-access models: Mistral-7B, Qwen3-8B, and Llama3.1-8B. Overall, LLMs have significant potential in automating security processes, helping organizations identify vulnerabilities and detect threats more effectively.

Further research and development are needed to address challenges associated with LLM integration, including bias mitigation, interpretability, and security considerations. Additionally, we plan to extend LLMs for different security purposes, such as integrating them into the MMT-DPI plugin [1] to automatically extract attributes from new protocols or employing LLMs for managing contradictions in predefined playbooks for Security Orchestration, Automation, and Response (SOAR) platforms [21].

Acknowledgments. This research is supported by the H2020 project AI4CYBER N° 101070450, CYBERSUITE N° 101145861, NERO N° 101127411 and INTACT N° 10126241.

References

1. Mmt-dpi (2025). https://github.com/Montimage/mmt-dpi
2. Mmt-probe (2025). https://github.com/Montimage/mmt-probe
3. Snort - network intrusion detection & prevention system (2025). https://www.snort.org/
4. Suricata - a high performance, open source network analysis and threat detection software (2025). https://suricata.io/
5. The zeek network security monitor (2025). https://zeek.org/
6. Ali, T., Kostakos, P.: Huntgpt: Integrating machine learning-based anomaly detection and explainable AI with large language models (llms). CoRR abs/2309.16021 (2023). https://doi.org/10.48550/arXiv.2309.16021
7. Ameri, K., Hempel, M., Sharif, H., Jr., J.L., Perumalla, K.: Cybert: cybersecurity claim classification by fine-tuning the BERT language model. J. Cybersecur. Priv. **1**(4), 615–637 (2021). https://doi.org/10.3390/JCP1040031
8. Balasubramanian, P., Seby, J., Kostakos, P.: Transformer-based llms in cybersecurity: an in-depth study on log anomaly detection and conversational defense mechanisms. In: IEEE International Conference on Big Data, BigData 2023, Sorrento, Italy, December 15-18 (2023)
9. Bayer, M., Kuehn, P., Shanehsaz, R., Reuter, C.: Cysecbert: a domain-adapted language model for the cybersecurity domain. CoRR abs/2212.02974 (2022). https://doi.org/10.48550/ARXIV.2212.02974
10. Ciesla, R.: The Book of Chatbots - From ELIZA to ChatGPT. Springer (2024). https://doi.org/10.1007/978-3-031-51004-5
11. Deng, G., et al.: Pentestgpt: an llm-empowered automatic penetration testing tool. CoRR abs/2308.06782 (2023). https://doi.org/10.48550/ARXIV.2308.06782
12. Ferrag, M.A., Battah, A., Tihanyi, N., Debbah, M., Lestable, T., Cordeiro, L.C.: Securefalcon: The next cyber reasoning system for cyber security. CoRR abs/2307.06616 (2023). https://doi.org/10.48550/ARXIV.2307.06616,

13. Ferrag, M.A., Ndhlovu, M., Tihanyi, N., Cordeiro, L.C., Debbah, M., Lestable, T., Thandi, N.S.: Revolutionizing cyber threat detection with large language models: a privacy-preserving bert-based lightweight model for iot/iiot devices. IEEE Access **12**, 23733–23750 (2024). https://doi.org/10.1109/ACCESS.2024.3363469

14. Garvey, B., Svendsen, A.: Can generative-ai (chatgpt and bard) be used as red team avatars in developing foresight scenarios? Analytic Research Consortium (ARC), August 2023

15. Hasib, K.M., Rahman, M.A., Masum, M.I., Boer, F.D., Azam, S., Karim, A.: Bengali news abstractive summarization: T5 transformer and hybrid approach. In: International Conference on Digital Image Computing: Techniques and Applications, DICTA 2023, Port Macquarie, Australia, November 28 - Dec. 1, 2023, pp. 539–545. IEEE (2023). https://doi.org/10.1109/DICTA60407.2023.00080,

16. Jang, M., Lukasiewicz, T.: Consistency analysis of chatgpt. In: Bouamor, H., Pino, J., Bali, K. (eds.) Proceedings of the 2023 Conference on Empirical Methods in Natural Language Processing, EMNLP 2023, Singapore, December 6-10, 2023, pp. 15970–15985. Association for Computational Linguistics (2023). https://doi.org/10.18653/V1/2023.EMNLP-MAIN.991,

17. Malbos, A., Desfontaines, D., Le Goff, J.: A survey of the applications of generative language models in cybersecurity. arXiv preprint arXiv:2310.05343 (2023)

18. Meng, R., Mirchev, M., Böhme, M., Roychoudhury, A.: Large language model guided protocol fuzzing. In: Proceedings of the 31st Annual Network and Distributed System Security Symposium (NDSS) (2024)

19. Motlagh, F.N., Hajizadeh, M., Majd, M., Najafi, P., Cheng, F., Meinel, C.: Large language models in cybersecurity: State-of-the-art. CoRR abs/2402.00891 (2024). https://doi.org/10.48550/ARXIV.2402.00891

20. Naveed, H., et al.: A comprehensive overview of large language models. CoRR abs/2307.06435 (2023). https://doi.org/10.48550/ARXIV.2307.06435

21. Nguyen, M.D., Mallouli, W., Cavalli, A.R., Montes de Oca, E.: Ai4soar: A security intelligence tool for automated incident response. ARES '24 (2024)

22. Omar, M., Shiaeles, S.: Vuldetect: A novel technique for detecting software vulnerabilities using language models. In: IEEE International Conference on Cyber Security and Resilience, CSR 2023, Venice, Italy, July 31 - Aug. 2, 2023, pp. 105–110. IEEE (2023). https://doi.org/10.1109/CSR57506.2023.10224924,

23. Sainz, O., Campos, J.A., García-Ferrero, I., Etxaniz, J., de Lacalle, O.L., Agirre, E.: NLP evaluation in trouble: On the need to measure LLM data contamination for each benchmark. CoRR **abs/2310.18018** (2023)

24. Sakaoglu, S.: Kartal: Web application vulnerability hunting using large language models: Novel method for detecting logical vulnerabilities in web applications with finetuned large language models (2023)

25. Sewak, M., Emani, V., Naresh, A.: CRUSH: cybersecurity research using universal llms and semantic hypernetworks. In: Proceedings of the Workshop on Enterprise Knowledge Graphs using Large Language Models (EKG-LLM 2023) co-located with 32nd ACM International Conference on Information and Knowledge Management (CIKM 2023), Birmingham, UK, October 22, 2023

26. Vörös, T., Bergeron, S.P., Berlin, K.: Web content filtering through knowledge distillation of large language models. In: Proceedings of the Conference on Applied Machine Learning in Information Security, Arlington, Virginia, USA, October 19-20 (2023)

27. Wang, H., Qin, J., Bastola, A., Chen, X., Suchanek, J., Gong, Z., Razi, A.: Visiongpt: Llm-assisted real-time anomaly detection for safe visual navigation. CoRR abs/2403.12415 (2024). https://doi.org/10.48550/ARXIV.2403.12415

28. Yang, H., Chen, Y., Zhang, Y., Wang, X.: Fortifying ai: Enhancing cybersecurity with large language models. arXiv preprint arXiv:2310.06688 (2023)
29. Yu, F., Martin, M.V.: Honey, I chunked the passwords: Generating semantic honeywords resistant to targeted attacks using pre-trained language models. In: Detection of Intrusions and Malware, and Vulnerability Assessment - 20th International Conference, DIMVA 2023, Hamburg, Germany, July 12-14, 2023, Proceedings
30. Zhang, H.Xiao, Q., Wan, X., Wang, B., Li, H.: Huatuogpt, towards taming language model to be a doctor. In: Findings of the Association for Computational Linguistics: EMNLP 2023, Singapore, December 6-10 (2023)
31. Zhang, X., Yang, Q.: Xuanyuan 2.0: A large chinese financial chat model with hundreds of billions parameters. In: Proceedings of the 32nd ACM International Conference on Information and Knowledge Management, CIKM 2023, Birmingham, United Kingdom, October 21-25 (2023)

A Decentralized PUF-Based Scheme for Remote Attestation

Mario Barbareschi⬤, Antonio Emmanuele$^{(\boxtimes)}$⬤, and Daniele Lombardi⬤

University of Naples Federico II - Dipartimento di Ingegneria Elettrica e delle
Tecnologie dell'Informazione, Naples, Italy
{mario.barbareschi,antonio.emmanuele}@unina.it

Abstract. With the continuous growth of edge computing, numerous
edge devices collaborate in decentralized groups to provide flexible and
reliable services while distributing computational workloads. However,
the presence of numerous devices requires the adaptation of existing end-
to-end security-procedures designed for resource-constrained edge-nodes.
Among them, Remote Attestation allows a remote server to directly
evaluate the trustworthiness of a node, by remotely verifying that no-
malicious code is being executed on the target. Unfortunately, attesting
groups of devices remains an open challenge, as it must minimize message exchanges to reduce network bandwidth consumption while ensuring
lightweight computation on both the server and device sides. For these
reasons, we propose DHERAP, a PUF-based remote attestation protocol targeted for groups of decentralized edge-nodes. We design DHERAP
to reduce message overhead by enabling different nodes to attest local
groups of nodes, removing the need for remote communication to a server.

Keywords: Physical Unclonable Functions · Remote Attestation ·
Internet of Things

1 Introduction

The growing ubiquity of the Internet of Things (IoT) paradigm in modern society is raising increasing concerns about the security of IoT nodes. A central
issue is the ability to remotely verify whether the code running on a device has
been compromised [1]. In this context, Remote Attestation (RA)—a process that
allows a trusted verifier to remotely evaluate the integrity of a software—plays
a key role in securing such systems [18].

Unfortunately, in this context the direct adoption of classical RA protocols
is impeded by the inherent characteristics of the IoT. Firstly, IoT networks are
usually composed of a large number of devices. Consequently, end-to-end RA
becomes unsuitable, as it would result in impractical completion times and
excessive network bandwidth consumption. For these reasons, RA protocols

---

Authors contributed equally and are listed in alphabetical order.

F. Skopik et al. (Eds.): ARES 2025 Workshops, LNCS 15999, pp. 167–180, 2025.
https://doi.org/10.1007/978-3-032-00644-8_10

for the IoT must attest entire groups of IoT nodes, minimizing the number of exchanged messages [1, 18].

Secondly, most IoT nodes—particularly those deployed at the edge—are low-cost Commercial Off The Shelf (COTS) devices, typically constrained in terms of computational power, memory, and energy, as they are often battery-powered [7]. Furthermore, due to their limited cost, these nodes generally lack embedded secure cryptoprocessors, such as Trusted Platform Module (TPM), which are commonly relied upon by traditional RA mechanisms [22].

In order to address these challenges, in this paper we propose a Group Remote Attestation protocol based on Physically Unclonable Function (PUFs). Silicon PUFs are lightweight cryptographic primitives that generate device-unique fingerprints by exploiting the nanoscale manufacturing variations inherently introduced during chip fabrication [26]. In addition, PUFs are tamper resistant cryptographic primitives, guaranteeing that if compromised by an attacker, then their behaviour is substatially altered [4]. By employing PUFs, our solution avoids the need for pre-stored cryptographic keys and costly cryptographic operations, both of which typically require additional hardware components, such as the TPM.

The remainder of this paper is structured as follows: Sect. 2 presents the preliminaries on PUFs and remote attestion. Section 3 introduces the adopted system model, the group key management schema employed and finally the proposed remote attestation schema. Section 4 evaluates the proposal against computational costs, communication costs and time overhead. Section 5 provides the related work. Finally Sect. 6 draws conclusion and future directions of this work.

2   Technical Background

2.1   Physical Unclonable Functions

Silicon PUFs are a category of hardware security primitives that harness inherent physical variations in semiconductor devices to produce unique and unpredictable cryptographic material. These variations arise from uncontrollable imperfections in the manufacturing process, leading to slight discrepancies in transistor characteristics, wire delays, and other physical properties [4, 26]. Specifically, PUFs function according to a challenge-response paradigm: upon receiving an input bit-string—referred to as the challenge—a PUF generates a corresponding bit-string—denoted as response—based on its distinct physical attributes. In other words, two distinct PUFs, even if logically implementing the same circuit, will yield different responses to the same challenges due to their unique physical characteristics.

With regard to their security benefits, by dynamically obtaining responses, PUFs remove the requirement of persistent Non-Volatile Memory (NVMs). Moreover, due to the random-nature of the response generation process, PUFs are both hard to clone, even for their manufacturer, and resistant to tampering.

Indeed, each attempt to modify a PUF will result in a modifying its challenge-response mapping [4]. These properties make particularly well-suited for applications requiring secure device authentication, cryptographic key generation, and remote attestation in environments with strict resource constraints [26]. However, it is important to note that, environmental factors such as temperature fluctuations, voltage variations, and aging effects can introduce noise in PUF responses. Therefore, responses usually necessitate error-correction techniques to ensure reliability [4].

PUFs can be categorized into two primary types based on their response behavior and security properties. Strong PUFs are characterized by a vast challenge-response space, meaning they can generate a large number of unique responses based on different input challenges [13]. This property makes them highly suitable for authentication applications, where a verifier can issue random challenges and expect unpredictable yet deterministic responses from a legitimate device [26]. Examples of strong PUFs include Arbiter PUFs [17], which leverage the inherent asymmetry in the delay paths of arbiter circuits, and Bistable Ring PUFs [14], which exploit the positive feedback loop in bistable circuits to amplify random threshold voltage variations introduced during manufacturing. Unfortunately, strong PUFs are vulnerable to modeling attacks, in which machine learning techniques are employed to derive a predictive model of the PUFs, enabling the attacker to accurately estimate future responses [23]. To counter such threats, various mitigation strategies have been proposed, including obfuscation techniques, controlled PUF architectures, and challenge-response pruning methods [26].

In contrast, weak PUFs support only a limited set of challenge-response pairs, often reduced to a single response derived from the physical properties of the device. They are primarily employed for secure key generation, where the PUF-derived response serves as a cryptographic key that does not need to be stored in memory [26]. A typical example of a weak PUF is the SRAM PUF, which exploits the random power-up states of volatile memory cells, determined by unpredictable threshold voltage variations [5]. It is worth noting that weak PUFs can serve as the foundation for constructing a strong PUF when combined with a cryptographic primitive, as demonstrated in [6].

2.2   PUF Based Protocols

Typically, authentication and key-agreement protocols based on PUFs operate in two distinct phases [4,26]. The first phase, referred to as enrollment, is executed in a secure environment. During this phase, a set of challenges is submitted to the PUF embedded within the device, and the corresponding responses are collected. Once a sufficiently large set of Challenge-Response Pair (CRPs) is acquired, it is stored in a secure database. The second phase occurs after the device is deployed in an untrusted environment. In this phase, a trusted remote server performs security protocols by submitting to the device the challenges previously stored during enrollment.

It is worth noting that this phase may involve several communication rounds, as achieving mutual authentication is non-trivial due to the fact that the device does not store the CRPs collected during enrollment. To address this issue, the authors of [8,11] introduce PHEMAP, a mutual authentication protocol that leverages an alternative enrollment procedure. In their approach, enrollment does not involve submitting random challenges. Instead, it consists of constructing PUF-chains—ordered sets of PUF responses, referred to as links, where each link l_i is the response to the challenge l_{i-1}. In other words, each response in the chain serves as the challenge for obtaining the next link. The protocol also includes an additional initialization phase, during which the device and the server agree on a common link in the chain, ensuring synchronization. As a result, mutual authentication can be achieved with just two messages per round, since both the device and the server only need to advance in their PUF chains to authenticate each other.

2.3   GK-PHEMAP

GK-PHEMAP [7] is a lightweight and efficient protocol designed to enable secure group communication in IoT environments, such as continuum computing [9], by leveraging PUF-chains, described in Sect. 2. It supports the distribution and dynamic update of group keys without relying on pre-stored cryptographic material, which is inherently susceptible to physical attacks and tampering. A key feature of GK-PHEMAP is its support for dynamic group membership, ensuring that key updates maintain both forward and backward security. Specifically, forward security ensures that devices which have left the group are unable to decrypt future communications, while backward security prevents newly added devices from accessing past transmissions.

The protocol supports two working modes: a centralized and a decentralized version. The centralized mode assumes the presence of a remote server and a group of N nodes. Each node, denoted as n^i, has completed the PHEMAP initialization procedure and is synchronized with the server on the link n^i_{j-1} of its PUF chain.

To generate the group key, the server computes:

$$K_G = \bigoplus_{i=1}^{N} n^i_{j+1} \oplus S_G,$$

where S_G is a random value introduced to ensure both forward and backward security. When sharing the key with node n^i, the server removes the node's contribution from the group key and adds an additional chain link, n^i_j, to obfuscate the message. Consequently, the partial key sent to node n^i is:

$$K^i = K_G \oplus n^i_j \oplus n^i_{j+1}.$$

Two additional links, n^i_{j+2} and n^i_{j+3}, are employed to authenticate the server and verify message integrity through lightweight HMAC-based procedures. Upon receiving the message, the node queries its PUF four times, starting from the synchronized link n_{j-1}^i, thereby retrieving the required PUF chain values used during message construction. The last two links are used to verify the integrity and authenticity of the message. If both checks pass, the node reconstructs the group key as:

$$K_G = K^i \oplus n_j^i \oplus n_{j+1}^i,$$

by removing the obfuscation value and reintroducing its own contribution. In addition to the group key, a unique and secret session identifier ID_G is also distributed during the initial sharing procedure. This identifier is used to authenticate nodes within the group and to verify the integrity of exchanged messages. Moreover, its value is updated after each group key change triggered by a node joining or leaving the group

Differently, the decentralized version of the protocol considers a network architecture in which nodes are partitioned into multiple subgroups, each managed by a Local Verifier (LV). Each LV, being a more computationally capable node, embeds its own PUF and is able to store the PUF chains of the nodes within its subgroup. It has been demonstrated that the PHEMAP protocol can be extended to decentralized architectures by delegating authentication tasks to intermediate nodes that are capable of managing portions of the PUF chains [11]. The decentralized protocol operates in three phases: i) LVs establish a group key among themselves and with the remote server, denoted as K_G^{LV}; ii) each subgroup, under the control of the l-th LV, establishes a local subgroup key using the centralized version of the protocol, denoted as K_G^l; and iii) each subgroup key is then shared among the LVs using K_G^{LV}. The global group key is computed as:

$$K_G = \bigoplus_{l=1}^{|LV|} K_G^l.$$

Similarly to the centralized protocol, each group shares both the global secret identifier ID_G and the local subgroup identifier ID_G^l.

2.4   Remote Attestation

Remote Attestation is a procedure that allows a remote server, known as the verifier, to assess the integrity of the software running on a target device, referred to as the prover, to ensure that it has not been compromised by malicious code [18]. The procedure consists of two phases: an offline phase, executed in a secure environment, and an online phase, performed in an untrusted setting. During the offline phase, certain values, known as measurements, are computed on the prover side, usually as hash values of various memory regions. At this point, measurements are stored on the server side to be used later in the online phase to verify the state of the prover.

Differently, the online phase takes place after the prover has been deployed in the field and follows a challenge-response scheme. It begins with the verifier sending an attestation request along with an authentication message to the prover. Authentication is included to prevent replay, impersonation, and Denial-of-Service attacks. Once the verifier is authenticated, the prover delegates a trusted component, usually software-based, to measure its internal state. These measurements are then signed in a process known as the quote operation and sent to the verifier. The verifier checks the message signature and compares the received measurements with the previously recorded ones. If they match, the prover is attested as trustworthy; otherwise, it is flagged as compromised.

However, the discussed end-to-end procedure suffers for scalability problems as the size of IoT networks increases [18]. For instance, as the number of devices grows, the number of message required to attestate each of them also increases. This leads in an increased use of the network bandwidth, resulting in an increased response-time for services, as IoT nodes usually collaborate in groups over the network. Moreover, as the server must challenge and validate the response of each single device, also its computational-time increases with the number of devices, further increasing the degradation of response-time.

For these reasons, Collective Remote Attestation tackles these challenge by allowing groups of IoT nodes, after the reception of a single broadcasted attestation request, to collaboratively forge a response message useful to attestate the entire group of IoT nodes in parallel. This approach reduces both the number of exchanged message, as the challenge response pair is directly executed for a group of devices, and the computational complexity on server-side, as it must validate only one response message [1, 18].

3   PUF-Based Group Remote Attestation

3.1   System Model

In this work, we consider a typical IoT network infrastructure, where groups of resource-constrained nodes are organized into decentralized subnetworks to collaborate. Moreover, we assume that in each subnetwork there is a node, denoted as LV, connected to all other subgroups and a remote server.

As for edge nodes, we target COTS microcontrollers that lack virtual memory management features, such as a Memory Management Unit, and dedicated security co-processors, such as the TPM. Nonetheless, we assume that these devices include hardware mechanisms for enforcing access permissions across different memory regions. In particular, they must support marking memory regions as read-only, write-only, or executable-only. We note that this functionality is already present in many COTS microcontrollers, typically through a Memory Protection Unit [10]. This feature is essential, as it enables the secure execution of the protocol, controlled access to the PUF, and trusted measurement evaluation.

Furthermore, we require the target device to include a True Random Number Generator (TRNG). In addition, it must embed an SRAM memory that serves as a weak PUF. As shown in previous research, weak PUFs can be enhanced by combining them with cryptographic primitives to construct strong PUFs, which form the foundation of the PHEMAP protocol family [6].

In contrast, for LVs, we consider COTS nodes equipped with fully-fledged microprocessors. We assume that these nodes provide the same security capabilities as the edge nodes. However, in addition, LVs are capable of provisioning tamper-proof secure memory, which is used to store the PUF chains of all nodes in the subgroup, as well as the cumulative measurement employed for attesting the subgroup.

Finally, we adopt the Dolev-Yao model as the attacker model. The latter assumes that an attacker is able to intercept communications, impersonate legitimate devices, and operate with no restrictions other than the cryptographic mechanisms implemented by the devices on the network [15].

3.2 Decentralized Hardware Enabled Remote Attestion Protocol

In this subsection, we present the *Decentralized Hardware-Enabled Remote Attestation Protocol* (DHERAP), a remote attestation scheme designed for IoT group attestation. DHERAP builds on the same foundational assumptions as the decentralized version of GK-PHEMAP, specifically regarding the network topology and the types of devices deployed. Moreover, the protocol assumes that the decentralized GK-PHEMAP protocol has been executed. Differently from GK-PHEMAP, DHERAP assumes that the network topology of each subgroup—i.e., the interconnection among nodes—follows a spanning tree structure. In this configuration, message dissemination, in addition to the classical broadcast, can occur hierarchically: the LV sends the message to a designated node, which then forwards it to its neighbors, and so on, until it reaches all child nodes, stopping at the leaves. Another key distinction is that LVs are required to store the memory measurements needed for attestation of each device within their respective subgroups. Indeed, as we target dynamic network topologies, when a node joins a subgroup, its LV must retrieve the memory measurements required for attestation from the remote server. This can be trivially achieved by leveraging the PUF-chain of the LV, as shown in Fig. 1.

Specifically, assuming that the LV is synchronized with the server on the chain link l_{i-1}, it can issue a remote attestation request for the newly joined node by forwarding the request along with the next chain link l_i. Upon receiving the request, the server authenticates it by verifying that the provided chain link l_i is the expected successor of l_{i-1}. The server then collects the requested memory measurements M_i for the newly joined node and transmits them to the LV. At this point the server forges a response message by appending the second subsequent link l_{i+2} to the message, and encrypts the entire content by leveraging l_{i+1}. It is important to note that this schema ensures not only the confidentiality of measurements, as they are encrypted, but also the integrity of the message. Indeed, even if one bit is flipped during transmission, then the decryption of the message will amplify the transmission errors, and, therefore, the decrypted l_{i+2} value will differ from the one computed by the node. After receiving the response, the LV queries its PUF to obtain l_{i+1}^*, decrypts the message, and verifies authenticity and integrity by computing l_{i+2}^* and checking

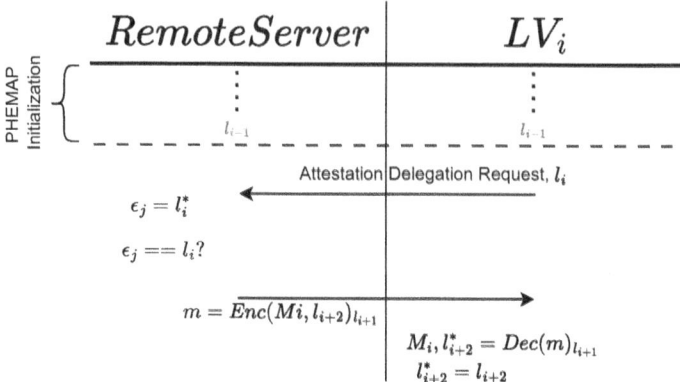

Fig. 1. Attestation Delegation procedure.

whether it matches the received value l_{i+2}. If the check is successful, the memory checksums M_i of the new node are securely stored in protected memory.

The second procedure of DHERAP consists of the group remote attestation. This is initiated by the Remote Server, which dispatches an attestation request to each LV. Upon reception, each LV attests its corresponding subgroup and returns the attestation result to the server. The procedure unfolds as follows: i) Upon receiving the attestation request, the LV computes a hash digest for each node's memory measurement and aggregates the results using a bitwise XOR operation, producing the cumulative attestation value $M = \bigoplus_{j=1}^{N} M_j$. Assuming the LV is synchronized on the chain link n_{i-1}^{j} for each node n^j in the subgroup, it also computes the following aggregates: $\Omega = \bigoplus_{j=1}^{N} n_i^j$ and $\Gamma = \bigoplus_{j=1}^{N} n_{i+1}^j$.

ii) The LV generates a nonce R, appends it to the current session identifier ID_G^l, and encrypts the message using the subgroup key K_G^l. The resulting attestation request is defined as $AttReq = Enc_{K_G^l}(ID_G^l, R)$ and is broadcast to the subgroup.

iii) Each node decrypts the message using the subgroup key, extracts ID_G^l and R, and verifies authenticity by ensuring that the received session identifier matches the one established during the GK-PHEMAP key management phase. iv) Each leaf node, as illustrated in Fig. 2, computes a hash digest of its memory measurement M_j, queries its PUF to obtain n_i^j, and derives $p_j = M_j \oplus n_i^j$. It subsequently queries the PUF again using n_i^j to retrieve n_{i+1}^j, and computes $a_j = R \oplus n_{i+1}^j$. The values p_j and a_j are then forwarded to the parent node in the spanning tree.

v) Each parent node n_k waits to receive all responses from its children, and then computes its own response as $p_k = \bigoplus_{j=1}^{N_{children}} p_j \oplus n_i^k \oplus M_k$, where M_k and n_i^k denote its own memory measurement and chain link, respectively. For the authentication value, if the number of child nodes is even, it computes $a_k = \bigoplus_{j=1}^{N_{children}} a_j \oplus n_{i+1}^k \oplus R$; otherwise, it computes $a_k = \bigoplus_{j=1}^{N_{children}} a_j \oplus n_{i+1}^k$ to ensure that the original value of R is not canceled in the XOR aggregation.

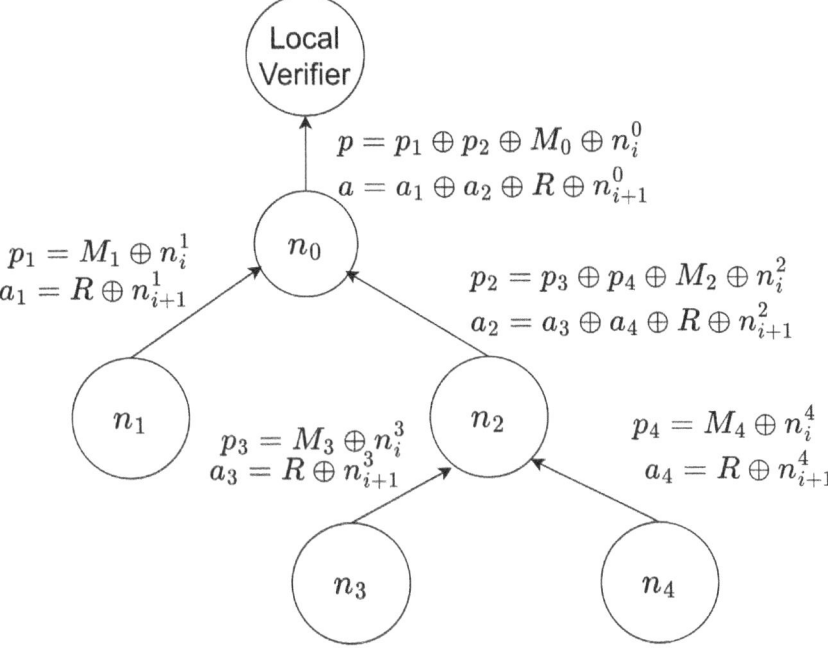

Fig. 2. Remote attestation response generation.

vi) Once the root node completes the aggregation, it forwards the final response p and a to the LV. vii) Upon receiving p and a, the LV verifies the freshness of the request by checking whether $\bigoplus_{j=1}^{N} a_j \oplus \Gamma = R$. If this check is successful, integrity is validated by verifying whether $p \oplus \Omega = M$. If both checks pass, the attestation of the entire subgroup is considered successful.

We point out that, upon receiving the *AttReq* message and verifying its authenticity, a node can speculatively begin measuring its memory region without waiting for its children's response. This parallelism reduces the overall time required for the group attestation process.

4   Protocol Evaluation

In this section, we assess the effectiveness of our proposal through two complementary approaches: simulation using the ns-3 simulator[1] to estimate network communication overhead, and a real-world implementation on an STM32H743 microcontroller. In the latter, we construct a strong PUF by combining an SRAM PUF with the lightweight cipher Chaskey, as done by the authors of [6]. For the computation of device measurements, we also employ the Chaskey algorithm to generate a cumulative hash over the entire flash memory. This process,

---

[1] https://www.nsnam.org/.

including the generation of p_j and a_j, requires on average 27.4 ms to both compute the measurement and construct the attestation response.

These empirical results are then integrated into the ns-3 simulator to analyze the overall timing performance of the communication protocol under varying subgroup sizes. Since each subgroup independently executes the full attestation procedure, the protocol is expected to scale efficiently with network size by increasing the number of subgroups.

The simulated network topology consists of a set of LVs interconnected via a CSMA-CD network. Each LV is additionally linked, through an LR-WPAN interface, to a secondary subnetwork comprising the resource-constrained IoT nodes to be attested. All relevant network parameters are detailed in Table 1.

Table 1. Configuration of the network in the ns-3 simulator

CSMA data rate	1 Gbps
CSMA Transmission delay	0,1 ms
LR-WPAN data rate	250 kbps
LR-WPAN Tx Power	20 dBm
LR-WPAN Channels' number	11

In this configuration, the number of subgroups is fixed to 20, while the number of nodes per subgroup varies from 5 to 50 in increments of five. Throughout the experiments, we assume that each non-leaf node, upon authenticating the *AttReq* message, immediately proceeds to compute its own measurement without waiting for responses from its children. For this operation, we directly account for the time required to construct the response message, as the time to query the PUF and perform the XOR operations is negligible compared to the cumulative hash computation.

For each configuration of the number of LVs and nodes, we measured the duration of the group attestation procedure as the time elapsed between the issuance of the initial request by the Remote Server and the completion of attestation by the last Local Verifier. These timings are presented in the scatter plot shown in Fig. 3. As anticipated, the completion time increases approximately linearly with the number of nodes in the initial range, but tends to plateau as the node count grows, demonstrating the scalability of the proposed approach.

5   Related Work

RA in the IoT remains an open challenge, primarily due to the limitations of resource-constrained nodes that lack embedded secure coprocessors [22]. To address this limitation, software-based attestation techniques aim to verify device integrity by either randomizing the memory regions checked during each attestation round or by analyzing performance timing during checksum computations

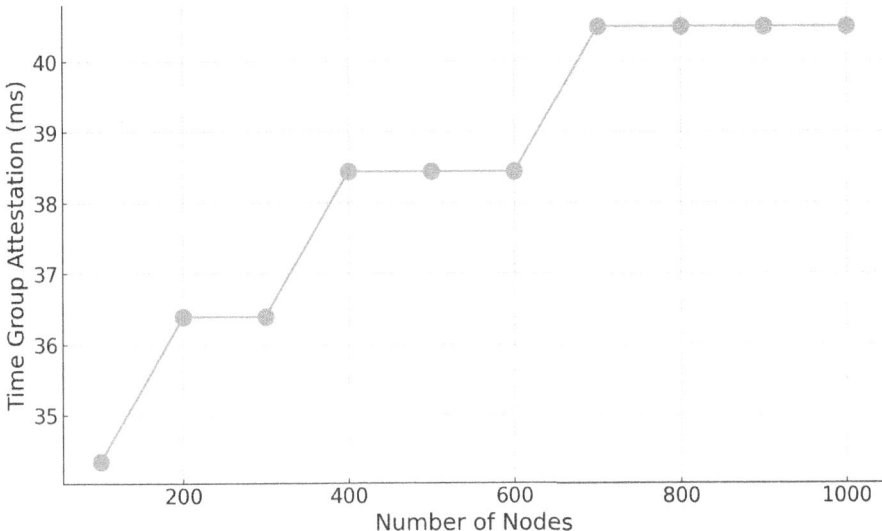

Fig. 3. Time required to complete the group remote attestation procedure.

to detect potential attacks [3]. For instance, the authors of [24] propose a protocol in which a random challenge serves as input to a Pseudo-Random Number Generator, which determines a pseudo-random memory traversal pattern for measurement. If the measurement process exceeds the expected timing—such as when an attacker modifies the checksum function to conceal injected code—the attestation procedure successfully detects the attack. Building on a similar approach, the authors of [25] address pre-computation attacks, in which an adversary attempts to pre-calculate the expected measurement, by embedding unpredictable values derived from the random challenge into the attestation process. Furthermore, to mitigate proxy attacks—where a compromised node forwards the attestation request to a more powerful device—the authors of [21] constrain the checksum area so that the measurement time remains shorter than the network transmission time. However, all these solutions are designed for end-to-end attestation and rely on strong assumptions about the environment and the adversary's capabilities, which often do not hold in the context of the IoT [2].

To overcome this limitation, the authors of [2] propose a group attestation procedure in which a server attests a set of nodes by forwarding an attestation request, along with a nonce, to a randomly selected node within the group. This node then propagates the request to its neighbors, which repeat the same operation. Unlike software-based attestation approaches, their solution relies on the presence of secure hardware technologies, such as TrustLite. Furthermore, to reduce the possibility of a single-point failure in attesting IoT networks, the authors of [19] propose a many-to-one attestation schema. Finally, to completely remove the need of secure hardware, the authors of [12] propose a software based attestation schema by multiple measurement rounds. Moreover, the introduce a memory filling at attestation time, to enhance resistance against Return Oriented programming attacks.

PUFs have also been investigated in the context of RA. For example, the authors of [16] present a PUF-based lightweight attestation protocol tailored for low-end microcontrollers, demonstrating its feasibility on the MSP430 platform. Similarly, [22] propose a quantum-resistant RA scheme relying solely on an SRAM PUF and an atomic Read Only Memory. Furthermore, [20] introduce a secure boot and RA mechanism that leverages PUFs to safeguard secrets even against a curious manufacturer seeking to extract private keys. Nonetheless, despite their promising features, PUFs are still not widely adopted for group remote attestation scenarios, leaving a significant portion of their potential in this domain unexplored.

6   Conclusion

In this paper, we presented a decentralized remote attestation scheme based on PUFs. The proposed solution enables devices to locally attest subgroups of nodes, minimizing the number of exchanged messages and improving communication efficiency. The entire approach relies on XOR operations and symmetric encryption, ensuring computational lightness and making it well-suited for IoT devices.

References

1. Ambrosin, M., Conti, M., Lazzeretti, R., Rabbani, M.M., Ranise, S.: Collective remote attestation at the internet of things scale: state-of-the-art and future challenges. IEEE Commun. Surv. Tutorials **22**(4), 2447–2461 (2020). https://doi.org/10.1109/COMST.2020.3008879
2. Asokan, N., Brasser, F., Ibrahim, A., Sadeghi, A.R., Schunter, M., Tsudik, G., Wachsmann, C.: SEDA: Scalable Embedded Device Attestation. In: Proceedings of the 22nd ACM SIGSAC Conference on Computer and Communications Security, pp. 964–975. CCS '15, Association for Computing Machinery, New York, NY, USA (2015) https://doi.org/10.1145/2810103.2813670, https://doi.org/10.1145/2810103.2813670
3. Banks, A.S., Kisiel, M., Korsholm, P.: Remote Attestation: A Literature Review (May 2021https://doi.org/10.48550/arXiv.2105.02466, http://arxiv.org/abs/2105.02466, arXiv:2105.02466 [cs]
4. Barbareschi, M.: Notions on Silicon Physically Unclonable Functions. In: Hardware Security and Trust: Design and Deployment of Integrated Circuits in a Threatened Environment, pp. 189–209, January 2017. https://doi.org/10.1007/978-3-319-44318-8_10, journal Abbreviation: Hardware Security and Trust: Design and Deployment of Integrated Circuits in a Threatened Environment
5. Barbareschi, M., Battista, E., Mazzeo, A., Mazzocca, N.: Testing 90 nm microcontroller SRAM PUF quality. In: 2015 10th International Conference on Design & Technology of Integrated Systems in Nanoscale Era (DTIS), pp. 1–6, April 2015. https://doi.org/10.1109/DTIS.2015.7127360, https://ieeexplore.ieee.org/abstract/document/7127360

6. Barbareschi, M., Casola, V., De Benedictis, A., Montagna, E.L., Mazzocca, N.: On the adoption of physically unclonable functions to secure IIoT devices. IEEE Trans. Industr. Inf. **17**(11), 7781–7790 (2021). https://doi.org/10.1109/TII.2021. 3059656

7. Barbareschi, M., Casola, V., Emmanuele, A., Lombardi, D.: A lightweight PUF-based protocol for dynamic and secure group key management in IoT. IEEE Internet Things J. **11**(20), 32969–32984 (2024). https://doi.org/10.1109/JIOT.2024. 3418207

8. Barbareschi, M., Casola, V., Emmanuele, A., Lombardi, D.: On the adoption of PUF for key agreement scheme in Internet of Things. In: Proceedings of the 21st ACM International Conference on Computing Frontiers: Workshops and Special Sessions, pp. 17–24. CF '24 Companion, Association for Computing Machinery, New York, NY, USA (Jul 2024).https://doi.org/10.1145/3637543.3654656, https://doi.org/10.1145/3637543.3654656

9. Barbareschi, M., Casola, V., Emmanuele, A., Lombardi, D.: PUF-based secure key management for continuum computing. In: Barolli, L. (ed.) Advanced Information Networking and Applications, pp. 390–399. Springer Nature Switzerland, Cham (2025). https://doi.org/10.1007/978-3-031-87778-0_38

10. Barbareschi, M., De Benedictis, A., La Montagna, E., Mazzeo, A., Mazzocca, N.: A PUF-based mutual authentication scheme for Cloud-Edges IoT systems. Future Generation Computer Systems **101**, 246–261 (2019). https://doi. org/10.1016/j.future.2019.06.012, https://www.sciencedirect.com/science/article/ pii/S0167739X19301293

11. Barbareschi, M., De Benedictis, A., Mazzocca, N.: A PUF-based hardware mutual authentication protocol. Journal of Parallel and Distributed Computing **119**, 107–120 (2018). https://doi.org/10.1016/j.jpdc.2018.04.007, https://www. sciencedirect.com/science/article/pii/S0743731518302582

12. Cao, J., Zhu, T., Ma, R., Guo, Z., Zhang, Y., Li, H.: A software-based remote attestation scheme for internet of things devices. IEEE Trans. Dependable Secure Comput. **20**(2), 1422–1434 (2023). https://doi.org/10.1109/TDSC.2022.3154887

13. Chatterjee, D., Pratihar, K., Hazra, A., R hrmair, U., Mukhopadhyay, D.: Systematically Quantifying Cryptanalytic Nonlinearities in Strong PUFs. IEEE Trans. Inf. Forensics Secur. **19**, 1126–1141 (2024). https://doi.org/10.1109/TIFS.2023. 3329438, https://ieeexplore.ieee.org/abstract/document/10304294

14. Chen, Q., Csaba, G., Lugli, P , Schlichtmann, U., R hrmair, U.: The Bistable Ring PUF: A new architecture for strong Physical Unclonable Functions. In: 2011 IEEE International Symposium on Hardware-Oriented Security and Trust, pp. 134–141, June 2011. https://doi.org/10.1109/HST.2011.5955011, https://ieeexplore. ieee.org/document/5955011/

15. Dolev, D., Yao, A.: On the security of public key protocols. IEEE Trans. Inf. Theory **29**(2), 198–208 (1983). https://doi.org/10.1109/TIT.1983.1056650

16. Feng, W., Qin, Y., Zhao, S., Feng, D.: AAoT: Lightweight attestation and authentication of low-resource things in IoT and CPS. Comput. Networks **134**, 167–182 (2018). https://doi.org/10.1016/j.comnet.2018.01.039, https://www.sciencedirect. com/science/article/pii/S1389128618300471

17. Gassend, B., Clarke, D., van Dijk, M., Devadas, S.: Silicon physical random functions. In: Proceedings of the 9th ACM Conference on Computer and Communications Security, pp. 148–160. CCS '02. Association for Computing Machinery, New York, NY, USA, November 2002. https://doi.org/10.1145/586110.586132, https:// doi.org/10.1145/586110.586132

18. Kuang, B., Fu, A., Susilo, W., Yu, S., Gao, Y.: A survey of remote attestation in Internet of Things: Attacks, countermeasures, and prospects. Comput. Secur. **112**, 102498 (2022). https://doi.org/10.1016/j.cose.2021.102498
19. Kuang, B., Fu, A., Yu, S., Yang, G., Su, M., Zhang, Y.: ESDRA: an efficient and secure distributed remote attestation scheme for IoT swarms. IEEE Internet Things J. **6**(5), 8372–8383 (2019). https://doi.org/10.1109/JIOT.2019.2917223
20. Lebedev, I., Hogan, K., Devadas, S.: invited paper: secure boot and remote attestation in the sanctum processor. In: 2018 IEEE 31st Computer Security Foundations Symposium (CSF). pp. 46–60, July 2018. https://doi.org/10.1109/CSF.2018.00011, https://ieeexplore.ieee.org/document/8429295/, iSSN: 2374-8303
21. Li, Y., McCune, J.M., Perrig, A.: VIPER: verifying the integrity of PERipherals' firmware. In: Proceedings of the 18th ACM conference on Computer and communications security, pp. 3–16. CCS '11. Association for Computing Machinery, New York, NY, USA (2011). https://doi.org/10.1145/2046707.2046711, https://doi.org/10.1145/2046707.2046711
22. Rom n, R., Arjona, R., Baturone, I.: A lightweight remote attestation using PUFs and hash-based signatures for low-end IoT devices. Future Generation Comput. Syst. **148**, 425–435 (2023). https://doi.org/10.1016/j.future.2023.06.008, https://www.sciencedirect.com/science/article/pii/S0167739X23002236
23. R hrmair, U., Sehnke, F., S lter, J., Dror, G., Devadas, S., Schmidhuber, J.: Modeling attacks on physical unclonable functions. In: Proceedings of the 17th ACM conference on Computer and Communications Security, pp. 237–249. CCS '10, Association for Computing Machinery, New York, NY, USA (2010). https://doi.org/10.1145/1866307.1866335
24. Seshadri, A., Perrig, A., van Doorn, L., Khosla, P.: SWATT: softWare-based attestation for embedded devices. In: IEEE Symposium on Security and Privacy, 2004. Proceedings. 2004, pp. 272–282, May 2004. https://doi.org/10.1109/SECPRI.2004.1301329, https://ieeexplore.ieee.org/abstract/document/1301329, iSSN: 1081-6011
25. Seshadri, A., Luk, M., Shi, E., Perrig, A., van Doorn, L., Khosla, P.: Pioneer: verifying code integrity and enforcing untampered code execution on legacy systems. In: Proceedings of the twentieth ACM symposium on Operating systems principles, pp. 1–16. SOSP '05. Association for Computing Machinery, New York, NY, USA (2005). https://doi.org/10.1145/1095810.1095812
26. Shamsoshoara, A., Korenda, A., Afghah, F., Zeadally, S.: A survey on physical unclonable function (PUF)-based security solutions for Internet of Things. Comput. Netw. **183**, 107593 (2020). https://doi.org/10.1016/j.comnet.2020.107593

Evaluating DAVS Approach for Docker Images Static Analysis

Ilnar Khasanov[1] and Andrey Sadovykh[2]

[1] Innopolis University, Innopolis, Russia
i.khasanov@innopolis.university
[2] Softeam, Courbevoie, France
andrey.sadovykh@softeam.fr

Abstract. Docker, the most widely used container platform, raises security concerns due to its layered image structure–vulnerabilities in a base image are inherited by all derived images. As a result, thorough and reliable image scanning is essential to maintaining system security.

The DAVS approach [4] improves static vulnerability detection by specifically targeting software installed manually in Docker images. By combining traditional static tools with scanning of suspicious layers, DAVS demonstrated higher detection efficiency.

This paper extends the DAVS work in three key ways. First, we developed an open-source implementation of the approach. Second, we validated it using multiple static analysis tools, including Trivy and Grype. Third, we constructed a recent dataset of 132 Docker images, including top-pulled, intentionally vulnerable, and randomly selected images.

Our results support previous findings [4] and show that our tool enhances existing scanners by detecting additional vulnerabilities–up to 751 previously missed issues, even in widely used images. By combining static and binary analysis, our method offers a more comprehensive solution for container image security.

Keywords: Docker · Cybersecurity · CVE · static analysis · binary analysis

1 Introduction

Containerization has revolutionized modern software deployment by enabling applications and their dependencies to be packaged into lightweight, portable units. Docker, the most prominent containerization platform, has become a foundational technology in DevOps, supporting consistent and scalable deployment across diverse environments. According to Majumder et al. [10], over 70% of organizations now utilize containers in production, underscoring their critical role in infrastructure today.

However, this ubiquity has also introduced significant security challenges. Docker images, particularly those hosted on public registries like Docker Hub,

F. Skopik et al. (Eds.): ARES 2025 Workshops, LNCS 15999, pp. 181–195, 2025.
https://doi.org/10.1007/978-3-032-00644-8_11

often suffer from outdated dependencies, misconfigurations, and insecure maintenance practices [11]. Because Docker images are layered, a vulnerability in a base image can propagate to a large number of descendant images, magnifying the impact of a single flaw throughout the ecosystem.

Static analysis tools such as Trivy[1], Grype[2], and Docker Scout[3] have emerged to detect known >vulnerabilities in container images. These tools are widely integrated into CI/CD pipelines and security workflows. Yet, they share a common limitation: reliance on package manager metadata. As highlighted in recent research [2], they often fail to detect vulnerabilities in software installed manually–through custom binaries, scripts, or compiled source code–bypassing conventional detection methods.

To address this gap, Doan and Jung introduced the DAVS (Dockerfile Analysis for Container Image Vulnerability Scanning) approach [4], which augments traditional static analysis by targeting image layers likely to contain manually added components. By applying binary scanners to these specific layers, DAVS increases the depth and breadth of vulnerability detection.

In this paper, we evaluate the effectiveness and practicality of the DAVS approach in real-world settings. Our contributions are threefold. First, we implement and open-source a robust prototype of the DAVS pipeline. Second, we systematically assess its performance across multiple scanners to measure its impact on detection accuracy. Third, we conduct a large-scale empirical evaluation on 132 diverse Docker images–spanning popular, vulnerable, and randomly selected containers. Our results demonstrate that DAVS significantly improves coverage, identifying up to 751 additional vulnerabilities missed by standard tools alone.

The remainder of this paper is organized as follows. Section 2 describes the proposed approach. Section 3 presents the evaluation methodology and results. Section 4 provides an analysis of the key findings. Finally, Sect. 5 discusses related work and situates our contribution within the existing literature.

2   Implementing DAVS Approach

Building on the results of DAVS [4], we propose a hybrid analysis strategy that combines a static analysis tool with a binary scanning utility. This approach addresses a key limitation of traditional static scanners: their inability to detect vulnerabilities in manually added binaries or software not managed by package managers.

Our prototype shows that existing static analysis tools can miss a significant number of vulnerabilities and evaluates how combining different tools can improve detection coverage.

The design of our system and an overview of the approach is shown in Fig. 1.

Our methodology for identifying vulnerabilities in Docker images consists of the following key steps:

---

[1] https://trivy.dev/.
[2] https://github.com/anchore/grype.
[3] https://docs.docker.com/scout/.

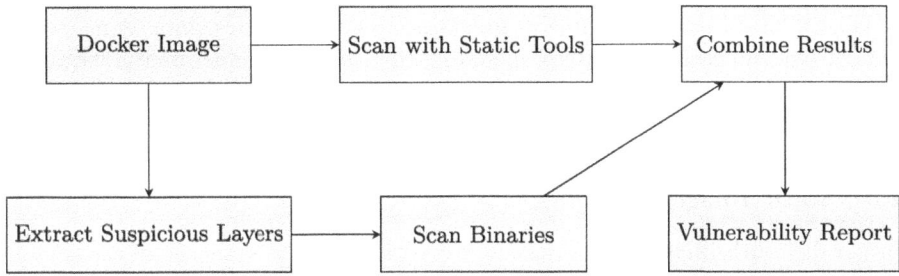

Fig. 1. Implementing DAVS [4] approach for Docker image scanning

2.1 Extracting Suspicious Layers

Docker offers a command-line interface to export an image's filesystem as a tar archive. Within this archive, image layers are located under the `blobs/sha256/` directory. By unpacking the archive, we gain direct access to these individual layers for analysis.

Building on the approach introduced by DAVS [4], we focus on Dockerfile instructions–specifically `FROM`, `COPY`, `ADD`, and `RUN`–that result in the creation of new layers. These instructions are examined to identify operations commonly associated with manual software installation, such as the use of tools like `make`, `wget`, and similar commands.

This targeted filtering allows us to narrow down the scope of our analysis to layers most likely to contain untracked or non-standard software components.

Additionally, the archive includes a `manifest.json` file. The "Config" key in this manifest points to a secondary JSON file that captures all build instructions and the corresponding layer identifiers. We extract these instruction-layer mappings into a structured representation, enabling systematic analysis.

Each instruction-layer pair is then evaluated for signs of potentially risky behavior. Layers generated via `COPY`, `ADD`, or those invoking network-related or build commands (e.g., `wget`, `curl`, `make`) are flagged as potentially vulnerable.

This step is performed using a filtering function designed to detect these suspicious patterns.

2.2 Scanning Suspicious Layers

Once relevant layers are identified, we extract their contents and subject them to binary-level vulnerability scanning. Each flagged layer corresponds to a specific directory in the unpacked Docker archive, typically found under `blobs/sha256/{layer_id}`.

For this analysis, we employ the `CVE-bin-tool`[4], an open-source scanner that examines compiled binaries for known security vulnerabilities. It generates a detailed JSON report enumerating detected issues.

---

[4] https://github.com/intel/cve-bin-tool.

The CVE-bin-tool is actively maintained and integrates data from multiple trusted vulnerability sources, including the National Vulnerability Database (NVD), Red Hat, OSV, GitLab, and Curl, ensuring up-to-date and comprehensive results.

2.3 Static Image Scanning

In parallel with binary-level analysis, we perform static vulnerability scanning across the entire Docker image using a suite of established tools:

1. Trivy[5]
2. Grype[6]
3. Snyk[7]
4. Docker Scout[8]

These scanners analyze packages installed via traditional package managers (e.g., `apt`, `apk`, `yum`) and compare them against known vulnerability databases. Unlike binary scanners, static tools are effective at detecting vulnerabilities in standard packages and libraries installed through official channels.

Each scanner's results are exported in a structured format, typically JSON, to facilitate aggregation and integration with other outputs.

2.4 Aggregating Results

After completing both static and binary scans, we consolidate the results into a unified dataset. Each tool produces a report containing vulnerability identifiers (e.g., CVE numbers), severity ratings, and affected components.

We implement a merging function that aligns vulnerabilities across tools based on CVE identifiers and component metadata. This step removes duplicate entries, highlights overlapping detections, and identifies findings unique to one method or the other.

This aggregation enables broader and more accurate vulnerability coverage by combining the strengths of both binary-level and static analysis.

2.5 Generating the Final Report

The merged findings are compiled into a comprehensive vulnerability report, which includes:

– Total number of detected vulnerabilities
– Breakdown by scanning tool (binary vs. static)
– Vulnerabilities uniquely identified through binary analysis

---

[5] https://trivy.dev/.
[6] https://github.com/anchore/grype.
[7] https://snyk.io/.
[8] https://docs.docker.com/scout/.

– Severity distribution (e.g., critical, high, medium, low)

This final report is intended to provide developers and security teams with a more holistic view of the security posture of a Docker image, particularly uncovering vulnerabilities associated with manually installed or custom-built software that may be overlooked by conventional scanners.

3   Evaluation

3.1   Selection of Docker Images

To evaluate the effectiveness of our system, we tested it on a curated dataset of 132 Docker images sourced from Docker Hub. The images were divided into three categories to capture a range of use cases and reduce selection bias:

Category 1: Popular Top-Pulled Images: This group consists of 20 Docker images with the highest download counts, such as `memcached:1.6.32`, which has been pulled over a billion times. These images are typically maintained by official teams and are assumed to follow established security practices. Analyzing this category provides a baseline for evaluating scanner performance on production-grade containers.

Previous work by Opdebeeck et al. [13] shows that many community-maintained images are derived from these base images, potentially inheriting their vulnerabilities.

Category 2: Intentionally Vulnerable Images: We include 10 images from the Vulhub project[9], each containing known and documented vulnerabilities. These serve as controlled test cases, allowing us to assess how effectively scanners detect known issues under ideal detection conditions.

Category 3: Random Community Images: This set includes 102 Docker images selected at random from Docker Hub. These images, such as `joehorn/phpunit:12-php8.3`, span a wide range of purposes and development practices. They are generally created by individual developers or small teams and vary in quality, complexity, and update frequency. This group represents a cross-section of typical real-world containers found in the Docker ecosystem.

This three-part categorization allows us to test our scanning approach across different image types:

– Well-maintained images with high adoption,
– Images intentionally embedded with known vulnerabilities,
– A diverse sample reflecting community usage.

By comparing scanner output across these groups, we can assess the generalizability and robustness of our method. Differences in CVE detection rates between categories help illustrate the strengths and limitations of individual tools and underscore the value of combining multiple scanning strategies.

---

[9] https://github.com/vulhub/vulhub.

3.2   Benchmark Results

All data collected from our scanning experiments, including detailed vulnerability reports for each Docker image, is publicly available on Zenodo [8] to support
transparency and reproducibility.

To demonstrate the benefits of incorporating binary-level scanning into container vulnerability detection, we highlight several representative examples.
These examples cover a range of scenarios:

1. When `cve-bin-tool` finds no additional vulnerabilities beyond those detected
   by static analysis tools.
2. When `cve-bin-tool` identifies numerous issues missed by static tools.
3. When both approaches reveal unique findings, with some overlap.

All tested images are version-pinned to ensure full reproducibility of the
results.

Table 1. Top-pulled images – total vulnerabilities discovered by each tool.

Image (Version)	Docker Scout	Grype	Snyk	Trivy	CVE-bin-tool
ubuntu:22.04	0	0	0	0	34
redis:7.2	74	135	164	138	52
centos:centos7	98	1207	1201	1208	790

Table 1 illustrates that `cve-bin-tool` can uncover vulnerabilities not
detected by conventional static tools. This is especially notable in the
`ubuntu:22.04` image, where binary scanning revealed 34 vulnerabilities despite
other tools reporting none.

Table 2. Top-pulled images – unique vulnerabilities found by `cve-bin-tool` in suspicious layers.

Image (Version)	Docker Scout	Grype	Snyk	Trivy
ubuntu:22.04	34	34	34	34
redis:7.2	7	9	52	8
centos:centos7	751	417	416	415

The unique vulnerabilities listed in Table 2 reinforce the importance of analyzing manually installed binaries, especially in complex or widely used base
images.

As shown in Table 3, vulnerable images such as those from VulHub often
contain more issues than official ones. Notably, `Docker Scout` failed to detect

Table 3. VulHub images – total vulnerabilities reported by each tool.

Image (Version)	Docker Scout	Grype	Snyk	Trivy	CVE-bin-tool
vulhub_activemq:5.17.3	182	433	659	404	184
vulhub_aria2:1.18.8	0	468	1222	309	276
vulhub_celery:3.1.23	9	521	962	311	331

Table 4. VulHub images – unique vulnerabilities detected in suspicious layers by `cve-bin-tool`.

Image (Version)	Docker Scout	Grype	Snyk	Trivy
vulhub_activemq:5.17.3	101	84	85	85
vulhub_aria2:1.18.8	276	193	193	231
vulhub_celery:3.1.23	324	193	244	273

any vulnerabilities in `vulhub_aria2:1.18.8`, while other tools flagged hundreds. This highlights inconsistencies between tools and the added value of binary scanning.

Table 4 confirms that vulnerabilities in VulHub images are not limited to package-managed software. A significant number of issues stem from manually installed components, underlining the need for binary-level inspection.

Table 5. Random community images – total vulnerabilities detected by each tool.

Image (Version)	Docker Scout	Grype	Snyk	Trivy	CVE-bin-tool
diodonfrost_ansible-almalinux:9	44	276	0	0	338
realsoft2023_backend-dev-design:10042025	116	3144	5814	603	1252
altinityinfra_test-base:1-...	1395	2131	506	1556	2537

The large number of vulnerabilities in randomly selected community images (Table 5) suggests that many users may lack the expertise or tools to build secure containers.

Table 6 shows that manually added software in community images is also a common source of vulnerabilities–often overlooked by traditional scanners.

These examples collectively demonstrate the complementary nature of static and binary analysis. By combining both approaches, practitioners can achieve broader and more reliable vulnerability coverage. This is crucial for securing containers used in production or security-sensitive environments.

Table 6. Random community images – unique vulnerabilities detected in suspicious layers by `cve-bin-tool`.

Image (Version)	Docker Scout	Grype	Snyk	Trivy
diodonfrost_ansible-almalinux:9	336	219	338	338
realsoft2023_backend-dev-design:10042025	1017	1025	1070	990
altinityinfra_test-base:1-...	2518	2525	2529	2529

4   Analysis

Tables 7, 8, and 9 summarize key statistics on vulnerabilities uniquely identified by applying CVE-bin-tool to suspicious layers within the analyzed images. These are vulnerabilities missed by static analysis tools, highlighting the added value of binary-level inspection.

Table 7. Top-pulled images: Summary of unique vulnerabilities discovered by applying `cve-bin-tool` to suspicious layers.

Metric	Trivy	Grype	Snyk	Docker Scout
Maximum unique vulnerabilities detected	415	417	416	751
Median number of unique CVEs	29	25.5	39	29

Table 8. VulHub images: Summary of unique vulnerabilities discovered by applying `cve-bin-tool` to suspicious layers.

Metric	Trivy	Grype	Snyk	Docker Scout
Maximum unique vulnerabilities detected	415	417	416	751
Median number of unique CVEs	196.5	133	132	226

The results demonstrate the substantial benefit of incorporating binary analysis into container security workflows. Even among top-pulled official images–assumed to follow rigorous security practices–CVE-bin-tool uncovered up to 751 vulnerabilities that static analysis tools failed to detect. This strongly suggests the presence of manually added or bundled binaries that are not visible through Software Bill of Materials (SBOM) or package metadata.

For VulHub images, which are intentionally insecure for testing purposes, the tool uncovered similarly high numbers of unique vulnerabilities. This again confirms that conventional static scanners may overlook substantial attack surfaces.

Table 9. Randomly selected images: Summary of unique vulnerabilities discovered by applying `cve-bin-tool` to suspicious layers.

Metric	Trivy	Grype	Snyk	Docker Scout
Maximum unique vulnerabilities detected	2518	2525	2529	2518
Median number of unique CVEs	9.5	6	13	9

Interestingly, the median number of additional vulnerabilities discovered in randomly selected images is lower (e.g., 13 for Snyk in Table 9) compared to top-pulled images (e.g., 25.5 for Grype in Table 7). This difference may be attributed to many of these community images being derived from minimal base distributions such as Alpine, which contain fewer binaries overall. It also suggests a potential bias in the dataset, which could be addressed by including more large and complex random images in future evaluations.

Another notable observation is that the maximum number of unique CVEs reported for both top and VulHub image groups is identical. This occurs because some VulHub images, such as `vulhub/apisix:2.9`, are based on `centos:7`, causing vulnerability inheritance from the base layer to the derivative image.

Collectively, these findings reinforce the importance of hybrid approaches. Relying solely on static vulnerability scanners like Trivy, Grype, or Snyk leaves significant blind spots, especially in images that include binaries installed manually or through custom build processes. Binary scanning complements static analysis by directly inspecting executables, revealing issues that would otherwise go undetected.

Our results align with prior research, including the DAVS framework [4], and provide further evidence for adopting comprehensive, multi-faceted vulnerability scanning strategies in Docker image security.

5   Related Work

5.1   Vulnerable Packages

Several studies have shown that Docker images often contain vulnerabilities. Shu et al. [18] introduced the DIVA framework, which scanned 356,218 images using Clair[10]. On average, official images had 185 vulnerabilities, while community images had 199. Most issues were inherited from base images, though some originated from the image itself. The study's reliance on a single scanner, Clair, limits the breadth of detection.

Zerouali et al. [22] examined 7,380 Debian-based images and found a median of 601 vulnerabilities per image. However, only 12.2% of packages were actually vulnerable, and over 80% of the images had up-to-date packages. Still, the scope was limited to Debian-based images, excluding ecosystems like PyPI, npm, and RubyGems.

---

[10] https://github.com/quay/clair

A related study focused on Alpine-based images [20], analyzing 2,245 images and 63,581 packages. It found that 94% of packages were outdated. While informative, the exclusive focus on Alpine limits generalization.

In another work, Zerouali et al. [21] used Snyk[11] to scan 961 images and 1,412 npm packages. Only 54 packages were vulnerable, but every image included at least one of them. This shows how easily vulnerable JavaScript libraries can spread, though reliance on a single tool is again a limitation.

Together, these studies show that vulnerabilities are common across Docker images, especially those built on Debian or Alpine [11]. However, many of these analyses use a single scanning tool or focus on specific ecosystems, which may overlook other risks.

5.2   Insecure Base Images

Docker images are typically built from base images. Vulnerabilities in these base layers are inherited by all child images, making them a critical point of concern.

Maruszczak et al. [11] compared base images and found that Distroless images usually contain fewer vulnerabilities than traditional options like Debian or Alpine. However, the results varied. Given the popularity of Debian and Alpine as base images, vulnerabilities in them can have a broad impact.

Opdebeeck et al. [13] analyzed 636,625 images and reported that 70% were built on outdated base images, with a median lag of 5.63 months. Debian and Alpine were the most commonly used, but the study only covered amd64 images, which may limit its generality.

Mullinix et al. [12] showed real-world threats by presenting examples of malicious images that used SSH for data exfiltration, underlining the risks tied to insecure base layers.

These works emphasize that updating application packages is not enough. Vulnerabilities in base images must also be addressed to ensure image security.

5.3   Static Analysis and the Need for Deeper Inspection

Static analysis tools are widely used to detect vulnerabilities before deploying containers. Popular tools include Trivy[12], Clair, Grype[13], Snyk, Docker Scout, and Microscanner[14].

A study by Boles et al. [2] compared Trivy and Grype across 927 images. Grype reported more vulnerabilities (603,259) than Trivy (473,661) in over 84% of cases. This discrepancy is largely due to their differing vulnerability databases– Grype also uses GitHub Advisories[15] in addition to CVEs. Issues like double-

---

[11] https://snyk.io/.

[12] https://trivy.dev/.

[13] https://github.com/anchore/grype.

[14] https://github.com/aquasecurity/microscanner.

[15] https://github.com/advisories.

counting and inconsistent updates from sources like the NVD[16] also affect accuracy.

However, these tools have limitations. Most depend on package manager metadata and often overlook manually installed or application-level software. Javed and Toor [7] found that tools like Clair and Microscanner focus only on OS-level packages. Even Anchore, which supports application scanning, misses about 34% of vulnerabilities. Their study, however, did not include newer tools like Trivy or Grype.

Doan and Jung [4] addressed this gap with the DAVS approach, which analyzes Dockerfiles to find layers that may include manually added software. These layers are then scanned using tools like CVE-bin-tool[17]. While DAVS improved detection coverage, it also introduced challenges such as slower performance and dependency on timely CVE database updates.

These limitations point to the need for better tools that combine different analysis methods. DAVS represents an important step in this direction by augmenting static scanning with Dockerfile-based inspection of suspicious layers.

5.4   Default Root Privileges

Unlike virtual machines, Docker containers share the host kernel, which raises concerns regarding privilege escalation–particularly when containers run with root privileges. Rajyashree et al. [14] highlight that Docker's default settings allow instructions to be executed with root privileges. To mitigate this risk, they recommend defining a non-root user in the Dockerfile and executing commands under that user.

Rosa et al. [15] support this by identifying the default root user as one of the most commonly observed security misconfigurations. Similarly, Bui [3] asserts that running containers as root is unnecessary in most scenarios and should generally be avoided.

To address this, Lu et al. [9] developed DFScan, a tool that detects and warns when an image uses the root user.

While dependency management does not directly affect user privilege levels within a container, it is considered a best practice to run Docker containers under a non-root user to reduce security risks.

5.5   Improper Dockerfile Instructions Usage

Findings from static analysis research indicate that solely scanning metadata or application packages is insufficient. It is also critical to examine Dockerfile instructions for insecure or inefficient practices.

---

[16] https://nvd.nist.gov/.
[17] https://github.com/intel/cve-bin-tool.

Wu et al. [19] analyzed over 6,000 GitHub repositories using Hadolint[18] and ShellCheck[19]. They discovered that 84% of Dockerfiles contained "smells" or bad practices, with about 62

Rosa et al. [15] studied 39,242 Dockerfiles and also employed expert review. One major issue identified was the lack of version pinning, which can result in unintentional use of vulnerable versions. However, the study also showed that only 36% of Hadolint-detected issues were deemed important by experts, suggesting some findings may lack practical relevance.

Doan and Jung [4] referenced the Dockerfile specification[20], which identifies only four instructions (FROM, RUN, COPY, ADD) as ones that modify the filesystem by creating new layers. These instructions are critical from a security perspective.

Durieux [6] examined 11,313 Dockerfiles using the Parfum framework [5], identifying 14 frequent Dockerfile smells that significantly inflate image sizes–such as failing to clean caches after installing packages. On average, fixing these issues reduced image size by 4.6% (48.06 MB), with some cases seeing up to 89% reduction, which also helps reduce attack surface.

In another study, Rosa et al. [16] emphasized version pinning for base images as one of the most frequent issues. Without it, rebuilding an image may unintentionally fetch a new, potentially vulnerable base version.

5.6   Dynamic Analysis

Dynamic analysis is increasingly recognized as a valuable complement to static methods in Docker security research.

Ajith et al. [1] introduced a hybrid approach combining static analysis (via Trivy) with dynamic analysis using Falco[21]. While static analysis detects vulnerabilities in dependencies, Falco monitors runtime behavior for anomalies such as unauthorized access–important in the context of securing IoT deployments.

Mullinix et al. [12] applied dynamic analysis through Shodan[22] for examining IP origins and VirusTotal[23] for monitoring suspicious file changes, CPU/memory statistics, and network behavior. However, these tools do not inspect installed dependencies directly.

While it is possible to configure dynamic tools like Falco for pre-deployment scanning, their primary role is anomaly detection during container runtime. In contrast, static analysis remains more effective for detecting package-related vulnerabilities before container execution.

---

[18] https://github.com/hadolint/hadolint.
[19] https://www.shellcheck.net/.
[20] https://docs.docker.com/reference/dockerfile/.
[21] https://github.com/falcosecurity/falco.
[22] https://www.shodan.io/.
[23] https://www.virustotal.com/gui/home/upload.

6 Conclusion

This study exposes a critical limitation of widely used static vulnerability scanners: their inability to detect issues in manually installed binaries. Our analysis reveals that this blind spot affects not only niche or poorly maintained containers, but also some of the most frequently pulled Docker images on Docker Hub–highlighting a serious and often underestimated security concern.

To address this shortcoming, the DAVS framework [4] introduced a hybrid vulnerability scanning approach that integrates static analysis with binary-level inspection using CVE-bin-tool. Our evaluation confirms that this combination significantly improves vulnerability coverage compared to static analysis tools alone.

Building on this foundation, our work expands the evaluation to a broader and more diverse dataset of 132 Docker images. We empirically compare four popular scanners–Trivy, Grype, Snyk, and Docker Scout–demonstrating how each performs when augmented with binary-level inspection. To facilitate transparency and reproducibility, we have made our implementation publicly available on GitHub[24], and our full benchmark dataset is released on Zenodo [8].

A striking example is the `ubuntu:22.04` base image, for which all static scanners reported zero vulnerabilities, while CVE-bin-tool detected 34. Given the widespread use of Ubuntu as a base layer in production containers, this discrepancy reveals an urgent blind spot in current scanning methodologies. Moreover, results from the random image set indicate that users frequently create and publish highly vulnerable images, posing broader systemic risks to software supply chains.

Our findings reinforce the importance of hybrid approaches that combine metadata-driven and binary-level analysis. No single method offers complete coverage; thus, layering complementary techniques is essential for robust container security.

Looking forward, we plan to enhance Software Bill of Materials (SBOM) integration by investigating standardization and improving interoperability across tools. Future work will also explore optimal combinations of static, binary, and potentially dynamic or AI-assisted scanning techniques to reduce blind spots and false positives. Embedding these enhanced scanning pipelines into CI/CD workflows will support real-time feedback and enforce security policies during development. Additionally, we aim to extend our dataset to encompass a wider range of applications and registries, enabling richer statistical insights and longitudinal analysis. Finally, integration with orchestration platforms such as Kubernetes will allow us to study container security at runtime and across distributed systems, providing a more holistic view of modern cloud-native security challenges. Overall, this work contributes to our general effort to maximise automation in all the stages of the DevSecOps methodology - from threat modelling, cybersecurity requirements extraction, formalisation and automated tests mapping [17].

---

[24] https://github.com/ilnarkhasanov/DockerScanner.

Acknowledgments. This research work has been partially funded by the Key Digital Technologies (KDT) Joint Undertaking through the project MATISSE, grant agreement No. 101140216.

References

1. Ajith, V., Cyriac, T., Chavda, C., Kiyani, A.T., Chennareddy, V., Ali, K.: Analyzing docker vulnerabilities through static and dynamic methods and enhancing iot security with aws iot core, cloudwatch, and guardduty. IoT **5**(3), 592–607 (2024). https://doi.org/10.3390/iot5030026
2. Boles, B., O Donoghue, E., Muneza, A.R.M., Perkins, G., Izurieta, C., Reinhold, A.M.: Deciphering discrepancies: A comparative analysis of docker image security. In: Proceedings of the SCAM 2024 Conference. https://www.cs.montana.edu/izurieta/pubs/SCAM2024.pdf. Accessed 01 Dec 2024
3. Bui, T.: Analysis of docker security (2015). https://arxiv.org/abs/1501.02967
4. Doan, P., Jung, S.: Davs: Dockerfile analysis for container image vulnerability scanning. Computers, Materials & Continua **72**, 1699–1711 (2022). https://doi.org/10.32604/cmc.2022.025096
5. Durieux, T.: Parfum: detection and automatic repair of dockerfile smells (2023). https://arxiv.org/abs/2302.01707
6. Durieux, T.: Empirical study of the docker smells impact on the image size. In: Proceedings of the IEEE/ACM 46th International Conference on Software Engineering, p. 1 12. ICSE 24. ACM, April 2024. https://doi.org/10.1145/3597503.3639143,
7. Javed, O., Toor, S.: Understanding the quality of container security vulnerability detection tools. CoRR abs/2101.03844 (2021). https://arxiv.org/abs/2101.03844
8. Khasanov, I., Sadovykh, A.: Dataset for "evaluating davs approach for docker images static analysis", May 2025. https://doi.org/10.5281/zenodo.15382902
9. Lu, H., Hao, J., Jiang, Y., Gupta, B.B., Almomani, A., Zhang, M., Tian, Z.: Dfscan: Security scanner of the dockerfile based on instruction coverage and attack perspective. Human-centric Computing and Information Sciences **14**, 10 (2024). https://doi.org/10.22967/HCIS.2024.14.010,
10. Majumder, S.H., Jajodia, S., Majumdar, S., Hossain, M.S.: Layered security analysis for container images: Expanding lightweight pre-deployment scanning. In: 2023 20th Annual International Conference on Privacy, Security and Trust (PST), pp. 1–10 (2023). https://doi.org/10.1109/PST58708.2023.10320152
11. Maruszczak, A., Walkowski, M., Sujecki, S.: Base systems for docker containers - security analysis. In: 2022 International Conference on Software, Telecommunications and Computer Networks (SoftCOM), pp. 1–5 (2022). https://doi.org/10.23919/SoftCOM55329.2022.9911523
12. Mullinix, S.P., Konomi, E., Townsend, R.D., Parizi, R.M.: On security measures for containerized applications imaged with docker. arXiv preprint arXiv:2008.04814 (2020). https://doi.org/10.48550/arXiv.2008.04814
13. Opdebeeck, R., Lesy, J., Zerouali, A., De Roover, C.: The Docker Hub Image Inheritance Network: Construction and Empirical Insights, pp. 198–208 (2023). https://doi.org/10.1109/SCAM59687.2023.00029

14. R, R., Mathi, S., G, S., M, S.: An empirical investigation of docker sockets for privilege escalation and defensive strategies. Procedia Comput. Sci. **233**, 660–669 (2024). https://doi.org/10.1016/j.procs.2024.03.255, https://www.sciencedirect.com/science/article/pii/S187705092400615X, 5th International Conference on Innovative Data Communication Technologies and Application (ICIDCA 2024)

15. Rosa, G., Scalabrino, S., Robles, G., Oliveto, R.: Not all dockerfile smells are the same: An empirical evaluation of hadolint writing practices by experts. In: Proceedings of the 21st International Conference on Mining Software Repositories, pp. 231 241. MSR '24. Association for Computing Machinery, New York (2024). https://doi.org/10.1145/3643991.3644905,

16. Rosa, G., Zappone, F., Scalabrino, S., Oliveto, R.: Fixing dockerfile smells: An empirical study. Empirical Softw. Eng. **29**(108) (2024). https://doi.org/10.1007/s10664-024-10471-7. Accessed 01 Dec 2024

17. Sadovykh, A., Ivanov, V.: Enhancing DevSecOps with continuous security requirements analysis and testing. Comput. Res. Modeling **16**, 1687–1702 (Dec 2024).https://doi.org/10.20537/2076-7633-2024-16-7-1687-1702

18. Shu, R., Gu, X., Enck, W.: A study of security vulnerabilities on docker hub. In: Proceedings of the Seventh ACM on Conference on Data and Application Security and Privacy, CODASPY '17, pp. 269 280. Association for Computing Machinery, New York (2017). https://doi.org/10.1145/3029806.3029832,

19. Wu, Y., Zhang, Y., Wang, T., Wang, H.: Characterizing the occurrence of dockerfile smells in open-source software: an empirical study. IEEE Access **8**, 34127–34139 (2020). https://doi.org/10.1109/ACCESS.2020.2973750

20. Zerouali, A.: Analyzing technical lag in docker images. In: BENEVOL 2018 (2018)

21. Zerouali, A., Cosentino, V., Mens, T., Robles, G., Gonzalez-Barahona, J.M.: On the impact of outdated and vulnerable javascript packages in docker images. In: 2019 IEEE 26th International Conference on Software Analysis, Evolution and Reengineering (SANER), pp. 619–623 (2019). https://doi.org/10.1109/SANER.2019.8667984

22. Zerouali, A., Mens, T., Robles, G., Gonzalez-Barahona, J.M.: On the relation between outdated docker containers, severity vulnerabilities, and bugs. In: 2019 IEEE 26th International Conference on Software Analysis, Evolution and Reengineering (SANER), pp. 491–501 (2019). https://doi.org/10.1109/SANER.2019.8668013

SAM-CyFra: A System for the Automated Management of Cybersecurity Frameworks

Raffaele Elia[1]([✉])[iD], Daniele Granata[2][iD], and Massimiliano Rak[3][iD]

[1] University of Campania Luigi Vanvitelli, 81031 Aversa, Italy
raffaele.elia@unicampania.it
[2] University of Naples Parthenope, 80125 Naples, Italy
daniele.granata@uniparthenope.it
[3] University of Naples Federico II, 80125 Naples, Italy
massimiliano.rak@unina.it

Abstract. Given the expanding threat landscape, protecting critical infrastructures and sensitive information has become a top priority. Organizations are increasingly emphasizing security risk assessments to safeguard their assets and maintain compliance with evolving standards and regulations. As a result, various cybersecurity frameworks have been developed to assist organizations assess and strengthen their security practices, promoting a proactive and strategic approach to risk management. However, cybersecurity frameworks present significant challenges in terms of complexity, scalability, and adaptability. On the one hand, they generally rely on manual assessment processes, with all limitations of manual evaluations. On the other hand, they are characterized by a heterogeneous nature that works at different levels of granularity, thus resulting in a complex landscape for companies. To address these challenges, this work proposes SAM-CyFra, a system designed to automate and streamline the management of cybersecurity frameworks. SAM-CyFra organizes security into three layers, providing a simplified and modular approach that enhances adaptability to each organization's specific needs. Some preliminary results are presented with a focus on U-space environments.

Keywords: Cybersecurity Framework · Security Assessment · U-space

1 Introduction

The ever-growing threat landscape makes protecting critical infrastructures and information a priority. Companies now focus on security risk assessments to safeguard their assets (i.e., valuable resources that require to be safeguarded) and ensure compliance with evolving standards and regulations. Consequently, various cybersecurity frameworks, such as the Cybersecurity Framework (CSF) developed by the National Institute of Standards and Technology (NIST) [16], have been introduced to help organizations evaluate and improve their security practices, ensuring a proactive and strategic approach to risk management. These

F. Skopik et al. (Eds.): ARES 2025 Workshops, LNCS 15999, pp. 196–212, 2025.
https://doi.org/10.1007/978-3-032-00644-8_12

frameworks have a broad scope of application, covering different areas such as Information Technology (IT), Cyber-Physical Systems (CPS), Industrial Control Systems (ICS), and Internet of Things (IoT), as discussed in [21].

However, while they aim to provide a comprehensive means to address cybersecurity issues, they also present significant challenges in terms of complexity, scalability, and adaptability. Cybersecurity frameworks generally rely on assessment processes, often handled manually, which introduces a range of limitations. These include potential inconsistencies in prioritizing activities required to handle security risks, discrepancies in establishing the maturity of security process and activities, a lack of standardized approaches for defining both the current and the target cybersecurity posture. On the other hand, manual processes may also lead to mistakes in selecting appropriate security controls, which are measures and actions implemented for an information system or organization to ensure the confidentiality, integrity and availability (CIA) requirements of the system and its information [20]. Such issues are further compounded by the heterogeneous nature of these frameworks that, varying in their granularity, operate at different layers and often require a time-consuming level of customization, creating a complex landscape for companies.

In response to these challenges, this work proposes SAM-CyFra, a System for the Automated Management of Cybersecurity Frameworks. SAM-CyFra is designed to fill the gaps in current frameworks by providing a structured approach that supports automation in security assessments. This system enables organizations to perform compliance checks, establish its security posture, and define targeted security roadmaps with greater accuracy and efficiency. SAM-CyFra organizes security into three layers, creating a simple and modular approach that makes security management adaptable to each organization's needs. This layered structure improves the accessibility of security assessments, also supporting more precise, data-driven evaluations, making it easier to highlight compliance gaps and understand where the company can improve in terms of security.

The remainder of the paper is structured as follows. Section 2 reviews key frameworks used in companies, providing background for our contributions, while Sect. 3 highlights open issues in the literature and outlines our research directions. Next, Sect. 4 introduces a taxonomy of the analyzed cybersecurity frameworks based on different layers. Section 5 illustrates the proposed formalism and notation that guide the analysis of the security assessment process, detailed in Sect. 6. It is partially illustrated in Sect. 7 to generate two contextualizations for U-space environments. Finally, Sect. 8 summarizes the conclusions and discusses future work.

2   Background

Cybersecurity frameworks, which are heterogeneous tools that operate at various granularity levels, are widely used by organizations of all sizes to perform a security assessment at different levels of detail. Generally, a security assessment based on established frameworks initiates by identifying the proper activities to manage cyber risk, and then evaluates which security controls are already in place to pinpoint further countermeasures required to achieve the desired cybersecurity posture, also specifying how they have to be applied. Accordingly, the background covers two areas: an analysis of frameworks addressing the entire cybersecurity risk management process (e.g., CSF), and an analysis of frameworks focusing on security controls (e.g., CIS Critical Security Controls [4]).

2.1 Cybersecurity Risk Management Frameworks

As for the frameworks addressing the cybersecurity risk management process, the Framework Nazionale per la Cybersecurity e la Data Protection (FNCDP) [14], developed by the Cyber Intelligence and Information Security Research Center (CIS) of the University of Rome "La Sapienza" and National Cybersecurity Laboratory of the National Interuniversity Consortium for Informatics (CINI), offers an operational instrument for structuring cybersecurity processes suitable for any scale organizations. It draws inspiration from the CSF, which provides a common organizational structure for multiple cybersecurity approaches by combining standards, guidelines, and practices that work effectively, designed by the NIST. Accordingly, it inherits Framework Core, Implementation Tiers, and Profile from CSF, introducing new concepts: priority level; maturity levels; and contextualization. Framework Core is a set of information security activities, desired outcomes, and applicable references common to all sectors of critical infrastructure. Specifically, it involves: (i) functions, the main themes for strategically addressing cyber risk management; (ii) categories, activities to be implemented to address functions; (iii) subcategories, more specific activities to be implemented to address functions; and (iv) informative references, references linking each subcategory to security practices required by existing standards or regulations. Implementation Tiers provide context on how an organization views cybersecurity risk and the processes in place to manage that risk. A Profile represents the results based on business needs that an organization has selected from the categories and subcategories of the framework. Profiles can be used to identify opportunities to improve cybersecurity posture by comparing a current profile, which denotes the security level of the analyzed organization, with a target profile, which indicates the activities to achieve a certain level of cybersecurity. Priority level defines a priority in the implementation of specific enabling activities. Maturity levels define a measure of the maturity of security processes. Contextualization refers to a defined set of functions, categories, and subcategories of interest, each associated with a specific priority level and a set of maturity levels. More details are available in [14].

For risk assessment and treatment, organizations may also refer to ISO/IEC 27005 [2], which provides structured guidance on identifying, analyzing, evaluating, and treating information security risks within an Information Security Management System (ISMS), published by the International Organization for Standardization (ISO) and the International Electrotechnical Commission (IEC). Unlike ISO/IEC 27001 [1], which focuses on the overall ISMS framework and adopts a PDCA (Plan-Do-Check-Act) model, ISO/IEC 27005 addresses risk management in detail and can support the selection of appropriate controls based on identified risks. It is important to recognize that the frameworks are designed to support organizations and should not be seen as a substitute for compliance with current regulations.

2.2 Security Control Frameworks

As for the frameworks focusing on security controls, NIST Special Publication 800-53 (NIST SP 800-53) [17] is a comprehensive catalogue of security and privacy controls for information systems and organizations with the purpose of protecting organizations' operations, assets, individuals from various threats, developed by NIST. In line with the security areas they cover, they are organized into 20 families, each containing controls related to its specific theme. Furthermore, NIST provides Security Content Automation Protocol (SCAP) [19], a framework that leverages specific standards to enable automated vulnerability management, measurement, and policy compliance evaluation of systems deployed in an organization, facilitating the implementation of security controls. As part of the ISMS process, organizations that choose to use ISO/IEC 27001, may select controls and control objectives from the framework to address identified risks. The controls are divided into ten clauses, each of which can have multiple control objectives, and each objective is associated with different controls aimed at achieving it. CIS Critical Security Controls are a set of 20 prioritized actions that collectively provide a defense-in-depth approach to mitigate the most common attacks on systems and networks, developed by the Center for Internet Security (CIS). Each control is divided into sub-controls, which specify various aspects of each control in detail. CIS also defines Implementation Groups (IGs), self-assessed categories that help organizations select relevant controls based on their cybersecurity maturity and risk profile. Each IG builds upon the previous one: IG2 includes all IG1 controls, and IG3 includes those from both IG1 and IG2. Furthermore, CIS provides CIS Benchmarks [3], which are specific guidelines for the secure configuration of operating systems, software applications, and network devices, aiding organizations harden their technologies. AgID Minimum Security Measures [7] are practical guidelines (i.e. technological, organizational and procedural controls) to help Italian public administrations assess and enhance their IT security levels, developed by Agency for Digital Italy (AgID) with the support of CERT-AgID, the structure specialized in cybersecurity. These measures are organized into specific control groups, each addressing different aspects of information security, with their implementation that may be structured across three progressive levels: minimum; standard; and advanced.

3 Challenges in Literature and Contributions

As evidenced by the previous section, security assessment is a complex task due to the heterogeneity of cybersecurity frameworks. They vary in structure, level of detail, and applicability, making it difficult to develop a unified approach for evaluating security posture. Existing techniques for compliance checking and risk assessment, such as those proposed by NIST [15], rely on predefined checklists but lack adaptability to different frameworks. While some automation efforts exist, they primarily focus on verifying compliance rather than providing a structured mechanism for guiding organizations through security improvements. A comprehensive review by Leszczyna [13] categorizes security assessment methods into four groups: (i) testing methods; (ii) evaluation and analysis methods; (iii) examination and review methods; and (iv) interviewing methods. For instance, WASMBOX [5] enhances isolation and resource efficiency in multi-tenant and embedded environments, while PriSIEM [6] applies Trusted Execution Environments and Homomorphic Encryption to enable privacy-preserving monitoring. These approaches, however, mainly address runtime enforcement and monitoring aspects rather than structured assessment or compliance evaluation.

Our work does not align with operative groups, but the second group. Still, it focuses on compliance checking and formal analysis, as these methods are widely used to assess security controls but are currently limited in automation and adaptability.

Since our work is based on a cybersecurity frameworks, one of the main challenges in securing an infrastructure is the composition of different contextualizations (each reflecting distinct domain aspects). Current approaches often attempt to merge different security models, but this integration is not always feasible [24]. Inconsistencies and misalignments emerge when combining different frameworks, leading to gaps in security evaluations. Assessments remain fragmented without a structured method for unifying security-related information, limiting their effectiveness in real-world applications.

Another critical issue is the absence of a clear criterion for determining the gap between the current security profile and the target profile. Security assessment should not only verify compliance but also quantify how far a system is from its desired security state. While some studies, such as [9], propose model-based methodologies for cybersecurity risk assessment, they do not offer a systematic way to measure this gap.

Even when security gaps are identified, the lack of a well-defined roadmap for implementing security controls further complicates the process. Compliance-checking frameworks, such as CyberSPL [25], automate rule validation but do not guide organizations in prioritizing security measures or determining the order in which they should be implemented. Furthermore, as security requirements change, systems need to upgrade or migrate between profiles while ensuring that security measures remain effective. However, there is no established method for handling these transitions in a structured manner.

To address these challenges, we propose a set of automated algorithms that enhance security assessment and profile management. Our approach introduces a fusion mechanism to integrate different security contextualizations, overcoming the limitations of existing composition-based methods. We also define an evaluation algorithm that establishes a measurable criterion for assessing the gap between current and target security profiles, providing a structured basis for security assessment. Furthermore, we propose a profile upgrade mechanism that enables organizations to construct a clear security controls roadmap. Finally, we introduce a migration strategy that facilitates the change to a different contextualization, defining a new roadmap accordingly.

4   Cybersecurity Framework Categorization

Due to the heterogeneous nature of cybersecurity frameworks, their employment results in assessments at various levels, as shown from the analysis reported in [24]. Consequently, we propose a three-layer categorization that aims to associate each cybersecurity framework with the granularity level it addresses. On the one hand, this categorization should allow security analysts to have a comprehensive and clear overview of the cybersecurity frameworks; on the other hand, it should guide them in choosing the most suitable tool to perform a security assessment in line with their purposes. The three levels we defined are: (i) Framework Layer (FL); (ii) Control Layer (CL); and (iii) Assessment Layer (AL).

The FL operates at a strategic level, focusing on two key aspects. On the one hand, it defines the steps required to conduct a security assessment; on the other hand, it establishes a pathway for implementing or enhancing an organization's cybersecurity posture in line with its purposes. Therefore, FL is structured into two sub-levels: (i) methodological level (FL-M), which addresses the adoption phases or steps defined by the frameworks; and (ii) requirement level (FL-R), which encompasses the specific concepts and terminologies that each framework defines (e.g., contextualization, subcategories). So, the FL includes FNCDP, CSF, and ISO/IEC 27001. In detail, the phases required for adopting a framework address the FL-M; while the concepts and terminologies defined by each framework address the FL-R.

The CL also operates at a strategic level, defining what should be implemented in terms of security controls, best practices, and general guidelines to manage cyber risk. Accordingly, it encompasses frameworks that provide an overview of security policies and organizational measures, including: NIST SP 800-53, ISO/IEC 27001, CIS Critical Security Controls, and AgID Minimum Security Measures. So, CL helps organizations establish a robust security foundation by aligning strategic objectives with risk management priorities.

Each framework within the CL group security controls following a specific categorization (e.g., families, subcontrols) in line with the maturity level the security controls address. Accordingly, we have defined three maturity levels (i.e. minimum, standard, and advanced) and uniformed each framework based on these levels. This contribution should provide a common language and systematic methodology to establish the maturity of the security process and activities, facilitating communication and collaboration both within the organization and with external stakeholders. Table 1 summarizes our work. It is important to note that ISO/IEC 27001 does not provide maturity levels, but companies often rely on different levels (e.g., Capability Maturity Model (CMM) [18] or Control Objectives for Information and related Technology (COBIT) [26]).

Table 1. Framework Uniformity based on Maturity Level

	NIST SP 800-53	CIS Controls	AgID Measures
Minimum	Low Baseline	IG1	Minimum
Standard	Moderate Baseline	IG2	Standard
Advanced	High Baseline	IG3	Advanced

The AL functions at an operational level, focusing on how security controls are implemented, configured, and verified in practice. It provides detailed technical guidance and tools for hardening systems and automating compliance assessments. Consequently, this level includes frameworks such as CIS Benchmarks and NIST SCAP, which ensure that the strategic directives defined at the CL are effectively translated into actionable and measurable security measures. Figure 1 illustrates the discussed categorization and emphasizes the progression in granularity from FL to AL.

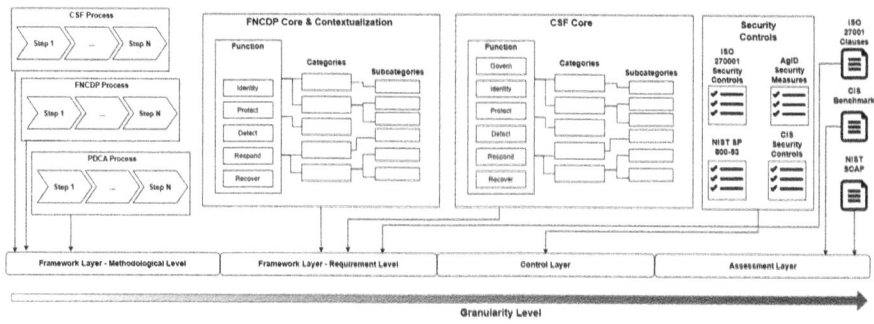

Fig. 1. Cybersecurity Framework Categorization.

5   Security Assessment Process Formalization

Before presenting the security assessment process, it is essential to define the formalism and notation that guides its analysis. Adopting a formal representation eliminates interpretative ambiguities by providing a rigorous and shared language, ensuring clarity and methodological reproducibility.

Let us denote the following: $\mathcal{C}$, a generic contextualization; $\mathcal{P}$, a current profile; $\mathcal{T}_{\mathcal{W}}$, the target profile with the overall maturity level $\mathcal{W}$; $\mathcal{R}_{\mathcal{W}}$, the security controls roadmap to achieve the target profile $\mathcal{T}_{\mathcal{W}}$; $\mathbb{S} = \{c_k\}$ the set of all N_S security controls with $k \in \{1, ..., N_S\}$; s_i, the i−th subcategory belonging to FNCDP, with $i \in \{1, ..., 117\}$; $\bar{c}_k$, the security controls array associated to s_i; p_j and m_j, the priority level and maturity level for s_i, respectively; $\overline{m}$ the array of maturity levels. Specifically, $\overline{c}_k = [c_{k_1}, c_{k_2}, ..., c_{k_L}]$ so that $c_{k_l} \in \mathbb{S}$ with $l \in \{1, ..., L\}$ and $1 \le L \le N_S$; $p_j \in \mathbb{P} = \{\mathcal{H}igh, Low, Medium\}$, the set of priority levels in line with FNCDP; $m_j \in \mathbb{M} = \{\mathcal{M}inimum, Standard, Advanced\}$, the set of maturity levels; $\overline{m} = [\mathcal{M}inimum, Standard, Advanced]$. It is worth noting that, in the proposed formalization, N_S includes all controls from the various frameworks under consideration, and 117 is the total number of subcategories defined in FNCDP.

A contextualization $\mathcal{C}$ involving N subcategories consists of an array of arrays, i.e.

$$\mathcal{C} = [[s_1, p_1, \overline{m}], [s_2, p_2, \overline{m}], ..., [s_N, p_N, \overline{m}]]. \tag{1}$$

$\mathcal{P}$, $\mathcal{T}_{\mathcal{W}}$ and $\mathcal{R}_{\mathcal{W}}$ are characterized by the same structure, i.e.

$$\mathcal{P} = [[s_1, p_1, m_1, \overline{c}_1], [s_2, p_2, m_2, \overline{c}_2], ..., [s_N, p_N, m_N, \overline{c}_N]]. \tag{2}$$

$$\mathcal{T}_{\mathcal{W}} = [[s_1, p_1, m_1, \overline{c}_1], [s_2, p_2, m_2, \overline{c}_2], ..., [s_N, p_N, m_N, \overline{c}_N]]. \tag{3}$$

$$\mathcal{R}_{\mathcal{W}} = [[s_1, p_1, m_1, \overline{c}_1], [s_2, p_2, m_2, \overline{c}_2], ..., [s_N, p_N, m_N, \overline{c}_N]]. \tag{4}$$

With respect to $\mathcal{C}$, each element of $\mathcal{P}$, $\mathcal{T}_{\mathcal{W}}$ and $\mathcal{R}_{\mathcal{W}}$ also includes a security controls array $\overline{c}$. Indeed, according to the definition of contextualization, it does not include security controls. Additionally, each item of $\mathcal{P}$, $\mathcal{T}_{\mathcal{W}}$ and $\mathcal{R}_{\mathcal{W}}$, replaces $\overline{m}$ with m_j. Indeed, our approach - described in Sect. 6 - involves that each s_i of $\mathcal{C}$ have to include the set of all maturity levels, which will be determined when a profile is defined.

Instead, the difference between $\mathcal{P}$, $\mathcal{T}_{\mathcal{W}}$ and $\mathcal{R}_{\mathcal{W}}$ is represented by $\overline{c}$: in the first case, for each element of $\mathcal{P}$, it refers to implemented security controls for s_i; in the second one, for each element of $\mathcal{T}_{\mathcal{W}}$, it refers to the set of security controls that must be implemented for s_i to have a target profile with the overall maturity level $\mathcal{W}$; in the third case, for each element of $\mathcal{R}_{\mathcal{W}}$, it refers the missing security controls that are necessary to implement to reach the wished target profile.

6   Security Assessment Process

A security assessment process, typically performed by a security analyst, involves several activities that provide a complete overview of the security level of the analyzed target, proposing the security countermeasures that should be implemented to improve its security level. In this section, following FNCDP as a baseline, we propose a description of a security assessment process detailing our contributions to support its automation. Figure 2 illustrates the step-by-step process, highlighting our contributions, and showing how the framework categorization supports the process.

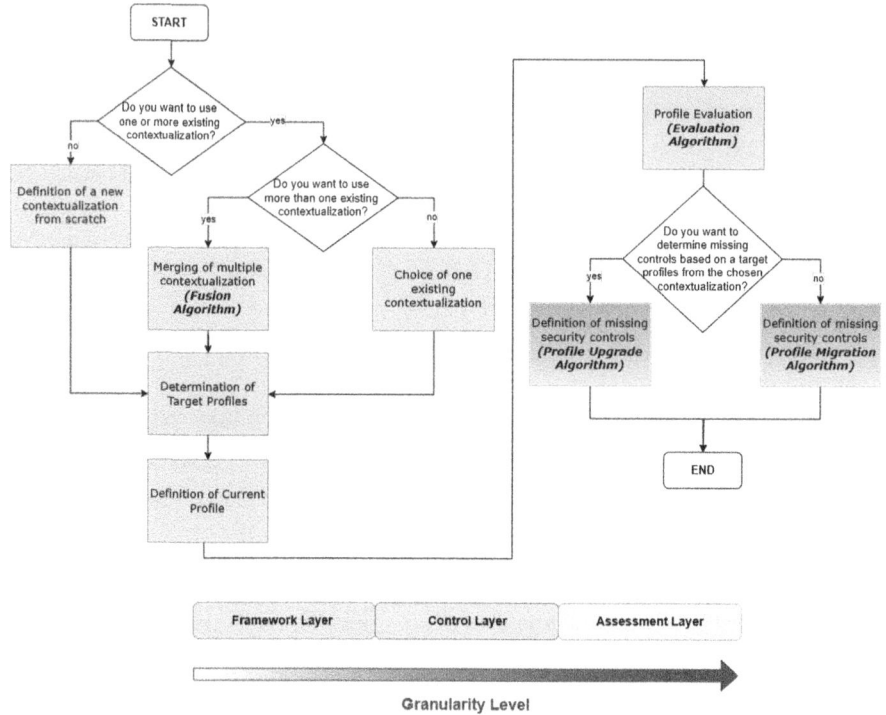

Fig. 2. Security Assessment Process.

6.1 Contextualization Definition

To improve the cybersecurity posture of a system under analysis using an app-roach based on a framework, it is first necessary to identify the proper contex-tualization, which consists of a set of subcategories - compliant with the ana-lyzed domain - each equipped with a priority level and a set of maturity levels. Some contextualizations are available in the literature, such as the GDPR (Gen-eral Data Protection Regulation) [11] contextualization [14]; however, a security analyst, in accordance with its purposes, may create a new one using specific criteria or merge more existing contextualizations. Specifically, the merger of more contextualizations aims to support an organization that wants to integrate contextualization belonging to different domains. Here, the idea is to obtain a contextualization involving all subcategories belonging to two or more existing contextualizations. So, we define the *fusion algorithm*, which is described below.

When a contextualization $\mathcal{C}$ is defined from scratch, the priority level for each s_i can be determined according to the criteria described in [8]. Here, a *high* prior-ity level is automatically assigned to all subcategories related to data protection or regulatory issues. For the remaining subcategories, to distinguish between *medium* and *low* priority levels, the authors propose a questions-and-answers approach focusing on: (i) the number of involved entities; (ii) the economic cost of the implementation; and (iii) the time required for the implementation. In detail, three questions are posed for each subcategory, with each answer being assigned a score ranging from 1 to 5. The final p_j is then determined by computing the average of these scores: if the average score is less than 3, the subcategory is classified as having a *medium* priority level; if it is equal to or greater than 3, it is classified as having a *low* priority level.

The *fusion algorithm* takes as input two contextualizations C_1 and C_2 and generates a new contextualization C_3, which is the result of the fusion of C_1 and C_2. It works by comparing the indeces of each subcategory s_i - of C_1 - with those of each s_l - of C_2 -. In detail, if i is lower than l, s_i will be added to C_3; if i is greater than l, s_l will be added to C_3; if i is equal to l, each item of s_i and s_l needs to be analyzed. Since i is equal to l, the subcategory that will be added to C_3 may be indistinctly s_i or s_l; p_j will be the higher priority between s_i and s_l; instead, $\overline{m}$ will be determined through the union of the maturity level array $\overline{m}_i$ belonging to s_i with the maturity level array $\overline{m}_l$ belonging to s_l. Lastly, when the items of one contextualization are over, the ones of the other contextualization will be added to C_3.

6.2   Target Profiles Determination

The target profiles represent the desired profiles in terms of cybersecurity posture. On one hand, they allow to determine the gap among the current profile and the desired profile; on the other hand, they support the definition of the security controls roadmap. Here, they are determined in compliance with the three maturity levels defined in Sect. 4. Accordingly, three target profiles are available: minimum target profile (i.e., $\mathcal{T_M}$), in which all minimum security countermeasures are implemented; standard target profile (i.e., $\mathcal{T_S}$), in which all minimum and standard security countermeasures are implemented; and the advanced target profile (i.e., $\mathcal{T_A}$), in which all security countermeasures are implemented.

The definition of $\mathcal{T_W}$, initiates from the chosen contextualization C. In detail, the following steps apply: (i) to select a subcategory s_i belonging to C; (ii) to define p_j, which may either align with the C or differ from it; (iii) to establish m_j according to $\mathcal{T_W}$ (i.e., if $\mathcal{T_W} = \mathcal{T_M}$, s_i will have *minimum* as maturity level); (iv) to add $[s_i, p_j, m_j, \overline{c}_k]$ to $\mathcal{T_W}$. Iterating for each s_i, $\mathcal{T_W}$ will be determined. However, a security analyst may choose to select subcategories and priority levels that align with the considered contextualization.

6.3   Current Profile Definition

The determination of the current profile $\mathcal{P}$ of the analyzed system also initiates from the identified contextualization C. In detail, the following steps have to be performed: (i) to select a subcategory s_i; (ii) to define p_j, which may either align with the C or differ from it; (iii) to define the set of security controls $\overline{c}_k$ implemented for s_i within the analyzed system; (iv) to determine m_j considering the implemented security controls. Specifically, m_j is determined through the criteria described in [8]: a subcategory s_i is assigned a specific maturity level m_j

if all security controls corresponding to m_j are fully implemented. At this point, $[s_i, p_j, m_j, \bar{c}_k]$ can be added to $\mathcal{P}$. Iterating for each s_i, $\mathcal{P}$ will be defined.

6.4 Current Profile Evaluation

Through the evaluation of the current profile, a security analyst should have an idea about the security level of the analyzed profile. Specifically, this step aims to associate an overall maturity level to the current profile. To address this step, we started from the algorithm described in [8]. Here, the authors propose to define the security level by means an evaluation of the subcategories' maturity levels, where the security level is equal to the lowest maturity level among the maturity levels linked with individual subcategories.

The *evaluation algorithm* works comparing the security controls implemented in the current profile $\mathcal{P}$ with those required for each target profile $\mathcal{T_W}$, starting from the $\mathcal{T_W}$ at the lowest level. Therefore, it takes as input four profiles: the current profile, i.e. $\mathcal{P}$; the target profile with the minimum level, i.e. $\mathcal{T_M}$; the target profile with standard level, i.e. $\mathcal{T_S}$; and the target profile with advanced level, i.e. $\mathcal{T_A}$.

The following steps are automatically performed to evaluate $\mathcal{P}$: (i) to select subcategory s_i for $\mathcal{P}$; (ii) to select subcategory s_l for the lowest target profile $\mathcal{T_W}$ so that $i = l$; (iii) to compare the security controls c_{k_l} implemented in s_i with the security controls c_{k_l} that have to be implemented in s_l; (iv) if at least one c_{k_l} associated to s_l is not implemented in the s_i, the overall maturity level of $\mathcal{P}$ will be *insufficient* and the algorithm ends; otherwise, the indices i and l have to be incremented and the algorithm restarts from the (i). When each s_i has been analyzed, the overall maturity level of $\mathcal{P}$ will be the lowest (i.e., *minimum*) and the algorithm restarts from (i), but considering the next target profile above. Clearly, if at least one c_{k_l} related to $\mathcal{T_W}$ is not implemented in $\mathcal{P}$, the overall maturity level will be the maturity level related to the analyzed target profile and the algorithm ends. Lastly, it is worth noting that, if the algorithm does not end, the comparison goes on till the last maturity level.

6.5 Determination of a Security Controls Roadmap

Starting from the overall maturity level related to $\mathcal{P}$, security analyst may upgrade $\mathcal{P}$ to the next maturity level by implementing missing security controls.

The algorithm we propose, referred to as *profile upgrade algorithm*, takes as input the current profile $\mathcal{P}$ and the target profile to reach $\mathcal{T_W}$, and works similarly with the *evaluation algorithm* through the comparison of the security controls c_{k_l} implemented in the current profile $\mathcal{P}$, with those required for the desired target profile $\mathcal{T_W}$. In detail, the following steps applies: (i) to select subcategory s_i for $\mathcal{P}$; (ii) to select subcategory s_l for the target profile to reach $\mathcal{T_W}$ so that $i = l$; (iii) to compare the security controls c_{k_l} implemented in s_i with the security controls c_{k_l} that have to be implemented in s_l; (iv) if all c_{k_l} are implemented, the indices i and l have to be incremented and the algorithm restarts from the (i), thus analyzing the next subcategory; otherwise, if at least one c_{k_l} is not implemented in s_i, $[s_l, p_j, m_j, \overline{c}_k]$ is added to $\mathcal{R}_\mathcal{W}$ with $\overline{c}_k$ including only the missing security controls. When all subcategories have been analyzed, the roadmap is complete, and the security analyst may start to implement the missing security controls to achieve the desired target profile.

It is worth noting that, during the security assessment process, a security analyst may want to generate a security controls roadmap based on a target profile from a different contextualization than the one used in the process. To address this, we defined a procedure, referred to as *profile migration algorithm*. Accordingly, it takes as input $\mathcal{P}$ from contextualization $\mathcal{C}_\mathcal{A}$, and the target profile to reach (i.e., $\mathcal{T}_\mathcal{W}$) from contextualization $\mathcal{C}_\mathcal{B}$. It works just like the *profile upgrade algorithm* but it also considers the subcategories that lack in $\mathcal{P}$. Specifically, in this case, each missing subcategory is marked as N/A, and $[s_l, p_j, m_j, \overline{c}_k]$ is added to $\mathcal{R}_\mathcal{W}$. Therefore, when the security level of the analyzed profile have to be upgraded, a security analyst must first implement the missing subcategories and then the related security controls.

7   Case Study

To examine some preliminary results, we generated two contextualizations for U-space environments. U-space is a European initiative designed to enable the management and integration of Unmanned Aerial Vehicles (UAVs), commonly known as drones, into airspace [23]. Specifically, U-space is a framework that supports UAV operations and provides a clear and effective interface with crewed aviation through fully automated drone-management systems [22]. With the revolution brought by U-space, drones are poised to transform both physical and cyberspace, giving rise to an ever-evolving threat landscape marked by significant cybersecurity risks. On one hand, U-space comprises a large number of cyber-physical systems that are inherently vulnerable to cyber threats; on the other hand, UAVs could be exploited as both physical and cyber weapons to target critical assets. Furthermore, drone-related incidents may cause different kinds of disruptions, potentially impacting public areas, essential infrastructure, and individuals' right to privacy [12]. These factors underscore the necessity to make U-space security a top priority. Consequently, it is essential to adopt a systematic and comprehensive approach to effectively handle security risks, as well as to establish and prioritize relevant activities, which are those whose implementation aids to address the risks. From an operational perspective, following a framework-based approach, results in the specification and prioritization of relevant subcategories (i.e., contextualization generation) for each function of the chosen framework.

However, to overcome the aforementioned limitations, the two U-space contextualizations have been generated through SAM-CyFra[1], a web application developed to implement the security assessment process detailed in Sect. 6. Building on FNCDP as baseline, SAM-CyFra extends FNCDP by incorporating the

---

[1] https://github.com/VSecLab/SAM-CyFra.

Table 2. Abstract of $\mathcal{C}_U$

Function	Category	Subcategory	Priority Level	Maturity Level
Identify (ID)	Data Management (DP-ID.DM)	DP-ID.DM-5: The processes for international data transfer are defined, implemented, and documented.	HIGH	Insufficient; Minimum, Standard, Advanced
Protect (PR)	Identity Management, Authentication and Access Control (PR.AC)	PR.AC-1: Digital identities and access credentials for users, devices, and authorized processes are managed, verified, revoked, and subjected to security audits.	LOW	Insufficient; Minimum, Standard, Advanced
	Identity Management, Authentication and Access Control (PR.AC)	PR.AC-2: Interdependencies and essential functions for the provision of critical services are identified and made known.	MEDIUM	Insufficient; Minimum, Standard, Advanced
	Information Protection Processes and Procedures (PR.IP)	PR.IP-5: Policies and regulations related to the physical environments where the organization's resources operate are respected.	HIGH	Insufficient; Minimum, Standard, Advanced
Respond (RS)	Response Planning (RS.RP)	RS.RP-1: A response plan exists and is executed during or after an incident.	LOW	Insufficient; Minimum, Standard, Advanced

fusion algorithm, the *evaluation algorithm*, the *profile migration algorithm*, and the *profile upgrade algorithm*. These enhancements enable automation of key steps in the security assessment processes, allowing to: automatically define contextualizations; guide the security analyst in the determination of target and current profiles based on the selected contextualization; automatically evaluate the current profile; automatically identify the missing security controls required to achieve a specific target profile. By providing a structured, three-layered approach to security, SAM-CyFRA assists security analysts evaluating the cybersecurity posture of a system, effectively addressing the inefficiencies and limitations of manual assessment approaches. SAM-CyFra features a client-server architecture and is developed in Python using the Django framework.

Specifically, we generated a U-space contextualization - $\mathcal{C}_U$ - from scratch; and then we applied *fusion algorithm* between $\mathcal{C}_U$ and GDPR contextualization - $\mathcal{C}_{GDPR}$ - to obtain $\mathcal{C}_{U-GDPR}$. Indeed, as far as we are aware, there are neither U-space-specific contextualizations nor adaptable contextualizations for U-space environments. It is important to highlight that both $\mathcal{C}_U$ and $\mathcal{C}_{U-GDPR}$ may be used by a security analyst to conduct a security assessment. Specifically, $\mathcal{C}_U$

Table 3. Abstract of $\mathcal{C}_{U-GDPR}$

Function	Category	Subcategory	Priority Level	Maturity Level
Identify (ID)	Data Management (DP-ID.DM)	`DP-ID.DM-5`: The processes for international data transfer are defined, implemented, and documented.	HIGH	Insufficient; Minimum, Standard, Advanced
Protect (PR)	Identity Management, Authentication and Access Control (PR.AC)	`PR.AC-1`: Digital identities and access credentials for users, devices, and authorized processes are managed, verified, revoked, and subjected to security audits.	HIGH	Insufficient; Minimum, Standard, Advanced
	Identity Management, Authentication and Access Control (PR.AC)	`PR.AC-2`: Interdependencies and essential functions for the provision of critical services are identified and made known.	HIGH	Insufficient; Minimum, Standard, Advanced
	Information Protection Processes and Procedures (PR.IP)	`PR.IP-5`: Policies and regulations related to the physical environments where the organization's resources operate are respected.	HIGH	Insufficient; Minimum, Standard, Advanced
Respond (RS)	Response Planning (RS.RP)	`RS.RP-1`: A response plan exists and is executed during or after an incident.	HIGH	Insufficient; Minimum, Standard, Advanced

may be used to evaluate U-space solutions not particularly critical (e.g., architectural photography in U-space environments [10]); instead, $\mathcal{C}_{U-GDPR}$ may be used in more critical solutions in which managed and exchanged data are particularly sensitive (e.g., pharmaceutical delivery in U-space environments [10]). To generate $\mathcal{C}_U$, we first have selected the relevant subcategories for the considered domain. Then, for each s_i, the priority level and the available maturity levels have been assigned according to what previous described. Specifically, `DP-ID.DM-5` and `PR.IP-5` have a *high* priority level since they involve data transfer and regulatory compliance, respectively. In contrast, `PR.AC-1` and `RS.RP-1` have a *low* priority level. While these activities are certainly crucial, their implementation is more complex and needs significant resources and time with respect to other activities. In particular, `PR.AC-1` involves multiple entities (i.e., users, devices, and processes), requiring technological solutions and audit processes, which means considerable costs and time. Similarly, `RS.RP-1` requires a significant commitment in terms of both economic resources and time. Lastly, `PR.AC-2` has a *medium* priority level since its implementation involves fewer entities (such as physical access systems and locks), is less costly compared to complex digital identity management solutions, and requires less implementation time. Table 2 reports an abstract of C_U. Then, by providing C_U and C_{GDPR} as input to the *fusion algorithm*, C_{U-GDPR} has been generated. Table 3 presents an abstract of C_{U-GDPR}, maintaining the same subcategories shown in Table 2 to highlight how the algorithm works. Indeed, the subcategories PR.AC-1, PR.AC-2, and RS.RP-1, which have *low, medium,* and *low* priority level in C_U, now have a *high* priority level, as they are assigned a *high* priority level in C_{GDPR}. Furthermore, since C_{GDPR} does not specify maturity levels, each subcategory in C_{U-GDPR} aligns with the three possible maturity levels previously defined. The outcomes have been validated by engaging representative U-space experts and stakeholders.

8   Conclusion

Cybersecurity frameworks have been developed to help organizations assess and strengthen their security practices, promoting a proactive and strategic approach to risk management. However, they are heterogeneous tools that function at various granularity levels and generally rely on manual assessment processes, with all the limitations of manual evaluations. Additionally, they are characterized by significant challenges in terms of complexity, scalability, and adaptability. To address these challenges, this work introduced SAM-CyFra, a system designed to automate and streamline the management of cybersecurity frameworks. To examine some preliminary results, SAM-CyFra has been used to generate two contextualizations for U-space environments: C_U and C_{U-GDPR}. While C_U was created from scratch, C_{U-GDPR} resulted from applying the *fusion algorithm* between C_U and C_{GDPR}. Both may be used by security analysts as starting points to evaluate U-space critical solutions, as well as U-space not critical solutions.

In future work, we plan to refine our approach by including modeling techniques to automatically generate a profile from a model of the analyzed system. An enhancement can involve different and detailed case studies in order to show the effectiveness of our approach. Additionally, we envisage establishing a criterion for developing a security controls roadmap that, starting from countermeasures targeting the most critical risks, suggests the necessary countermeasures based on the extent to which each mitigates those risks.

Acknowledgments. We would like to thank the experts and stakeholders of the Italian Aerospace Research Centre (CIRA) for their invaluable contribution to the case study that significantly enhanced this work. We are especially grateful to MSc. Lucia Migliaccio for her contributions. This work was partially supported by the SERICS project (PE00000014) âĂŞ Spoke 2 "Misinformation and Fakes" (D43C22003050001) and the SecCo-OC project (D33C22001300002), within the SERICS framework, both funded by Italian MUR. Additional support was provided by the DEFEDGE project (E53D23016380001) under the PRIN program, funded by the Italian MUR.

Disclosure of Interests. The authors have no competing interests to declare that are relevant to the content of this article.

References

1. ISO/IEC 27001:2013 information technology – security techniques – information security management systems – requirements. Tech. Rep. 27001:2013 (2013)
2. ISO/IEC 27005:2022 information security, cybersecurity and privacy protection guidance on managing information security risks. Tech. rep. (2022), https://www.iso.org/standard/80585.html, adopted in Europe as EN ISO/IEC 27005:2024
3. CIS Benchmarks. https://www.cisecurity.org/cis-benchmarks, April 2024, [online]
4. Center for Internet Security: CIS Controls, Version 7.1 (2019). http://www.cis.org
5. Coppolino, L., D'Antonio, S., Mazzeo, G., Nardone, R., Romano, L., Schmitt, M.: Wasmbox: a lightweight wasm-based runtime for trustworthy multi-tenant embedded systems. IEEE Trans. Emerging Top. Comput., 1–14 (2024). https://doi.org/10.1109/TETC.2024.3409817
6. Coppolino, L., D Antonio, S., Mazzeo, G., Romano, L., Sgaglione, L.: Prisiem: enabling privacy-preserving managed security services. J. Network Comput. Appl. **203**, 103397 (2022). https://doi.org/10.1016/j.jnca.2022.103397, https://www.sciencedirect.com/science/article/pii/S108480452200056X
7. DI MASSIMO, D.: Misure minime di sicurezza ict per le pubbliche amministrazioni (2019)
8. Elia, R., Granata, D., Rak, M.: Threat analysis and security assessment of an HPC system. In: Gang, L., Joaquim, F., Zhiwei, X. (eds.) Communications in Computer and Information Science. Springer International Publishing (2025). forthcoming
9. Elia, R., Rak, M., Pascarella, D.: A First Step Towards an Automated Methodology for the Security Risk Assessment of U-Space Solutions. In: 2024 IEEE 21st International Conference on Mobile Ad-Hoc and Smart Systems (MASS), pp. 676–681 (2024)https://doi.org/10.1109/MASS62177.2024.00108
10. EUROCONTROL: U-space ConOps and architecture (edition 4). CORUS-XUAM Project Deliverable D4.2, 01.00.02, July 2023. https://www.sesarju.eu/sites/default/files/documents/reports/U-space%20CONOPS%204th%20edition.pdf
11. European Parliament and Council of the European Union: General Data Protection Regulation (GDPR) Regulation (EU) 2016/679. Tech. Rep. L 119, European Union, May 2016. https://eur-lex.europa.eu/eli/reg/2016/679/oj, official Journal of the European Union, pp. 1–88
12. Karlos, V., Larcher, M.: Protection against Unmanned Aircraft Systems. Handbook on UAS risk assessment and principles for physical hardening of buildings and sites. Tech. rep., Joint Research Centre (European Commission) (2023). https://doi.org/10.2760/969680, https://op.europa.eu/en/publication-detail/-/publication/21cb95e2-6bca-11ee-9220-01aa75ed71a1/language-en
13. Leszczyna, R.: Review of cybersecurity assessment methods: applicability perspective. Comput. Secur. **108**, 102376 (2021). https://doi.org/10.1016/j.cose.2021.102376
14. Angelini, M., Ciccotelli, C., Franchina, L., Spaccamela, A.M., Querzoni, L.: Framework Nazionale per la Cybersecurity e la Data Protection. White Paper, CIS-Sapienza, CINI Cybersecurity National Lab (Feb (2019))
15. Mell, P.: The nist definition of cloud computing. NIST Special Publication, pp. 800–145 (2011)
16. National Institute of Standards and Technology: Framework for improving critical infrastructure cybersecurity. NIST Cybersecurity Framework Version 1.1 NIST CSWP 04162018, National Institute of Standards and Technology (2018). https://nvlpubs.nist.gov/nistpubs/CSWP/NIST.CSWP.04162018.pdf

17. National Institute of Standards and Technology: Security and Privacy Controls for Federal Information Systems and Organizations. Tech. Rep. SP 800-53 Revision 5, National Institute of Standards and Technology (2020). https://doi.org/10.6028/NIST.SP.800-53r5

18. Paulk, M.C., Curtis, B., Chrissis, M.B., Weber, C.V.: Capability maturity model, version 1.1. IEEE Softw. **10**(4), 18–27 (1993)

19. Quinn, S., Waltermire, D., Johnson, C., Scarfone, K., Banghart, J.: The technical specification for the security content automation protocol (scap): Scap version 1.0. Tech. Rep. 800-126, National Institute of Standards and Technology (NIST), Gaithersburg, MD (2009). https://doi.org/10.6028/NIST.SP.800-126, https://doi.org/10.6028/NIST.SP.800-126

20. Ross, R., Pillitteri, V., Graubart, R., Bodeau, D., Mcquaid, R.: Developing cyber-resilient systems: a systems security engineering approach. Tech. Rep. 800-160, Volume 2 Revision 1, National Institute of Standards and Technology (2021). https://doi.org/10.6028/NIST.SP.800-160v2r1

21. Saritac, U., Liu, X., Wang, R.: Assessment of cybersecurity framework in critical infrastructures. In: 2022 IEEE Delhi Section Conference (DELCON), pp. 1–4 (2022). https://doi.org/10.1109/DELCON54057.2022.9753250

22. SESAR JU: European ATM Master Plan. Digitalising Europe's Aviation Infrastructure. Executive view. 2020 Edition (2020). https://doi.org/10.2829/695700, https://www.sesarju.eu/sites/default/files/documents/reports/European%20ATM%20Master%20Plan%202020%20Exec%20View.pdf

23. SESAR JU: U?space. Supporting safe and secure drone operations in Europe. Consolidated report on SESAR U?space research and innovation results (2020). https://doi.org/10.2829/55322, https://www.sesarju.eu/sites/default/files/documents/reports/U-space%20research%20innovation%20results.pdf

24. Syafrizal, M., Selamat, S.R., Zakaria, N.A.: Analysis of cybersecurity standard and framework components. Int. J. Commun. Networks Inf. Secur. **12**(3), 417–432 (2020)

25. Varela-Vaca, A.J., Gasca, R.M., Ceballos, R., G mez-L pez, M.T., Torres, P.B.: Cyberspl: a framework for the verification of cybersecurity policy compliance of system configurations using software product lines. Appl. Sci. **9**(24) (2019). https://doi.org/10.3390/app9245364, https://www.mdpi.com/2076-3417/9/24/5364

26. Wolden, M., Valverde, R., Talla, M.: The effectiveness of cobit 5 information security framework for reducing cyber attacks on supply chain management system. IFAC-PapersOnLine **48**(3), 1846–1852 (2015). https://doi.org/10.1016/j.ifacol.2015.06.355. https://www.sciencedirect.com/science/article/pii/S2405896315005947 IFAC Symposium onInformation Control Problems in Manufacturing

An Intelligent Network Fuzzer for Protocol Testing in Healthcare Systems

Manh-Dung Nguyen[1]([✉])[iD], Huu Nghia Nguyen[1][iD], Lethycia Maia de Souza[1][iD], Stylianos Karagiannis[2,3][iD], Ana Rosa Cavalli[1][iD], and Edgardo Montes de Oca[1][iD]

[1] Montimage EURL, 37 rue Bobillot, 75013 Paris, France
{manhdung.nguyen,huunghia.nguyen}@montimage.eu
[2] PDMFC, Rua Fradesso da Silveira, n. 4, Piso 1 B, 1300-609 Lisbon, Portugal
[3] Department of Informatics, Ionian University, Plateia Tsirigoti 7, 49100 Corfu, Greece

Abstract. Testing the robustness and security of network protocol implementations is essential across all domains. We present NETWORK-FUZZER, a generic, feedback-driven network fuzzer designed to test and analyze protocol implementations by operating directly on real traffic. Unlike traditional code coverage-based fuzzers, NETWORKFUZZER works at the network level and employs a closed-loop fuzzing mechanism that dynamically adapts based on server responses. The system incorporates three key components: (i) response-aware fuzzing operators that perform protocol-specific packet mutations, (ii) a Conditional Tabular GAN (CTGAN) model that learns from both normal and abnormal traffic to generate diverse and protocol-compliant test cases, and (iii) Large Language Models (LLMs) that automate the generation of testing rules from protocol specifications. While NETWORKFUZZER is protocol-agnostic and applicable to a wide range of network protocols, in this paper we focus on its application to the Digital Imaging and Communications in Medicine (DICOM) protocol, which is commonly used for medical image exchange, to demonstrate its utility in healthcare cybersecurity. Our evaluation shows that NETWORKFUZZER effectively executes real-world attacks and generates realistic synthetic traffic, thus enhancing the robustness of testing and training for security systems.

Keywords: Network Fuzzing · Traffic Engineering · Attack Injection · GAN · LLM · DICOM Protocol Testing · Synthetic Traffic

1 Introduction

Context. Medical imaging is a cornerstone of modern healthcare, essential for accurate diagnosis, treatment planning, and patient management. The DICOM protocol serves as the global standard for the exchange, storage, and retrieval of medical images and related data [8]. By enabling interoperability among diverse medical imaging devices and systems, DICOM ensures that healthcare providers can efficiently access and interpret imaging data, regardless of the vendor or

F. Skopik et al. (Eds.): ARES 2025 Workshops, LNCS 15999, pp. 213–231, 2025.
https://doi.org/10.1007/978-3-032-00644-8_13

institution. Central to the DICOM ecosystem is the Picture Archiving and Communication System (PACS), which facilitates the secure storage, retrieval, and distribution of medical images and associated information. Even though PACS is not directly connected to the internet, it can still be vulnerable via internal networks. Exposed PACS servers face significant risks, such as network intrusions, denial-of-service attacks, and other threats that compromise the confidentiality, integrity, and availability of medical images [13, 24].

Recent years have revealed critical vulnerabilities within DICOM systems, exposing them to potential cyberattacks [1, 3, 12]. These vulnerabilities threaten both the confidentiality of sensitive patient data and the integrity of medical images, which are vital for clinical decision-making. For instance, in 2017, researchers from Massachusetts General Hospital discovered thousands of unprotected DICOM servers worldwide, including hundreds in the United States, leaving patient information vulnerable to unauthorized access [12]. These incidents highlight the alarming consequences of inadequate security measures in DICOM implementations. Given the critical role of DICOM in healthcare and its growing exposure to sophisticated cyber threats, this underscores the importance of adopting advanced solutions, such as smart network fuzzers, to systematically probe DICOM systems for flaws.

Challenges. Several studies have been conducted on the detection and prediction of cyberattacks in stateful protocols [11, 16] and in DICOM server implementation, such as the DCMTK library [23]. There is a lack of open-source solutions that enable the manual creation or editing of existing DICOM network protocol packets and their injection into a network, allowing researchers and practitioners to easily test proposed detection schemes. Tools like TCPREPLAY, SCAPY, and others have been employed for network testing, but they exhibit limitations when applied to the DICOM protocol. An open-source tool, 5GREPLAY, was recently introduced to forward network packets - unmodified or with basic modifications - between network interface cards (NICs) to trigger abnormal behaviors, provides an effective solution to fuzz testing 5G network [21] and HTTP/2 [10], extending this tool to test new protocols is not straightforward. Although, this tool has some limitations, as detailed below:

C1 **Lack of context-awareness.** 5GREPLAY does not account for the server's responses after injecting packets, resulting in a lack of context-awareness that could otherwise improve the precision and effectiveness of the injections. DICOM is a stateful protocol where interactions between the client and server involve specific sequences and negotiations (e.g., A-ASSOCIATE and P-DATA). Without dynamically analyzing server responses, critical insights are missed, limiting the accuracy of the tests. Furthermore, 5GREPLAY supports only a limited set of basic atomic operations, such as deleting or duplicating packets and modifying attributes [21]. It lacks critical capabilities, such as reordering packets or dynamically adjusting attributes based on server feedback, which are essential for comprehensive protocol testing.

C2 **Lack of intelligent fuzzing mechanisms.** The absence of AI mechanisms in 5GREPLAY limits its ability to adapt to dynamic and complex protocol behaviors. Modern protocols like DICOM involve hierarchical data structures and stateful communications that require sophisticated and intelligent fuzzing strategies to uncover vulnerabilities. Incorporating AI, such as a GAN-based smart fuzzer, can enable the automated generation of diverse and realistic malformed packets.

C3 Manually crafting test rules. Manually crafting test rules for protocol validation is a time-intensive and error-prone process, particularly for complex protocols like DICOM, which include intricate attribute hierarchies, nested data structures, and strict communication sequences. The reliance on manual rule generation limits scalability and introduces potential human biases and oversights.

Proposal. In this paper, we introduce NETWORKFUZZER, a smart fuzzer for network traffic protocol, with a focus on the DICOM protocol. Unlike existing coverage-based fuzzers that rely on code coverage to generate new inputs for testing server binary executables [7,9,17,20], our smart fuzzer is designed to test the network functionalities of the DICOM protocol with respect to its specifications. The core idea is to alter network packets either online or offline in a highly flexible manner, inject them into the server, and adapt the modification process based on the server's responses, thereby creating an efficient *closed-loop fuzzing* mechanism. To address thee challenges mentioned above, we design and build NETWORKFUZZER on top of 5GREPLAY with following extensions: (i) takes into account server's responses for an efficient fuzzing closed-loop with new atomic operators, (ii) incorporates a GAN approach for generating diverse and realistic test cases by learning patterns from both normal and abnormal network traffic, and (iii) employs LLMs to automate the generation of security testing rules.

The fuzzer uses server responses after each injection to guide a feedback-driven fuzzing loop that refines packet modifications in real time. By analyzing reactions, such as errors, state transitions or server-related metrics, NETWORKFUZZER adapts its strategy to better explore protocol behaviors and uncover hidden vulnerabilities. Furthermore, the GAN-based fuzzer enhances protocol testing by generating realistic packets that closely mimic valid traffic but with variations to expose edge-case vulnerabilities. It also leverages known DICOM attack patterns to craft malicious traffic, supporting both vulnerability discovery and the creation of synthetic datasets for training AI-based Intrusion Detection and Prevention Systems (IDPS) [18,19]. Finally, NETWORKFUZZER integrates LLMs to automate the generation of testing rules from protocol documentation, boosting both efficiency and accuracy while reducing manual effort.

Contributions. Our contributions are as follows.

– We design and implement NETWORKFUZZER, which is an open-source fuzzer for modifying and replaying any protocol network traffic using attack injection, fuzzing and generative AI.

- We evaluate the effectiveness of NETWORKFUZZER in real-world healthcare scenarios, demonstrating its ability to test DICOM servers and enhance network security testing.
- We construct a dataset containing DICOM traffic in pcap format to facilitate the analysis and testing of DICOM servers and security tools.

The rest of this paper is organized as follows. Section 2 provides a background on the DICOM protocol and discusses relevant work in this research area. Next, Sect. 3 discusses the design of NETWORKFUZZER to address challenges **C1-C3**. We then present the implementation and evaluate our tool in different scenarios for Sect. 4. Finally, Sect. 5 concludes the paper and offers insight into potential future directions for research and development.

2   Background & Related Work

We provide a brief overview of the DICOM protocol to understand the process of connection establishment, discuss related approaches for protocol testing, especially the network fuzzer 5GREPLAY, and then delve into our framework and its extensions in Sect. 3.

2.1   DICOM Protocol

The DICOM protocol is an application-layer standard designed for the exchange, storage, and retrieval of medical images, typically in the DICOM format. Operating over the TransmissionControl Protocol (TCP), DICOM ensures reliable and stateful communication between healthcare devices, such as PACS, imaging modalities, and workstations.

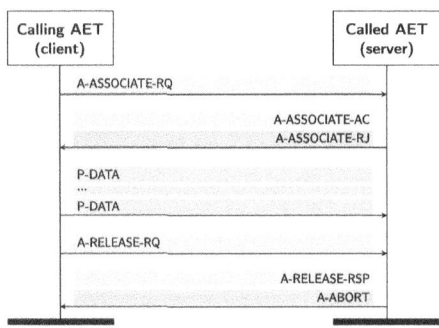

Fig. 1. DICOM basic communication protocol between a Calling AET (client) and a Called AET (server) with Association/Release , Error and Data Transfer packets.

DICOM Communication. Figure 1 illustrates the DICOM communication protocol between a Calling Application Entity Title (AET) (client) and a Called AET (server), consisting of three main phases: Association, Data Transfer, and Release. In the Association phase, the Calling AET initiates the connection by sending an A-ASSOCIATE-RQ packet with parameters, such as Application Entity Titles, Presentation Contexts, and the list of supported services and transfer syntaxes. The Called AET responds with either A-ASSOCIATE-AC (Accept) to establish the connection or A-ASSOCIATE-RJ (Reject) if the request is invalid. Once associated, the Data Transfer phase begins, where the Calling AET transmits P-DATA packets containing DICOM payloads, such as medical images or metadata. Multiple P-DATA packets can be exchanged to support large datasets. Finally, in the Release phase, the Calling AET ends the session with an A-RELEASE-RQ packet, which the Called AET confirms with an A-RELEASE-RSP. For abrupt terminations, an A-ABORT packet may be sent.

DICOM Attacks. Some of the key threats [3,12] targeting DICOM communications and systems are as follows:

- *Man-in-the-Middle attack and packet manipulation*: Since traditional DICOM communication often lacks encryption, attackers can intercept, modify, and inject malicious DICOM packets into the network. This enables them to alter attributes such as patient ID, study metadata, or image data, leading to data tampering, patient data exposure, unauthorized modifications, or incorrect medical diagnoses.
- *Replay attack*: Attackers can capture and replay previously recorded DICOM communications to a PACS server. This can result in duplicate image storage, incorrect medical records, or inconsistencies in patient management systems.
- *Denial-of-Service (DoS) attack*: By sending malformed DICOM packets or overwhelming the PACS server with excessive requests, attackers can degrade or completely disrupt medical imaging services, impacting hospital operations and patient care.
- *Malware hidden in DICOM files*: Since DICOM images support embedded metadata and private attributes, attackers can embed malware or other malicious payloads within DICOM files. If executed on a vulnerable system, this could lead to ransomware infections, data breaches, or system compromise.
- *Unauthorized access and weak authentication*: Many DICOM implementations rely on AETs for authentication, which can be easily guessed or spoofed. Without proper access controls, attackers can impersonate legitimate DICOM nodes to retrieve, modify, or delete medical images.

2.2 Related Work

Protocol Fuzzing. In general, there are approaches to fuzz and test network protocols, such as black-box fuzzing [6,14], symbolic execution [22] and grammar-based fuzzing [20]. Recently, ChatAFL [15] leverages pre-trained LLMs to perform grammar-aware mutations and predict the next input when fuzzing protocols to produce more effective inputs.

DICOM Testing. Wang et al. [23] addressed the security risks inherent in the implementation of the DICOM protocol by proposing a fuzzing-based vulnerability mining framework targeting open-source DICOM libraries. The authors developed a prototype system, DICOM-Fuzzer, featuring modules for test case generation, automated testing, and exception monitoring. Testing on the DCMTK library revealed a vulnerability causing buffer overflows with large input files, leading to DoS conditions in PACS systems.

Mirsky et al. [16] demonstrated how an attacker could exploit PACS servers by employing two conditional GAN models: one to inject false medical evidence into healthy images and another to remove evidence of tumors from diagnostic images. This method poses a significant threat as it could lead to misdiagnoses of serious medical conditions. High-resolution pathologies, which rely on precise imaging, are particularly vulnerable to such CTGAN-based attacks.

5GREPLAY. 5GREPLAY [21] is an open-source network fuzzer designed for fuzz testing 5G networks. It enables the evaluation of 5G components by replaying and modifying network traffic, as well as creating and injecting network scenarios into a target, which can be either a 5G core service or a Radio Access Network. Technically, 5GREPLAY can be viewed as a one-way bridge between NICs or can accept pre-captured packets saved in a PCAP-format file as input. The user defines rules that explicitly specify which packets should pass through the bridge and how they should be modified. The configuration file also allows for specifying default actions for packets that do not match any rules, determining whether they should be forwarded or dropped. 5GREPLAY relies on MMT-DPI [4], which is a C library that implements Deep Packet Inspection (DPI) techniques to analyze network packets, classify the network protocol in use or the application a packet belongs to, and extract network and application-based events.

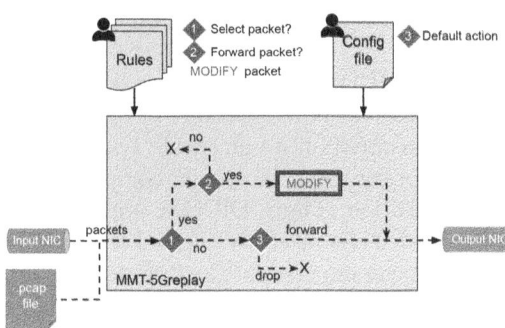

Fig. 2. 5GREPLAY global architecture [21].

Figure 2 depicts the global architecture of 5GREPLAY. For each incoming packet, 5GRE-PLAY classifies the packet to identify its protocol, extracts relevant protocol attributes used in the rules, and checks if any of the rules are satisfied. If no rules match, 5GREPLAY applies the default action as specified in the configuration file. The default action is either FORWARD, which sends the packet to the output NIC without modification, or DROP, which discards the packet. If the packet matches a rule, 5GREPLAY applies the action defined by the rule. If the action is FORWARD, the packet is modified according to the rule before being sent to the output NIC. 5GREPLAY currently supports several fundamental mutation operators for network traffic, including deleting or duplicating packets and modifying specific attributes in the headers of network packets.

We adopt and extend the 5GREPLAY to fuzz and test the DICOM protocol. Importantly, we address the limitations of the current fuzzer, as discussed in Sect. 1, to build a smart network fuzzer for DICOM targets.

3   NetworkFuzzer Design

In this section, we will present the architecture of NETWORKFUZZER and discuss how the design addresses the challenges **C1**-**C3** discussed in Sect. 1.

3.1   Architecture

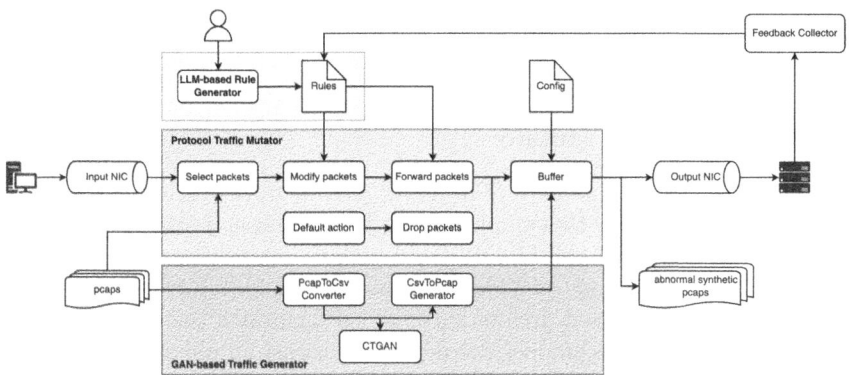

Fig. 3. Architecture of NETWORKFUZZER.

Figure 3 presents an overview of NETWORKFUZZER and the fuzzing loop. Similar to traditional network traffic fuzzers, NETWORKFUZZER takes network traffic as input, either directly from a NIC or from pre-captured traffic in PCAP format, and performs various mutations on this traffic before sending it to the output NIC. Unlike existing network fuzzers like 5GREPLAY, where users manually create rules to modify traffic of interest and then manually observe the server's reactions via logs after injecting the modified traffic, our smart fuzzer automates and enhances this process. Our fuzzer intelligently generates mutation rules and dynamically adapts its behavior based on real-time responses from the server under test through a *closed-loop* fuzzing process. This adaptation is enabled by a Feedback Collector module, which monitors various forms of feedback such as server response packets, performance metrics under stress, and system behavior after receiving malformed or abnormal packets sent from the client. Specifically, our smart fuzzer, NETWORKFUZZER, integrates three key components to address the challenges **C1-C3**:

1. **Protocol Traffic Mutator** analyzes legitimate network traffic to extract protocol-specific attributes and applies mutation operators, such as delete, forward, duplicate, and reorder. By systematically modifying traffic, the mutator generates diverse test cases that simulate realistic and edge-case scenarios, addressing **C1** (*diversity in traffic generation*).
2. **GAN-based Traffic Generator** employs GANs to generate synthetic traffic samples to complement the deterministic mutations from the Protocol Traffic Mutator. By learning patterns from real network traffic, the GAN-based Generator creates realistic yet novel packet sequences, effectively addressing **C2** (*intelligent traffic synthesis*) and expanding the test coverage.
3. **LLM-based Rule Generator** leverages a LLM to generate testing rules dynamically based on protocol specifications, extracted attributes, and past testing results. The LLM-based Rule Generator ensures the fuzzer adapts to new protocols and scenarios, tackling **C3** (*adaptability* and *scalability*).

By leveraging automated analysis and feedback mechanisms, it ensures a more efficient, scalable, and thorough exploration of potential vulnerabilities, significantly reducing the need for manual intervention and increasing testing accuracy. In the next subsections, we will discuss the technical details of the three principal components.

3.2 Protocol Traffic Mutator

Protocol Analysis. Similar to 5GREPLAY, NETWORKFUZZER utilizes MMT-DPI [4], a C-based library that employs Deep Packet Inspection (DPI) techniques to analyze network traffic. MMT-DPI has a plugin architecture for easily adding new protocols and analysis techniques including machine learning techniques. Leveraging its plugin-based architecture, which facilitates the addition of new protocols and analysis techniques, we developed a custom plugin for MMT-DPI to extract attributes specific to the DICOM protocol.

Figure 4 presents the attributes of DICOM packets extracted by the MMT-DPI library. These attributes include identifiers and metadata crucial for understanding and analyzing DICOM traffic. Specifically, attributes 1âĂŞ15 correspond to the headers of DICOM packets, including fields such as Protocol Data Unit (PDU) type, Called or Calling AET, presentation context, etc., which are essential for decoding the structure and semantics of DICOM communications. The remaining attributes are general-purpose attributes applicable to all packets, providing valuable

```
Protocol id 701 --- Name dicom
        Attribute id 1 --- Name pdu_type
        Attribute id 2 --- Name pdu_len
        Attribute id 3 --- Name proto_version
        Attribute id 4 --- Name called_ae_title
        Attribute id 5 --- Name calling_ae_title
        Attribute id 6 --- Name application_context
        Attribute id 7 --- Name presentation_context
        Attribute id 8 --- Name max_pdu_length
        Attribute id 9 --- Name implementation_class_uid
        Attribute id 10 --- Name pdv_length
        Attribute id 11 --- Name pdv_context
        Attribute id 12 --- Name pdv_flags
        Attribute id 13 --- Name command_group_length
        Attribute id 14 --- Name command_field
        Attribute id 15 --- Name patient_name
        Attribute id 4096 --- Name p_hdr
        Attribute id 4097 --- Name p_data
        Attribute id 4098 --- Name p_payload
        Attribute id 4099 --- Name packet_count
        Attribute id 4100 --- Name data_count
        Attribute id 4101 --- Name payload_count
        Attribute id 4102 --- Name first_packet_time
        Attribute id 4103 --- Name last_packet_time
        Attribute id 4104 --- Name p_data_len
        Attribute id 4105 --- Name stats
```

Fig. 4. Key attributes of DICOM packets extracted by MMT-DPI.

insights into the temporal and statistical characteristics of the traffic.

Once that key attributes are extracted through MMT-DPI, NETWORKFUZZER can use them for generating the attack traffic. By extracting these attributes, the plugin enables comprehensive analysis and manipulation of DICOM traffic, supporting use cases such as protocol evaluation, performance monitoring, and network testing. The modularity of MMT-DPI ensures that this extension integrates seamlessly with existing tools and workflows for DICOM traffic analysis.

Mutation Operators. The Protocol Traffic Mutator module processes incoming network traffic, applies different mutation operations, and optionally reorders packets before forwarding them to an output NIC. Initially, the algorithm loads a set of rules and a configuration file, which define the actions to be taken for different types of packets. A new buffer, as shown in Fig. 3, is also initialized to temporarily store packets that are modified or forwarded for potential reordering. As packets are received, a packet processing algorithm similar to that of 5GRE-PLAY, is applied to modify them. Once all packets have been processed, the module optionally reorders the buffered packets by applying a random reorder operator, depending on the configuration. The use of a buffer, along with the additional reordering step, allows for random shuffling of multiple packets before they are injected into the network, providing greater flexibility and control over the traffic mutation process.

3.3   GAN-Based Traffic Generator

This module focuses on the generation of synthetic DICOM network traffic by leveraging CTGAN [25]. The process consists of three main steps, as shown in Fig. 5: (i) processing and labeling DICOM flows from normal and abnormal PCAPs into structured CSV files, (ii) training a CTGAN model to generate synthetic DICOM-specific features while preserving key network identifiers, and (iii) modifying real PCAPs with synthetic values to create replayable traffic for testing DICOM servers.

Dataset Preprocessing. We first construct a dataset of legitimate and abnormal DICOM communications by capturing traffic in PCAP format. Each PCAP file was processed to extract flow-level features using a combination of standard and protocol-specific tools. Specifically, CICFlowMeter and Zeek were employed to extract general network flow statistics, such as flow duration, packet size, inter-arrival time, TCP flag counts, etc. Additionally, MMT-DPI and Wireshark were used to extract fine-grained DICOM-related attributes from packet headers, such as PDU type, PDU length, command field, etc. The extracted features were merged and aggregated into two CSV files: one containing normal DICOM flows and another containing abnormal ones, obtained through prior mutation and injection testing using NetworkFuzzer. Non-DICOM flows were filtered out using port-based heuristics and application-layer protocol identification, ensuring only relevant traffic was retained. Each record was labeled accordingly: 0 for normal flows and 1 for abnormal ones. Specifically, the dataset contains 146 features, including 84 general features and 72 DICOM-related features.

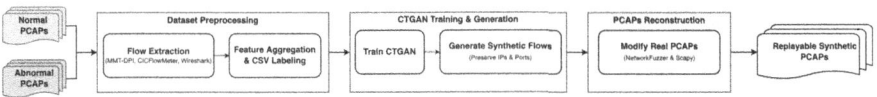

Fig. 5. Architecture of GAN-based Traffic Generator module.

Training the CTGAN. To enrich the dataset with realistic synthetic samples, we applied a CTGAN, which is particularly suited for generating structured tabular data with mixed data types and imbalanced class distributions, which are common in network traffic datasets. The GAN was trained using both normal and abnormal CSV datasets, learning conditional relationships between protocol-specific features. During generation, the model was constrained to preserve static fields, such as `src_ip`, `dst_ip`, `src_port`, `dst_port`, while allowing CTGAN to synthesize plausible values for the remaining DICOM-related fields. This ensures that generated flows remain consistent with real-world addressing while simulating novel variations in DICOM semantics. The synthetic flows produced by CTGAN were labeled based on the conditioning parameters used during generation (normal or abnormal) and exported as new CSV files for further processing.

Synthetic PCAP Generation. The final stage involves converting synthetic CSV flows into full PCAP files. This is accomplished by modifying real PCAPs using NETWORKFUZZER and Scapy, guided by synthetic values generated by CTGAN. Specifically, selected DICOM-related fields, such as command codes, message IDs, and dataset attributes, are rewritten to reflect the synthetic data, while preserving the original packet structure and timing. General static fields, such as source/destination IPs and ports, remain unchanged to facilitate consistent testing. The resulting PCAPs represent a realistic blend of legitimate and synthetic traffic, suitable for replay and injection into testbed environments to assess DICOM server robustness. These PCAPs can also support anomaly detection and IDPS evaluations under diverse, high-fidelity traffic conditions.

3.4 LLM-Based Rule Generator

To address the manual process of creating rules, especially for non-experts, we utilize LLMs to automate test rule generation.

Preprocessing Documentation. The first step of the LLM-based module involves understanding the DICOM protocol, its key attributes, and the valid and invalid values associated with them. To extract relevant information, we leverage advanced LLMs such as OpenAI GPT-4, which have been trained on extensive data from websites and technical documents. To evaluate its effectiveness, we test the model by asking a set of specific DICOM-related questions and manually verifying the responses using trusted resources [2], especially part 8 – DICOM network communication support for message exchange. Our observations indicate that LLM models are capable of interpreting the DICOM protocol specifications, performing reasoning and inference across multiple sections, and answering non-trivial questions about various DICOM attributes correctly.

Prompt Design. To ensure that the LLM-based rule generation module produces structured and syntactically correct XML rules for testing DICOM attributes, we design a well-defined prompt as shown below. The prompt below provides a clear instruction to the LLM, specifying its role as an expert in DICOM protocol testing and network fuzzing. It includes example rules, for example in Listing 1.1, to guide the model in generating similar rules based on user requests. The prompt emphasizes key aspects such as embedding meaningful comments within the generated C function, correctly setting the required attributes (e.g., `property_id`, `description`, and `if_satisfied`), and ensuring the appropriate use of helping functions (e.g., `replace_dicom_attribute()`), with protocol DICOM with ID 701 and the corresponding attribute ID. Additionally, the prompt enforces constraints on attribute selection by providing a predefined list of valid attributes, as shown in Sect. 3.2. If a user requests a rule for an unsupported attribute, the LLM is instructed to return a predefined error message.

Example prompt provided to the LLM

You are an expert in DICOM protocol testing and network fuzzing. Your task is to generate XML rules for testing DICOM attributes with valid or invalid values. Below are example rule structures:: {EXAMPLE_RULE}.

There are two main types of rules you can generate:
1. Drop Rules: Use #drop() to drop specific DICOM packets [redacted]
2. Modification Rules: Use replace_dicom_attribute() to modify packet contents [redacted]

Please generate a similar rule based on the user's request. The rule should:
1. Include proper embedded C function with meaningful comments
2. Set appropriate property_id, description, and if_satisfied attributes
3. Define correct boolean_expression based on the attribute being tested
4. Use replace_dicom_attribute() with protocol ID 701 and the correct attribute ID
5. Properly set is_string to 1 for string values and 0 for numeric values

IMPORTANT: You can ONLY use the following DICOM attributes: {valid_attributes}. If the user requests an attribute that is not in this list, respond with: "The requested attribute is not supported in the current DICOM implementation. Please choose from the list of supported attributes: {valid_attributes}".

Return ONLY the XML rule without any additional explanation if the attribute is supported, or ONLY the error message if it's not supported.

```
<beginning>
<!-- Property 32: Modify the PDU length to increase the payload size -->
<embedded_functions><![CDATA[
    static void em_modify_dicom_pdu_len(const rule_info_t *rule, int verdict
        , uint64_t timestamp, uint64_t counter, const mmt_array_t * const
        trace) {
        int is_string = 0;
        int new_val = 10000;  // Set PDU length to 10000 bytes
        replace_dicom_attribute(701, 2, &new_val, is_string);
        forward_packet();
    }
]]></embedded_functions>
<property property_id="32" type_property="FORWARD"
        description="Modify DICOM PDU length to invalid value (10000)"
        if_satisfied="em_modify_dicom_pdu_len">
    <event description="Got any DICOM packets"
        boolean_expression="((dicom.pdu_type &gt; 0) &amp;&amp; (dicom.
            pdu_type &lt; 8))"/>
</property>
</beginning>
```

Listing 1.1. One of several example rules provided to the LLM

4   Implementation and Evaluation

4.1   Implementation

DICOM Simulator. We implement the DICOM simulator in Python using the *Pydicom* (version 2.4.4) and *Pynetdicom* (version 2.1.1) libraries. The simulator replicates legitimate DICOM communication functionalities, including establishing a connection, sending and retrieving DICOM files, and releasing the connection to a PACS server. Additionally, we account for all potential scenarios in which the server may return error responses, such as A-ASSOCIATE-RJ and A-ABORT. This comprehensive approach enables us to capture all possible cases of DICOM communication between the Calling and Called AET in PCAP format, forming a dataset of legitimate DICOM traffic for further analysis.

MMT-DPI Plugin for DICOM. We develop a new plugin for MMT-DPI to extract key attributes of the DICOM protocol. The plugin is tested against a dataset of legitimate PCAP files captured on the server after executing the DICOM simulator. The extracted values are verified by cross-checking with the DICOM communication documentation and validating them using other packet analysis tools, such as Wireshark.

textbfNETWORKFUZZER. NETWORKFUZZER extends 5GREPLAY (version 0.0.8, commit 86f2074) by integrating new mutation operators, a GAN-based Traffic Generator, and a LLM-based Rule Generator. The GAN-based Traffic Generator utilizes CTGAN (version 0.11.0) to generate synthetic traffic. While the LLM-based Rule Generator employs a GPT-4 model for learning and generating mutation rules, it can also use open-source LLM models such as LLaMA 2 or Mistral.

4.2   Experimental Setup

Attack Modeling. We consider the threat model for an attacker targeting a DICOM system within an internal network. We assume that the attacker has gained unauthorized access to the internal network, either through an insider threat, or by exploiting a vulnerability in another networked device. With this level of access, the attacker can conduct reconnaissance, interceptDICOM communications, and launch targeted attacks against the PACS server and connected devices. Additionally, we assume that the DICOM server lacks certain security enhancements and is misconfigured, making it vulnerable to attacks that could compromise data integrity, confidentiality, and availability.

Testbed Setup. Fig. 6 illustrates the simulated environment used to evaluate the capabilities of NETWORKFUZZER in different DICOM protocol testing scenarios, as discussed below in this section. The testbed consists of three key components: a client machine, a server machine, and a traffic capturing and analysis framework. The client machine is an

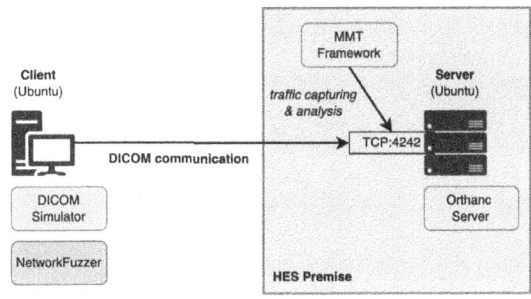

Fig. 6. The DICOM testbed.

Ubuntu Virtual Machine (VM) (version 22.04) running the DICOM simulation, where NETWORKFUZZER is installed and executed to generate and inject test traffic, including potential attack scenarios. On the HES premise, the server machine is another Ubuntu VM (version 22.04) hosting Orthanc [5], a free and open-source lightweight DICOM server deployed as a service to process and respond to DICOM requests. Additionally, the MMT security monitoring framework is installed on the server machine for packet sniffing and analysis. Furthermore, we utilize additional open-source tools, such as tcpdump and Wireshark, on the server machine to capture and analyze network traffic, complementing the MMT framework.

Research Questions. In this section, we conduct experiments to evaluate effectiveness of NETWORKFUZZER in testing the DICOM protocol. These experiments aim to answer the following research questions: (i) efficiency and reliability of LLM-based Rule Generator (Sect. 4.3); (ii) real attack scenario performed by NETWORKFUZZER (Sect. 4.4); and (iii) effectiveness of GAN-based approach in synthetic traffic generation (Sect. 4.5).

4.3   RQ1: Efficiency and Reliability of LLM-Based Rule Generator

To assess the effectiveness of the LLM-based rule generator, we conducted an evaluation focusing on correctness, execution feasibility, and its impact on security testing efficiency. By employing this module, we automatically generated 40 test rules, each designed to either drop specific DICOM packets or modify specific DICOM attributes using valid or invalid values. All generated rules conformed to the expected XML structure. Furthermore, the rules were compiled and executed by our fuzzer without requiring manual corrections, enabling direct manipulation of corresponding attributes in real DICOM network traffic (Fig. 7).

```
Generating rule for: 'Make a rule that sends invalid protocol version of DICOM packets A-ASSOCIATE-RQ'

Generated Rule (Property ID: 107):
-------------------------------------------------------------------------
<beginning>
<!-- Property 107: Modify the protocol version to an invalid value -->
<embedded_functions><![CDATA[
    static void em_modify_dicom_proto_version(
        const rule_info_t *rule, int verdict, uint64_t timestamp,
        uint64_t counter, const mmt_array_t * const trace) {
        int is_string = 0;
        int new_val = 9999;   // Set protocol version to an invalid value
        // Replace protocol version field (attribute ID 3 in protocol 701)
        replace_dicom_attribute(701, 3, &new_val, is_string);
        forward_packet();
    }
]]></embedded_functions>
<property property_id="107" type_property="FORWARD"
        description="Modify DICOM protocol version to invalid value (9999)"
        if_satisfied="em_modify_dicom_proto_version">
    <event description="Got A-ASSOCIATE-RQ DICOM packets"
        boolean_expression="((dicom.pdu_type == 1) &amp;&amp; (dicom.proto_version != 9999))"/>
</property>
</beginning>
-------------------------------------------------------------------------
Rule saved to: rules/dicom_rule_modify_dicom_protocol_version_to_invalid_value_9999.xml
Property ID: 107 (automatically assigned to avoid conflicts)

You can now use 'networkfuzzer compile' to compile the rule.
```

Fig. 7. Example of a rule generated by our module based on the user's request.

This automation significantly reduced the time and effort required by security engineers. To validate the accuracy of the generated rules, we executed our fuzzer with these rules and captured the modified PCAP files for verification using the MMT-DPI and external tools such as Wireshark. The results demonstrated that the automated approach consistently produced functionally equivalent rules while maintaining adherence to DICOM protocol specifications, thereby facilitating the testing of DICOM implementations. Furthermore, generating all potential rules using our module takes approximately 131 s in total and costs $0.37, demonstrating its great efficiency and cost-effectiveness.

This experiment highlights the efficiency and reliability of our LLM-based approach, demonstrating its potential to enhance automated security testing of network protocols in general, and the DICOM protocol in particular.

4.4 RQ2: Real DICOM Extraction Attack Scenario

The DICOM Extraction Attack is a real multi-phase intrusion scenario targeting medical imaging servers like Orthanc through the DICOM protocol, aiming to silently extract sensitive patient data and images. The scenario contains five main steps, as depicted in Fig. 8. The attack begins with step 1 Discovery, where the attacker scans the network using tools like nmap to identify active DICOM endpoints on port 4242. Once a server is located, the attacker initiates step 2 Called AET Brute-Force, where our NETWORKFUZZER is used to attempt different Called AET values through repeated A-ASSOCIATE-RQ packets. Once a valid Called AET is found and a session is established, the attack proceeds to step 3 Patient Metadata Enumeration, where NETWORKFUZZER issues crafted C-FIND queries to the Orthanc server to retrieve indexed patient data. Responses from the server expose sensitive metadata including patient names, study dates, and unique identifiers such as StudyInstanceUID. These identifiers become the foundation for step 4 DICOM File Extraction, where the attacker sends C-MOVE requests to download actual DICOM images associated with selected patients. Finally, in step 5 Optional Analysis, the attacker may locally analyze, modify,

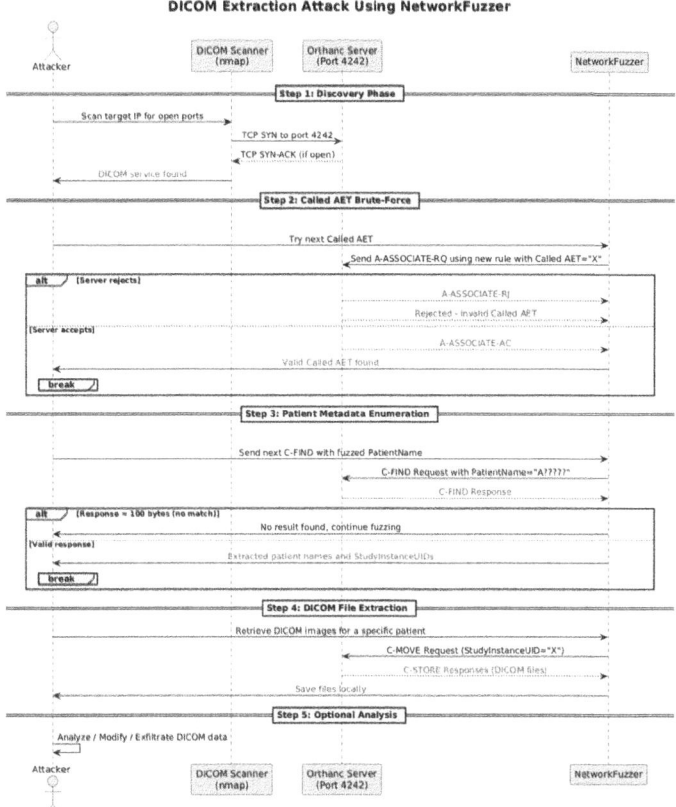

Fig. 8. DICOM extraction attack.

or exfiltrate the collected DICOM files for malicious purposes, such as patient data leaks, tampering with diagnostics, or insurance fraud.

The two most critical steps in this sequence are step 2 and step 3, which are not intended to crash the server, but rather to extract sensitive medical metadata that can later be exploited. Using closed-loop fuzzing, NETWORKFUZZER dynamically adapts its inputs based on server feedback, fine-tuning its behavior through *on-the-fly rule generation*, thanks to rules produced by the LLM-based Rule Generator module, in order to gather the maximum amount of information. In step 2, rather than sending random values, NETWORKFUZZER iterates over plausible Called AET candidates (e.g., 'ORTHANC', 'PACS', 'IMAGING', etc.), constructing minimal but valid A-ASSOCIATE-RQ packets. Figure 9a shows the fuzzing packets sent by NETWORKFUZZER to the DICOM server. For each trial, it observes the server's response, if A-ASSOCIATE-ACCEPT indicates a valid Called AET, while a rejection or no response leads to refinement.

In Step 3, NETWORKFUZZER exploits the DICOM C-FIND service to query indexed patient information stored on the server. Since the server enforces restric-

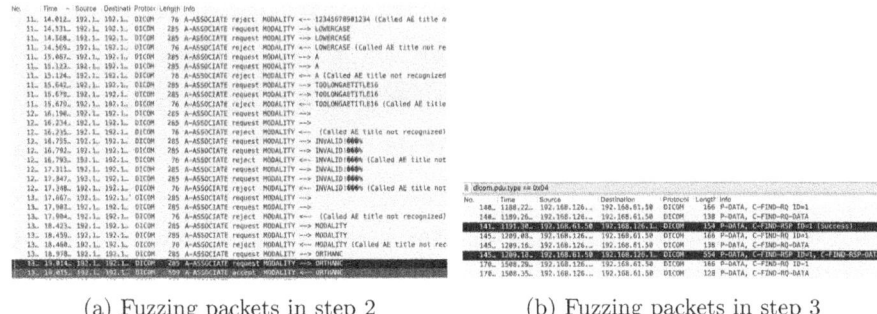

(a) Fuzzing packets in step 2   (b) Fuzzing packets in step 3

Fig. 9. Packets captured on the DICOM server during the attack.

tions that prevent the use of the wildcard character '*' to retrieve all patient records, only the single-character wildcard '?' is allowed. To work around this limitation, NETWORKFUZZER begins by fuzzing the `PatientName` field incrementally, starting with '?', then '??', and so on, to infer the length of valid patient names. Once the approximate length is determined, it proceeds to brute-force the initial characters (e.g., for length 5: 'A????', 'B????', etc.), analyzing the length of server responses to identify valid entries. A response packet with a total size of 154 bytes containing 100 bytes of DICOM payload indicates that no results were found, while longer responses suggest the presence of valid patient data. Through closed-loop fuzzing, NETWORKFUZZER dynamically refines its queries, specifically adjusting the patient name values in rules, to efficiently extract metadata, as shown in Fig. 9b.

This real scenario demonstrates how an attacker can exploit weaknesses in DICOM implementations through a feedback-driven process using our NETWORKFUZZER. By leveraging closed-loop fuzzing, NETWORKFUZZER modifies packets and injects them in real time based on server responses, using on-the-fly rule generation to maximize data extraction.

4.5   RQ3: Effectiveness of GAN-Based Module

To evaluate the quality of synthetic PCAP files generated by our GAN-based module, we adopted a *post-hoc replacement* approach in which all DICOM-related features were replaced with synthetic values generated by CTGAN. We applied a set of statistical metrics to assess the similarity between original and synthetic datasets, grouped by feature type:

- Total Variation Distance (TVD): Measures the difference between the original and synthetic categorical distributions.
- Chi2 p-value: Assesses whether the observed categorical distribution is statistically different from the expected distribution.
- Category Coverage (CatCov): Evaluates the diversity of categories in the synthetic data compared to the original.

- Discrete Kullback-Leibler Divergence (D-KLD): Quantifies the divergence between the original and synthetic categorical distributions.
- Integrated Kullback-Leibler Similarity (IKS): Measures the similarity between the original and synthetic continuous feature distributions.
- Pearson Correlation Coefficient (PCC): Assesses the linear correlation between the continuous features in the synthetic and original datasets.
- Statistical Similarity (StatSimilarity): Measures the overall statistical similarity between the continuous feature distributions.
- Continuous Kullback-Leibler Divergence (C-KLD): Quantifies the divergence between the original and synthetic continuous feature distributions.

The results in Table 1 indicate that the GAN-based module performs effectively in modeling continuous DICOM features. High values of *IKS* (0.9847), *StatSimilarity* (0.9925), and *C-KLD* (0.9793) demonstrate strong similarity between synthetic and original distributions for continuous features. For discrete features, although some divergence is observed, the high *Chi2 p-value* suggests that these differences are not statistically significant. The *Category Coverage* (0.3936) reveals limited diversity in categorical values, suggesting room for improvement in capturing rare categories. However, during injection of synthetic PCAPs generated by modifying multiple values using CTGAN, we observed warnings and errors in the DICOM server logs, suggesting potential structural inconsistencies or invalid field lengths. This highlights the need for tighter protocol-conformant constraints during generation, which we plan to address in future work.

Table 1. Summary of evaluation metrics (mean values) for synthetic DICOM data

Feature	Mean Value
Discrete Features	
TVD	0.6076
Chi2_pvalue	0.8042
CatCov	0.3936
D-KLD	0.4187
Continuous Features	
IKS	0.9847
PCC	0.0188
StatSimilarity	0.9925
C-KLD	0.9793

The CTGAN model is effective at generating realistic synthetic data for both categorical and continuous features but had limitations in preserving the full diversity of categories in discrete features. The GAN-based module shows potential for augmenting protocol-level datasets in cybersecurity and DICOM analysis.

5   Conclusion and Future Work

In this paper, we design and implement a network fuzzer, NETWORKFUZZER, to test network protocols, with a focus on the DICOM protocol in the healthcare domain. NETWORKFUZZER is built on top of the existing open-source fuzzer 5GREPLAY, but has been extended to enhance traffic diversity, enable intelligent generation, and improve adaptability for a broader range of protocols. We employ NETWORKFUZZER to execute real attack scenarios against a DICOM server, aiming to extract patient metadata and simulate further malicious actions. This demonstrates NETWORKFUZZER's ability to modify traffic dynamically, generate rules on the fly based on server responses, and produce synthetic malicious traffic.

In the future, we plan to extend the network fuzzer to make it more generic for testing additional protocols, particularly those used in 5G and 6G networks. Enhancing NETWORKFUZZER, especially by integrating LLMs into MMT-DPI plugins to automatically extract attributes from new protocols, will significantly reduce the manual effort required when dealing with unfamiliar protocol structures. We also plan to integrate the fuzzer with AI4SOAR [19] to simulate and evaluate real-time mitigation strategies against protocol-specific attacks.

Acknowledgement. This research is supported by the H2020 project AI4CYBER N° 101070450, NATWORK N° 101139285, CYBERSUITE N° 101145861, NERO N° 101127411 and INTACT N° 10126241.

References

1. Dicom demystified: Exploring the underbelly of medical imaging (2025). https://claroty.com/team82/research/dicom-demystified-exploring-the-underbelly-of-medical-imaging
2. The dicom standard (2025). https://www.dicomstandard.org/current
3. Healthcare s anatomy: Exposing dicom and critical vulnerabilities in healthcare systems (2025). https://www.gatewatcher.com/en/lab/healthcares-anatomy-attacking-dicom/
4. Mmt-dpi (2025). https://github.com/Montimage/mmt-dpi
5. Orthanc, open-source, lightweight dicom server (2025). https://www.orthanc-server.com/index.php
6. Peach fuzzing platform (2025). https://gitlab.com/gitlab-org/security-products/protocol-fuzzer-ce
7. Ba, J., Böhme, M., Mirzamomen, Z., Roychoudhury, A.: Stateful greybox fuzzing. In: 31st USENIX Security Symposium (USENIX Security 22) (2022)
8. Bidgood Jr, W.D., Horii, S.C., Prior, F.W., Van Syckle, D.E.: Understanding and using dicom, the data interchange standard for biomedical imaging. J. Am. Med. Inform. Assoc. (1997)
9. Böhme, M., Pham, V.T., Nguyen, M.D., Roychoudhury, A.: Directed greybox fuzzing. In: CCS '17 (2017)
10. Caccavale, F.G., Nguyen, H.N., Cavalli, A., Montes De Oca, E., Mallouli, W.: Http/2 attacks generation using 5greplay. In: ARES '23
11. Daniele, C., Andarzian, S.B., Poll, E.: Fuzzers for stateful systems: survey and research directions. ACM Computing Surveys (2024)
12. Desjardins, B., et al.: Dicom images have been hacked! now what? Am. J. Roentgenol. (2020)
13. Eichelberg, M., Kleber, K., Kämmerer, M.: Cybersecurity challenges for pacs and medical imaging. Academic Radiology (2020)
14. Gascon, H., Wressnegger, C., Yamaguchi, F., Arp, D., Rieck, K.: PULSAR: stateful black-box fuzzing of proprietary network protocols. In: Thuraisingham, B., Wang, X.F., Yegneswaran, V. (eds.) SecureComm 2015. LNICSSITE, vol. 164, pp. 330–347. Springer, Cham (2015). https://doi.org/10.1007/978-3-319-28865-9_18

15. Meng, R., Mirchev, M., Böhme, M., Roychoudhury, A.: Large language model guided protocol fuzzing. In: Proceedings of the 31st Annual Network and Distributed System Security Symposium (NDSS) (2024)

16. Mirsky, Y., Mahler, T., Shelef, I., Elovici, Y.: {CT-GAN}: malicious tampering of 3d medical imagery using deep learning. In: 28th USENIX Security Symposium (USENIX Security 19) (2019)

17. Nguyen, M.D., Bardin, S., Bonichon, R., Groz, R., Lemerre, M.: Binary-level directed fuzzing for Use-After-Free vulnerabilities. In: 23rd International Symposium on Research in Attacks, Intrusions and Defenses (RAID 2020)

18. Nguyen, M.D., Bouaziz, A., Valdes, V., Rosa Cavalli, A., Mallouli, W., Montes De Oca, E.: A deep learning anomaly detection framework with explainability and robustness. In: Proceedings of the 18th International Conference on Availability, Reliability and Security (2023)

19. Nguyen, M.D., Mallouli, W., Cavalli, A.R., Montes de Oca, E.: Ai4soar: a security intelligence tool for automated incident response. ARES '24 (2024)

20. Pham, V.T., Böhme, M., Roychoudhury, A.: Aflnet: a greybox fuzzer for network protocols. In: 2020 IEEE 13th International Conference on Software Testing, Validation and Verification (ICST) (2020)

21. Salazar, Z., Nguyen, H.N., Mallouli, W., Cavalli, A.R., Montes de Oca, E.: 5greplay: a 5g network traffic fuzzer-application to attack injection. In: Proceedings of the 16th International Conference on Availability, Reliability and Security (2021)

22. Stephens, N., et al.: Driller: Augmenting fuzzing through selective symbolic execution. In: NDSS (2016)

23. Wang, Z., Li, Q., Wang, Y., Liu, B., Zhang, J., Liu, Q.: Medical protocol security: dicom vulnerability mining based on fuzzing technology. In: Proceedings of the 2019 ACM SIGSAC Conference on Computer and Communications Security (2019)

24. Widup, S., Bassett, G., Hylender, D., Rudis, B., Spitler, M.: Verizon protected health information data breach report (2015)

25. Xu, L., Skoularidou, M., Cuesta-Infante, A., Veeramachaneni, K.: Modeling tabular data using conditional gan (2019)

Detection of Adversarial Examples by Adversarial Training: A Study on the Suitability of FGSM for Hardening NIDS Against Problem-Space Attacks

Marta Catillo$^{(\boxtimes)}$[iD], Antonio Pecchia[iD], and Umberto Villano[iD]

Dipartimento di Ingegneria, Università degli Studi del Sannio, Benevento, Italy
{marta.catillo,antonio.pecchia,villano}@unisannio.it

Abstract. Network intrusion detection systems (NIDS) can leverage machine and deep learning techniques to monitor network traffic and recognize potential intrusions. Although valuable, deep learning-based NIDS are vulnerable to adversarial attacks. Adversarial training, which consists in integrating adversarial examples into the training process, is a means to improve the robustness of NIDS. The literature has largely demonstrated that adversarial examples can be successfully crafted in the feature space through the perturbation of the network traffic features used by NIDS. This paper puts forward the intuition that the use of feature-space perturbations for improving the robustness of NIDS by adversarial training is questionable. This aspect is exacerbated when the network traffic is perturbed prior to the feature extraction step, in the problem space. The experiment reported in the paper is based on the application of both a feature-space and a problem-space adversarial attack to normal and Denial of Service network traffic collected in a controlled testbed. The results obtained aim to promote a critical reflection on the use of feature-space perturbations in the context of network intrusions and suggest the need for more foundational research on protecting NIDS from problem-space adversarial attacks.

Keywords: Intrusion detection · Deep learning · Denial of Service · Adversarial attacks

1 Introduction

Network intrusion detection systems (NIDS) based on machine learning (ML) and deep learning (DL) are valuable to monitor network traffic and recognize potential intrusions. A common approach in NIDS consists in the extraction of various features from the network traffic that are used for ML and DL purposes [13]. Features, such as *payload length*, *number of packets*, *bytes sent*, *mean time between packets*, can be extracted either from individual packets or traffic flows (i.e., aggregations of packets pertaining to the same connection between a source computer and a destination across a network). In this study, we focus on **flow-based** NIDS, where real-world *traffic flows* (i.e., the **problem space**)

F. Skopik et al. (Eds.): ARES 2025 Workshops, LNCS 15999, pp. 232–249, 2025.
https://doi.org/10.1007/978-3-032-00644-8_14

are transformed into "synthetic" n–dimensional records (or *examples*, in the following) called *flow records* (i.e., the **feature space**) suited for ML and DL applications. Although valuable in NIDS, it is a fact that ML and DL models are vulnerable to **adversarial examples**, i.e., examples obtained by applying imperceptible perturbations to input data in order to alter the prediction expected from the model [25]. In the NIDS domain, adversarial attacks can be leveraged to cause various forms of **evasion**, such as intrusions going undetected or normal activity that generates false alerts [8].

Adversarial training, which consists in integrating adversarial examples into the training process [28], is a means for hardening and improving the robustness of NIDS against adversarial attacks. The literature has largely demonstrated that adversarial examples against NIDS can be successfully crafted in the feature space through the perturbation of the network traffic features of the flow records. To this aim, an ever-growing body of papers leverage various adversarial attacks from the image classification domain, such as Fast Gradient Sign Method (FGSM) [11], Jacobian-based Saliency Map Attack (JSMA) [19], DeepFool [16], CarliniâĂŞWagner (CW) [3] and Projected Gradient Descent (PGD) [14], in the context of network intrusions. However, feature-space perturbations (although successfully devised in the image classification domain) are fraught with major issues – partially summarized in Sect. 2.1 – when applied to flow-based NIDS [12,13,21]. As a result, in spite of the widespread adoption of feature-space perturbations, their usage for improving the robustness of NIDS by adversarial training is questionable. This aspect is exacerbated when the network traffic is perturbed prior to the feature extraction step, i.e., in the problem space.

This paper documents an experiment based on the application of both a feature-space and a problem-space adversarial attack to normal and Denial of Service (DoS) network traffic collected in a controlled testbed. As for the feature-space attack, we perturb the flow records by means of FGSM (a mainstream in adversarial machine learning); for completeness' sake we tried four parameterizations of FGSM, which regulate the magnitude of the perturbation from negligible to substantial. On the other hand, the problem-space attack is based on our preliminary proposal of using the *traffic control* utility (available in modern networking toolkits) to shape the normal and attack traffic generated by a source node [5]. At first, the "original" flow records obtained in our testbed – not subject to any form of perturbation at all, either feature- or problem-space – are used to train a supervised deep neural network serving as a *baseline* NIDS model to detect either normal and DoS classes of traffic. The baseline model is re-trained on top of both the (i) original flow record examples and (i) the corresponding FGSM adversarial examples in order to generate an "adversarial-trained" NIDS (AT-NIDS) model, which is capable of detecting both the original classes of traffic (either normal or DoS) and their adversarial versions. The baseline NIDS and AT-NIDS models are tested with original examples, feature-space adversarial examples and problem-space adversarial examples *held-out* from training. The key outcome of our experiment is that the integration of feature-space adversarial examples into the training process allows a NIDS to detect feature-space adversarial examples of the same type and magnitude of those used at training time; however, it is ineffective at detecting the problem-space adversarial examples. As a byproduct of our experiment, we also noted that an excessively low perturbation of the examples used for training purposes could be detrimental to the detection performance.

It is worth noting that this paper is not a critique of adversarial training *per se*. Adversarial training has been proven to improve the robustness of ML and DL models; however, the use of feature-space perturbations for training NIDS – though "apparently" robust – should be approached with caution. The experiment documented in this paper is not intended to address the entirety of open issues in the area of adversarial machine learning in NIDS. In this respect, we are aware that our results are based on a single feature-space attack (i.e., FGSM) and a specific problem-space approach based on traffic shaping. Moreover, at the current stage of development we are more concerned about the suitability of applying feature-space perturbations against NIDS rather than the detection of problem-space adversarial examples. In consequence, the results of this paper should be contextualized with respect to the network datasets, ML models and techniques assessed. For example, the adversarial perturbations were tuned in order to impact the baseline NIDS; however, different tuning, i.e., even weaker or stronger than the range assessed, may reflect in different values of the evaluation metrics. Although the results obtained might not appear fully conclusive, they provide evidence of the need for a critical reflection on the use of feature-space perturbations in the context of network intrusions and more foundational research on protecting NIDS from problem-space adversarial attacks.

The rest of the paper is organized as follows. Section 2 provides the background and discusses some related work in the area. Section 3 describes the testbed, workloads and the dataset collected. Section 4 presents the methodology. Section 5 assesses the NIDS models and provides results and findings of our experiment. Conclusions and future work are presented in Sect. 6.

2   Background and Related Work

A **traffic flow** is an aggregation of packets exchanged between a source computer and a destination across a network; a traffic flow is logically equivalent to a *call* or a *connection* according to the Internet Engineering Task Force (IETF) RFC 2722[1]. The set of "valid" traffic flows – exchanges of packets implementing *real* and *meaningful* conversations between two nodes – forms the **problem space**. Machine and deep learning techniques mostly work on numerical records, which means that a problem-space object – a traffic flow in this study – has to be transformed into a n–dimensional record in the **feature space** [21]. In the context of network traffic, the feature extraction step is done through a *traffic meter*, i.e., a function that transforms a traffic flow into a **flow record**, which holds the values of categorical and numeric features computed from the packets of a traffic flow.

---

[1] https://datatracker.ietf.org/doc/html/rfc2722.

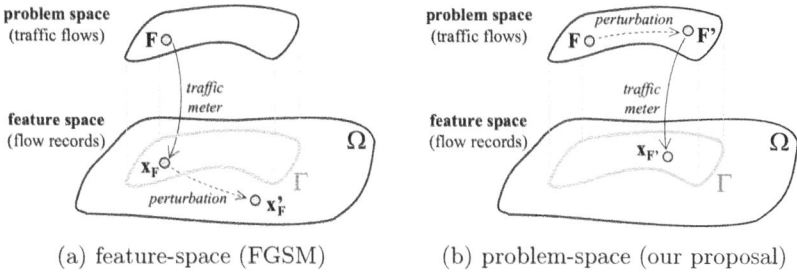

(a) feature-space (FGSM)   (b) problem-space (our proposal)

Fig. 1. Attacks used in this paper to generate the adversarial examples.

2.1 Feature-Space *vs* Problem-space Adversarial Attacks

Let F be a traffic flow in the problem space and m the *traffic meter* function: we obtain the feature-space object $x_F = m(F)$, where $x_F \in \Gamma$ (with $\Gamma \subseteq \mathbb{R}^n$ being the set of all feature-space objects that represent the mapping of real-world traffic flows). Adversarial attacks can be formulated as a function A such that $x'_F = A(x_F)$ is misclassified by a ML(DL)-based system. Often A is defined as an additive mapping $x'_F = x_F + \delta$ where δ is the feature-space perturbation vector. Overall the approach is represented in Fig. 1a along with the relationships among F, x_F, x'_F and Γ.

There are many adversarial attacks in the literature – mostly focused on image and object recognition, such as Fast Gradient Sign Method (FGSM) [11], Jacobian-based Saliency Map Attack (JSMA) [19], DeepFool [16], and Carlin-iâ Ă ŞWagner (CW) [3]; however, they are unsuited for the feature-space perturbation of the network traffic (although misused by the related literature on NIDS). In fact, feature-space attacks implement the *similarity* constraint between x_F and x'_F mostly through a geometric "artifact" in the feature space, e.g., features are perturbed within an ℓ_p–norm ball [13] with no awareness of the real-world network traffic, protocols and packets. In consequence, x'_F – although a valid $\mathbb{R}^n$ point for ML(DL) purposes – will end up outside of Γ (i.e., *unrealistic* feature values, which are not the mapping of real-world traffic flows).

In a previous paper [5] we documented a preliminary proposal of a novel adversarial attack against NIDS, which aims to overcome the issues above. Given the traffic flow F, we conduct a **problem-space** perturbation, at first. The perturbation is done by means of a *traffic control* (c) function, which transforms F into $F' = c(F)$. It is worth noting that traffic control is a well-established utility of modern networking toolkits and assures the *plausibility* of F', i.e., F' is still a valid member of the problem space (i.e., a realistic traffic flow implementing a conversation between two endpoints of a network). Second, the traffic meter is applied to F' in order to obtain the feature-space object $x_{F'} = m(F')$, where $x_{F'} \in \Gamma$ – by construction – as shown in Fig. 1b. As a result, $x_{F'}$ is used as the adversarial counterpart of F.

2.2 Related Work in the NIDS Domain

Work on adversarial attacks from a security perspective can be found in many references, such as [9] and [23]; the interested reader is also referred to the survey by He et al. [13] for a taxonomy of adversarial machine learning for network intrusion detection systems. Papers as [2,15,27] broadly discuss ongoing efforts, challenges and guidelines in modeling realistic adversarial attacks in the context of NIDS; however, they do not provide specific proposals of problem-space attacks.

In spite of the issues above, an ever-growing body of literature attempts to infer lessons on adversarial *robustness, training* and *defense* of NIDS based on the use of feature-space attacks. Some examples are discussed in the following. The authors of [22] assess ML-based IDS models against adversarial attacks in the Internet of Things (IoT) domain. Adversarial examples are generated using five white-box attacks, e.g., JSMA, FGSM and CW. In [1] the authors propose a methodology based on adversarial training and XAI to increase the accuracy of deep neural models. They use the FGSM approach to generate adversarial examples. Four popular white-box evasion attack algorithms (FGSM, PGD, BIM and CW) are tested against an ANN-based IDS in [20], where the authors propose a technique for detecting those attacks using neural activations.

Currently a relatively small body of literature focuses on realistic *problem-space* evasion attacks against ML(DL)-based intrusion detection. For example, the paper [12] proposes a practical traffic-space adversarial attack on ML-based NIDS under gray and black-box assumptions, formulated as a bi-level optimization problem with a two-step solution. Similarly, the reference [29] proposes a two-step black-box evasion attack against ML-based NIDS. First, a Generative Adversarial Network (GAN) is applied to generate forged data packets that can evade anomaly detection. Second, the forged data packets are mixed in the network traffic to help real malicious data packets evade detection. An evasion strategy for live network traffic that relies solely on the manipulation of outbound packets is presented in [26]. The overall architecture consists of three components. Finally, an adversarial attack framework to generate malicious practical traffic with little prior knowledge is proposed in [24]: the proposal aims to modify the temporal-spatial features of traffic by delaying the sending time of traffic packets and increasing the length of packets by padding the payload.

3   Testbed and Data Collection

3.1   Testbed Description

We developed a controlled testbed made by Docker **containers** connected by the *bridge* network driver. The testbed allows us both to (i) collect "original" – not subject to perturbation – network traffic and (ii) perform problem-space attacks via traffic control according to our previous proposal. The testbed is shown in Fig. 2 and consists of:

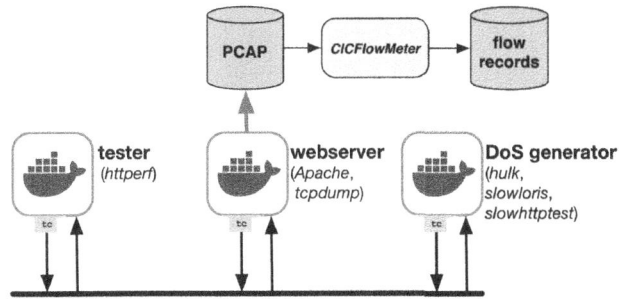

Fig. 2. Experimental testbed.

- **webserver**: it hosts (i) an Apache2 web server (version 2.4.57, default con-figuration), which receives the normal traffic from the *tester* and DoS traffic from the *DoS generator*, and (ii) the `tcpdump` utility to capture and store the traffic in packet capture data (`pcap`) files.
- **tester**: it runs `httperf`[2] in order to accomplish two functions depending on the data to be collected (i) it issues randomized web requests to collect a normal baseline and (ii) it collects response statistics during an attack to check if the DoS is successful.
- **DoS generator**: generates DoS traffic by means of various tools, such as `hulk`, `slowloris` and `slowhttptest` (presented in Sect. 3.2).

The outgoing traffic of each container is controlled by means of `tc`[3] (i.e., the *traffic control* utility placed at the outgoing links of the containers), which makes it possible to mimic a network given its shaping parameters.

3.2 Normal and DoS Workloads

The **normal traffic** is generated by a script that leverages `httperf` to generate random sessions of requests that access assorted content (*small, medium* and *large* HTML files, images, PDF documents, and so forth) pre-uploaded to the webserver. The normal traffic collection has a duration of around 40 min. As for the generation of **DoS traffic**, the tools used are:

- `hulk`[4]: it generates an HTTP flood, spawning a large volume of obfuscated and unique requests;
- `slowloris`[5]: a `GitHub` implementation by Yaltirakli et al. of a DoS attack that continuously issues *partial* HTTP requests to maintain many simultaneous connections to the target;

---

[2] https://github.com/httperf/httperf.
[3] https://man7.org/linux/man-pages/man8/tc.8.html.
[4] https://github.com/grafov/hulk.
[5] https://github.com/gkbrk/slowloris.

Table 1. Number of examples by class of traffic.

traffic class	ORIG dataset		PS_ADV dataset	
	label	examples	label	examples
normal	NOR orig	4,259	NOR adv	9,074
hulk	HLK orig	153,342	HLK adv	326,475
slowloris (GitHub)	GSL orig	6,280	GSL adv	2,935
slowloris (slowhttptest)	HSL orig	11,027	HSL adv	11,106
slow POST	HSP orig	10,891	HSP adv	10,953
total		*185,799*		*360,543*

- **slowhttptest**[6]: it supports different modes. We use the tool both in the (i) "slowloris" mode, which sends incomplete HTTP requests to the victim, and (ii) "slow POST" mode, which sends message bodies at very slow speed.

For each tool, the corresponding DoS attack has a duration of 300 s, enough to collect a significant sample of traffic.

3.3 Original and Problem-Space Adversarial Datasets

The datasets collected and parameters of tc are presented in the following:

- **original (ORIG) dataset**: the five traffic captures – normal, hulk, slowloris and slowhttptest (slowloris and slow POST mode) – are carried out by setting tc at all the containers with the parameters inspired by a real-life network [10], i.e., 1 Gbit/s rate, 5 ms packet delay and 1 ms jitter, no lost, corrupted or duplicated packets. These initial captures lead to five pcap files.
- **problem-space adversarial (PS_ADV) dataset**: the five traffic captures are carried out by setting tc at the tester and DoS generator with higher delay and jitter, and with lost, corrupted and duplicated packets (i.e., 100 Gbit/s rate, 20 ms packet delay and 25 ms jitter, 5% lost, 5% corrupted and 2% duplicated packets). The captures lead to additional five pcap files.

The pcap files obtained from the (i) original and (ii) problem-space adversarial data collections are processed with the CICFlowMeter tool – the "traffic meter" of Fig. 1 – to obtain the flow record features. It should be remarked that here we use the freshly-revised version of CICFlowMeter[7]. The number of original and problem-space adversarial examples obtained is reported in Table 1 along with the **label** of each class of traffic for supervised learning. It is worth noting that we use two different labels for the same class of traffic, e.g., NOR orig and NOR adv (for the normal traffic), to distinguish the original examples of a given class from the corresponding adversarial examples.

---

[6] https://tools.kali.org/stress-testing/slowhttptest.
[7] https://github.com/GintsEngelen/CICFlowMeter.

It is worth noting that the testbed is made by three nodes; moreover, the use of containers surely simplifies monitoring and deployment [4]. Although the testbed might not capture the complexity of real-world settings [6], the traffic collected is not affected by strong sources of uncertainty or other uncontrollable factors. In consequence, we make sure that the attacks stand out from the normal traffic and the perturbations we intend to study do not confound with other phenomena, such as traffic spikes, transitory behaviors or data drifts.

4   Methodology

The methodology adopted in this paper is depicted in Fig. 3 and consists of three steps. At first, a baseline NIDS model of the classes of traffic is learned from the original examples (Fig. 3a). The baseline NIDS model and a set of original examples held-out from training are provided to an FGSM attack to generate the feature-space adversarial test set (Fig. 3b). Finally, the baseline NIDS model and the set of original training examples are used by an FGSM attack to generate an adversarial training set: the model is re-trained on both original and adversarial training examples to obtain an "adversarial-trained" NIDS (AT-NIDS) model (Fig. 3c), which is capable of detecting both the original classes of traffic (either normal or DoS) and their adversarial versions.

In the following, we present the data preparation steps and the methodology. The use of the original, feature- and problem-space test sets against the NIDS – along with the metrics obtained – is addressed in Sect. 5.

4.1   Data Preparation

The original and problem-space adversarial examples are "prepared" before the experiments as for any machine learning study. In this respect, non-relevant or biasing features, i.e., *id*, *timestamp* and *protocol* of the flow records, *source IP address* and *port*, *destination IP address* and *port*, are removed. Removal leads to 87 features out of 94 (label included). The set of original examples is split into the typical *training*, *validation* and *test* set. To this aim, the total 185,799 examples are divided in (i) ORIG_TRAIN (133,774 records), (ii) ORIG_VAL (14,862 records) and (iii) ORIG_TEST (37,163 records), i.e., 80% training-validation (with 10% of the training examples reserved for validation) and 20% test. Similarly, we reserve 20% of the total 360,543 problem-space examples for test purposes; this set is denoted by PS_ADV_TEST in the rest of the paper.

4.2   Generation of the Baseline NIDS Model (Fig. 3a)

We use a supervised **deep neural network** to serve as the NIDS model. A deep neural network is made of many interconnected *neurons*; each neuron is characterized by a set of *weights*. The learning process involves adjusting the weights of the neurons, iteratively, based on a training set where each example is annotated with the corresponding class. We implement the deep neural network

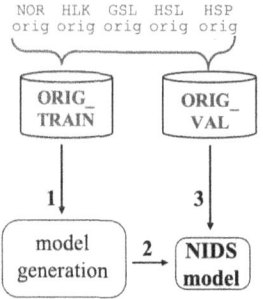

(a) generation of the baseline NIDS model with the original examples

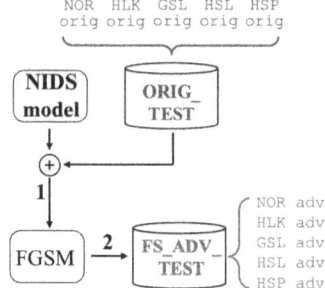

(b) generation of the feature-space adversarial test examples

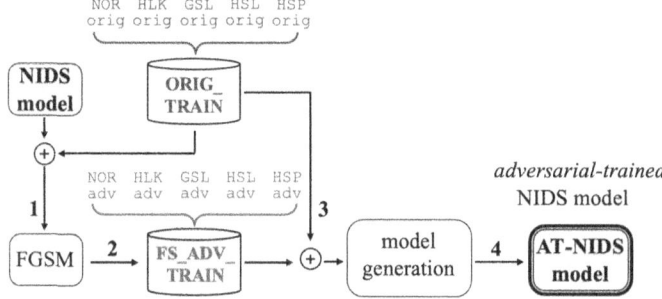

(c) generation of the "adversarial-trained" NIDS (AT-NIDS) model with the original and feature-space adversarial training examples

Fig. 3. Representation of the proposed methodology.

with the ubiquitous Keras[8] library. The baseline NIDS model is learned with ORIG_TRAIN (training set) and ORIG_VAL (validation set) as represented in Fig. 3a. The former is used to train the model; after training, the "goodness" of the model, parameters and overfitting are checked with the latter. We start with an initial mixture of parameters and then apply again the learning procedure to come up with the final parameterization. Following up the learning procedure, a suitable deep neural network for the data at hand is made of four hidden layers (each made by 48 neurons), the rectified linear unit (ReLU) activation function for all the layers except of the output layer (that uses the softmax function), the Adam optimizer, the categorical crossentropy loss function, 48 epochs and batch size equal to 1,024. It is worth noting that the ORIG_TEST portion of data is held-out from the training procedure.

---

[8] https://keras.io.

4.3   Feature-Space Adversarial Test Sets (Fig. 3b)

The feature-space adversarial test sets are generated under a white-box adversarial attack model, which underlies the assumption of having complete knowledge of the NIDS to be attacked. While some studies put forth the transferability of the adversarial examples, such as [17,18], in this paper we purposely opt for a white-box approach in order to make sure that the results are not biased by the interposition of a *surrogate* model in lieu of the actual model.

We generate the adversarial test sets with the **fast gradient sign method** (FGSM) attack available in the ART library[9], i.e., a Python library for the evaluation and defense of ML models. FGSM, proposed in [11], is widely used in the literature on adversarial machine learning in NIDS. FGSM adds a small perturbation to the original input example. More formally, let $\boldsymbol{\theta}$ be the parameters of the model, $\boldsymbol{x}$ the input to the model and y the targets associated with $\boldsymbol{x}$. Given the loss function $J(\boldsymbol{\theta}, \boldsymbol{x}, y)$ the adversarial perturbation is obtained as:

$$\boldsymbol{\eta} = \epsilon \cdot sign(\nabla_x J(\boldsymbol{\theta}, \boldsymbol{x}, y)) \tag{1}$$

where ϵ (*eps*, in the following) is a hyperparameter that controls the magnitude of the perturbation. Moreover, we apply FGSM by *clipping* the adversarial examples in order to assure that the feature values stay within plausible ranges. The FGSM algorithm is provided with (i) the model to be attacked (i.e., the NIDS model obtained as presented in Sect. 4.2) and (ii) a set of original examples to be perturbed against the model, namely ORIG_TEST, as represented in Fig. 3b (*step 1*).

In this paper we assess four values of *eps*, i.e., *eps*={0.0005, 0.001, 0.01, 0.1} – ranging from negligible to substantial perturbation of the input examples – which leads to four parameterizations of FGSM and, in turn, four distinct feature-space adversarial test sets being generated, i.e., FS_ADV_TEST$_{0.0005}$, FS_ADV_TEST$_{0.001}$, FS_ADV_TEST$_{0.01}$, FS_ADV_TEST$_{0.1}$. As for the labels available in the FS_ADV_TEST$_{eps}$ test files, they encompass the token 'adv' following to the name of the class of traffic as shown in Fig. 3b.

4.4   Generation of the AT-NIDS Models (Fig. 3c)

The baseline NIDS model obtained according to Sect. 4.2 and the original training examples (i.e., ORIG_TRAIN) are provided to the FGSM algorithm to obtain the feature-space adversarial examples for training purposes (i.e., FS_ADV_TRAIN) according to the representation in Fig. 3c (steps 1–2). It is worth noting that the original examples used to perform the FGSM attack are different from those used for the generation of the feature-space test sets in Sect. 4.3.

The NIDS model is re-trained on 10 (5 original and 5 adversarial) classes of traffic, i.e., Fig. 3c (steps 3), which encompass both the original and adversarial training examples: the result is an "adversarial-trained" NIDS (AT-NIDS). It is worth noting that this step consists solely of re-training; no changes are made to

---

[9] https://adversarial-robustness-toolbox.readthedocs.io/en/latest/.

the deep neural network in terms of number of layers, activation functions or the optimizer. Similar to the feature-space adversarial test sets, adversarial training is iterated over $eps=\{0.0005, 0.001, 0.01, 0.1\}$, which leads to four variants of the AT-NIDS model trained under different parameterizations of FGSM, i.e., $\text{AT-NIDS}_{0.0005}$ $\text{AT-NIDS}_{0.001}$, $\text{AT-NIDS}_{0.01}$, $\text{AT-NIDS}_{0.1}$.

5   Results

The performance of a NIDS model – either baseline or adversarial-trained – to classify the examples in a given test set is measured by the typical metrics of *recall* (R), *false positive rate* (FPR) and *F1 score* (F1) computed as:

$$R = \frac{TP}{TP + FN} \qquad FPR = \frac{FP}{FP + TN} \qquad F1 = 2 \cdot \frac{P \cdot R}{P + R}$$

where True Positive (TP), True Negative (TN), False Positive (FP) and False Negative (FN) refer to the **multiclass** classification setting and P, i.e., the *precision*, is $\frac{TP}{TP+FP}$. For example, given a class of traffic C, TP is the number of records of C that are actually classified as C by the NIDS model; FP is the number of records of any other class but C that are classified as C by the NIDS model. The computation of the metrics is complemented by an in-depth analysis of the confusion matrices obtained.

5.1   No Adversarial Training

The baseline NIDS model obtained solely from the original examples (i.e., no adversarial training) is tested with the original test set (ORIG_TEST), problem-space adversarial test set (PS_ADV_TEST) and each of the feature-space adversarial test sets obtained by varying *eps*, i.e., $\text{FS\_ADV\_TEST}_{0.0005}$, $\text{FS\_ADV\_TEST}_{0.001}$, $\text{FS\_ADV\_TEST}_{0.01}$ and $\text{FS\_ADV\_TEST}_{0.1}$. The confusion matrices obtained are shown in Fig. 4. It is worth noting that $\text{FS\_ADV\_TEST}_{0.001}$ and $\text{FS\_ADV\_TEST}_{0.01}$ are not shown because they are very similar to Fig. 4c. Given a matrix, any cell $c_{i,j}$ (where i is the row and j the column) shows (i) the number of examples of the class C_i (the "true" class, *row*) that are classified as C_j (the "predicted" class, *column*) by the NIDS model, and (ii) the ratio of $c_{i,j}$ over the total examples in C_i. For example, 852 NOR orig examples are correctly classified as NOR orig by the model (Fig. 4a); on the other hand, 865 NOR adv problem-space adversarial examples are misclassified as HSL orig by the model (Fig. 4b).

The model achieves excellent results on ORIG_TEST, i.e., the test set made by only original examples: both R and F1 are in 0.91–1 in four classes of traffic, and the FPR is in the range 0–0.01 for all the classes. These values are backed by the confusion matrix in Fig. 4a, where most of the examples lie on the diagonal of the left half of the matrix (enclosed by the "predicted as: original" solid rectangle). Not surprisingly – due to the lack of any specific training-time countermeasure – the NIDS model is not capable of detecting any adversarial example, either problem-space or feature-space. The matrices in Fig. 4b, 4c and 4d show that the

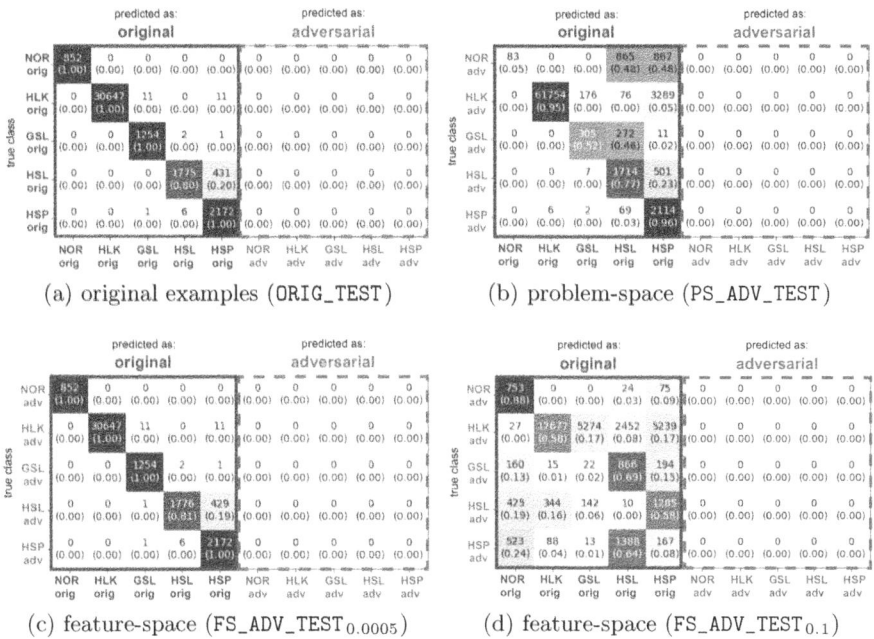

(a) original examples (ORIG_TEST)

(b) problem-space (PS_ADV_TEST)

(c) feature-space (FS_ADV_TEST$_{0.0005}$)

(d) feature-space (FS_ADV_TEST$_{0.1}$)

Fig. 4. Detection of original (Fig. 4a) and adversarial examples (Fig. 4b, 4c, and 4d) in case of no adversarial training (baseline NIDS).

NIDS model attempts to fit the adversarial classes into any of the original classes, which means that the right half of each matrix (enclosed by the "predicted as: adversarial" dashed rectangle) does not account for any cell different from zero. The results convey further interesting findings. For example, almost all normal problem-space adversarial examples (i.e., NOR adv in Fig. 4b) are misclassified as either HSL orig (865) or HSP orig (867), which means that the NIDS model will generate plenty of false alerts (also known as *overstimulation*) when elicited with the problem-space normal adversarial traffic. In this respect, it is worth stressing again that the normal traffic remains normal also after the traffic shaping.

As for FGSM, the misclassifications observed depend on the value of *eps*. Figure 4c (test set obtained with *eps*=0.0005) indicates that most of the feature-space adversarial examples of a given class C adv are predicted as the corresponding original class C orig (e.g., 30,647 HLK adv examples predicted as HLK orig). At the other end of the spectrum in Fig. 4d (test set obtained with *eps*=0.1), the feature-space adversarial examples of a given adversarial class C adv tend to be misclassified into any of the original classes D orig with C ≠ D. For example, out of the total GSL adv examples, we obtain 160 NOR orig, 866 HSL orig and 194 HSP orig predictions. One exception in Fig. 4d is the NOR adv class, still mostly recognized as NOR orig.

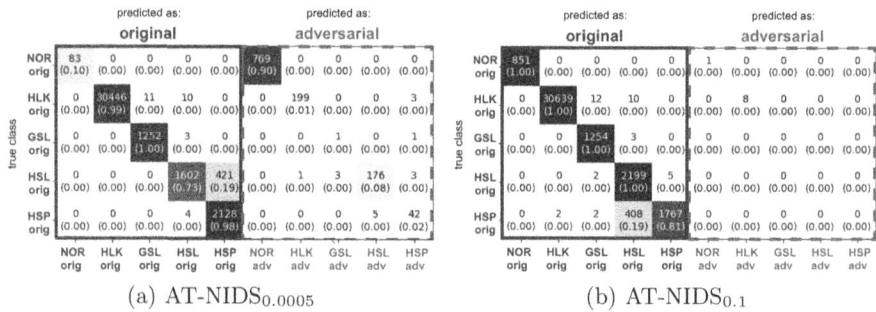

(a) AT-NIDS$_{0.0005}$ (b) AT-NIDS$_{0.1}$

Fig. 5. Detection of the original examples (`ORIG_TEST`) with adversarial training.

5.2   Adversarial Training

Each "adversarial-trained" variant AT-NIDS$_{eps}$ is tested with the original test set (`ORIG_TEST`), the feature-space test set obtained at the same value of eps (i.e., `FS_ADV_TEST`$_{eps}$) and the problem-space test set (`PS_ADV_TEST`). We show only the confusion matrices obtained for AT-NIDS$_{0.0005}$ and AT-NIDS$_{0.1}$ because the remaining ones are similar to those presented in the following.

Figure 5 shows the confusion matrices obtained by classifying the original test set (`ORIG_TEST`). It is worth observing that a "desirable" AT-NIDS is expected to achieve robustness against adversarial examples without compromising its correctness when tested with the original examples. The results indicate that most of the examples of a given original class are predicted correctly, which means that they lie on the diagonal of the left half of the matrix (enclosed by the "predicted as: original" solid rectangle); the matrices obtained with AT-NIDS$_{0.001}$ and AT-NIDS$_{0.01}$ – not shown – are almost the same as Fig. 5b. One particular case is the `NOR orig` class in case of AT-NIDS$_{0.0005}$ (Fig. 5a), where almost all the examples (i.e., 769 out of 852) are badly predicted as `NOR adv`. Although valuable, the use of feature-space adversarial examples during training should be approached with caution.

Finding: The integration of the feature-space adversarial examples into the training process does not interfere with the detection of the original examples as long as the magnitude of the perturbation *is not* excessively low (e.g., 0.0005 in our experiment).

Figure 6   shows   the   confusion   matrices   obtained   by   classifying `FS_ADV_TEST`$_{eps}$ in case of adversarial training. The key outcome is that almost all the feature-space adversarial examples are correctly predicted as adversarial, regardless of the magnitude of the perturbation. The examples of a given adversarial class `C adv` (row) are correctly predicted as the class `C adv` (column) both in Fig. 6a and 6b, which means that they all lie on the diagonal of the right half of the matrix (enclosed by the "predicted as: adversarial" dashed rectangle). It is worth mentioning again that all the feature-space adversarial examples were

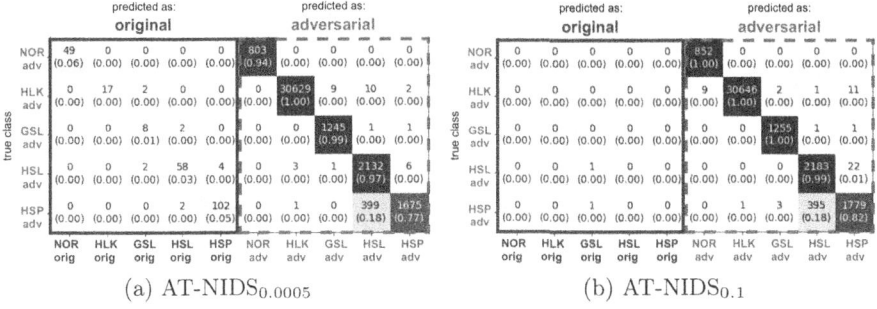

Fig. 6. Detection of the feature-space adversarial examples (`FS_ADV_TEST`$_{eps}$) with adversarial training.

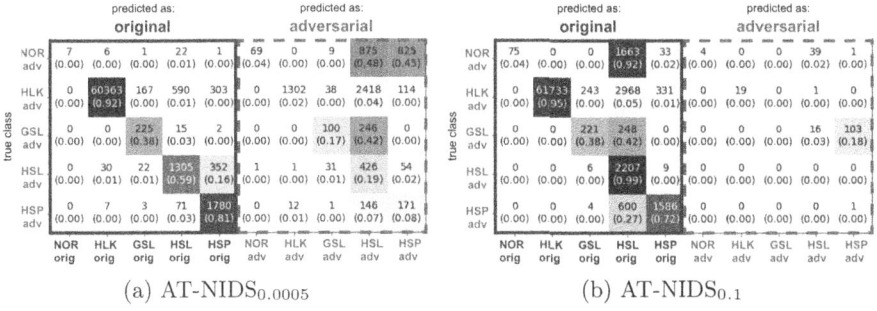

Fig. 7. Detection of the problem-space adversarial examples (`PS_ADV_TEST`) with adversarial training.

poorly assigned to any of the original classes in case of *no* adversarial training (Fig. 4c and 4d). We hypothesize that the original and feature-space adversarial examples are inherently different: those differences are conveniently learnt by the AT-NIDS models during the training process.

> **Finding**: The integration of the feature-space adversarial examples into the training process allows to detect feature-space adversarial examples of the same type and magnitude of those used at training time.

Finally, Fig. 7 shows the confusion matrices obtained by classifying the problem-space adversarial examples `PS_ADV_TEST` in case of adversarial training. Surprisingly, the examples of a given adversarial class C `adv` (row) are now predicted as any of the original classes both in Fig. 7a and 7b, which means that most of the examples fall in the left half of the matrix (enclosed by the "predicted as: original" solid rectangle); again, the matrices obtained with the AT-NIDS$_{0.001}$ and AT-NIDS$_{0.01}$ models – not shown – are very similar to Fig. 7b (i.e., most of the examples falling in the left half of the matrix). We note a peculiar tendency of AT-NIDS$_{0.1}$ (Fig. 7b) to classify the problem-space adversarial examples as `HSL orig`, which will require future investigation. One interesting

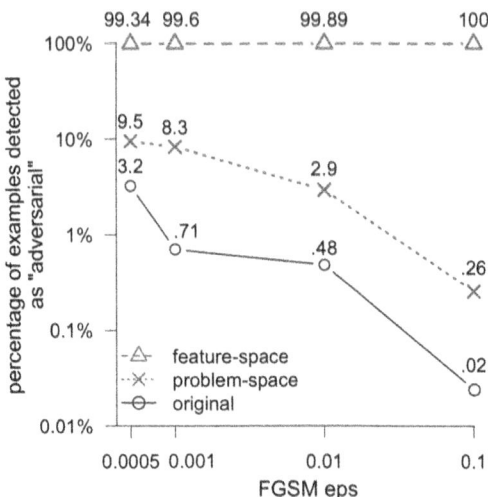

Fig. 8. Percentage of examples detected as "adversarial" by the AT-NIDS model with respect to the *eps* parameter.

case in Fig. 7a is the NOR adv class, whose examples appear to be predicted as *adversarial* (although in a class different than NOR adv): 875 HSL adv and 825 HSP adv predictions. In theory, it could be concluded that the AT-NIDS$_{0.0005}$ model is capable to detect normal problem-space adversarial examples; however, it must be observed that AT-NIDS$_{0.0005}$ also misclassified the normal original examples as *adversarial* (as shown in Fig. 5a).

> **Finding**: Regardless of the magnitude of perturbations, the integration of the feature-space adversarial examples into the training process appears ineffective to detect problem-space adversarial examples generated through traffic shaping.

5.3   Final Remarks

The results of our experiment are summarized in Fig. 8. The x-axis shows the value of the *eps* parameter used to train the AT-NIDS$_{eps}$ models; the y-axis shows the percentage of examples being detected as "adversarial" by AT-NIDS$_{eps}$ out of the total examples in FS_ADV_TEST$_{eps}$ ($\triangle$-*marked* data series), PS_ADV_TEST ($\times$-*marked* data series) and ORIG_TEST ($\circ$-*marked* data series), respectively. It is worth noting that both the x-axis and y-axis are in logarithmic scale. The most striking outcome is that an AT-NIDS model is capable to detect almost all the feature-space adversarial examples regardless of the value of *eps*: the percentage of detections goes from 99.34% (*eps*=0.0005) up to 100% (*eps*=0.1). Apparently, the lower *eps*, the higher the percentage of problem-space adversarial examples detected. For example, AT-NIDS$_{0.0005}$ detects 9.5%

problem-space adversarial examples. Unfortunately, this apparently-promising – although minor – improvement against problem-space adversarial examples, is strongly diminished by the fact that lowering too much *eps* is detrimental to the correctness of the AT-NIDS model when tested with the original examples.

6   Conclusion and Future Work

Intrusion detection is a pivotal mechanism in monitoring and safeguarding network security. ML(DL)-based solutions can achieve remarkable performance in the NIDS domain; however, they remain susceptible to adversarial attacks. In this paper, we investigated the use of feature-space perturbations – widely applied in the NIDS literature – for improving the robustness of NIDS by adversarial training. The results indicate that adversarial training based on feature-space adversarial examples is capable of detecting feature-space adversarial examples of the same type and magnitude of those integrated at training time; however, it is ineffective at detecting problem-space adversarial examples. The results of our experiment must be contextualized with respect to the network datasets, ML models and adversarial attacks (both feature- and problem-space) assessed; in consequence, they should not be generalized to all adversarial attacks. Although the results documented represent just an initial step, they provide evidence of the need for a critical reflection on the use of feature-space perturbations in the context of network intrusions and more foundational research on protecting NIDS from problem-space adversarial attacks.

Adversarial machine learning in NIDS underlies many open issues that are beyond the scope of this paper. Our future research will explore a wider range of parameterizations of the models and adversarial attacks under test, the impact of class imbalance and the effect of the network scenario used to collect the data. Future work will be also devoted to fully exploring the topic, by addressing a wider spectrum of feature-space attacks and learning paradigms. For example, NIDS models may be considered based on their ability to detect classes of intrusions held-out from training [30], such as those involving the use of unsupervised and semi-supervised learning approaches (e.g., by means of deep autoencoders [7]). One more direction will be the design of more sophisticated adversarial attacks against NIDS models, including a better understanding of the relationship between the traffic control parameters and the effectiveness of the attack. Finally, we plan to define a method – possibly based on adversarial training and the combination of both feature- and problem-space adversarial examples – for the detection of problem-space attacks.

Acknowledgments. This work has been partially funded by the European Union – Next-GenerationEU – National Recovery and Resilience Plan (NRRP) – MISSION 4 COMPONENT 2, INVESTMENT N. 1.1, CALL PRIN 2022 PNRR D.D. 1409 14-09-2022 – (Threat-driven security testing and proactive defense identification for edge-cloud systems) CUP N. F53D23009270001 (CUP Master N. E53D23016380001).

Disclosure of Interests. The authors have no competing interests to declare that are relevant to the content of this article.

References

1. AL-Essa, M., Andresini, G., Appice, A., Malerba, D.: An XAI-based adversarial training approach for cyber-threat detection. In: Proc. Intl Conf on Dependable, Autonomic and Sec. Comp., Intl Conf on Pervasive Intelligence and Comp., Intl Conf on Cloud and Big Data Comp., Intl Conf on Cyber Science and Tech. Cong., pp. 1–8. IEEE (2022)
2. Apruzzese, G., Andreolini, M., Ferretti, L., Marchetti, M., Colajanni, M.: Modeling realistic adversarial attacks against network intrusion detection systems. Digital Threats **3**(3), 31 (2022)
3. Carlini, N., Wagner, D.: Towards evaluating the robustness of neural networks. In: Symposium on Security and Privacy, pp. 39–57. IEEE (2017)
4. Catillo, M., Rak, M., Villano, U.: Auto-scaling in the cloud: Current status and perspectives. In: Barolli, L., Hellinckx, P., Natwichai, J. (eds.) Advances on P2P, Parallel, Grid, Cloud and Internet Computing, pp. 616–625. Springer (2020)
5. Catillo, M., Pecchia, A., Repola, A., Villano, U.: Towards realistic problem-space adversarial attacks against machine learning in network intrusion detection. In: Proc. International Conference on Availability, Reliability and Security, p. 113. ACM (2024)
6. Catillo, M., Pecchia, A., Villano, U.: Machine learning on public intrusion datasets: Academic hype or concrete advances in NIDS? In: Proc. International Conference on Dependable Systems and Networks - Supplemental Volume (DSN-S), pp. 132–136. IEEE (2023)
7. Catillo, M., Pecchia, A., Villano, U.: Successful intrusion detection with a single deep autoencoder: theory and practice. Softw. Quality J. **32**, 95 123 (2024)
8. Corona, I., Giacinto, G., Roli, F.: Adversarial attacks against intrusion detection systems: taxonomy, solutions and open issues. Inf. Sci. **239**, 201–225 (2013)
9. De Lucia, M.J., Cotton, C.: Adversarial machine learning for cyber security. J. Inf. Syst. Appl. Res. **12**(1), 26 (2019)
10. Fulkerson, J.: 9 sets of sample tc commands to simulate common network scenarios (2017). https://www.badunetworks.com/9-sets-of-sample-tc-commands-to-simulate-common-network-scenarios/. Accessed 11 June 2025
11. Goodfellow, I.J., Shlens, J., Szegedy, C.: Explaining and harnessing adversarial examples. arXiv (2015)
12. Han, D., et al.: Evaluating and improving adversarial robustness of machine learning-based network intrusion detectors. IEEE J. Sel. Areas Commun. **39**(8), 2632–2647 (2021)
13. He, K., Kim, D.D., Asghar, M.R.: Adversarial machine learning for network intrusion detection systems: a comprehensive survey. IEEE Commun. Surv. Tutorials **25**(1), 538–566 (2023)
14. Madry, A., Makelov, A., Schmidt, L., Tsipras, D., Vladu, A.: Towards deep learning models resistant to adversarial attacks. arXiv (2019)
15. Merzouk, M.A., Cuppens, F., Boulahia-Cuppens, N., Yaich, R.: Investigating the practicality of adversarial evasion attacks on network intrusion detection. Ann. Telecommun., 1–13 (2022). https://doi.org/10.1007/s12243-022-00910-1
16. Moosavi-Dezfooli, S., Fawzi, A., Frossard, P.: Deepfool: a simple and accurate method to fool deep neural networks. In: Proc. Conference on Computer Vision and Pattern Recognition, pp. 2574–2582. IEEE (2016)
17. Papernot, N., McDaniel, P., Goodfellow, I.: Transferability in machine learning: from phenomena to black-box attacks using adversarial samples. arXiv (2016)

18. Papernot, N., McDaniel, P., Goodfellow, I., Jha, S., Celik, Z.B., Swami, A.: Practical black-box attacks against machine learning. In: Proc. of the ACM on Asia Conference on Computer and Communications Security, p. 506 519. ACM (2017)
19. Papernot, N., McDaniel, P., Jha, S., Fredrikson, M., Celik, Z.B., Swami, A.: The limitations of deep learning in adversarial settings. In: European Symposium on Security and Privacy, pp. 372–387. IEEE (2016)
20. Pawlicki, M., Choraś, M., Kozik, R.: Defending network intrusion detection systems against adversarial evasion attacks. Future Generation Comput. Syst. **110**, 148–154 (2020)
21. Pierazzi, F., Pendlebury, F., Cortellazzi, J., Cavallaro, L.: Intriguing properties of adversarial ml attacks in the problem space. In: Proc. Symposium on Security and Privacy, pp. 1332–1349. IEEE (2020)
22. Rashid, M.M., et al.: Adversarial training for deep learning-based cyberattack detection in IoT-based smart city applications. Comput. Secur. **120**, 102783 (2022)
23. Rosenberg, I., Shabtai, A., Elovici, Y., Rokach, L.: Adversarial machine learning attacks and defense methods in the cyber security domain. ACM Comput. Surv. **54**(5), 108 (2021)
24. Sun, P., Li, S., Xie, J., Xu, H., Cheng, Z., Yang, R.: Gpmt: Generating practical malicious traffic based on adversarial attacks with little prior knowledge. Comput. Secur. **130**, 103257 (2023)
25. Szegedy, C., et al.: Intriguing properties of neural networks. In: Proc. International Conference on Learning Representations, pp. 1–10 (2014)
26. Tan, S., Zhong, X., Tian, Z., Dong, Q.: Sneaking through security: mutating live network traffic to evade learning-based nids. IEEE Trans. Netw. Serv. Manage. **19**(3), 2295–2308 (2022)
27. Vitorino, J., Pra a, I., Maia, E.: Sok: realistic adversarial attacks and defenses for intelligent network intrusion detection. Comput. Secur. **134**, 103433 (2023)
28. Zhao, M., Zhang, L., Ye, J., Lu, H., Yin, B., Wang, X.: Adversarial training: a survey. arXiv (2024)
29. Zhu, Y., Cui, L., Ding, Z., Li, L., Liu, Y., Hao, Z.: Black box attack and network intrusion detection using machine learning for malicious traffic. Comput. Secur. **123**, 102922 (2022)
30. Zoppi, T., Ceccarelli, A., Puccetti, T., Bondavalli, A.: Which algorithm can detect unknown attacks? comparison of supervised, unsupervised and meta-learning algorithms for intrusion detection. Comput. Secur. **127**, 103107 (2023)

NERO Training Methodology and Initial Results

Pedro R. Tomas[1,2]([⊠]) [ID], Diogo Fevereiro[2] [ID], Tiago Cruz[1] [ID],
and Luis Cordeiro[2] [ID]

[1] DEI, CISUC, University of Coimbra, Coimbra, Portugal
{tomas,tjcruz}@dei.uc.pt
[2] OneSource, Coimbra, Portugal
{pedro.tomas,duarte.fevereiro,cordeiro}@onesource.pt

Abstract. Small and medium enterprises represent the backbone of the European economy, yet these are exposed to significant cyber-security risks. Strengthening the cyber-awareness and hygiene of such enterprises is critical to protecting sensitive information and ensuring business continuity. This paper presents the training methodology developed within NERO, an EU-funded project which aims to increase cybersecurity awareness among European SMEs. The methodology combines a tailored curriculum–covering topics such as threat recognition, safe digital practices, and regulatory compliance–with a blended delivery model utilizing both online and in-person sessions. Preliminary results from pilot sessions conducted across several European countries indicate a significant improvement in participants' cyber-awareness and hygiene practices. These findings underscore the importance of training initiatives and provide actionable insights for further empowering SMEs to face evolving cyber threats.

Keywords: Cybersecurity Training · SMEs · Cybersecurity awareness · Cybersecurity hygiene

1 Introduction

In an era of escalating cyber threats and increasingly sophisticated cyber attacks, ensuring awareness for cyber hygiene and cyber awareness has become paramount for all organisations. Small and medium-sized enterprises (SMEs) across Europe are particularly susceptible due to limited resources and often insufficient security postures. As digital transformation accelerates and attackers become more adept, the need to equip European SMEs with essential cybersecurity knowledge and practices is urgent to protect critical information, maintain business continuity, and preserve stakeholder trust.

European SMEs make up a significant portion of the continent's economy, serving as engines of innovation, employment, and growth. However, many lack the capacity to invest in dedicated cybersecurity teams or advanced protective measures. This vulnerability is exacerbated by a widespread lack of cyber-awareness and cyberhygiene among staff, which contributes to a high rate of successful cyber incidents driven by human error. Addressing this gap requires tailored training solutions that are accessible, practical, and responsive to the unique needs of SMEs operating in diverse regulatory and cultural contexts across Europe.

Within the framework of NERO, a comprehensive training methodology was developed and piloted to enhance cyber hygiene and cyber-awareness among European SMEs and is presented in this document.

This paper is structured as follows: Sect. 2, Training Planning, presents the backbone of the training planning, with a brief presentation of the methodology, objectives, strategy and assessment method used. Section 3, Results, presents the initial results collected in the early stage of the training activities, while Sect. 4, KPIs Evaluation, provides an overview on the considered KPIs. Lastly, Sect. 5, Conclusion, concludes this paper.

2   Training Planning

2.1   Methodology

The training planning methodology has been designed under the pillars of user-friendliness, flexibility, sector-specific guidance, and direct industry relevance. The training syllabus was designed to be accessible and clear, with comprehensible materials that facilitate learning for participants from diverse backgrounds. Recognising that cybersecurity threats–and the technological landscape–are continually evolving, NERO's training plan incorporates flexibility and an evolutionary stance. The structure is broken down into progressive stages with ongoing assessments, enabling regular updates and the refinement of content to stay ahead of new challenges.

A dedicate syllabus with 9 modules has been carefully designed, with each module being carefully mapped to the distinct requirements of sectors such as Finance, Healthcare, and Transport & Logistics, covering from the fundamentals of cybersecurity up to intrusion detection systems, including gamification-based cybersecurity and cyber ranges training exercises, for easier and more comprehensive learning. The complete training methodology has been laid out in deliverable 5.1 of the NERO project "NERO training planning" [NERO(2025)].

2.2   Objectives

The training plan has been developed with the following objectives:

- **Deliver Industry-Relevant Cybersecurity Knowledge**: The backbone of the training is enhancing the cybersecurity proficiency of SMEs, directly addressing vulnerabilities and sector-specific challenges through content informed by up-to-date threat landscapes.
- **Offer a Structured, Engaging Learning Experience**: NERO delivers a blended curriculum combining virtual and face-to-face activities, built around a structured, clearly defined syllabus.
- **Cater to Critical Sectors**: The focus on Finance, Healthcare, and Transport & Logistics ensures that training addresses the pressing risks in sectors where cyberattacks can have especially severe consequences.
- **Promote Practical Skills Development**: By integrating hands-on exercises, simulation scenarios (cyber ranges), and gamified elements (such as scoring, badges, and leaderboards), the programme not only makes learning engaging but also ensures skills are practical and transferable to real-world situations.
- **Continuously Evaluate and Improve**: Pre and post training assessments–through quizzes or practical exercises–determine the effectiveness of the programme and spotlight areas for enhancement, creating a feedback loop that continually raises standards.
- **Align with European Standards**: By mapping training offerings with the European Cybersecurity Skills Framework (ECSF) [ECSF(2025)], NERO strengthens the alignment of its outcomes with EU-wide workforce development priorities, especially targeting SME requirements.

2.3   Strategy

To achieve its objectives, NERO adopts a multifaceted, innovative training strategy. The training follows a blended learning model–merging online and physical sessions–to accommodate diverse learning preferences and maximise accessibility, particularly for participants spread across different locations.

Assessment is a cornerstone of the NERO strategy. Trainees undergo evaluations before and after training to measure progress, ensure knowledge retention, and help instructors fine-tune the course content, thus enabling an adaptive, continually improving programme.

The strategy also foresees the attribution of micro-credentials, assigning recognised ECTS credits for completed modules, making the achievements portable and immediately valuable for career progression. This encourages ongoing professional development without overwhelming learners.

NERO's curriculum is intentionally informative and hands-on. It leverages a diverse set of training materials and methods to engage learners, recognise different styles, and foster active participation. The inclusion of cyber range exercises allows trainees to practice threat detection, prevention, and response in a risk-free but realistic environment.

Gamification is also part of the strategy, not just to boost motivation, but also to cement learning by transforming complex theoretical concepts into immersive, interactive experiences. Enhanced scenarios reflect the latest threats, ensuring relevance and real-world applicability.

2.4   Questionnaire Design

All training evaluations within NERO consider a pre and post training questionnaire. The pre-questionnaire was designed to capture the participant's pseudonym, profiling data (age, gender, sector, ICT background, etc.), and initial cybersecurity knowledge and awareness. The post-questionnaire (linked by pseudonym) included further knowledge questions, dedicated questions to each training and training-specific feedback, and overall satisfaction. Special attention was given to anonymising all the collected data, so it would not be possible to identify any trainee from their answers in the questionnaires.

2.5   Data Collection and Analysis

All the questionnaires were delivered via Google Forms, and the responses were entered into a dedicated analysis sheet, with filters for *ICT background* and *Organisation Sector* to enable detailed subgroup analysis, as presented in Fig. 1.

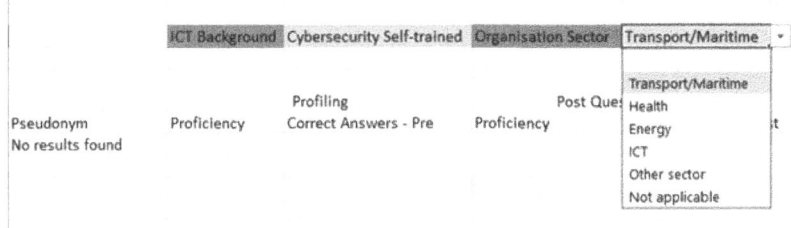

Fig. 1. SpreadSheet filters

3   Results

3.1   Training Sessions Overview

Table 1 presents an overview of some relevant data about the major training sessions conducted until April 15th, including those conducted under Training Round 1, below referred to as "TR1".

In the table, the "TR1-ONE" training session refers to the "DeepGuardian Framework: Hands-On" session provided by OneSource, while the "TR1-MONT" refers to the "Cyberranges training and exercises" provided by Montimage.

Table 1. Summary of major NERO Training Sessions

Training Session	Satisfaction Rate	Answers	Attendees
TR1-ONE	77.14%	7	7
TR1-MONT	83.33%	7	13
TR1-MDS	86.43%	7	10
TR1-TRUSTILIO	88.08%	13	21
Train the Trainers	91.27%	35	12*
CyberHot 2024	85.02%	146	18*

In addition, "TR1-MDS" refers to the "Gamified Scenario-Based Cybersecurity Training" provided by Massive Dynamic Sweden (MDS) and the session mentioned by "TR1-TRUSTILIO" corresponds to the "Software Security" session, provided by TRUSTILIO.

On one hand, for the "Train the Trainers" and for the "CyberHot 2024" sessions, the presented satisfaction rate corresponds to an average for the satisfaction rates collected individually for each sub-training session, the number of answers corresponds to the total number of answers collected and the attendees corresponds to an average value of trainees per sub-training session. On the other hand, the values presented for the "TR1" sessions were individually collected (for each training session).

3.2   DeepGuardian Framework: Hands-On (ONE)

Figure 2 presents the results obtained for the questions used to assess the satisfaction rate of this training. The majority of the trainees confimed that the training was clear and undertood, and 57% fully agree that this training helped increased their technical capabilities. Moreover, 72% of the trainnes fully agree that this training was helpful for their work or academic progress, while 43% felt fully confident about the topics learned during the training. A global satisfaction rate of 77.14% was registered.

3.3   Cyberranges Training and Exercises (MONT)

Figure 3 presents the satisfaction analysis related statistics. Thirteen trainees provided their feedback on pre questionnaire, yet only seven trainees provided their feedback to the post questionnaire, leading to a droup-out percentage of 46.15%. Within the universe of those that provided the final feedback, 71% of them fully agree that this training was clear and understood, while 72% agree that this training was helpful for their work or academic progess. Moreover, 57% full agree they feel confident about the topics learnt during the training session and 72% agree that this training raised their technical capabilities and cyber-security awareness. The global satisfaction rate was of 83.33%.

Fig. 2. Satisfaction analysis for DeepGuardian Framework: Hands-On

3.4 Gamified Scenario-Based Cybersecurity Training (MDS)

Figure 4 presents the results obtained for the satisfaction related questions. In this training, 71% of the trainees fully agree that the training was clear and understood and 72% agreed that the training was helpful for their work or academic progress. Moreover, the majority (57%) fully agree they feel confident about the topics covered during the training sessions, while 72% also agree the training raises their technical capabilities and cyber-security awareness. As such, the global satisfaction rate for this training was 86.43%.

3.5   Software Security (Trustilio)

Figure 5 presents the results obtained for the satisfaction analysis related questions for this training. Twenty-one answers were collected to the pre training part of the questionnaire and thirteen for the post part. From the data collected, 77% of the inquiries fully agree that the training was clear and understood, and 54% agree they feel confident about the topics learnt. Moreover, 46% agree that the training was helpful for their work or academic progress, while 54% agree that this training raised their technical capabilities. The global satisfaction rate for this training was of 88.08%.

4   KPIs Evaluation

Several KPIs have been used to measure the impact of the training sessions conducted and are listed hereafter:

Fig. 3. TR1 - Cyberranges Training and Exercises (MONT)

Fig. 4. TR1 - Gamified Scenario-Based Cybersecurity Training (MDS)

– **TR1_KPI1**: Number of trainings conducted
  TR1_KPI2: Number of (unique) participants
– **TR1_KPI3**: Training completion rate (target 80%)
– **TR1_KPI4**: Participant satisfaction (target 80%)
– **TR1_KPI5**: Average knowledge/awareness score improvement (target 15% increase)
– **TR1_KPI6**: Participant confidence (target 55%)

Table 2 presents a summarised version of the collected KPIs for all the training sessions involved in Training Round I. The obtained values show the effectiveness of the different training sessions, with elevated satisfaction rates and considerable increases in cybersecurity awareness and hygiene.

The training was clear and understood

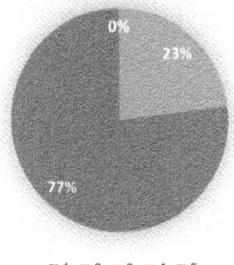

■1 ■2 ▪3 ▪4 ▪5

This training raised my technical capabilities and cyber-security awareness

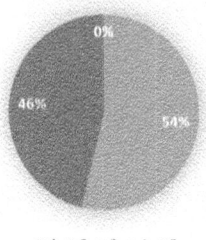

■1 ■2 ▪3 ▪4 ▪5

This training was helpful for my work or for my academic progress

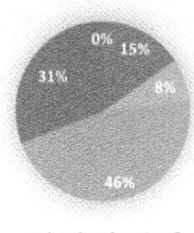

■1 ■2 ▪3 ▪4 ▪5

I feel confident about the topics that I have learnt

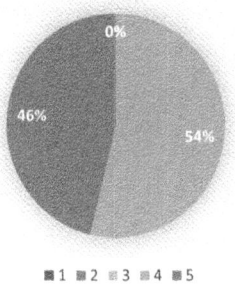

■1 ■2 ▪3 ▪4 ▪5

Fig. 5. TR1 - Software Security (TRUSTILIO)

Table 2. Target and achieved KPI values for NERO training sessions

KPI ID	Target value	Achieved value
DeepGuardian Framework		
TR1_KPI3	80%	100%
TR1_KPI4	80%	72%
TR1_KPI5	15% increase	30.55%
TR1_KPI6	55%	57%
Cyberranges Training and Exercises		
TR1_KPI3	80%	53.85%
TR1_KPI4	80%	86%
TR1_KPI5	15% increase	—*
TR1_KPI6	55%	93%
Gamified Scenario-Based Cybersecurity Training		
TR1_KPI3	80%	70%
TR1_KPI4	80%	83%
TR1_KPI5	15% increase	17.86%
TR1_KPI6	55%	93%
Software Security		
TR1_KPI3	80%	61.9%
TR1_KPI4	80%	88%
TR1_KPI5	15% increase	5.9%
TR1_KPI6	55%	100%

5   Conclusion

This work has presented the methodology, objectives and strategy of the NERO training programme, which aims to improve cybersecurity awareness and hygiene among European SMEs. The training curriculum, built on principles of flexibility, accessibility, and sectoral relevance, was planned to be delivered through a blended learning approach and evaluated using a pre-defined set of KPIs. The initial evaluation results demonstrate that the majority of participants reported high satisfaction, increased confidence, and measurable knowledge gains, underscoring both the demand for and the impact of tailored cybersecurity training in the SME community.

Despite the encouraging outcomes, the evaluation has also highlighted specific areas in need of further attention. Notably, completion rates and average knowledge improvements varied between sessions, with some modules falling short of established targets. This variation can be attributed to factors such as participant engagement levels, varying baseline expertise, and the format of specific training modules. These insights confirm the necessity of continuous programme refinement, by incorporating more interactive elements, practical exercises, and updated scenarios.

In conclusion, the initial deployment of the NERO training programme demonstrates substantial progress toward bolstering cyber-awareness and resilience within the European SME landscape. The evidence-based approach using structured feedback and KPI assessment enables targeted enhancements and a responsive training model. As cyber threats become increasingly sophisticated, ongoing investment in scalable, adaptable cybersecurity education remains essential. The feedback collected from this first round will inform the iterative development of NERO and similar initiatives, paving the way for more effective and sustainable protection of Europe's vital SME sector against digital risks.

Acknowledgements. The authors would like to acknowledge the financial support provided by the following project: 'Advanced Cybersecurity Awareness Ecosystem for SMEs' (NERO) project, which has received funding from the European Union's DEP programme under grant agreement No. 10112741. The views expressed in this paper represent only the views of the authors and not of the European Commission.

References

ECSF 2025. European Cybersecurity Skills Framework (ECSF). https://www.enisa.europa.eu/publications/european-cybersecurity-skills-framework-ecsf. Accessed 15 Apr 2025

NERO 2025. Advanced cybersecurity Awareness ecosystem for SMEs. https://nerocybersecurity.eu/. Accessed 15 Apr 2025

Proceedings of the Eighth International Workshop on Emerging Network Security (ENS 2025)

ENS 2025 Preface

It is our great pleasure to introduce research papers presented at the 8th International Workshop on Emerging Network Security (ENS 2025), co-located with the 20th International Conference on Availability, Reliability, and Security (ARES 2025). The conference was held in Ghent, Belgium during August 11–14, 2025.

The ENS 2025 workshop focused on the evolving field of network security for 5G, beyond 5G, and emerging 6G systems, addressing the challenges posed by increasingly complex and high-capacity communication networks. It aimed to bring together researchers, industry experts, and practitioners to explore secure architectures, protocols, and technologies that ensure privacy, trust, and data protection in advanced networks incorporating concepts like SDN, NFV, IoT, AI, and cloud computing. Building on the success of previous 5G-NS workshops, ENS 2025 also sought to foster collaboration across communities, particularly between the 5G and AI sectors, to fully realize the potential of next-generation communication infrastructures.

This year ENS received 10 submissions, of which 50% were accepted. Each paper was peer-reviewed by our experts from the Technical Program Committee (TPC) and, on average, received 3.5 reviews. This year, our TPC consisted of fifteen experts from eight countries around the world (China, France, Finland, Greece, Italy, Poland, the UK, and the USA). The whole review process was conducted using double-blind methodology, and assisted by five Workshop Chairs.

August 2025

Pascal Bisson
Krzysztof Cabaj
Wojciech Mazurczyk
Edgaro Montes de Oca
Ilsun You

ENS 2025 Organization

Workshop Chairs

Pascal Bisson	Thales, France
Krzysztof Cabaj	Warsaw University of Technology, Poland
Wojciech Mazurczyk	Warsaw University of Technology, Poland
Edgaro Montes de Oca	Montimage, France
Ilsun You	Kookmin University, South Korea

Program Committee

Chafika Benzaid	University of Oulu, Finland
Grzegorz Blinowski	Warsaw University of Technology, Poland
Daniele Bringhenti	Politecnico di Torino, Italy
Luca Caviglione	Institute for Applied Mathematics and Information Technologies CNR, Italy
Michał Choraś	ITTI Ltd, Poland
Gilles Guett	Institut Mines-Télécom Atlantique, France
Georgios Karopoulos	Joint Research Centre, Greece
Zbigniew Kotulski	Warsaw University of Technology, Poland
Sławomir Kukliński	Warsaw University of Technology, Poland
Amitabh Mishra	University of Delaware, USA
Paweł Rajba	University of Wroclaw, Poland
Leonardo Regano	Università degli Studi di Cagliari, Italy
Stavros Shiaeles	University of Portsmouth, UK
Jani Suomalainen	VTT Technical Research Centre of Finland, Finland
Hui Tian	National Huaqiao University, China

Proposition of IT Platform for Combating Wildfires with Decision Support System

Krishna Chandramouli[1], Rafał Kozik[2], Marcin Przybyszewski[3],
Dominika Grunwald[3], and Michał Choraś[2(✉)]

[1] Venaka TReLeaf GbR (VTG), Berlin, Germany
[2] Bydgoszcz University of Science and Technology, Bydgoszcz, Poland
chorasm@pbs.edu.pl
[3] ITTI Sp. z o.o., Poznań, Poland

Abstract. In this paper, we present and describe a new innovative platform designed and develop to combat the increasing effects of wildfires. The development of the platform reflects upon the need of the end users for adopting an interdisciplinary approach. The proposed platform brings together experience from experts with diverse backgrounds, such as information technology (IT), Geographical Information System (GIS), climate change researchers, foresters, firefighters, state authorities, municipalities, nature protection authorities and organizations, policy makers. The overall effectiveness of the platform has been demonstrated through dedicated pilot exercises that were carried out across nine (9) different pilot sites in several countries. The platform design considers the need for developing an integrated fire management (IFM) approach that will allow the stakeholders to take necessary interventions at every stage of wildfire management. The platform integrates 12 technologies, each of which corresponds to the interdisciplinary innovations.

Keywords: Integrated Fire Management (IFM) System · Geographical Information System (GIS) · Earth Observation (EO) · Crisis Management toolkit · Artificial Intelligence (AI) · Internet of Things (IoT)

1 Introduction and Context

Landslides, tornadoes, earthquakes, and hurricanes—these are just a few examples of disasters that have a significant impact on land, property, and civilian lives. According to a recent article in Forbes, natural disasters cost the United States approximately $165B in 2022. Hurricane Ian alone was responsible for nearly $113B in damages in September 2022. However, the true impact of disasters is far more evident when looking at them in the long term. According to the National Centers for Environmental Information, 341 events (approximately 8 per year) have been categorized as disasters since 1980. So far, these events have cost 15,821 lives and approximately $2.4 trillion in damages. Considering the impact disasters have from both a financial standpoint and on the nation's mortality rate, several organizations and sectors of government are redoubling their

© The Author(s), under exclusive license to Springer Nature Switzerland AG 2025
F. Skopik et al. (Eds.): ARES 2025 Workshops, LNCS 15999, pp. 265–280, 2025.
https://doi.org/10.1007/978-3-032-00644-8_16

efforts in terms of emergency preparedness [**Error! Reference source not found.**], including establishing and implementing an effective disaster communication plan [2]. Technology in disaster management and recovery will also continue to play a key role in overall preparedness, enabling first responders to do their jobs more efficiently while mitigating loss of human life.

Disasters increasingly threaten communities at a global scale, necessitating innovative approaches to risk reduction, response, recovery, preparedness, adaptation, and mitigation [3]. Over the past few decades, the frequency and intensity of these events has escalated, highlighting the critical need for enhanced disaster management strategies. Between 2000 and 2019, over 7000 major disaster events were recorded globally, affecting more than four billion people, and causing approximately $2.97 trillion in economic losses. Such statistics highlight the urgency of developing effective disaster management solutions. The Sendai Framework for Disaster Risk Reduction 2015–2030, developed by the United Nations Office for Disaster Risk Reduction (UNISDR), represents an important shift towards planning and investing for risk reduction to build community resilience.2 The Framework advocates for such people-centred preventive approach to disaster risk management. This approach involves engaging with relevant stakeholders, such as civil society at large, and creating synergies across different groups, including academia and research institutions. This engagement allows for the appropriate and participatory design and implementation of policies, plans, and standards. Additionally, it contributes to raising awareness about a culture of prevention and education, and advocates for resilient communities within inclusive societies. Crucially, the Framework also emphasizes the importance of integrating advanced digital solutions and fostering inclusive community engagement to build resilience and mitigate the impacts of disasters.

Historically, disaster management practices have focused on reactive measures for post-disaster response and recovery, rather than proactive measures to prevent or reduce disaster risks [5]. However, the advent of digital technologies is transforming the disaster management field, enabling more proactive and data-driven approaches. Technologies such as remote sensing, radars, satellite imaging, the Internet of Things (IoT), smartphones, and social media platforms are now integral to modern disaster management. These technologies facilitate real-time data collection and dissemination, enabling effective communication and coordination during disasters [6]. Consequently, they can monitor and predict disasters, provide real-time data for early warning systems, and assess damage in the aftermath of catastrophic events. Two factors likely contributed to this positive development [3]: general advances in disaster preparedness and response and the increased use of technology in disaster management. Early warning systems and artificial intelligence (AI) have protected many people from disasters. Drones and remote sensing reduce the time it takes to find and rescue victims. Cloud storage and crowdsourcing help humanitarian responders receive information faster. This increase in frontier technologies has shown the potential to improve prevention measures, increase response efficiency and speed up recovery. While natural hazards affect many people's lives, it is often man-made factors that determine how severe their consequences are. Although technologies have reduced many risks associated with natural hazards, they come with their own risks and challenges that must be considered before their use is mainstreamed in disaster management activities.

One of such disasters that is increasingly affecting globally is wildfires. Wildfires are an ancient phenomenon [7], and many plant species have acquired adaptive traits that help them survive and reproduce under recurrent fire events [8]. Wildfires regimes vary across the ecosystem, especially in relation to productivity [9], and because of human activities [10] and other global changes, including climate change. It is safe to state that climate change is one of the biggest challenges of mankind. The effects of climate change are already being felt, with the resulting damage having a worldwide impact. Global impacts vary due to multiple factors, with a country's economic power playing one of the biggest roles in preparedness, resulting in vulnerable nations. Decisions must be made to mitigate climate change consequences by increasing preparedness in vulnerable areas against the presumed impacts. Climate change will undoubtedly affect the entire planet and calls for international collective actions [11]. Most human activities, particularly the combustion of fossil fuels, have accelerated the rise in carbon dioxide emissions and thus the increase in global warming, with tangible impacts on humans, animals, and the ecological balance around the world. The immediate environmental consequence of global warming is the increase in natural hazards that result in disasters, e.g., melting glaciers, more extreme and more frequent floods, wildfires, storms, droughts, and heatwaves. The indirect consequences include threats to human health, and the reduction of biodiversity and habitable areas, leading to migration and deterioration of community, public health, and socioeconomic conditions in most countries of the world [12]. The impacts of climate change will lead to socioeconomic and political instability, which will change the living conditions of many communities. The reduction of the rate of climate change progress and the mitigation of its consequences requires the creation of a profound scientific basis and the involvement of experts who cover all areas of climate change. These areas range from ecology, life sciences, meteorology, health care, social, and economic sciences, mathematics and computer science to energy, food, and transport. Interdisciplinary approaches deliver huge amounts of data to create reliable future scenarios. They should provide a comprehensive understanding of the problem and possible measures at all levels. All climate change models show significant geographical differences.

Addressing the threat of wildfire, this paper aims to present the notion of adopting integrated fire management (IFM) using the latest development in technological innovations [13]. The adoption of IFM strategy within SILVANUS reflects the three phases in wildfire management, namely (i) prevention and preparedness; (ii) detection and response coordination; (iii) restoration and adaptation. All of these phases are integrated into a single platform that provides the stakeholder with the relevant information necessary to efficiently combat wildfire. For the prevention and preparedness phase, AI based algorithms for detecting and forecasting the fire danger index has been developed thus allowing the end-users to identify regions of high vulnerability. The information available is then used to increase the preparedness of the regional and local fire fighters by delivering training using AR/VR technology. Additionally, the use of mobile application is used to gather information on any fire incident along with identifying the biodiversity information of the region. As the threat of fire incident increases, the stakeholders are recommended to undertake higher frequency surveillance using UAVs (or drones) and collect information on any potential fire incident.

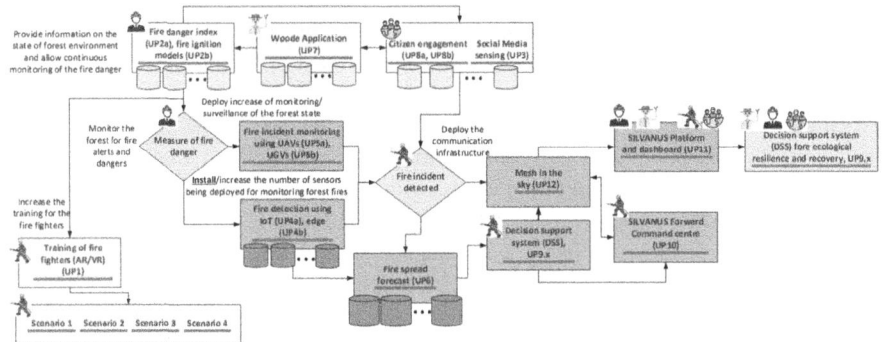

Fig. 1. SILVANUS adoption of integrated fire management (IFM)

Also, the platform offers the capability to install IoT devices equipped with the capability of detecting fire incidents and raising automated alarms. Once the fire incident is being detected, the response coordination is carried out through the deployment of forward command center (FCCs), which are equipped with the tools and services necessary to coordinate the resource deployment to combat the spread of wildfire. The impact of restoration and adaptation strategy has been proposed to be monitored with earth observation and satellite data sources. The IFM approach that has been adopted within the project is presented in Fig. 1 and explained in further sub-sections.

The rest of the paper is structured as follows. In Sect. 2, an overview of the SILVANUS rings of protection (referred to as "lines of defense") is presented, followed by the reference architecture adopted for the integration of the platform. In Sect. 3 a brief review of the stakeholder interest and the assets identified for integration within the platform is presented. Subsequently, in Sect. 4, the overall platform demonstration and the organization of the field exercises is presented, followed by conclusions and future work in Sect. 5.

2   SILVANUS Rings of Protection

Building on the approach of SILVANUS IFM (as presented in Sect. 1), in this section, an overview of the decision support system (DSS) as implemented and integrated is presented. The DSS interventions that are being offered to the stakeholders correspond to the four rings of protection, each one depicting the use of new information sources that has been considered for processing additional knowledge. To this end, the first line of defense offers the relevant stakeholder the ability to gain insight into the environmental threat of the forest landscape where a potential fire outbreak could take place. This is achieved using advances in hardware sensors for detecting smoke, fuel load, temperature and other devices. The second line of defense offers the stakeholders the ability to conduct (or increase) aerial surveillance to monitor any fire incidents and smoke sightings. This will assist in reducing the time for response coordination. The third line of defense offers the ability to use ground robots to disperse water to contain the fire spread. The last line of defense is the use of water bombs that will be focused and targeted for specific regions.

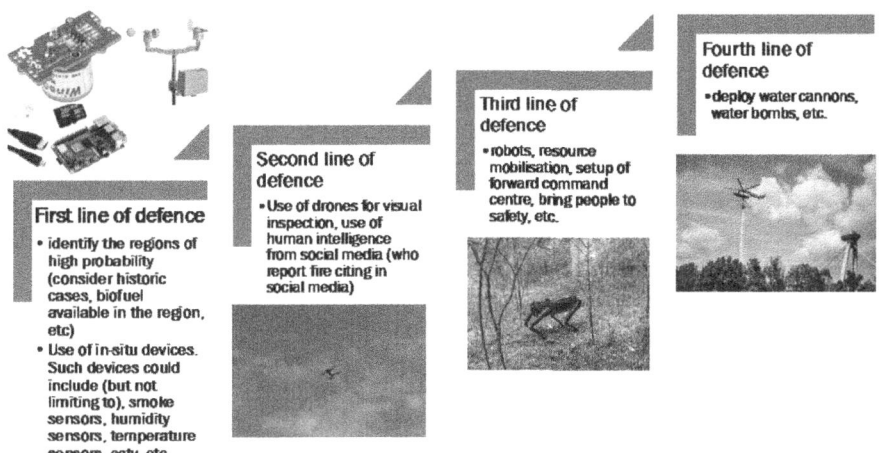

Fig. 2. SILVANUS rings of protection (1st–4th lines of defence) deployed during the pilot demonstrations

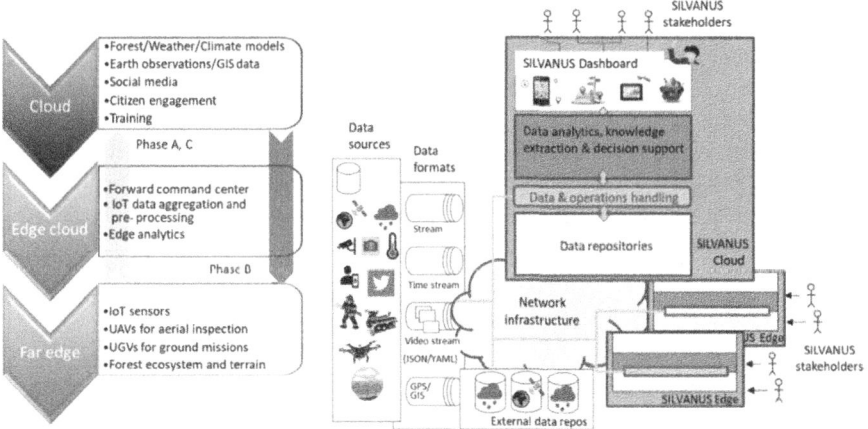

Fig. 3. SILVANUS final architecture with DSS

The different rings of protection is presented in Fig. 2, while the overall platform architecture is being presented in Fig. 3. The added value of the SILVANUS platform is the consideration of needs for different end-users and limit the amount of information that is required for the specific end-user category. The four categories of end-users namely (i) civil protection authority; (ii) fire fighters; (iii) foresters and researchers; and (iv) citizens is presented in detail in Sect. 3. An exhaustive list of different software and hardware components that have been integrated within the project platform has been summarized in Table 1. Each of the components is referred to as a user product (UP) as they are being designed to address the needs of the relevant stakeholder. Each of the user products are categorized to tackle the three phases of wildfire management, namely Phase A addressing the need for enhancing prevention and preparedness against wildfire; Phase B addressing the need for improved detection and response coordination; and Phase C addressing the need for establishing restoration and rehabilitation strategy to restore the loss of natural resources.

3 SILVANUS Platform Validation

For the demonstration of the platform capabilities, four (4) different user categories have been selected, who will be able to directly interact with the platform. A high-level summary of these four categories is presented in Table 2. These roles have been selected to simplify the platform demonstration and to enable the platform visualization to the relevant stakeholders[1].

One of the key observations from SILVANUS activities is the need for a close collaboration among all the key constituents of integrated wildfire management. To this end, the period1F to be undertaken for the recommended activities and the associated close coordination action is presented in Fig. 4. The approach adopted in the second phase of the trial period relates to the presentation of the stakeholder roles in IFM along with presenting the assets which have been integrated within the project. A list of software and hardware assets that have been developed (and integrated from existing infrastructure) is summarized as an itemized list. The list of assets relates to the availability of the "command center", in which the visualization dashboard is presented.

Additionally, for the second phase of the trials, the use of forward command centers has been included, which have been distributed to the technical partners and the associated pilot owners. The use of mobile applications developed in the project has also been shared. The list of IoT and environmental sensors have been identified to be integrated. The use of the firefighting resources has also been included which will be made use of in the pilot activities.

SILVANUS assets:

- Command center
- Forward command centers
- Mobile apps (Woode, citizen engagement)
- List of IoT sensors (air quality, humidity, temperature)
- List of weather stations
- Camera sensors
- Fire trucks
- Unmanned aerial vehicles (UAVs)
- Unmanned ground robots (UGVs)
- Communication infrastructure (Mesh in the Sky)

---

[1] In consultation with the stakeholders of the project, it is noted that there are larger number of participants involved in combating against wildfires.

Table 1. List of user products (UPs) which has been integrated into the SILVANUS platform

UP#	Description	Phase	Functionality
UP1	AR/VR training toolkit for responders	A	Offers a digital platform to train the fire fighters for combating wildfires. Different scenarios have been constructed using an authoring tool to deliver advanced training to the participants
UP2	Fire danger tool	A/B	The AI based component is able to generate a map based on the parameters to forecast the threat of a fire incident
UP3	Fire detection based on social sensing	B	The social media-based crawler generates an alert based on the analysis of real-time feed from X (previously known as Twitter) and other social media platforms
UP4	Fire detection from IoT devices	A/B/C	The on-demand IoT device deployment within the forest allows the fire fighters and other stakeholders to gain insight on the environmental status. The edge-based analytics embedded within the IoT device allows for further customisation to generate fire alerts and monitor the effectiveness of the restoration programs
UP5	UxV Monitoring for Wildfire Behaviour	A/B	The use of aerial vehicles showcases the effectiveness of fire incident and severity detection, while the ground robots have been used to create a wet line and prevent the spread of wildfire
UP6	Fire spread forecast	A/B	The AI based model is able to generate predictive forecast for modelling the fire spread using environmental and historical records
UP7	Woode Mobile Application	A/B/C	The mobile application is designed as a crowd sourced app, that allows to create and establish social communities for the protection of forest against fire incidents

(continued)

Table 1. (*continued*)

UP#	Description	Phase	Functionality
UP8	Citizen engagement and information sharing application	A/B/C	The citizen engagement app allows for the regional stakeholders to promote fire safety measures among public and has the ability to generate user alerts upon fire incident reports
UP9	Decision Support System	A/B/C	The DSS is one of the main components of project platform, that integrates several features, such as resource planning, air quality assessment and evacuation route planning, among others
UP10	Forward Command Center	B	The forward command centre is a uniquely designed hardware component, which can be integrated within the fire fighter resources, such as fire truck. The multi-layered software layers are designed to collect information from the on-field deployment of hardware sensors and to generate alert and recommendations on the fire extinguishing actions that are required
UP11	SILVANUS UI Dashboard	A/B/C	The single point of entry into the system is offered by the dashboard, which is powered by the GIS layers
UP12	Mesh in the sky	B	The component offers communication infrastructure to establish link between the forward command centres, to coordinate among the fire fighters deployed on the field

The launch of the platform demonstration required planning along with information needed for the technical partners to assist in the configuration of the cloud and forward command center deployment to each of the pilot sites. As a total of nine (9) pilots were planned, at the planning stage, each pilot owner selected a site in which the field exercise activity would be carried out. For each of the field exercises to be carried out, a set of key locations and the resource mobilization and logistics to be coordinated to the pilot site were systematically documented as depicted in Fig. 5. This information provided by the respective pilot owners then assisted the technical partners in coordinating the platform configuration that will enable the scenario development. The novelty of the platform design was to enable the visualization of multiple layers of information on top of each other (as depicted in Fig. 6) that allows the corresponding stakeholder to be

Table 2. SILVANUS stakeholders

Civil Protection Authority *will undertake the role of the civil protection authority. The actor will be responsible for the protection of a forest region. At a regional level necessary interventions will be carried out to promote prevention and preparedness against wildfire*
Forester/Researcher *will undertake the role of the forester and researcher involved in the activities of landscape management. The actor will represent the need to strengthen the forest restoration activities, strengthening the post fire restoration*
Fire fighters *will act provide input on behalf of the firefighter and incident commanders. The actor will represent the needs of on the field and incident command centre data analytics to undertake effective fire suppression and extinction strategy*
Citizens *will represent the interest of citizens. As an active participant of the society, the citizen will represent the interest of the public in learning about forest and protecting it against fire incidents*

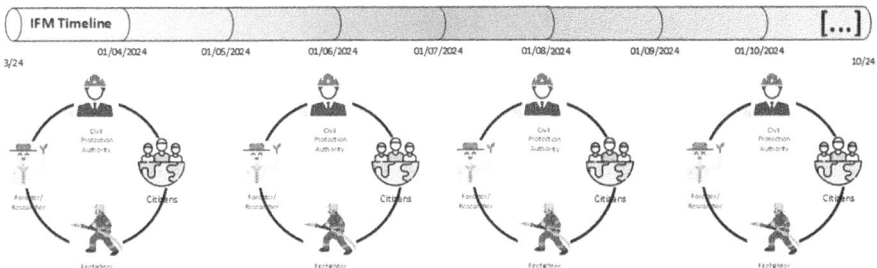

Fig. 4. The approach of SILVANUS to demonstrate the adoption of integrated fire management

able to enable or disable the information to be overlayed. It is also worth mentioning that SILVANUS platform was designed and developed with SbD (Security by Design) principles in order to ensure digital security [14].

4   SILVANUS Platform Demonstration

SILVANUS Dashboard as presented in Fig. 6, is a web-based interface created to provide useful information, enabling users to quickly understand the situation in the field to make informed and good decisions. The interface is designed to be used mainly by trained personnel e.g. firefighters, analysts or public administration representatives to facilitate Integrated Fire Management. It combines prevention and firefighting strategies, considering social, economic, cultural and ecological analyses. Its goal is to minimize losses caused by fires and maximize the benefits that may come from them. In addition, it also covers four stages of crisis management: mitigation, preparedness, response and recovery. To use the Dashboard, a person must successfully undergo training conducted by a specialist. They also must demonstrate an understanding of fires, forest fires, legal regulations and how firefighting units operate in the served area.

For the successful demonstration of the project platform, a set of field exercises have been organized across the nine (9) pilot sites in Europe (France, Portugal, Croatia, Slovakia, Czechia, Greece, Romania, Italy (Puglia, Sardinia). Each of the pilot site developed a scenario in which the location of the fire incidents was determined along with the location of the SILVANUS assets and the citizens who should be brought to safety. An example of the planning is presented in Fig. 5, which was carried out using Google Earth. Following several iterations of the planning, the information from the pilot site was then used to configure the project platform to accurately map and model the information associated to the geo-spatial location and the timestamp series as the data is ingested into the system. To efficiently ensure the relevant information from the specific component has been ingested into the platform, the project has developed a GeoJSON [15] based standard for exchange of data within the project along with the information being gathered from external sources.

Fig. 5. SILVANUS Platfrom demonstration and logistics coordination

The SILVANUS dashboard displays a map with several layers representing the work of different User Products (UP). The main view of the dashboard is presented in the Fig. 7.

Depending on the data collected, layers are divided into those displayed in the form of pins, routes and those that represent a certain area. All layers can be enabled simultaneously and each separately. They are listed in the Table 3 with assigned categories.

Fig. 6. SILVANUS dashboard with multiple layers being activated

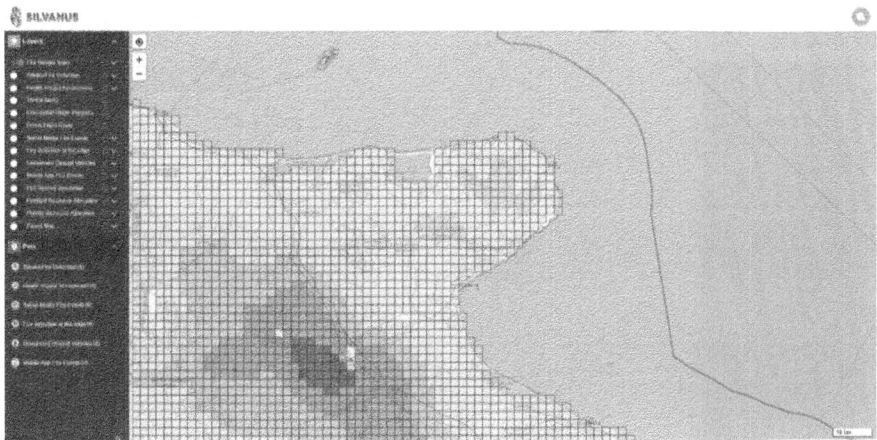

Fig. 7. SILVANUS dashboard with different features of the platform

In response to these questions, the technical partners of the project then subsequently presents a detailed discussion on the ability of the platform to cater to the needs of the end-users.

Table 3. Data layers in the SILVANUS platform categorized by spatial representation

Pins	Routes	Areas
Smoke/Fire Detection	Evacuation Route Planning	Fire Danger Index
Health Impact Assessment	Drone Flight Route	Threat Alerts
Social Media Fire Events		Fire Spread Simulation
Fire Detection At The Edge		Firefight Resource Allocation
Unmanned Ground Vehicles		Forest Map
Mobile App Fire Events		Priority Resource Allocation

The list of questions have been selected to be representative of the end-user needs and the response provided by the technical partners is summarized in Figs. 8, 9, 10, 11 and 12.

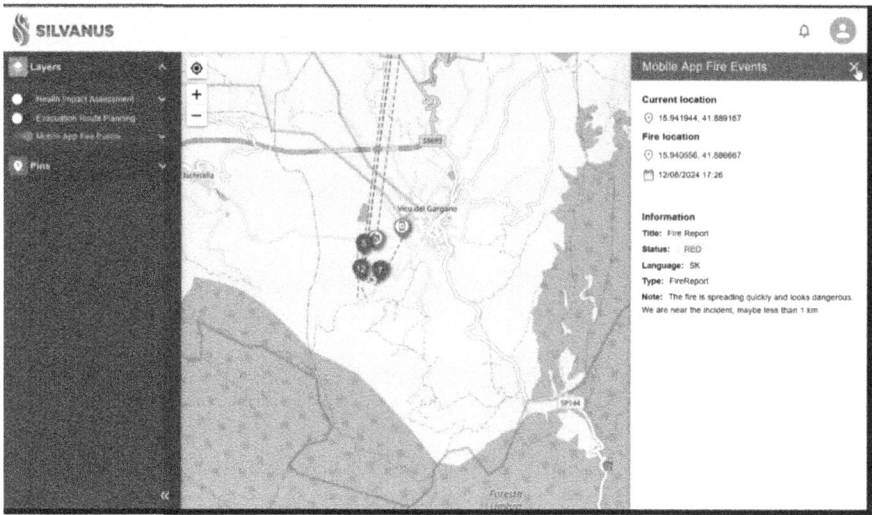

Fig. 8. SILVANUS platform demonstration with fire alerts recevied from mobile application

Across each of the pilot demonstration organized through field exercises all the platform features have been demonstrated to the relevant stakeholders who were participating in the event. In complementary to the field exercises, all the pilot owners have also active engaged in the promotion of SILVANUS activities through stakeholder engagement, educational campaigns and other related events.

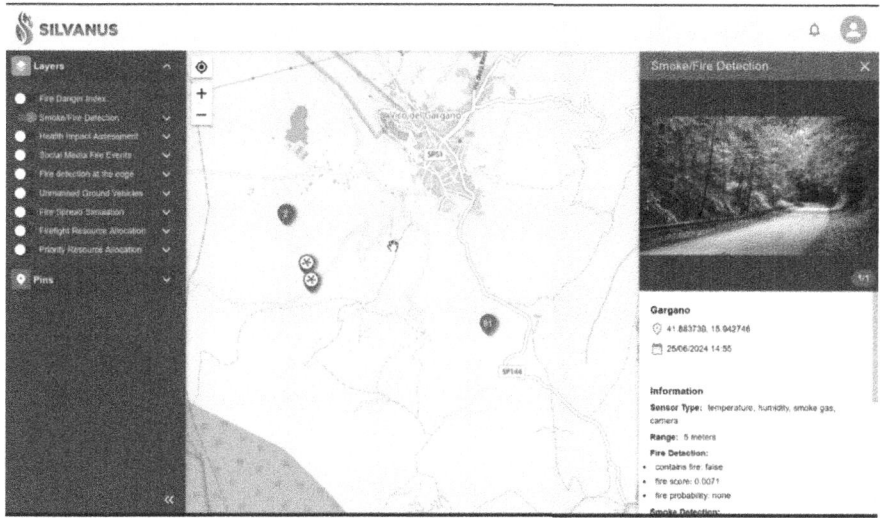

Fig. 9. SILVANUS platform with point data being installed on the field

Fig. 10. SILVANUS fire spread model and the associated resource planning

Fig. 11. SILVANUS user product for monitoring restoration and rehabilitation

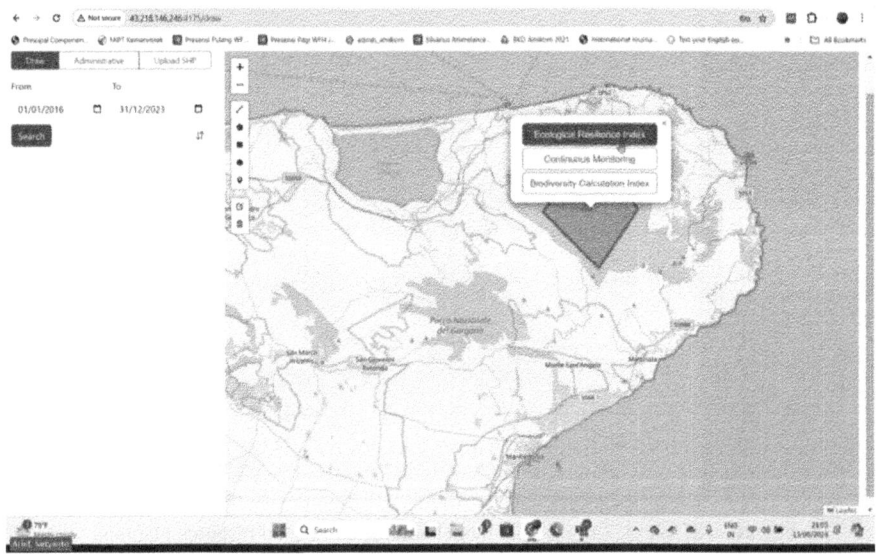

Fig. 12. SILVANUS user product for monitoring the effectiveness of policy interventions

5   Conclusions and Lessons Learnt

At the beginning of 2024, the SILVANUS consortium developed an overall approach to IFM which was presented and summarized in Fig. 1. The process of adoption came after a series of internal discussions among the experts representing the interdisciplinary nature of the research activities that were being carried out. After the adoption of the IFM, the key highlight of the second phase of the project trial resulted in the development and showcase of (i) Decision Support System (DSS) and (ii) the integration of forward command centers. The second platform release achieved in May 2024 was subsequently validated by the external advisory board members in September 2024, which was then used across all pilot locations for conducting the field exercises. It is notable that in every pilot activity that was carried out, some of the unique strengths of the project was demonstrated and collectively the lessons learnt from the experience has been shared among the consortium partners representing the interest of the stakeholders.

The timely release of the platform was tested at Czechia. The field exercise showcased the performance of the platform and the application of the DSS in countering the spread of wildfire. The next pilot was conducted in Romania in which the use of the training activities using AR/VR was extensively tested. Subsequently, in both the Italian pilots (organized in Puglia and in Sardinia), enabled the project to demonstrate and validate the effectiveness of the platform that was validated by the external stakeholders.

The pilot demonstration in Portugal paved the pathway to showcase the effectiveness of adopting the use of nature-based solutions in maintaining the landscape. Additionally, the pilot also paved a pathway to showcase the effectiveness of the use of activities such as prescribed burning, forest grazing and the necessity to implement fire breaks. The comprehensive undertaking of the activities in Portugal has been fully disseminated across the consortium and the rest of the community.

Subsequent pilot organized in France provided the demonstration and use of operational standards which are critical to be adopted in dealing with emergency crisis management. The pilot demonstration in Slovakia led to the showcase on the use of robots for combating against wildfire. The Croatian pilot allowed for the integration of forward command center within the firefighter resources and infrastructure that allowed the on-field demonstration of the use of forward command center. The transmission of data collected from the IoT and other on-field devices was successfully ingested and showcased within the forward command center which was installed within the fire truck. This demonstration paved the pathway to showcase the use of SILVANUS on-field for combating the spread of wildfire and dynamically place resource at a safe distance from the fire front. The final pilot that took place was in Greece. In this pilot demonstration the overall effectiveness of the DSS was demonstrated to the relevant stakeholders.

Across all of the pilot demonstration and the field exercises that were carried out, many of the common solutions developed in the project was continually promoted. Especially the use of the citizen engagement app for a constant feature across the pilot demonstrations which was also accompanied with the launch of the citizen engagement course on raising awareness among the public to promote knowledge on preventing wildfire incidents. It is notable that the course content was updated to reflect the positive use of fire in protecting the biodiversity of the region. Along with the use and promotion of citizen engagement app, the collection and indexing of natural resources available across the regions was also continually carried out resulting in the knowledge representation of the biodiversity index of the region.

Acknowledgments. This study has been conducted in the framework of SILVANUS project. This project has received funding from the European Union's Horizon 2020 research and innovation program under grant agreement No 101037247. The contents of this publication are the sole responsibility of the authors and can in no way be taken to reflect the views of the European Commission.

Disclosure of Interests. The authors have no competing interests.

References

1. Technology in Disaster Management and Recovery: Types and Impact - School of Public Health (2024). https://publichealth.tulane.edu/blog/technology-disaster-management
2. Emergency Preparedness Coordinator: Role and Requirements (2022). https://publichealth.tulane.edu/blog/emergency-preparedness-coordinator
3. Developing a Disaster Communication Plan (2023). https://publichealth.tulane.edu/blog/developing-disaster-communication-plan
4. Baraldo, M., Di Giuseppantonio Di Franco, P.: Place-centred emerging technologies for disaster management: a scoping review. Int. J. Disaster Risk Reduction **112**, 104782 (2024). https://doi.org/10.1016/j.ijdrr.2024.104782
5. Majlingova, A., Brodrechtova, Y., Balikova, K., Hillayova, M.K.: Existing Sustainable Forest Management Services and Formalization of Functional requirements (2022). https://silvanus-project.eu/wp-content/uploads/2023/12/SILVANUS-D2.1.pdf
6. Mancini, M.: Demonstration of data collection, aggregation of Earth Observations, weather/climate models and in-situ environmental sensors for forest fire risk/threat assessment (2023). https://silvanus-project.eu/wp-content/uploads/2023/12/SILVANUS-D4.1.pdf
7. Dikmener, G., et al.: Innovation in Disaster Management (2023). https://www.undp.org/sites/g/files/zskgke326/files/2024-03/innovation_in_disaster_management_web_final_compressed.pdf. Accessed 12 Jan 2025
8. Scott, A.C.: Burning Planet. Oxford University Press (2018). https://global.oup.com/academic/product/burning-planet-9780198734840?cc=gb&lang=en&
9. Pausas, J., Ribeiro, E.: The global fire–productivity relationship. Glob. Ecol. Biogeogr. **22** (2013). https://doi.org/10.1111/geb.12043
10. Keeley, J.E., Pausas, J.G.: Distinguishing disturbance from perturbations in fire-prone ecosystems. Int. J. Wildland Fire **28**(4), 282–287 (2019). https://doi.org/10.1071/WF18203
11. Klingelhöfer, D., Müller, R., Braun, M., Brüggmann, D., Groneberg, D.A.: Climate change: does international research fulfill global demands and necessities? Environ. Sci. Eur. **32**(1), 137 (2020). https://doi.org/10.1186/s12302-020-00419-1
12. Watts, N., et al.: The 2019 report of the lancet countdown on health and climate change: ensuring that the health of a child born today is not defined by a changing climate. The Lancet **394**(10211), 1836–1878 (2019). https://doi.org/10.1016/S0140-6736(19)32596-6
13. Chandramouli, K.: A Systemic Framework for the adoption of Integrated Fire Management TIEMS 2024 Virtual Annual Conference (2024). https://www.tiems.info/images/pdf/TIEMS_2024_Virtual_Annual_Conference_Accepted_Submissions.pdf
14. Orzechowski, N., et al.: Security architecture in the SILVANUS project. In: Proceedings of the 18th International Conference on Availability, Reliability and Security, Benevento, Italy (2023). https://doi.org/10.1145/3600160.3605082
15. Butler, H., Daly, M., Doyle, A., Gillies, S., Hagen, S., Schaub, T.: The GeoJSON Format (2016). https://datatracker.ietf.org/doc/html/rfc7946

Steganographic Channels in Body Area Networks

Markus Walter[1] and Jörg Keller[2(✉)]

[1] Federal Office for Information Security, Bonn, Germany
Markus.Walter@bsi.bund.de
[2] FernUniversität in Hagen, Hagen, Germany
Joerg.Keller@fernuni-hagen.de
https://feu.de/pv/en

Abstract. Wireless Body Area Networks get more widespread and deal with sensitive patient data. Despite that, they are connected to the Internet and processing is partly outsourced into the cloud, raising security concerns. An aspect that seems to have been neglected is the possibility of steganographic transmissions via network covert channels in such networks, and which countermeasures could mitigate or even eradicate such channels. Such investigation seems necessary as network steganographic channels are often used by malware to harm functionality of devices or exfiltrate data to attackers. The present research seeks to fill this gap by performing a hiding pattern analysis which reveals that network covert channels are possible in wireless body area networks based on IEEE 802.15.6. We support the analysis by a simulation that demonstrates feasibility of one of the identified network covert channels. Furthermore, we discuss countermeasures against network covert channels in body area networks such as compartmentalization through virtualization.

Keywords: body area networks · steganographic channels · covert channels · countermeasures · virtual networks

1 Introduction

Body Area Networks (BANs, aka Wireless BANs or WBANs) are widespread in highly developed and aging societies. As one of their applications, they connect sensors and monitoring devices worn at or within the body of a patient with a monitoring station where the different patient data are compared, analyzed, correlated and stored for future use [19]. The security features and problems of such networks are of interest, given that sensitive patient data are collected and transmitted. Exfiltration of sensitive data via steganographic methods has been investigated, e.g., by [11], however either used image, video or text steganography, i.e., on application level, or used network steganography in conventional IP-based network stacks. A corner that seems to have been overlooked in previous research is stealthy exfiltration of patient data via network steganographic approaches in

F. Skopik et al. (Eds.): ARES 2025 Workshops, LNCS 15999, pp. 281–291, 2025.
https://doi.org/10.1007/978-3-032-00644-8_17

protocols of body area networks. We fill this gap with the present paper. To this end, we first perform an analysis whether a widespread BAN-specific protocol (IEEE 802.15.6) is vulnerable to network steganographic approaches, by applying the most frequently used hiding patterns to the protocol's header fields. Next, we implement one of the identified covert channels into this protocol and demonstrate in a simulation that stealthy transmission is possible. Finally, we investigate countermeasures against such channels and discuss to use a virtualization layer, i.e., software-defined networking (SDN), which has been proposed for BANs, as a countermeasure against stealthy data exfiltration.

The remainder is structured as follows. In Sect. 2, we summarize background information on BAN protocols and network steganography, and discuss related work. Section 3 presents an analysis of BAN protocols. Applying frequently used hiding patterns reveals vulnerabilities for network steganographic approaches and example scenarios to exploit these weaknesses are presented. Section 4 presents the simulations we performed to implement one of the steganographic channels from the previous analysis. In Sect. 5, we sketch countermeasures against network covert channels in BANs, in particular through the use of a virtualization layer. Section 6 gives conclusions and an outlook to future work.

2   Background

Wireless body area networks describe a system of interconnected network devices either located within or attached to the human body. Originally, Zimmermann introduced a personal area network (PAN) connecting devices worn by humans on or near the body so that collected personal information could be shared amongst them [29]. Since then, electronic devices have progressed considerably in terms of size, computing power and efficiency. As a result, medical devices and sensors in form of wearables or even implants are becoming increasingly popular to monitor vital signs and improve the medical condition of patients. To implement body area networks, such devices and sensors could be connected via wireless network protocols like WiFi or mobile technologies such as 5G. Beyond those general protocols, there exists a specific set of standards defined by IEEE 802.15 Working Group which deals with wireless speciality networks, especially with wireless PANs and BANs. The network stack used by wireless personal area networks (WPAN) is defined in IEEE 802.15.1 which specifies OSI layers 1 and 2 of a WPAN based on Bluetooth. The coexistence of such personal area networks with other wireless networks like WLANs is standardized in IEEE 802.15.2. Additionally, IEEE also specifies the physical layer and medium access control for high rate WPAN (IEEE 802.15.3) and low rate WPAN (IEEE 802.15.4). Meshing of high rate and low rate WPANs is addressed in IEEE 802.15.5. The most relevant standard for devices within a wireless body area network is IEEE 802.15.6. It defines the physical layer as well as medium access control used by BAN devices placed on the surface of the human body, as an implant or as an external device that is carried within a certain range. [19]

Network Steganography , as a major branch of information hiding, is the art and science of hiding a secret message in an innocent cover object (here overt network traffic or carrier), thus concealing not only the content but also the existence of the secret message [9]. Mostly, covert channels are used, i.e., channels that were never intended for communication and that break a security rule [12]. We denote the sender and receiver of the secret message as covert sender and receiver. They can be identical to the sender and receiver of the overt network traffic that is used to transmit the secret message, or they can be on the communication path [16]. We distinguish storage channels, that explicitly modify some bits of network packets, and timing channels, that encode secret message bits via modifications of packet timing. In storage channels, we distinguish channels that modify header bits and those that modify packet payload. Furthermore, we distinguish channels that are reversible, i.e., where the covert receiver not only extracts the secret message but can also undo the modifications done by the covert sender, before the packet is ultimately forwarded to the overt receiver [14]. A covert channel can be further characterized by its *capacity* or *bandwidth*, i.e., the number of secret bits that can be transferred per packet or per second, respectively, by its *robustness*, i.e., how likely it is that the covert receiver can still extract the secret information in a packet, and by its *stealthyness*, i.e., how likely it is that a countermeasure (see below) can detect the presence of this channel. These three parameters cannot be simultaneously optimized, as there are conflicts between them.

The different approaches to network steganography are categorized in hiding patterns [23–25]. This avoids re-inventions and allows systematic analysis of protocols for vulnerabilities (cf., e.g., [17]), even in the phase of standardization [3,10]. Despite the revision, the network-specific taxonomy of Wendzel et al. [25] remains valid. Because the focus of our analysis is on network covert channels we use the legacy taxonomy. Most known covert channels employ only four hiding patterns [25]: Add Redundancy, Value Modulation, Reserved/Unused and Random Value. Hence, we will focus on these in the sequel. Additionally, we consider the Sequence pattern, as this seems to be growing in importance. All of these patterns are patterns for storage channels, so we leave an analysis for timing channels as future work. The *Add Redundancy* pattern involves adding extra data that appears redundant but actually contains hidden information. This added redundancy is typically ignored by the receiving system but can be decoded by a covert receiver to extract the hidden message. The *Value Modulation* pattern comprises three sub-patterns, of which we will focus on the *least significant bit* pattern as it seems easiest to apply. Fields that are used to count, e.g. TTL in IPv4, will not suffer in functionality if their lowermost bit is set to a different value, as long as this secret data can be extracted by the covert receiver before the field is again modified by a device on the communication path. The *Reserved/unused* pattern hides pieces of a secret message in reserved or unused header fields. Modification of such a field will not hamper the functionality of the network protocol, yet may compromise stealthyness if countermeasures (see below) check for default values and may even compromise robustness if deviating packets are dropped by countermeasures. The *Random Value* pattern replaces a random value by a piece of the secret message, possibly encrypted to look random. Random values in network protocols have been exploited in kleptography attacks, cf. [27] as first paper on the topic, and still is not resolved in many protocols. The *Sequence* pattern exploits the possibility of optional header fields in various network protocols. If optional fields might be structured in an arbitrary order, a specific order can be used to encode a hidden message, i.e., using the *Position* sub-pattern. None of the above patterns requires reversibility, thus enabling wider use as only the covert sender needs to modify packet content. Also, neither pattern threatens network forward capabilities if properly applied.

The most frequent countermeasure against covert channels is deployment of a *warden* which is a network function present in a router or gateway [16]. A *passive* warden checks network packets to find indicators for the presence of a covert channel, while an *active* warden can also modify packets, such as setting unused or reserved header bits to a default value, to mitigate or even eradicate covert channels. A certain handicap of wardens is that actions are mostly specific to particular pattern instances which necessitates hundreds of possible actions while only a limited number of actions is possible for reasons of performance and throughput. This can partly be mitigated by using dynamic wardens [15].

Related Work. Jabeen et al. [8] survey security of healthcare data on BANs and Thiruchelvam et al. [21] propose to use AI to detect attacks of the above kind. Zhou et al. [28] investigate encryption for cloud-assisted BANs, yet neither work mentions steganographic approaches or covert channels. Masdari et al. [13] give a survey about steganography approaches in BANs, yet use this term as a means to protect patient data similar to encryption, and not as a tool for stealthy exfiltration. Oh et al. [18] present a covert channel in bluetooth, yet do not focus on bluetooth for BANs. Galal et al. [5] and Hasan et al. [6] investigate, among others, the use of software-defined networking for BANs. Preethichandra et al. [19] review SDN use for BANs with respect to security, but neither work considers stealthy data exfiltration via network covert channels.

3   Covert Channel Possibilities in BAN Protocols

In this section, we first analyze BAN protocols if they are vulnerable to network steganographic approaches. This is done by systematically applying the selected hiding patterns (cf. Sect. 2) to all header fields. We focus on IEEE 802.15.6 [7] as other protocols have already been investigated, such as bluetooth by [18] or 5G by [22], although not in a systematic way and/or not in the context of body area networks. Furthermore, in the following analysis, we focus on the header fields of the MAC layer as shown in Fig. 1. Afterwards, we sketch some example scenarios how protocol vulnerabilities could be exploited to exfiltrate patient data in a stealthy manner.

3.1   Hiding Pattern Analysis

Add Redundancy. In general, there are no redundant header fields in a MAC frame of IEEE 802.15.6 WBAN. Therefore, the *Add Redundancy* pattern cannot be applied to create a covert channel within the MAC header.

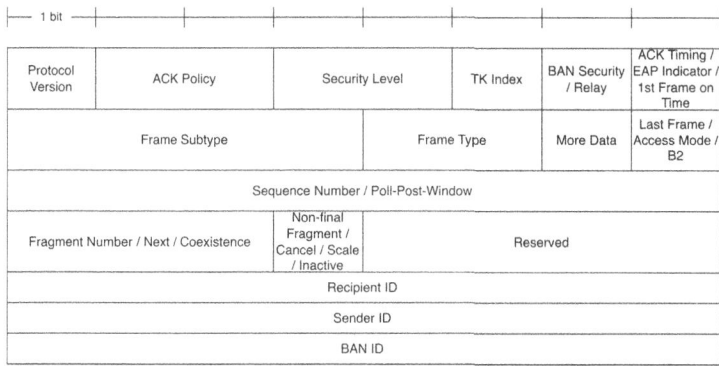

Fig. 1. Structure of WBAN MAC Header [7]

Value Modulation. The only header field that counts is the sequence number. Hence, the least significant bit (LSB) of the sequence number in a MAC frame could probably be used to apply the *Value Modulation* pattern. However, if this LSB is changed, the overt receiver most likely rejects the MAC frame since he expects a different sequence number. Even if the receiver accepts, a deviation in sequence number LSB can raise suspicion if applied too often. Consequently, only a small portion of MAC frames could be used for the transmission of covert information. To avoid the reject possibility altogether, only the initial sequence number of a packet stream should be utilized to apply this pattern. This means that the covert capacity would be very limited.

Reserved/Unused. According to IEEE 802.15.6-2012, reserved bits are given the value 0 by the sender and ignored by the receiver. However, ignoring reserved bits on the receiver side does not prevent covert communication. As proposed in [10], packets deviating from the given value within a reserved header field should either be normalized or discarded to avoid transmission of covert bits to higher layers (Rule 1). In that respect, the BAN protocol is definitely susceptible to the *Reserved/Unused* pattern. The structure of the MAC header shows that there is always at least one reserved field containing four reserved bits regardless of the specific frame type and subtype. In the remaining 16 header fields, depending on the constellation of frame type and frame subtype, there are further options to use reserved bits for a covert channel, e.g. the BAN Security/Relay header field is also reserved in data frames that are sent from a node to the hub.

Random Value. The MAC header fields in IEEE 802.15.6 do not use any random values. Consequently, the *Random Value* pattern cannot be applied. Possibly, Rule 2 proposed in [10] was applied during their specification. However, to perform security operations, randomly drawn nonces are used within the payload of a MAC frame. Potentially, these random values could also be exploited to create covert channels, but they are outside the scope of this analysis that focusses on header fields.

Sequence. The size and order of MAC header elements in body area networks is clearly specified in IEEE 802.15.6 [7], meaning the number as well as the position of header fields are defined bit-exactly. Any deviation from this standardized order leads to malformed MAC frames. Also, no optional header fields are available within a MAC frame. Consequently, the *Sequence* pattern cannot be applied to create a covert channel.

3.2   Application Scenario

Having a means for transport is a necessary requirement, yet alone not sufficient to establish a covert channel. Hence, we sketch an application scenario how the revealed protocol vulnerabilities could be exploited for various forms of data exfiltration via network covert channels. As a simple example, data exfiltrated from malicious sensors could be stealthily forwarded via the BAN to a compromised access point where the BAN is connected to the Internet or the cloud, and forwarded from there via conventional network covert channels in IP networks.

More complicated scenarios are possible. A malicious sensor might be able to compromise another sensor which then would have to act as a temporary covert storage, and from where the data would either be sent to the covert receiver, i.e., attacker, in times with good internet connection or retrieved again by the malicious sensor before that sensor is removed and returned to the malicious manufacturer.

In a similar way, indirect covert channels might be possible where an intermediate node, that acts, e.g., as a gateway, could be misused for communication between two sensors that are not allowed to communicate directly. For example, one sensor could send more packets than usual for a certain timespan and the other sensor would experience an increased response time of the intermediate gateway. Thus, an indirect timing channel could be established even without exploiting protocol vulnerabilities.

3.3   Covert Channel Capacity

Prior to implementation and simulation, the following is a simple example to demonstrate the potential capacity of such a covert storage channel within a body area network. We apply the *Reserved/Unused* pattern to the MAC header of every packet that is to be transmitted in a BAN data stream. In this case, the covert channel capacity depends on the number of MAC frames transmitted and the data rate of this transmission. Therefore, we assume that each MAC frame has a length of 255 octets (2040 bits) which is the maximum length according to [7]. In order to be able to transmit the ever-increasing amounts of data in a short time, the radio frequencies for BAN have been selected so that data rates of up to 10 Mbps are supported. In our hypothetical example, we assume that BAN devices transmit data at an average rate of 5 Mbps.

In reality, medical applications have vastly different Quality of Service (QoS) requirements. Among other things, the required data rate depends heavily on the type of medical data generated by the BAN sensor. In Sect. 4 we will therefore use a realistic simulation, but for this simple scenario we assume a data rate of 5 Mbps. This implies that approximately 2450 MAC frames at maximum size can be transmitted in one second. If the *Reserved/Unused* pattern is applied in its simplest form and thus only the four reserved bits available in a MAC frame are used to embed covert data, then the covert channel capacity, i.e. the rate with which covert data can be transmitted, is approximately 9800 bits per second.

However, this is the minimum capacity as we have assumed the maximum length of a MAC frame is used. If less payload is transmitted within a frame, then the number of frames transferred to the receiver and consequently also the capacity of the covert channel increases. Furthermore, to avoid raising suspicion on the receiver side, only a small number of frames in the data stream will most likely be used to embed covert data. This makes it more difficult for wardens to recognize whether a covert channel exists on the basis of anomalies in the MAC header fields, yet reduces steganographic bandwidth accordingly.

4   Simulations

Although the BAN standard IEEE 802.15.6 was first published in 2012, the use of compliant products is not yet fairly widespread. While this will rapidly change in the coming years as production costs decrease and hardware and software become more efficient, currently it is not yet possible for us to conduct tests in a real-world BAN. Therefore, we use the Body Network Simulator (BNS)[1] proposed by Caballero et al. [2] that implements the BAN MAC layer as defined in IEEE 802.15.6. It is an extension of the Castalia[2] BAN simulator which is based on the OMNeT++[3] library.

We implement a covert channel within a realistic medical application scenario integrated in the BNS framework to evaluate whether the implementation of our steganographic channel is a suitable approach and how the capacity compares to the example of Sect. 3.3. As visualized in Fig. 2, a BAN scenario containing 11 medical devices is simulated. All of these medical devices are already in widespread use in everyday healthcare, albeit mostly in the form of larger external devices. In the BAN simulation, the medical sensors are placed in and on the human body and connected to a central hub, which acts as a gateway for internal communication between the sensors. In a real-world scenario, such a hub could also provide connectivity to external networks, e.g. via 5G to a telemedicine server that controls the patient's healthcare.

To implement the covert channel, we applied the *Reserved/Unused* pattern within the MAC layer of all nodes. We assume that every node acts as overt and covert sender, while the hub is the overt and covert receiver in our simulated scenario. The sensors distributed over the body collect and send their medical data to the hub as overt traffic. At the same time, all nodes also transmit covert traffic, e.g. falsified health data, to the hub which receives both the overt and

---

[1] https://github.com/midiacom/BNS-Framework.
[2] https://github.com/boulis/Castalia.
[3] https://omnetpp.org/.

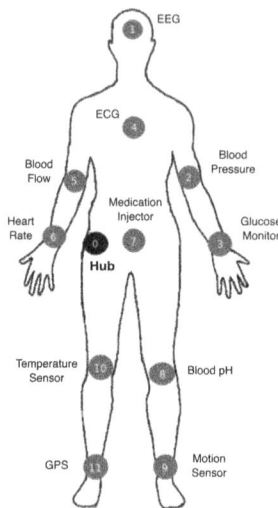

Fig. 2. Medical Application Scenario for BAN Simulation [2]

covert traffic. The hub, on the other hand, could forward the falsified health data, e.g. by using a covert channel within the 5G air link as proposed by Walter and Keller [22], to external covert receivers residing in a telemedicine server and influencing patient's healthcare. To create a steganographic channel with our approach it is necessary to modify the device code in such a way that the covert data to be transmitted is embedded in the reserved bits of the MAC header. The attack could be performed either before the medical sensors are implanted or via an over-the-air update if the devices are already placed in the human body. Furthermore, the hub has to be able to extract covert data from the Reserved header field of the MAC frames he receives. Since countermeasures such as logging or normalization of reserved bits were not implemented within the BNS framework, our covert channel remains undetected. However, this is not a weakness in the BAN implementation but rather a specification weakness, cf. Sect. 3.1.

Unfortunately, the header fields in the MAC layer of the BNS framework are not implemented in a standard-compliant way, e.g. instead of 4 reserved bits as in IEEE 802.15.6, an integer variable is used, which the C compiler translates into at least 16 bits. Nevertheless, we can make a realistic prediction of the covert capacity based on the configuration provided by the simulation, as we implemented our steganographic channel within the BNS framework using only the 4 bits given in the standard, which demonstrates that the transmission of covert data embedded in the reserved field of the MAC header works. In the BAN simulation, all nodes are configured with data rates representing the current requirements for transmission of data generated by medical sensors, i.e. 192 Kbps for ECG or 48 bps for Heart Rate monitor. Consequently, the covert capacity

$$C = (\text{overt data rate [bps]} \div \text{packet size [bpp]}) \times 4 \text{ reserved bits [bpp]}$$

also varies. As the packet size is fixed in the simulated BAN scenario and configured to be 100 bytes, the covert capacity of our proposed covert channel is for example $C_{ECG} = 960$ bps or $C_{Glucose} = 5$ bps. This is far from the covert capacity calculated in our simple scenario sketched in Sect. 3.3, as we have assumed an average data rate of 5 Mbps. However, it seems only a matter of time until data rates of medical sensors will exceed this threshold.

5   Protection of BANs

Countermeasures against covert channels in BANs start with usual countermeasures, i.e., network normalizers [16] that for example set reserved bits to default values and report or even drop packets with other values. Yet, such normalizer would have to sit at the hub to the internet and thus not be able to control direct communication between devices. To overcome this, we propose to apply virtualization to add an additional layer of difficulty for steganographic channels. Virtualization in the form of software-defined networks has been used in the past for wired and mobile networks to secure network parts by separation into network segments such as virtual LANs [1,20] and has also been proposed for BANs [19, Sect. II.A], e.g., to act as an interface between sensors and the Internet [5]. If a network packet carrying part of a secret message must cross the border of a virtual LAN, it must pass a virtual router that could also take the function of an active or passive warden and thus either fight or at least detect traces of such a covert channel [16]. As re-configuration is easier in software-defined networks than in hard-coded networks, the warden might even be frequently re-configured to perform functions of a dynamic or adaptive warden [4,15] and thus even fight adaptive covert channels that employ network environment learning to evade warden functions [26]. Yet, we admit that some scenarios need a more detailed, individual analysis to plan countermeasures, e.g., if an off-band channel such as 5G is used by a malicious sensor to send out stolen sensitive data that have previously been collected from sensors in the same virtual LAN.

6   Conclusions

By applying hiding patterns to BAN protocols, we have revealed that BANs are vulnerable to steganographic attacks such as exfiltration of patient data. Based on one such pattern, we have implemented a covert channel in IEEE 802.15.6 protocol within an example scenario and demonstrated its feasability in a simulation. Furthermore, we have made a proposal for countermeasures to make such secret data transfers more difficult, e.g., by introducing virtualization in the form of virtual LAN segmentation. Future work will comprise to extend our analysis to all storage patterns and to timing patterns. Furthermore, we plan to implement one of the steganographic channels that our analysis revealed in a real device, and to simulate a BAN protocol modified with segmentation, to demonstrate that this measure prevents the steganographic channels in BANs.

References

1. Ahmad, I., et al.: An overview of the security landscape of virtual mobile networks. IEEE Access **9**, 169014–169030 (2021). https://doi.org/10.1109/ACCESS.2021.3133319

2. Caballero, E., Ferreira, V., Lima, R.A., Soto, J.C.H., Muchaluat-Saade, D., Albuquerque, C.: BNS: a framework for wireless body area network realistic simulations. Sensors **21**(16) (2021). https://doi.org/10.3390/s21165504

3. Caviglione, L., Mazurczyk, W.: You can't do that on protocols anymore: analysis of covert channels in IETF standards. IEEE Netw. **38**(5), 255–263 (2024). https://doi.org/10.1109/MNET.2024.3352411

4. Chourib, M., Wendzel, S., Mazurczyk, W.: Adaptive warden strategy for countering network covert storage channels. In: 46th IEEE Conference on Local Computer Networks, LCN 2021, Edmonton, AB, Canada, 4–7 October 2021, pp. 148–153 (2021)

5. Galal, A., Hesselbach, X., Tavernier, W., Colle, D.: SDN-based gateway architecture for electromagnetic nano-networks. Comput. Commun. **184**, 160–173 (2022). https://doi.org/10.1016/J.COMCOM.2021.12.017

6. Hasan, K., et al.: Control plane optimisation for an sdn-based WBAN framework to support healthcare applications. Sensors **20**(15), 4200 (2020). https://doi.org/10.3390/S20154200

7. Institute of Electrical and Electronics Engineers: IEEE Standard for local and metropolitan area networks - part 15.6: Wireless body area networks. IEEE Std 802.15.6-2012, pp. 1–271 (2012). https://doi.org/10.1109/IEEESTD.2012.6161600

8. Jabeen, T., Ashraf, H., Ullah, A.: A survey on healthcare data security in wireless body area networks. J. Ambient. Intell. Humaniz. Comput. **12**(10), 9841–9854 (2021). https://doi.org/10.1007/S12652-020-02728-Y

9. Katzenbeisser, S., Petitcolas, F.A.P. (eds.): Information Hiding, 2nd edn. Artech House, Norwood (2015)

10. Keller, J., Spiekermann, D., Walter, M.: Protocol design rules from hiding patterns to avoid steganographic channels in wireless communication. In: IEEE Wireless Communication and Networking Conference (WCNC), Milan, Italy, 24–27 March 2025 (2025)

11. King, J., Bendiab, G., Savage, N., Shiaeles, S.: Data exfiltration: methods and detection countermeasures. In: IEEE International Conference on Cyber Security and Resilience, CSR 2021, Rhodes, Greece, 26–28 July 2021, pp. 442–447 (2021). https://doi.org/10.1109/CSR51186.2021.9527962

12. Lampson, B.W.: A note on the confinement problem. Commun. ACM **16**(10), 613–615 (1973). https://doi.org/10.1145/362375.362389

13. Masdari, M., Band, S.S., Qasem, S.N., Sayed, B.T., Pai, H.T.: ECG signals-based security and steganography approaches in WBANs: a comprehensive survey and taxonomy. Sustain. Comput. Informat. Syst. **41**, 100937 (2024)

14. Mazurczyk, W., Szary, P., Wendzel, S., Caviglione, L.: Towards reversible storage network covert channels. In: 14th International Conference on Availability, Reliability and Security, ARES 2019, Canterbury, UK, 26–29 August 2019, pp. 69:1–69:8. ACM, New York (2019). https://doi.org/10.1145/3339252.3341493

15. Mazurczyk, W., Wendzel, S., Chourib, M., Keller, J.: Countering adaptive network covert communication with dynamic wardens. Future Gener. Comput. Syst. **94**, 712–725 (2019). https://doi.org/10.1016/J.FUTURE.2018.12.047

16. Mazurczyk, W., Wendzel, S., Zander, S., Houmansadr, A., Szczypiorski, K.: Information Hiding in Communication Networks: Fundamentals, Mechanisms, and Applications. Wiley-IEEE Press (2016)
17. Mileva, A., Velinov, A., Hartmann, L., Wendzel, S., Mazurczyk, W.: Comprehensive analysis of MQTT 5.0 susceptibility to network covert channels. Comput. Secur. **104**, 102207 (2021). https://doi.org/10.1016/J.COSE.2021.102207
18. Oh, Y., Lee, Y., Jang, J., Choi, H., Lee, I.: Implementation and analysis of covert channel using iBeacon. In: 10th International Conference on Information Systems, Security and Privacy, ICISSP, Rome, 26–28 February 2024, pp. 861–868. SCITEPRESS (2024). https://doi.org/10.5220/0012457800003648
19. Preethichandra, D.M.G., Piyathilaka, L., Izhar, U., Samarasinghe, R., De Silva, L.C.: Wireless body area networks and their applications-a review. IEEE Access **11**, 9202–9220 (2023). https://doi.org/10.1109/ACCESS.2023.3239008
20. Qiu, Q., Xu, S., Liu, S., Xu, T., Zhao, B.: Network virtualization security: threats, measures, and use cases. In: ITU Kaleidoscope, New Delhi, India, 21–23 October 2024, pp. 1–7. IEEE (2024). https://doi.org/10.23919/ITUK62727.2024.10772977
21. Thiruchelvam, V., Jegatheswaran, R., Binti Juremi, J.: Safeguarding patient data: advanced security in wireless body area networks and AI-driven healthcare systems. In: Applied Informatics, pp. 119–131. Springer, Cham (2025). https://doi.org/10.1007/978-3-031-75144-8_9
22. Walter, M., Keller, J.: 5G UnCovert: hiding information in 5G new radio. In: Sicherheit, Schutz und Zuverlässigkeit: Proceedings of 12th Conference of Security Section of German Informatics Society (GI), Worms, Germany, 9–11 April 2024. LNI, vol. P-345, pp. 33–46. GI (2024). https://doi.org/10.18420/SICHERHEIT2024_002
23. Wendzel, S., et al.: A revised taxonomy of steganography embedding patterns. In: 16th International Conference on Availability, Reliability and Security (ARES), pp. 67:1–67:12. ACM (2021). https://doi.org/10.1145/3465481.3470069
24. Wendzel, S., et al.: A generic taxonomy for steganography methods. ACM Comput. Surv. **57**(9) (2025). https://doi.org/10.1145/3729165
25. Wendzel, S., Zander, S., Fechner, B., Herdin, C.: Pattern-based survey and categorization of network covert channel techniques. ACM Comput. Surv. **47**(3), 50:1–50:26 (2015). https://doi.org/10.1145/2684195
26. Yarochkin, F.V., Dai, S., Lin, C., Huang, Y., Kuo, S.: Towards adaptive covert communication system. In: 14th IEEE Pacific Rim International Symposium on Dependable Computing, PRDC 2008, Taipei, Taiwan, 15–17 December 2008, pp. 153–159. IEEE Computer Society (2008). https://doi.org/10.1109/PRDC.2008.26
27. Young, A., Yung, M.: Kleptography: using cryptography against cryptography. In: Fumy, W. (ed.) EUROCRYPT 1997. LNCS, vol. 1233, pp. 62–74. Springer, Heidelberg (1997). https://doi.org/10.1007/3-540-69053-0_6
28. Zhou, Y., Zhao, L., Jin, Y., Li, F.: Backdoor-resistant identity-based proxy re-encryption for cloud-assisted wireless body area networks. Inf. Sci. **604**, 80–96 (2022). https://doi.org/10.1016/j.ins.2022.05.007
29. Zimmerman, T.G.: Personal area networks: near-field intrabody communication. IBM Syst. J. **35**(3.4), 609–617 (1996). https://doi.org/10.1147/sj.353.0609

SHAP Insights into Domain Adaptation in Netflow-Based Network Intrusion Detection Powered by Deep Learning

Marek Pawlicki[1,2]([✉]), Sebastian Szelest[1], Rafal Kozik[1,2], and Michał Choraś[1,2]

[1] ITTI sp. z o.o., Poznań, Poland
marek.pawlicki@pbs.edu.pl
[2] Bydgoszcz University of Science and Technology, Bydgoszcz, Poland

Abstract. The wide adoption of supervised-learning–based network intrusion detection systems is hindered by their reliance on labelled traffic, which is costly to obtain in real-world scenarios. In this work, five unsupervised domain adaptation methods are evaluated in an attempt to alleviate this problem. First, the severity of source-target divergence is quantified on two benchmark datasets(CICIDS2018 and UNSW-NB15 netflow datasets) using Maximum Mean Discrepancy, per-feature Wasserstein distances, and Kolmogorov–Smirnov tests. Next, a common neural-network backbone is trained on the source, and each DA method is used to attempt to bridge the source - target domain gap. Finally, SHAP is used to compare feature-importance patterns before and after adaptation, to assess the DA effect on model decision logic. The results demonstrate that conventional DA methods fail to deliver robust cross-domain NIDS.

Keywords: Domain Shift · Unsupervised Domain Adaptation · Network Intrusion Detection Systems · NetFlow Data · SHAP Explainability

1 Introduction

Supervised-learning-based Network intrusion detection systems (NIDS) are at the frontline of defending modern networks against malicious actors, merging high detection capabilities with high volume of processed traffic [1]. However, their significant weakness lies in the laborious process of obtaining labelled data. Hand-labeling millions of flows is not feasible [3,23]. As a result, researchers turn to open benchmark datasets to train intrusion detectors [6]. However, models trained on such data stumble when confronted with the realities of production traffic, or even when encountering traffic from different open datasets, whose feature distributions diverge [20].

This divergence, called "domain shift", manifests when the statistical fingerprint of traffic of one network fails to match that of another. Traditional ML models promise accurate detection, only to underperform when the assumption of test data coming from the same distribution as train data breaks down [21].

F. Skopik et al. (Eds.): ARES 2025 Workshops, LNCS 15999, pp. 292–309, 2025.
https://doi.org/10.1007/978-3-032-00644-8_18

Studies consistently show significant drops in detection rates when, for example, a classifier trained on campus traffic is redeployed on a corporate backbone, or when changes in user behavior and protocol usage reshape the traffic landscape [4,8].

Domain adaptation (DA) [11,22,27] emerges as a remedy to this predicament, aiming to bridge the gap between a labelled source domain and an unlabeled target domain. At its core, DA seeks a shared feature space in which the source and target data distributions align. Techniques such as Domain-Adversarial Neural Networks (DANN) [33] encourage formulating representations of samples that an adversarially-trained domain discriminator cannot distinguish. The success of the fusion of deep learning and domain adaptation in computer vision and natural language processing promises deployable and resilient NIDS frameworks.

Building on this promise of bridging train-test mismatches, this paper takes a hard look at whether unsupervised DA techniques truly live up to their promises when applied to real NIDS netflow data. Rather than assuming that marginal alignment translates into better detection, this paper first quantifies the severity of source-target shifts using Maximum Mean Discrepancy, Wasserstein distance and the Kolmogorov-Smirnov test. Next, five unsupervised DA methods - CORAL [31], deepCORAL [30], DANN [33], ADDA [32] and CDAN [12] are subjected to cross-domain NIDS evaluation, training only on CICIDS2018 netflow and testing on UNSW-NB15, with no target labels.

This paper also goes beyond aggregate performance metrics to inspect how each method reshapes the decision logic of the model. By computing per-feature Shapley-value explanations (SHAP) before and after adaptation, the authors expose which features remain misaligned even after DA is performed. This perspective reveals the limits of feature alignment - an aligned feature can still be semantically dislodged. Thus, the paper asks and seeks to answer the following three research questions:

1. [RQ1] How severe is the source->target shift in NIDS netflow features as measured by MMD, Wasserstein distance, and K-S tests?
2. [RQ2] Can standard unsupervised DA methods reduce that shift *and* improve detection performance on the unlabeled target?
3. [RQ3] How do per-feature importances (via SHAP) reconfigure after adaptation—and what does that tell us about the limits of "feature alignment"?

This paper is structured as follows: Sect. 2 reviews related work on cross-domain NIDS and DA, Sect. 3 describes the used methods, Sect. 4 quantifies the source–target shift, Sect. 5 details datasets, preprocessing and model setup, Sect. 6 presents classification and SHAP results; and Sect. 7 concludes with key insights.

2 Related Works

The authors of [9] introduce DI-NIDS, a Domain Invariant Network Intrusion Detection System. It is a truly unsupervised, imbalance-aware cross-domain intrusion detector. By first training a lightweight adversarial network to learn a 10-dimensional "domain-agnostic" embedding of NetFlow records (lab vs. live) without any target labels, and then fitting a One-Class SVM solely on benign source flows in that space—so anomalies anywhere get flagged, they reduce the source-target domain f1 score by only 6 f1-score points.

In [15] few-shot IoT intrusion detection is tackled by marrying adversarial domain adaptation to a novel dual-domain pairing scheme: instead of requiring large amounts of unlabeled target traffic, they generate "hybrid" and "concatenated" samples that approximate the joint source–target distribution, then leverage those pairs to train a supervised ADDA backbone toward truly shared features. On top of that, the authors design a super-lightweight LEFE-Net extractor and revamp the ADDA loss and discriminator. The authors of [34] present a semi-supervised adversarial DA framework tailored to industrial control system (ICS) that, unlike classical DANNs or partial/adversarial DA models, simultaneously classifies both shared and domain-specific attack categories under severe class imbalance. Their key innovation is a sample-discriminant module which fuses the domain-classifier confidence with label-classifier outputs to compute per-sample weights and filter private-label target samples, thereby enabling a weighted loss that counteracts negative transfer and guides supervised learning on rare attack types.

In [2] DA in NIDS is formulated as a transfer learning problem in which source and target flows may follow arbitrarily different distributions. The authors introduce two novel multi-kernel algorithms: DetMKTL and StoMKTL, that jointly minimise a Maximum Mean Discrepancy term over a convex combination of M kernels to align source and target domains.

The authors of [10] deliver the first systematic, explainable cross-domain benchmarking of ML-based NIDSs by reformatting four recent public datasets into a common NetFlow feature space and evaluating eight supervised and unsupervised models "train-on-A, test-on-B" across all domain pairs; they reveal that no model generalizes universally, that source-target swaps yield highly asymmetric performance shifts, and that, overall, unsupervised detectors hold an edge—and, by applying SHAP, demonstrate that successful cross-domain transfer hinges on the degree to which key flow features preserve their distributional separation of Attack vs. Benign across environments.

In [28] a GAN-based feature aligner plus a joint attack/benign classifier is used to transfer a deep-learning NIDS from one dataset to another with virtually no new labels, even when the two datasets use different feature sets. By pre-processing both source and target flows (including PCA to equalize dimensions), training a generator to map them into a domain-invariant subspace and a discriminator to distinguish domains, and then using the generator as a binary attack detector, they achieve near-source performance on UNSW-NB15 and NSL-KDD with as few as 100 target samples.

3 Materials and Methods

This section introduces the tools used in this study, starting from visualisation and xAI techniques, through the statistical tools to identify domain shift, and finally, unsupervised domain-adaptation approaches.

3.1 T-Distributed Stochastic Neighbour Embedding (t-SNE)

The goal of t-SNE [16] is to turn each multidimensional vector into a dot on a two-dimensional plane, so that dots close together correspond to similar datapoints, and dots that are apart convey dissimilarity. This is achieved through Stochastic Neighbour Embedding (SNE) - a process which turns the distances between every pair of high-dimensional points into a probability, where a bigger probability means the samples are more similar. The unique aspect of t-SNE is that it prevents the dots from clumping up by using a heavy-tailed Student t-curve, instead of a Gaussian. The benefit of t-SNE is that it reveals both tiny local neighbourhoods and larger cluster structures in one single map, without you having to choose a fixed scale ahead of time.

3.2 SHAP

SHAP [14] values quantify, using a game-theoretic approach, the individual contribution each feature makes to moving the prediction away from a neutral baseline. By treating every feature as a player and the output of the model as the collective contribution, SHAP evaluates every possible ordering in which features could contribute to the result. The summary plot of SHAP is dependent on the explained set of samples, it aggregates per-sample SHAP values across all features, so one cannot expect the summary plots to align perfectly even for samples drawn from the same distribution. However, the summary plot of SHAP provides an overview of feature importance, their overall magnitude and the contribution of which features matter to the model in that set. By plotting SHAP summaries for the same model (or adapted model) on both source and target samples side by side, one can immediately see whether adaptation has actually shifted the reliance of the model on particular features. Traditional metrics, like MMD, WD and K-S test, inform if the distributions have diverged

SHAP shows the decision logic of the model. In principle, a successful DA should produce a model whose feature contributions line up between source and target. In other words, after DA, the SHAP summary plot on the target should look almost the same as on the source, showing that the model is relying on similar signals in both domains. If, after the DA procedure, SHAP produces different summary plots, it could suggest that even though the covariances of the domains were aligned, the model did not translate the semantics of the features from one domain to the other.

4   Domain Shift Analysis

In domain adaptation, the difficulty of transferring a model trained on a source dataset can be related to the magnitude of the differences in data distributions. In this section, the differences between the source and target feature distributions are analysed using Maximum Mean Discrepancy (MMD), Wasserstein distance (WD), and Kolmogorov-Smirnov (K-S)tests, supported by a t-SNE visualisation. This multi-metric approach reveals both the magnitude and structure of source–target divergences.

4.1   Maximum Mean Discrepancy MMD

Maximum Mean Discrepancy [5] is a statistic that measures the distance between two probability distributions. In the context of domain adaptation, computing MMD between a source domain and a target domain provides a direct, interpretable measure of how much the feature distributions have shifted. A larger MMD indicates a greater shift, which often results in degraded performance when applying a model trained on the source to the target data. To put the source–target MMD into context, a baseline distribution of MMD values was first obtained by computing the MMD between two random splits of the source domain data. This was repeated over 50 independent splits to capture the natural variability ("noise-floor") arising purely from sampling. Comparing the source–target MMD against the mean and standard deviation of these 50 source–source MMD values ensures that the observed discrepancy is not just an artefact of random sampling. The source–source MMD quantifies the level of divergence one would expect if both samples were drawn from the same distribution, providing a reference point against which to assess the domain shift.

4.2   Wasserstein Distance

The Wasserstein distance [24] - WD - (also called the earth-mover's distance) treats each distribution as a pile of mass spread over some space and asks: how much work is required to reshape one pile into the other? The cost of each move is the amount of mass times the distance it travels. The Wasserstein distance is then the minimum total cost needed to carry out this reshaping. Because it respects both how much mass differs and how far it must go, it provides a geometry-aware measure of distributional difference rather than just counting pointwise mismatches. By computing the Wasserstein distance for each feature, one can get a quantitative score of how much the distribution of that feature has shifted between the source and target domains. However, raw Wasserstein values can vary wildly in scale, so the observed range of each feature has to be reported.

4.3   The Kolmogorov–Smirnov Test

The Kolmogorov–Smirnov (K-S) [13] test is a way to compare two sets of observations by looking at how their cumulative distributions differ. The resulting D statistic is the largest vertical gap between those cumulative distributions. A D close to 1 means they diverge almost completely at some point. The accompanying p-value signifies how likely it would be to observe a gap that large if both samples came from the same distribution. A p-value near zero means one can confidently conclude the distributions differ. In the context of domain comparison in ML, the two-sample K-S test provides a check on whether each feature distribution has shifted between the source and target domains.

4.4 Correlation Alignment for Unsupervised Domain Adaptation and DeepCORAL

CORrelation ALignment (CORAL) [30] is an unsupervised domain-adaptation approach. It adapts a labeled source domain to an unlabeled target domain by aligning covariances. CORAL does not require labels for the target domain.

DeepCORAL [31] extends into deep neural networks by introducing a differentiable CORAL loss directly into the training objective. This allows for end-to-end unsupervised domain adaptation. Rather than performing a separate feature alignment step before classifier training, DeepCORAL simultaneously fine-tunes a pre-trained network on labeled source data and unlabeled target data aiming at achieving an encoding that is both discriminative in terms of classification and domain-invariant. The network performs domain adaptation by jointly aligning covariance and training on the task-relevant features.

4.5 Domain-Adversarial Neural Network

DANN [33] is a domain adaptation technique that focuses on aligning features between domains. The objective of DANN is to acquire a representation of features that does not allow for differentiation by a discriminator network. This is achieved with adversarial training, by training an encoder on the labelled source domain samples and unlabelled target domain samples, so it is able to fool the discriminator. Thus, DANN extends a standard feed-forward network, which is used as the encoder, by adding two heads - **TaskClassifier** with task-loss $\mathcal{L}_{task}$, trained on source-domain labels, which is utilised for the classification of samples according to their labels and **DomainDiscriminator** with adversarial-loss, trained to distinguish source from target samples. $\mathcal{L}_{dom}$.

The adversarial training is performed using a `GradientReversal` layer (GRL). The GRL is inserted before the DomainDiscriminator head. The GRL multiplies the gradient by $-\lambda$ during backpropagation, causing the encoder and the discriminator networks to be optimised with opposing objectives, with the discriminator gradient getting scaled by λ.

4.6 Adversarial Discriminative Domain Adaptation ADDA

The Adversarial Discriminative Domain Adaptation (ADDA) [32] unsupervised domain-adaptation technique allowing the user to train a classifier on a labelled source dataset and adapt that classifier to an unlabelled target dataset. The approach features a standard supervised training to formulate the 'source ecoder' network for feature extraction and a 'source classifier', then trains a discriminator to be able to tell apart the source and the target domain samples, and at the same time trains an encoder for the target domain, which adversarially learns to translate the target domain features into the source domain features, until it is able to reliably fool the discriminator.

4.7 Conditional Adversarial Domain Adaptation CDAN

In Conditional Adversarial Domain Adaptation (CDAN) [12] the discriminator used the label guesses of the model source-trained model along with the feature vector. The method is set up as follows: a feature extractor/encoder and a softmax classifier head are trained on the labelled source data, and a discriminator model is trained adversarially. The trade-off weight λ is set as a hyperparameter.

Table 1. Wasserstein distances with observed ranges, normalized scores, and qualitative comments

Feature	WD	Range	Norm'd WD	Comment
IN_BYTES	0.044180	99.645432	0.000443	Negligible difference: inbound byte-size distributions are almost identical
OUT_BYTES	0.208096	412.440658	0.000505	Negligible difference: outbound byte-size distributions are almost identical
IN_PKTS	0.041520	63.098035	0.000658	Negligible difference: inbound packet counts are highly similar
OUT_PKTS	0.348679	421.471227	0.000827	Negligible difference: outbound packet counts are highly similar
FLOW_DURATION MILLISECONDS	0.988960	2.003586	0.493595	Moderate difference: flow durations differ by roughly half their observed span
L4_SRC_PORTEnc	0.312277	3.816163	0.081830	Low difference: source-port usage shows only slight divergence
L4_DST_PORTEnc	0.982127	2.694890	0.364441	Moderate difference: destination-port distributions differ noticeably
PROTOCOLEnc	0.450333	3.308432	0.136117	Low difference: network-layer protocol mix shifts are modest
L7_PROTOEnc	1.246894	2.341427	0.532536	High difference: application-layer protocol usage shifts are substantial
TCP_FLAGSEnc	6.464376	10.426296	0.620007	High difference: TCP flag patterns show large-scale variation

4.8   Classification Metrics

This paper uses the standard Accuracy, Precision, and Recall evaluation metrics [7,29]. Accuracy is the proportion of correctly classified instances among all samples, widely used due to its simplicity. While it is intuitive, it is misleading in imbalanced settings.

Precision (also known as Positive Predictive Value) conveys the proportion of true positive predictions among all positive predictions. Useful when the cost of false positives is high, it reflects how often positive predictions are correct.

Recall (also referred to as Sensitivity or True Positive Rate) measures the proportion of actual positives that are correctly identified. It is important in detection tasks.

The Matthews Correlation Coefficient (MCC) considers all components of a confusion matrix—true positives (TP), true negatives (TN), false positives (FP), and false negatives (FN), to deliver an evaluation of classification performance. Its value ranges from –1 to 1, where 0 indicates random prediction, 1 signifies a perfect classification, and –1 denotes complete disagreement.

Balanced Accuracy is a metric used in datasets with imbalance of classes, it is the average of sensitivity and specificity.

The Geometric Mean (G-Mean) is a performance metric that evaluates the balance between classification sensitivity (recall for the positive class) and specificity (recall for the negative class). It is particularly useful for imbalanced datasets, as it ensures that the model performs well across both classes. The G-Mean ranges from 0 to 1, with higher values indicating better overall classification performance. A G-Mean of 1 reflects perfect sensitivity and specificity.

5   Experimental Setup

5.1   Datasets and Data Preprocessing

The experiment was performed on the publicly available CICIDS2018 [26] and UNSW-NB15 [17] subsets of the Netflow Collection converted into Netflow format [25]. Two comma-separated value (CSV) files constitute the source (CSE-CIC-IDS2018) and target (UNSW-NB15) domains. Each used dataset is a well-regarded cybersecurity benchmark.

Any label containing "benign" is classified as "Benign," while all others are collapsed under the "Attack" class. This is to reduce complexity, to evaluate the domain adaptation methods in the easiest viable scenario. To address source-domain imbalance, the majority "Benign" class is downsampled without replacement to match the number of attack instances (1:1 ratio). The target domain is left as-is to simulate a real-world situation where no labelled samples are available. Infinite values are replaced with NaN, and all NaNs and duplicates are removed. Five categorical columns (source/destination ports, protocol identifiers, application–layer protocol, TCP flags) are frequency-encoded. The un-encoded categorical features are then discarded along with the IP information. Stratified sampling partitions each domain into training (80%) and testing

(20%) subsets. A StandardScaler is fitted on source training subset and applied to the source test set and both target sets.

5.2   Classifier Backbone

Table 2. Configuration of the baseline model, also used as the encoder in the evaluated domain adaptation methods.

Component	Specification
Hidden layer 1	Dense(128, activation='relu')
Hidden layer 2	Dense(64, activation='relu')
Hidden layer 3	Dense(32, activation='relu')
Output layer	Dense(1, activation='sigmoid')
Optimizer	Adam
Loss function	binary_crossentropy
Metrics	['accuracy']
Validation split	0.1
Epochs	30
Batch size	32
Verbose level	1

Table 2 summarises the configuration of the baseline ANN. The model begins with an input layer that matches the dimensionality of the source feature set. It then passes through three fully connected hidden layers with 128, 64, and 32 neurons, each employing a ReLU activation function. A final output layer with a single neuron and sigmoid activation produces the binary classification. The model is compiled using the Adam optimiser, a binary cross-entropy loss (matching the binary classification and the sigmoid in the ultimate layer), and accuracy as the evaluation metric. During training, 10% of the source data is reserved for validation. The training proceeds for up to 30 epochs, with a batch size of 32. A batch size of 32 was selected as a practical compromise between GPU memory utilisation and the statistical quality of gradient estimates. The remainder of the hyperparameters was selected as a result of previous extensive research [18,19]. This baseline is trained on the source training set, the weights are saved, and to control for the encoder variability in training, the pre-trained ANN will be loaded as an encoder for each domain adaptation method (that uses an encoder model).

6   Results

Table 3 shows the baseline MMD, source-target MMD and the z-score for the two evaluated NIDS datasets. The z-score of 2590 means that the observed MMD

Table 3. MMD Results with Baseline Comparison

Metric	Value
Baseline MMD^2 (source vs. source)	0.000358 ± 0.000153
Source–target MMD^2	0.397458
Z-score	2590.10

is over 2590 standard deviations above what could be expected from random sampling noise alone. The source-target MMD is 3 magnitudes larger than the source-source MMD. That basically means there is no plausible way that the source and target sets came from the same distribution.

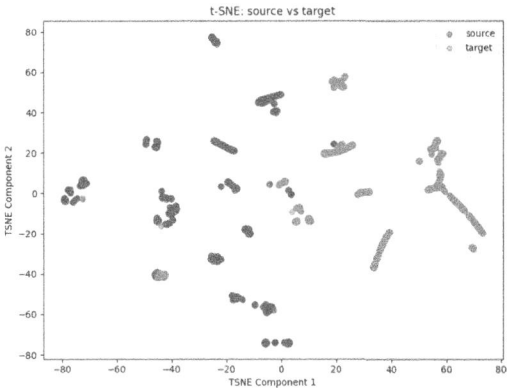

Fig. 1. t-SNE plot of the source and the target domain. (Color figure online)

The t-SNE plot in Fig. 1 illustrates that the source (blue) and target (orange) are, for the most part, out of alignment. The majority of source points cluster on the left, while target points cluster on the right, indicating a significant domain shift.

In Table 1, each row shows the feature name, its raw Wasserstein distance (WD), the full span of observed values (max-min), and the distance divided by that span (the normalised WD score). It also provides a qualitative comment, ranging from "negligible" for almost identical distributions up to "high" for substantial shifts.

Overall, the byte- and packet-level features (IN_BYTES, OUT_BYTES, IN_PKTS, OUT_PKTS) show almost no shift between the two domains: all normalised WD are well below 0.001, indicating that the traffic volume and packet counts are essentially unchanged. This suggests that whatever shifts are observed are not due to a difference in overall data throughput, but rather to changes in how traffic is structured. FLOW_DURATION exhibits a moderate shift -normalised WD around 0.49 - meaning that typical connection lifetimes have changed by about half of their overall span. Similarly, destination-port distributions (L4_DST_PORTEnc, with normalised WP around 0.36) have shifted noticeably, which conveys that different services or endpoints are being contacted. The largest shifts are present at the application layer protocols and in TCP flag patterns, indicating a substantial change in which application protocols are in use (new web service, streaming platform, novel cloud API), and in the way TCP sessions are being established or killed. A set of quick preliminary experiments shows that simply deleting the shifted features results in an over 10-percentage-point drop in accuracy in the source domain.

Table 4. K–S Test Results by Feature

Feature	D_statistic	pvalue
IN_BYTES	0.396419	0.0
OUT_BYTES	0.666933	0.0
IN_PKTS	0.433315	0.0
OUT_PKTS	0.659379	0.0
FLOW_DURATION_MILLISECONDS	0.494592	0.0
L4_SRC_PORTEnc	0.502191	0.0
L4_DST_PORTEnc	0.574708	0.0
PROTOCOLEnc	0.795696	0.0
L7_PROTOEnc	0.734357	0.0
TCP_FLAGSEnc	0.958192	0.0

The D statistic and its p-value, give a quick map of where the biggest distributional changes occur. In Table 4, every p-value is effectively zero, so all features show statistically significant drift. The D statistics rank them by the maximum pointwise difference. Features like IN_BYTES and IN_PKTS have moderate D values (around 0.4), indicating noticeable but not overwhelming shifts in volume. By contrast, PROTOCOLEnc with D around 0.80 and TCP_FLAGSEnc with D around 0.96 are signalling that the mix of network protocols and TCP-flag patterns has changed dramatically.

The classification metrics are as unforgiving as the stark domain mismatch measures. The baseline ANN (Table 5, left) achieves near-perfect performance on source domain, but collapses on the target. The techniques of unsupervised adaptation deliver, at best, marginal improvements, but most often fail catastrophically, where attack recall hovers at or below 0.35, and often at zero (Tables 5, right, 7, 6. Neither aligning covariances nor adversarially blurring domains helped the ability of the detector to spot malicious flows.

Before adaptation (Fig. 2a), source predictions draw heavily on port encodings and TCP flags. After adaptation, mostly the same feature dominate - with the exception of flow_duration falling in importance in the target domain, and

Table 5. Comparison of classification metrics for source vs. target domains under two approaches.

(a) Baseline ANN model			(b) CORAL approach		
Metric	Source	Target	Metric	Source	Target
Attack			*Attack*		
Precision	1.00	0.50	Precision	0.47	0.02
Recall	0.91	0.01	Recall	0.79	0.35
F1-score	0.95	0.01	F1-score	0.59	0.04
Benign			*Benign*		
Precision	0.95	0.96	Precision	0.76	0.92
Recall	1.00	1.00	Recall	0.43	0.32
F1-score	0.97	0.98	F1-score	0.55	0.48
Macro average			*Macro average*		
Precision	0.97	0.73	Precision	0.61	0.47
Recall	0.96	0.50	Recall	0.61	0.33
F1-score	0.96	0.50	F1-score	0.57	0.26
Weighted average			*Weighted average*		
Precision	0.97	0.94	Precision	0.64	0.89
Recall	0.97	0.96	Recall	0.57	0.32
F1-score	0.97	0.94	F1-score	0.56	0.46
Accuracy	0.9661	0.9611	Accuracy	0.5694	0.3220
Balanced Accuracy	0.9571	0.5033	Balanced Accuracy	0.6076	0.3338
G-Mean (macro)	0.9571	0.5033	G-Mean (macro)	0.6076	0.3338
Matthews Corr. Coef.	0.9302	0.0556	Matthews Corr. Coef.	0.2209	-0.1362

out_pktstaking its place - (Fig. 2b). Firstly, CORAL and deepCORAL (Fig. 3a and 4a) do not influence the original classifier, so the Source SHAP remain identical. The remainder of the methods use the encoder in the adversarial training, changing its weights, and thus the decision process. This is visible in both the degraded detection results and the SHAP scores (Fig. 7a, 5a, 6a). All three SHAP plots differ from the SHAP of the baseline model. In terms of the internal decision logic, all DA methods transformed the models in a way that emphasises the TCP_FLAGS feature significantly (Fig. 3b, 4b, 5b, 6b, 7b). The SHAP plots show that the DA approaches consistently alter the decision-making process of the models. However, with the brutal classification results, the message they convey is clear: unless the DA approach understands the semantic drift of features, not just their raw statistics, the detector will stumble.

Table 6. Classification metrics for source vs. target domains under ADDA and CDAN models.

(a) ADDA model			(b) CDAN model		
Metric	Source	Target	Metric	Source	Target
Attack			*Attack*		
Precision	0.00	0.00	Precision	1.00	0.38
Recall	0.00	0.00	Recall	0.91	0.00
F1-score	0.00	0.00	F1-score	0.95	0.00
Benign			*Benign*		
Precision	0.61	0.96	Precision	0.95	0.96
Recall	1.00	1.00	Recall	1.00	1.00
F1-score	0.76	0.98	F1-score	0.97	0.98
Macro average			*Macro average*		
Precision	0.30	0.48	Precision	0.97	0.67
Recall	0.50	0.50	Recall	0.96	0.50
F1-score	0.38	0.49	F1-score	0.96	0.49
Weighted average			*Weighted average*		
Precision	0.37	0.92	Precision	0.97	0.94
Recall	0.61	0.96	Recall	0.97	0.96
F1-score	0.46	0.94	F1-score	0.97	0.94
Accuracy	0.6075	0.9611	Accuracy	0.9659	0.9611
Balanced Accuracy	0.5000	0.5000	Balanced Accuracy	0.9567	0.5005
G-Mean (macro)	0.5000	0.5000	G-Mean (macro)	0.9567	0.5005
Matthews Corr. Coef.	0.0000	0.0000	Matthews Corr. Coef.	0.9298	0.0189

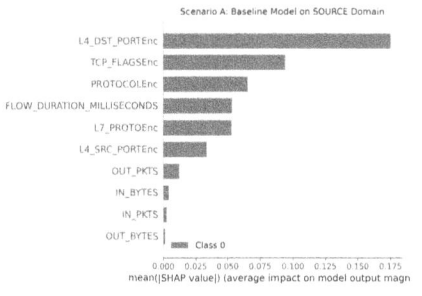

(a) Global SHAP on the source set

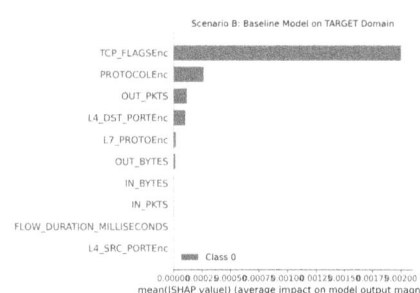

(b) Global SHAP on the target set

Fig. 2. Global SHAP summaries for (a) the source and (b) the target sets.

Table 7. Classification metrics for source vs. target domains under deepCORAL and DANN.

(a) deepCORAL model			(b) DANN model		
Metric	Source	Target	Metric	Source	Target
Attack			*Attack*		
Precision	1.00	0.00	Precision	1.00	0.07
Recall	0.11	0.00	Recall	0.87	0.00
F1-score	0.19	0.00	F1-score	0.93	0.00
Benign			*Benign*		
Precision	0.63	0.96	Precision	0.92	0.96
Recall	1.00	1.00	Recall	1.00	1.00
F1-score	0.78	0.98	F1-score	0.96	0.98
Macro average			*Macro average*		
Precision	0.82	0.48	Precision	0.96	0.51
Recall	0.55	0.50	Recall	0.93	0.50
F1-score	0.48	0.49	F1-score	0.94	0.49
Weighted average			*Weighted average*		
Precision	0.78	0.92	Precision	0.95	0.93
Recall	0.65	0.96	Recall	0.95	0.96
F1-score	0.55	0.94	F1-score	0.95	0.94
Accuracy	0.6491	0.9611	Accuracy	0.9472	0.9609
Balanced Accuracy	0.5531	0.5000	Balanced Accuracy	0.9329	0.5001
G-Mean (macro)	0.5531	0.5000	G-Mean (macro)	0.9329	0.5001
Matthews Corr. Coef.	0.2587	-0.0007	Matthews Corr. Coef.	0.8922	0.0022

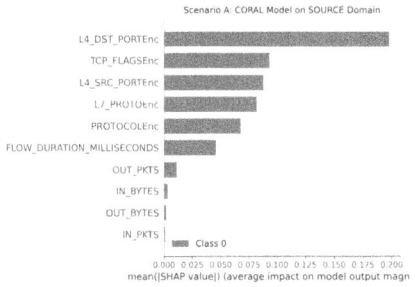 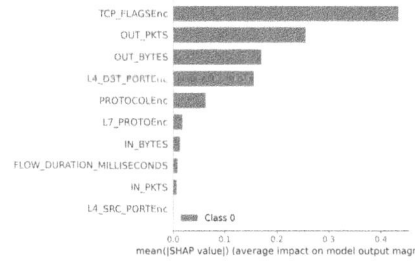

(a) SHAP plot for the source domain for the model trained on source domain data after CORAL adaptation

(b) SHAP plot for the target domain for the model trained on source domain data after CORAL adaptation

Fig. 3. Global SHAP summaries for the CORAL-adapted model on (a) the source and (b) the target domains.

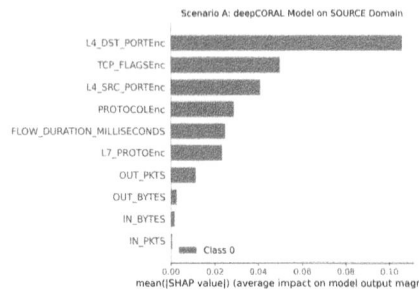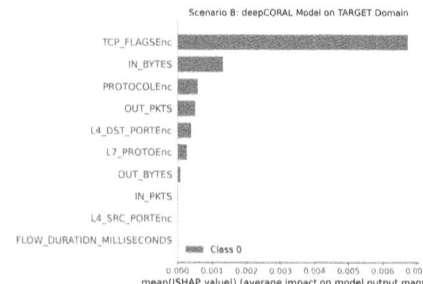

(a) SHAP of the deepCORAL model on the source data

(b) SHAP of the deepCORAL model on the target data

Fig. 4. SHAP summaries for the deepCORAL model on (a) the source and (b) the target data.

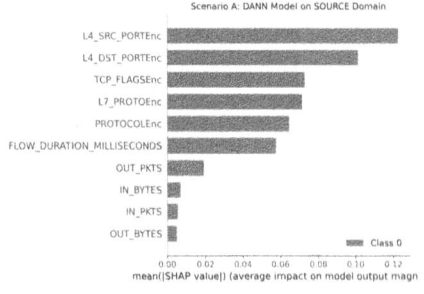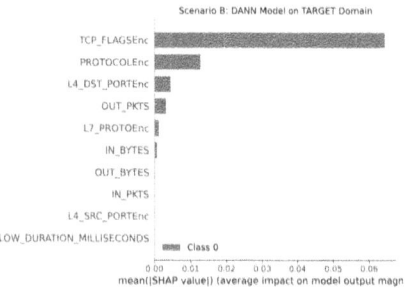

(a) SHAP of the DANN model on the source data

(b) SHAP of the DANN model on the target data

Fig. 5. SHAP summaries for the DANN model on (a) the source and (b) the target data.

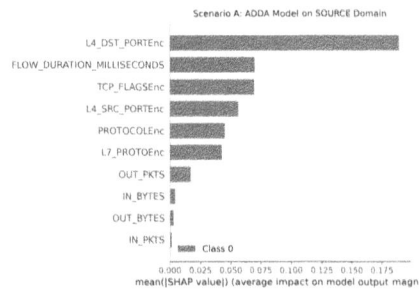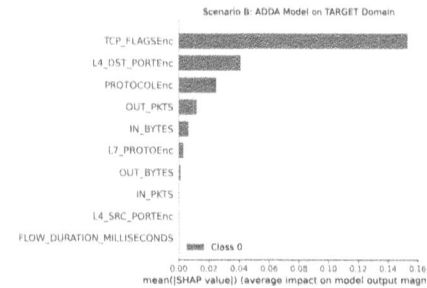

(a) SHAP of the ADDA model on the source data

(b) SHAP of the ADDA model on the target data

Fig. 6. SHAP summaries for the ADDA model on (a) the source and (b) the target data.

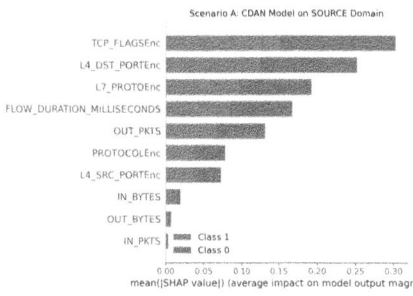 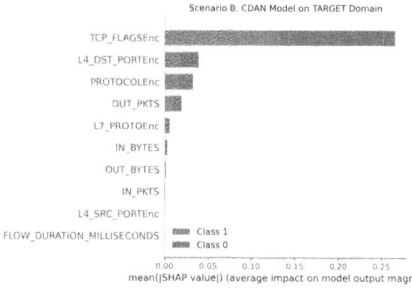

(a) SHAP of the CDAN model on the source data

(b) SHAP of the CDAN model on the target data

Fig. 7. SHAP summaries for the CDAN model on (a) the source and (b) the target data. Because CDAN requires a softmax, the figures have two colours, signifying the two classes.

7 Conclusions

This study revealed a significant disparity between the CICIDS2018 source domain and the UNSW-NB15 target domain, answering RQ1: Source–target $MMD^2 \approx 0.397$ providing clear evidence of a severe shift. WD and K–S are also highly significant. The t-SNE plot (Fig. 1) further substantiates this finding, showing that the two domains occupy largely disjoint regions in feature space. During this study, five canonical DA techniques, CORAL, deepCORAL, DANN, ADDA, and CDAN, were evaluated. The results were sobering - Attack recall seldom surpassed 0.35 and in some instances drops to zero. This answers RQ2. Finally, the study employed SHAP explanations to investigate the effect of DA approaches on the ML decision-making process. The results underscore a key insight: aligning statistical measures without accounting for their semantic meaning is not necessarily the best way to adapt ML-based NIDS (answering RQ3). The findings suggest that effective DA for NIDS requires more than conventional covariance alignment or adversarial training. We do acknowledge that the experiment was run on only two datsets, and the source domain 'benign' class was downsampled significantly, which might have an effect on DA.

Acknowledgements. This research is funded under the Horizon Europe AI4CYBER Project, which has received funding from the European Union's Horizon Europe research and innovation programme under grant agreement No. 101070450.

References

1. Ahmad, Z., Shahid Khan, A., Wai Shiang, C., Abdullah, J., Ahmad, F.: Network intrusion detection system: a systematic study of machine learning and deep learning approaches. Trans. Emerg. Telecommun. Technol. **32**(1), e4150 (2021)
2. Amamra, A., Terrelonge, V.: Multiple kernel transfer learning for enhancing network intrusion detection in encrypted and heterogeneous network environments. Electronics **14**(1), 80 (2024)
3. Dutta, V., Choraś, M., Kozik, R., Pawlicki, M.: Hybrid model for improving the classification effectiveness of network intrusion detection. In: Herrero, Á., Cambra, C., Urda, D., Sedano, J., Quintián, H., Corchado, E. (eds.) CISIS 2019. AISC, vol. 1267, pp. 405–414. Springer, Cham (2021). https://doi.org/10.1007/978-3-030-57805-3_38
4. Ghosh, S., Jameel, A.S.M.M., El Gamal, A.: Improving transferability of network intrusion detection in a federated learning setup. In: 2024 IEEE International Conference on Machine Learning for Communication and Networking (ICMLCN), pp. 171–176. IEEE (2024)
5. Gretton, A., Borgwardt, K.M., Rasch, M.J., Schölkopf, B., Smola, A.: A kernel two-sample test. J. Mach. Learn. Res. **13**(1), 723–773 (2012)
6. Hamid, Y., Balasaraswathi, V.R., Journaux, L., Sugumaran, M.: Benchmark datasets for network intrusion detection: a review. Int. J. Netw. Secur. **20**(4), 645–654 (2018)
7. Hossin, M., Sulaiman, M.N.: A review on evaluation metrics for data classification evaluations. Int. J. Data Mining Knowl. Manag. Process **5**(2), 1 (2015)
8. Kim, H., Park, S., Hong, H., Park, J., Kim, S.: A transferable deep learning framework for improving the accuracy of internet of things intrusion detection. Future Internet **16**(3), 80 (2024)
9. Layeghy, S., Baktashmotlagh, M., Portmann, M.: DI-NIDS: domain invariant network intrusion detection system. Knowl.-Based Syst. **273**, 110626 (2023)
10. Layeghy, S., Portmann, M.: Explainable cross-domain evaluation of ml-based network intrusion detection systems. Comput. Electr. Eng. **108**, 108692 (2023)
11. Liu, X., et al.: Deep unsupervised domain adaptation: a review of recent advances and perspectives. APSIPA Trans. Signal Inf. Process. **11**(1) (2022)
12. Long, M., CAO, Z., Wang, J., Jordan, M.I.: Conditional adversarial domain adaptation. In: Bengio, S., Wallach, H., Larochelle, H., Grauman, K., Cesa-Bianchi, N., Garnett, R. (eds.) Advances in Neural Information Processing Systems, vol. 31. Curran Associates, Inc. (2018)
13. Lopes, R.H., Reid, I., Hobson, P.R.: The two-dimensional kolmogorov-smirnov test (2007)
14. Lundberg, S.M., Lee, S.I.: A unified approach to interpreting model predictions. Adv. Neural Inf. Process. Syst. **30** (2017)
15. Ma, W., Liu, R., Li, K., Yan, S., Guo, J.: An adversarial domain adaptation approach combining dual domain pairing strategy for iot intrusion detection under few-shot samples. Inf. Sci. **629**, 719–745 (2023)
16. Van der Maaten, L., Hinton, G.: Visualizing data using t-sne. J. Mach. Learn. Res. **9**(11) (2008)
17. Moustafa, N., Slay, J.: Unsw-nb15: a comprehensive data set for network intrusion detection systems (unsw-nb15 network data set). In: 2015 Military Communications and Information Systems Conference (MilCIS), pp. 1–6. IEEE (2015)

18. Pawlicki, M., Kozik, R., Choraś, M.: Artificial neural network hyperparameter optimisation for network intrusion detection. In: Huang, D.-S., Bevilacqua, V., Premaratne, P. (eds.) ICIC 2019. LNCS, vol. 11643, pp. 749–760. Springer, Cham (2019). https://doi.org/10.1007/978-3-030-26763-6_72

19. Pawlicki, M., Kozik, R., Choraś, M.: A survey on neural networks for (cyber-) security and (cyber-) security of neural networks. Neurocomputing **500**, 1075–1087 (2022)

20. Pawlicki, M., Kozik, R., Choraś, M.: Towards deployment shift inhibition through transfer learning in network intrusion detection. In: Proceedings of the 17th International Conference on Availability, Reliability and Security, pp. 1–6 (2022)

21. Quiñonero-Candela, J., Sugiyama, M., Schwaighofer, A., Lawrence, N.D.: Dataset Shift in Machine Learning. Mit Press, Cambridge (2022)

22. Redko, I., Morvant, E., Habrard, A., Sebban, M., Bennani, Y.: A survey on domain adaptation theory: learning bounds and theoretical guarantees. arXiv preprint arXiv:2004.11829 (2020)

23. Rodofile, N.R.: Generating attacks and labelling attack datasets for industrial control intrusion detection systems. Ph.D. thesis, Queensland University of Technology (2018)

24. Rubner, Y., Tomasi, C., Guibas, L.J.: The earth mover's distance as a metric for image retrieval. Int. J. Comput. Vision **40**, 99–121 (2000)

25. Sarhan, M., Layeghy, S., Moustafa, N., Portmann, M.: NetFlow datasets for machine learning-based network intrusion detection systems. In: Deze, Z., Huang, H., Hou, R., Rho, S., Chilamkurti, N. (eds.) BDTA/WiCON -2020. LNICST, vol. 371, pp. 117–135. Springer, Cham (2021). https://doi.org/10.1007/978-3-030-72802-1_9

26. Sharafaldin, I., Lashkari, A.H., Ghorbani, A.A.: Toward generating a new intrusion detection dataset and intrusion traffic characterization. ICISSp **1**, 108–116 (2018)

27. Singhal, P., Walambe, R., Ramanna, S., Kotecha, K.: Domain adaptation: challenges, methods, datasets, and applications. IEEE Access **11**, 6973–7020 (2023)

28. Singla, A., Bertino, E., Verma, D.: Preparing network intrusion detection deep learning models with minimal data using adversarial domain adaptation. In: Proceedings of the 15th ACM Asia Conference on Computer and Communications Security, pp. 127–140 (2020)

29. Sokolova, M., Lapalme, G.: A systematic analysis of performance measures for classification tasks. Inf. Process. Manag. **45**(4), 427–437 (2009)

30. Sun, B., Feng, J., Saenko, K.: Correlation alignment for unsupervised domain adaptation. In: Domain Adaptation in Computer Vision Applications, pp. 153–171 (2017)

31. Sun, B., Saenko, K.: Deep CORAL: correlation alignment for deep domain adaptation. In: Hua, G., Jégou, H. (eds.) ECCV 2016. LNCS, vol. 9915, pp. 443–450. Springer, Cham (2016). https://doi.org/10.1007/978-3-319-49409-8_35

32. Tzeng, E., Hoffman, J., Saenko, K., Darrell, T.: Adversarial discriminative domain adaptation. In: Proceedings of the IEEE Conference on Computer Vision and Pattern Recognition, pp. 7167–7176 (2017)

33. Yu, C., Wang, J., Chen, Y., Huang, M.: Transfer learning with dynamic adversarial adaptation network. In: 2019 IEEE International Conference on Data Mining (ICDM), pp. 778–786. IEEE (2019)

34. Zhang, J., Yu, L., Zhang, F.: Network intrusion detection system based on domain adaptation for industrial control system. In: Artificial Intelligence Technologies and Applications, pp. 430–441. IOS Press (2024)

Real-World Identity and Access Management Scenarios Simulations in the SILVANUS Project

Paweł Rajba$^{(\boxtimes)}$ ⓘ, Natan Orzechowski ⓘ, and Dawid Nastaj ⓘ

Warsaw University of Technology, Warsaw, Poland
pawel.rajba@pw.edu.pl, natan.orze@gmail.com, daw.nas@o2.pl

Abstract. Wildfires caused by global climate change are an increasing problem and require applying a comprehensive global fire prevention strategy. To support these efforts, a SILVANUS project has been established with more than 50 parties engaged. However, such a large-scale initiative introduces complexity of collaboration and architecture, so introducing any security-related processes and components is challenging, including identity and access management ones. In this paper, we continue the efforts on building a robust and efficient identity and access management architecture (IAM). As both the platform and IAM architecture are distributed with scattered components across a wide geographical area, including regions with limited connectivity, we wanted to verify if certain aspects of synchronization are going to work properly in such a demanding environment. We build the test environment to simulate real-world challenges and propose two approaches for ensuring the IAM components are synchronized. The conducted tests confirm the feasibility of the proposed solutions as well as their robustness and efficiency.

Keywords: Identity and Access Management · Security Architecture · Network Security · Keycloak · Simulation · Performance tests

1 Introduction

Nowadays, every IT solution needs to be designed with applying appropriate security elements, and that includes respective identity and access management approach, which among others means strong authentication, a governed users' management, structured approach to access rights management with a special focus on the access to sensitive information [19]. More and more leading experts are stating that *identity is a new perimeter* and that principle is being applied in more and more enterprise companies. As a result, a reduced risk of unauthorized access and security breaches is expected. On top of that, there is also a trend for cloud-based and centralized authentication IAM services supported by standardized protocols like SAML or OAuth2/OpenID Connect [7], Single Sign-On, acknowledged architectures, and hosted by well-known cloud providers [1,14].

F. Skopik et al. (Eds.): ARES 2025 Workshops, LNCS 15999, pp. 310–325, 2025.
https://doi.org/10.1007/978-3-032-00644-8_19

The above considerations are also important in the SILVANUS project, where one of the main outcomes is a platform supporting efforts for introducing a fire prevention strategy for wildfires caused by global climate change. The platform also includes a toolkit for sustainable forest management with the aim of supporting collaboration between stakeholders from different countries. As the project consists of more than 50 partners, the platform is based on many IT systems, which finally need to be protected in a consistent and complete way, also applying comprehensive and proactive identity and access rights management.

In response to these needs, a general overview of the security architecture in the SILVANUS project was discussed in [15], and the identity and access management architecture was discussed in [17]. Certain parts of the security deployment baseline introduced in the project were described in [4], where identity and access management was also partially covered. The core IAM component for authentication and access rights management is based on Keycloak, supported by PostgreSQL DBMS, which are both open-source software. Due to the scattered and distributed architecture of the platform, the IAM architecture also needs to respond to this, and for that reason, there are many Keycloak instances that need to be in sync. However, for solutions with many Keycloak instances, the main consideration in the community is to support load-balancing scenarios [11], and we didn't find any automated approach for keeping dozens of or even hundreds of Keycloaks synchronized to the selected master one. In this work, we are trying to close that gap, considering a specific real-world deployment environment, and the main contributions of this paper are as follows:

- proposed two approaches for the Keycloak instances synchronization,
- introduced a test environment that simulates the real-life network bandwidth limitations,
- performed tests to ensure that the proposals are feasible and efficient in the established test environments,

by which we continue the efforts toward a robust and efficient identity and access management architecture in the SILVANUS platform.

The rest of this paper is structured as follows. In Sect. 2 we discuss the most relevant related work. Next, in Sect. 3 we introduce SILVANUS cloud architecture, including the identity and access management domain. Then, Sect. 4 includes the main proposals of Keycloak instances' synchronization as well as the description of the real-world variants we want to verify. In Sect. 5, details of the test environment are described, followed by the results of the experiments in Sect. 6. Finally, Sect. 7 concludes our work.

2 Background and Related Work

As described in detail in [17], the IAM solution in the SILVANUS platform is based on certain key components, protocols, and patterns. The overall architecture is based on the OASIS XACML standard [21], where respective functions are structured and defined appropriately following the consideration discussed in

[16], where certain partial adoption is proposed. The rights management is based on the Role-Based Access Control (RBAC) [18] and the Attribute-Based Access Control (ABAC) [9], and the authentication is primarily based on OpenID Connect (OIDC) [5], which is authentication protocol based on OAuth2 framework [7], however if necessary, Security Assertion Markup Language 2.0 (SAML 2.0) [10] is also supported. Finally, the key infrastructure component for supporting all the above is Keycloak, hosted in the SILVANUS Cloud domain.

The key consideration in this paper is to perform certain simulations in a test environment that depends on the following items: OpenShift [8] to support the complete hosting environment and Docker [2] to support the virtualization. We considered other options, for instance inspired by [4] where authors developed a Zero Trust infrastructure [20] in Kubernetes using Keycloak, we started with Minikube [12], however after experiencing certain configuration challenges, we decided to apply Docker in favor of simplicity and control. Finally, all tests have been orchestrated by creating respective Python [6] scripts, which give a lot of flexibility and control.

3   Architecture of the SILVANUS Platform

The SILVANUS platform consists of many components delivered by different consortium partners, which are structured into several functional and infrastructure domains. The main infrastructure areas are the central SILVANUS Cloud and multiple Edge Clouds deployed in the firefighters' Forward Command Centers (FFCs). An interesting part of the infrastructure is the Mesh-in-the-Sky network, which uses UAV-carried radio transmitters to provide network access to firefighters in remote areas, especially in case of emergency where the regular connectivity is broken. All that and the overall architecture of the SILVANUS Platform are presented in Fig. 1.

Considering functional domains, including the end user perspective, the main entry point is the SILVANUS Dashboard. The Dashboard is a web application hosted in the SILVANUS Cloud where users can find various results generated by many modules, a.k.a. the User Products (UPs). Each UP is an analytical application that provides fire-related analysis to the end users, and examples UPs are fire danger index or fire detection for IoT and UAV/UGV monitoring. Having that, users can see in the dashboard, e.g., a map generated by the fire danger index, with places where IoT devices detect fire.

All these infrastructure components, as well as functional areas in applications, require respective identity and access management implemented in a consistent, complete, and efficient way. The baseline IAM architecture has already been discussed in [15] and [17]. It is based on Keycloak, which is a core component for authentication, authorization, and access control tasks. Moreover, due to the scattered nature of the architecture as mentioned previously, many Keycloak instances are expected: the master Keycloak in the SILVANUS Cloud and a single Keycloak in each Edge Cloud. The main assumption is that all the IGA (Identity Governance and Administration) and access management activities should be performed on the master Keycloak and then further synchronized with all other slave Keycloaks. Unfortunately, Keycloak doesn't offer this kind of synchronization, and in this paper, we present two proposals for solving this problem. Moreover, we also performed a series of tests to verify and compare the proposed solutions.

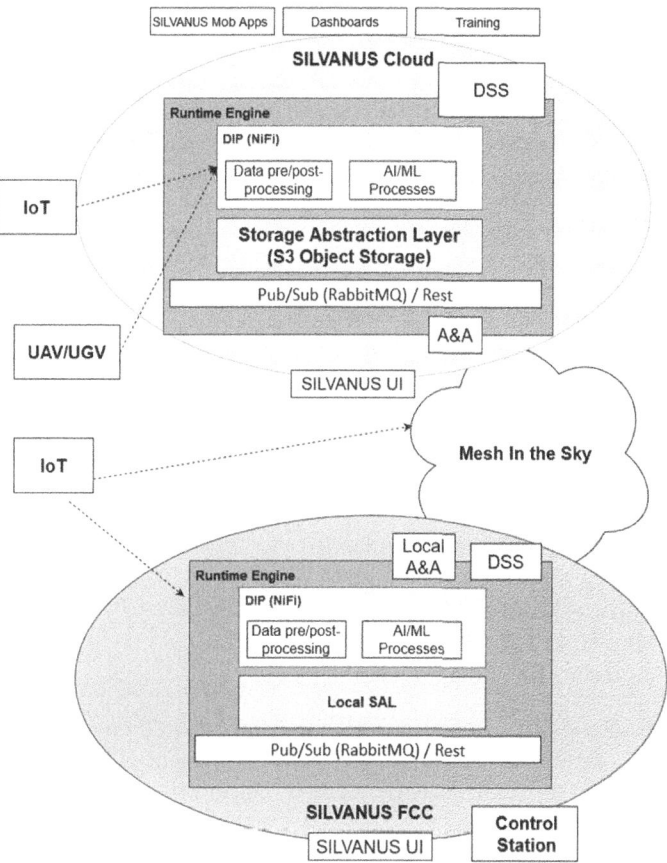

Fig. 1. SILVANUS platform architecture ([17]

4   Solution Proposals and Real-World Scenarios

Referring to the SILVANUS Platform Architecture, we have a single master Keycloak instance where all the accounts and permissions are managed, and there are many slave Keycloak instances used locally either to reduce the load of the master instance or to ensure the availability of IAM services in case of disruption. Moreover, these slave instances are distributed in many different locations, including those with very limited network bandwidth.

Our goal is to synchronize the Keycloak database, i.e., users and permissions from the master Keycloak instance to slave Keycloak instances, and this mechanism is not offered by Keycloak in a native way, so we need to introduce that. We propose two approaches to solve the problem:

- based on the Keycloak import and export functionality and the data transfer using the SFTP protocol. In this approach, the complete Keycloak database is exported, then it is transferred to Keycloak slave instances using the SFTP protocol, and finally imported into each of the Keycloak slave instances,
- based on the PostgreSQL database replication mechanism. In this approach, underlying Keycloak databases are configured to be replicated, and based on that, Keycloak instances are synchronized as well.

To sum up, in our experiments, we consider both described synchronization variants, i.e., based on:

- Keycloak import/export functionality,
- Replication of the underlying PostgreSQL databases.

At the current stage of the investigation, we have covered the test scenarios where we verify whether the synchronization between master and slave instances is timely and correct, considering the above-mentioned network limitations.

The baseline configurations for both variants are as follows:

- Bandwidth limit (download & upload):
  - 8 Mbp/s/2 Mbp/s (3G),
  - 32 Mbp/s/8 Mbp/s (4G),
  - 180 Mbp/s/45 Mbp/s (5G).
- Number of users: 100, 1000, 5000.

All other parameters, like RAM or CPU, are fixed for all created containers.

For each configuration of parameters, the experiment is performed 50 times, and based on that, the analysis is performed. During the experiment, the following measures are collected:

- Time of task completion (i.e., Keycloak instances synchronization),
- Confirmation that synchronization succeeded.

Despite the fact that our experiments are executed in the connected environment, we can briefly reflect on the situation where any of the slave Keycloaks is not available for some time. Due to the fact that any changes can be applied only on the master Keycloak, there will be no conflicts in the data synchronization. Once connectivity is back, either an import will be performed (always a complete database is exported from the master, so there is no risk of data loss), or a PostgreSQL synchronization will be executed. In case the master is not available, no changes will be applied at all, so there is no need for any synchronization.

5 Test Environment

The main purpose of the test environment is to simulate the real-world environment where IAM activities are executed. To achieve the goal, we apply the following solution. The whole test environment is based on Docker containers, and each component is hosted in a separate container, including the network gateway component, where key measurements are executed. On top of that, in the network gateway component, the respective network bandwidth limitations are applied to simulate the limitations of the real-world mobile environment. Finally, the overall environment is hosted on a single physical computer with RedHat OpenShift as a primary virtualization platform, where a single Ubuntu instance serves as an environment for conducting experiments.

To support the scenarios described in the previous section, we can distinguish two different configurations with respective combinations of the required components, and these are presented in Fig. 2 and Fig. 3.

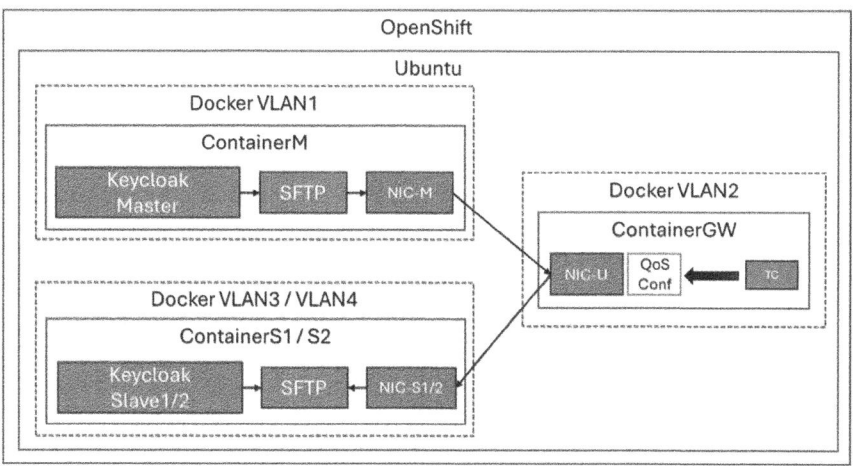

Fig. 2. Test environment architecture for scenario 1

5.1 Network Bandwidth Limitations

Network bandwidth limitation is implemented using the *tc* (traffic control, [13]) tool, which is a dedicated Linux utility for managing network traffic, including shaping, scheduling, and policing bandwidth on network interfaces. Applying this tool to the network component interfaces enables precise control over both upload and download bandwidths.

The basic usage of the tool is the execution of the following command:

```
$ tc qdisc <action> dev <interface> root
```

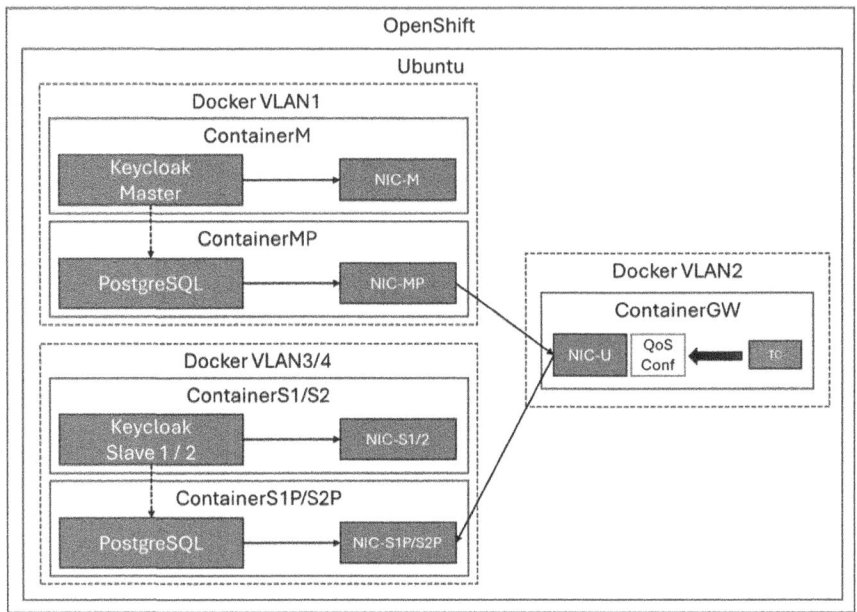

Fig. 3. Test environment architecture for scenario 2

A qdisc (queueing discipline) is a mechanism in the Linux networking stack that manages how packets are queued and scheduled for transmission. Various qdisc options offer different queuing and shaping strategies, one of which is HTB (Hierarchical Token Bucket) - a qdisc specifically designed for traffic shaping.

HTB enables precise bandwidth control by organizing traffic into a hierarchical structure where different classes can be assigned guaranteed or restricted bandwidth. In this context, *class* refers to a category or type of network traffic. It is used to classify and describe traffic based on specific characteristics. For example, labeling traffic as *originates from eth1* associates it with a designated network interface, allowing further processing or prioritization. This approach ensures efficient resource allocation, making HTB well-suited for the requirements of this work. Its key features include:

- hierarchical bandwidth distribution, ensuring fair resource allocation across different classes,
- defining minimum and maximum bandwidth limits for various types of traffic,
- prioritization of critical traffic, allowing high-priority flows to receive additional bandwidth when necessary.

As a first step, we execute the following command: By that, any existing queuing discipline *qdisc* on network interfaces (such as *eth0, eth1,* or *eth2*) is removed to ensure a clean configuration.

```
$ tc qdisc del dev <interface> root
```

Then, a new queuing discipline is assigned to the specific interface using the HTB algorithm with

```
$ tc qdisc add dev <interface> root handle 1: htb default 1
```

Breaking down this command:

- `tc qdisc add dev <interface>` – adds a new queuing discipline (qdisc) to the specified network interface (¡ interface ¿),
- `root handle 1:` – sets HTB as the queuing discipline for all outgoing traffic on the interface. The handle 1: acts as a reference identifier, allowing further configurations to be applied to this qdisc,
- `htb` – specifies that the HTB queuing discipline is being applied,
- `default 1` – ensures that any packets not explicitly classified into specific traffic classes are assigned to the default class (identified as class 1).

By establishing HTB as the root queuing discipline, the system gains control over bandwidth allocation and prioritization. The **handle 1:** parameter makes it possible to define multiple subclasses for different types of traffic, each with unique bandwidth constraints. Additionally, the default class (1) serves as a fallback, meaning packets that do not match predefined rules will still be processed without being dropped.

To define both the download and upload bandwidth limit, a traffic class **1:1** is added under HTB main class 1 with a command:

```
$ tc class add dev <interface> parent 1: classid 1:1 htb rate <fixed
rate limit> mbit ceil <fixed ceil limit> mbit
```

The specified class is linked to the root qdisc and enforces a strict bandwidth limitation. Both *fixed rate limit* and *fixed ceil limit* parameters are declared: `fixed rate limit` parameter specifies the guaranteed bandwidth, while the `fixed ceil limit` parameter defines the maximum allowable bandwidth. By applying this configuration, upload and download traffic can be effectively restricted to a fixed bandwidth.

5.2 Scripts for Test Execution

Conducting each test execution requires certain preparations, triggering data transfer, performing measurements, and finally collecting results.

At this point, we have an environment that enables the deployment of selected applications using Docker Compose, facilitates communication between these applications through a virtualized network layer, and imposes limits on system resources and network bandwidth for the applications. However, we need a solution that coordinates a single test execution as well as ensures an automation that executes complete scenarios described earlier. We decided to create a solution as a set of Python scripts that interact with the test environment components using Docker API [3] and the OS shell.

We also need to ensure the repeatability of each test instance, so in both scenarios, before each test instance execution, we need to configure Keycloak to a certain initial state, so we can draw conclusions and calculate statistics based on the obtained results. All that needs to be secured in the scripts.

During the configuration of the environment and the development of software capable of executing such scenarios, numerous challenges were encountered. These issues arose at various stages, requiring adjustments in both infrastructure setup and code implementation to ensure seamless execution.

Creating a complete configuration copy and uploading it to another instance requires the complete shutdown of the Keycloak process, resulting in downtime for the IAM system. Although this downtime was relatively short (on the order of a few seconds) and did not present a business obstacle within the context of our use case, it remains a noteworthy limitation. However, terminating the Keycloak process within a container that utilizes the RUN directive is not feasible, as this process acquires PID 1, becoming the parent process. Initially, an attempt was made to run two instances of Keycloak within a single container–one serving as the parent process, while the other participated in the simulation, specifically undergoing activation and deactivation for configuration import. This approach, however, proved impractical due to shared binary files between the two processes. A significantly simpler solution involved initializing the container with the bash shell process, followed by executing Keycloak within the established environment. This adjustment required modifications in container build scripts and in environment initialization procedures. The finalized setup first constructed a Linux-based image with pre-installed dependencies (such as SFTP support packages and Java), then generated a container from this image, which initially launched with the bash shell process before ultimately executing Keycloak. While this approach is not considered elegant, it was the only viable method to ensure progress.

The implementation of network restrictions also posed challenges, given the multiple approaches available. Since Docker does not natively support such functionality, additional software was required to impose restrictions and enable network traffic monitoring. The adopted solution involved the creation of an auxiliary container acting as a router for existing Keycloak instances. This router container regulated and monitored traffic at its level, ensuring controlled communication.

During preliminary experiments, the configuration import time measurement was inaccurate, as configurations were sequentially imported for Keycloak slave instances rather than being processed concurrently. This issue was addressed by establishing a clear distinction between sequential preparation/simulation tasks and concurrent execution. Any operations intended for Keycloak slave instances were structured to execute in parallel, optimizing overall performance.

Having the above, there are two main scripts to support SFTP and Post-greSQL replication scenarios.

The scripts for the import/export scenario implementing the experiments perform the following tasks:

- The current state of the infrastructure is verified against the desired state, which includes stopped application containers, no network filters on the host system, and the existence of a Docker virtual network for each Keycloak instance.
- Images for the Docker Compose environment are built.
- The Docker Compose environment for network devices is launched.
- The Docker Compose environment for Keycloak instances is launched.
- It is verified whether each Keycloak instance is operational and responding to HTTP requests.
- Default gateways are configured to facilitate communication between Keycloak instances.
- The test scenario is initiated. Each iteration (for 1 out of 50 test cases) includes the following tasks:
  - Stopping the Keycloak master instance.
  - Exporting the configuration of the Keycloak master.
  - Resuming the Keycloak master instance.
  - Distributing the Keycloak master configuration to all Keycloak slaves using the SFTP protocol.
  - Stopping all Keycloak slave instances.
  - Importing the configuration on Keycloak slaves.
  - Resuming the Keycloak slave instances.
  - Verifying the correctness of the configuration distribution (ensuring the master and slave configurations are identical).
- After completing the final experiment, all application containers are stopped and removed (the infrastructure is reused between experiments).

In the case of the PostgreSQL synchronization scenario, the following steps are performed:

- The current state of the infrastructure is verified against the desired state, which includes stopped application containers, no network filters on the host system, and the existence of a Docker virtual network for each Keycloak-PostgreSQL pair.
- Images for the Docker Compose environment are built.
- The Docker Compose environment for network devices is launched.
- The Docker Compose environment for Keycloak master and PostgreSQL instances is launched.
- Default gateways are configured to facilitate communication between Keycloak and PostgreSQL instances.
- The logical replication configuration is performed, including:
  - Configuring the appropriate schema in PostgreSQL databases.
  - Setting the streaming properties with the PostgreSQL configuration file (postgresql.conf).
  - Creating a publication object on the master database.
  - Creating a subscription object on the replica databases.
- The Docker Compose environment for Keycloak slaves is launched.

- It is verified whether each Keycloak-PostgreSQL pair is operational and responding to HTTP requests.
- The test scenario is initiated. Each iteration (for 1 out of 50 test cases) includes the following tasks:
  - Adding users directly to the PostgreSQL master database using transactions to ensure all users are added at the same time.
  - Logical replication between PostgreSQL databases.
  - Verifying the correctness of the configuration distribution (ensuring the master and slave configurations are identical).
  - Removal of previously added users to perform the next test iteration.
- After completing the final experiment, all application containers are stopped and removed (the infrastructure is reused between experiments).

5.3 Validation

One of the key aspects of the whole experiment was to ensure that the environment is providing reliable results and to check that and increase our confidence in the obtained results. We conducted the validation by copying 50 times a file of size 50MB and ensuring that the applied limitations on network bandwidth work.

The obtained results of the validation tests are summarized in Table 1.

Table 1. Summary of environment validation tests

Upload [MB/s]	Avg. Time [s]	StdDev. Time [s]	Avg. Transfer [MB/s]
2	220.25	0.05	1.82
8	55.57	0.11	7.20
45	11.69	0.86	34.20

There are two most important observations in these results. First, we can see that the average transfer is just below the threshold defined in the upload values. The second observation is that the transfer is very stable, i.e., the copying time in all iterations is very similar to what can be observed by reviewing the standard deviation values. At this point, we can conclude that the environment is ready to execute the experiments.

6   Results of Experiments

In the analysis, we focused on two main aspects: feasibility of the considered scenario, time required to synchronize Keycloak instances, and correctness of the synchronization in case the bandwidth of the network is limited. First, we can conclude that the feasibility is confirmed as both scenarios have been completed successfully. Next, we can also cover the correctness aspect, as it turned out that in all the conducted experiments, data was synchronized correctly, both in the import/export as well as the PostgreSQL replication scenarios. We also don't provide any comparison to other similar solutions, as we couldn't find any in the context of Keycloak systems.

Now, let us review the time needed to complete the synchronization. Due to the different nature of both investigated scenarios and, in consequence, the slightly different experimental setup, the results are not fully comparable. However, we can still conclude the following: (a) the execution time difference between various bandwidth limits, (b) the general time difference between scenarios, as even if they are not fully comparable, the gap size between the result values is still insightful.

6.1 Import/Export Scenario

In this scenario, we can distinguish three stages of the synchronization process:

- export, which happens locally on the master machine,
- SFTP transfer, which utilizes the network,
- import, which again happens locally on the slave machine.

Having the above, we want to primarily focus on measuring the middle stage, as it is when limitations of the mobile network may occur. Nevertheless, we also provide the export and import times for getting the complete view of the process.

In Fig. 4, average mean times of data transfer over SFTP are summarized. Results are grouped per number of users, and within each group, we can compare the results for each type of network: 3G, 4G, and 5G. We can easily observe that the results follow the expectation, i.e., the faster the network, the shorter the time; moreover, the bigger the number of users, the longer the time. Finally, we can also see that the total time is not too long, assuming that synchronization is executed, e.g., once per day or even once per 6 h.

In Fig. 5, there are again mean times of data transfer over SFTP, but presented in box plot view, providing more details. Here we can observe (what could be missed in average values) that data points are very focused around each mean value, and by that we can conclude that transfer time is quite predictable (of course, assuming network stability).

In Fig. 4, we can find the time needed to perform the export and import on a Keycloak instance. In this diagram, there is no split on different network types, as both activities are executed locally, either before or after the data transfer. As expected, the bigger the number of users, the longer the time needed to perform the operation. What is worth noting is the fact that from the end-to-end perspective, the time needed for export and import is significantly longer than the actual data transfer.

6.2 PostgreSQL Replication Scenario

In Fig. 7, a summary of the replication time is presented for the PostgreSQL replication scenario. The structure of the diagram is analogous to the one for

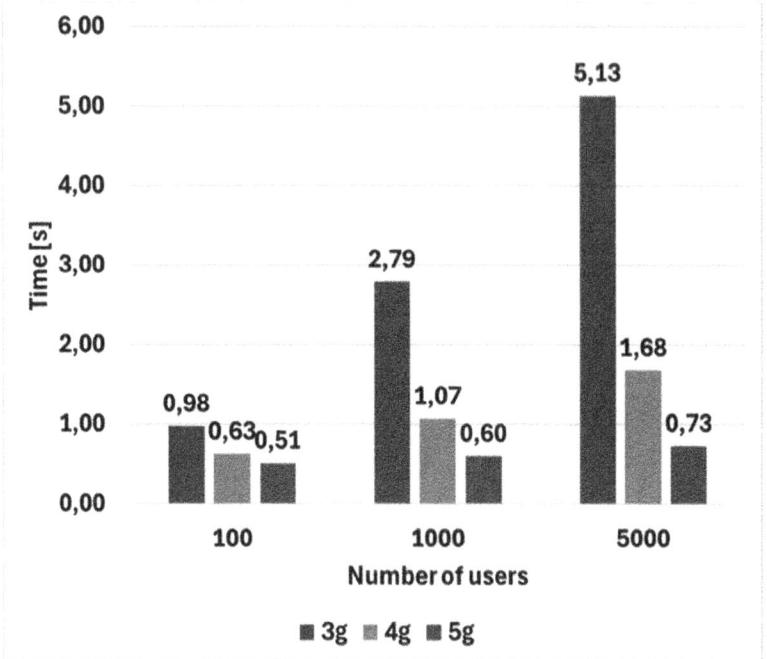

Fig. 4. Average time for the SFTP data transfer

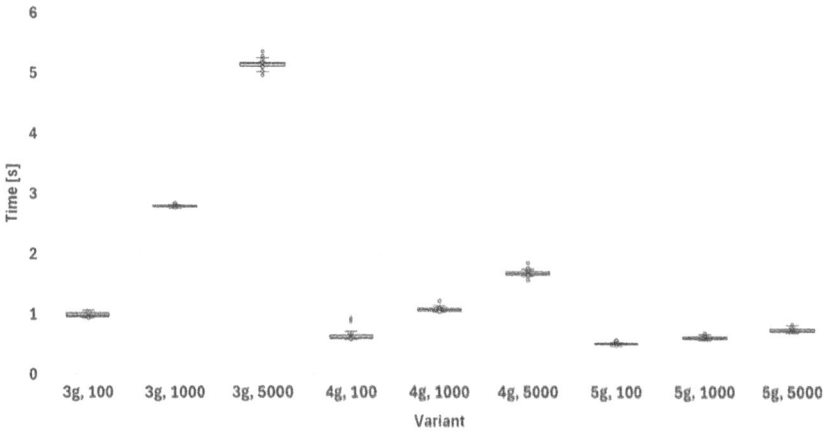

Fig. 5. Time for the SFTP data transfer with more detailss

the SFTP scenario, so results are grouped per number of users, and within each group, we can compare the results for each type of network: 3G, 4G, and 5G. We can easily observe that the results follow the expectation, i.e., the faster the network, the shorter the time; moreover, the larger the number of users, the

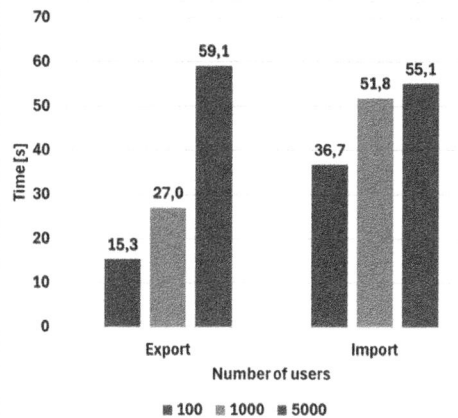

Fig. 6. Time for export and import on a Keycloak instance

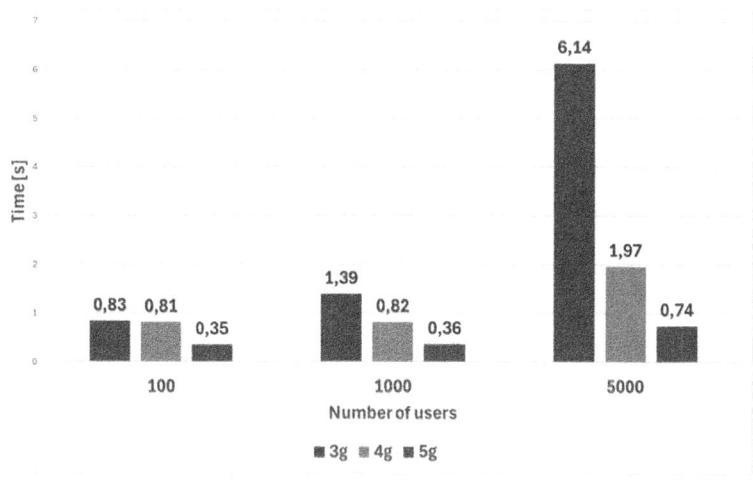

Fig. 7. Average synchronization time for the PostgreSQL replication scenario

longer the time. Finally, we can also see that the time is very similar to the one from the SFTP scenario, so it is not too long, assuming that synchronization is executed, e.g., once per day or even once per 6 h.

In Fig. 5, there are again mean times of PostgreSQL replication, but presented in a box plot view, providing more details. Here we can observe a little more dispersion of results, but it is still focused quite well around the mean value, so we can conclude that transfer time is quite predictable (of course, assuming network stability).

Finally, compared to the SFTP scenario, there is a significant advantage to this approach: while the data transfer time is similar, there is no need for export

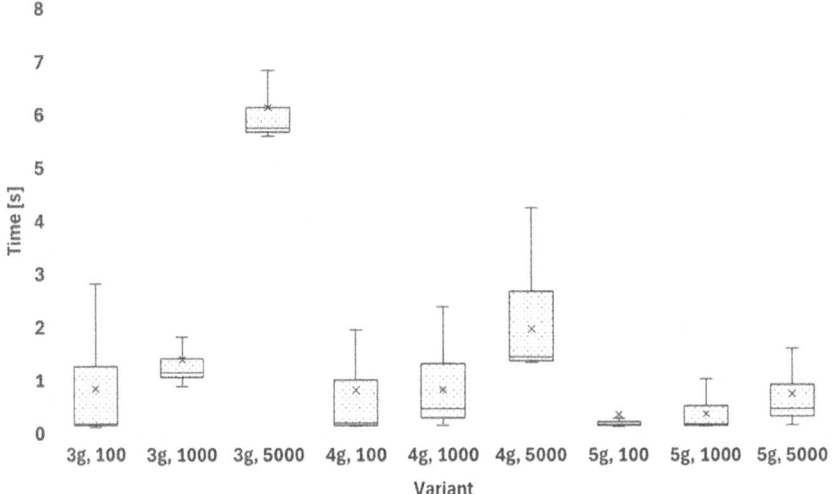

Fig. 8. Synchronization time with more details for the PostgreSQL replication scenario

and import activities; therefore, this approach is much quicker overall. Moreover, the import/export operation makes Keycloak slave/master instances unavailable for some time, which does not occur in the case of database replication in the background.

7 Conclusions

In this paper, we proposed 2 approaches for keeping multiple Keycloak instances in sync, introduced a test environment with real-world network bandwidth limitations applied, and presented results of tests for both presented approaches executed in the introduced test environment. Finally, we concluded with a short comparison showing that both solutions are feasible, but the database replication is significantly faster.

Future work will be devoted to considering other factors in the real-world environment, like limited memory or CPU power. Moreover, we also plan to consider introducing random disruptions in the network connectivity to simulate an even more realistic way of the real world environment. Finally, we also plan to introduce end-user devices in tests simulating daily usage of these in a challenging environment with applied limitations.

Acknowledgment. This work was funded under the SILVANUS project, which has received funding from the European Union's Horizon 2020 research and innovation program under grant agreement No. 101037247.

References

1. AWS: AWS IAM (2025). https://aws.amazon.com/iam/. Accessed 10 June 2025
2. Docker: Docker (2025). https://www.docker.com/. Accessed 10 June 2025
3. Docker: Docker Documentation (2025). https://docs.docker.com. Accessed 10 June 2025
4. D'Silva, D., Ambawade, D.D.: Building a zero trust architecture using kubernetes. In: 2021 6th International Conference for Convergence in Technology (I2CT), pp. 1–8 (2021). https://doi.org/10.1109/I2CT51068.2021.9418203
5. Foundation, O.: OIDC Documentation (2025). https://openid.net/connect/. Accessed 10 June 2025
6. Foundation, P.S.: Python (2025). https://www.python.org/. Accessed 10 June 2025
7. Hardt, D.: The oauth 2.0 authorization framework. Technical report, Internet Engineering Task Force (IETF) (2012)
8. Hat, R.: Openshift (2025). https://www.redhat.com/en/technologies/cloud-computing/openshift. Accessed 10 June 2025
9. Hu, V.C., et al.: Guide to attribute based access control (abac) definition and considerations (draft). NIST Spec. Publ. **800**(162), 1–54 (2013)
10. Hughes, J., Maler, E.: Security assertion markup language (saml) v2. 0 technical overview. In: OASIS SSTC Working Draft SSTC-SAML-TECH-overview-2.0-Draft-08, vol. 13, p. 12 (2005)
11. Keycloak: Keycloak documentation: configuring database (2025). https://www.keycloak.org/high-availability/introduction. Accessed 10 June 2025
12. Kubernetes: Minikube (2025). https://minikube.sigs.k8s.io/docs/. Accessed 10 June 2025
13. Linux Foundation: Linux manual – tc command (2025). Accessed 10 June 2025
14. Microsoft: Microsofot Entra ID (2025). https://www.microsoft.com/en/security/business/identity-access/microsoft-entra-id. Accessed 10 June 2025
15. Orzechowski, N., et al.: Security architecture in the silvanus project. In: Proceedings of the 18th International Conference on Availability, Reliability and Security. ARES '23. Association for Computing Machinery, New York (2023). https://doi.org/10.1145/3600160.3605082
16. Rajba, P.: Tackling access control complexity by combining XACML and domain driven design. In: Zamojski, W., Mazurkiewicz, J., Sugier, J., Walkowiak, T., Kacprzyk, J. (eds.) DepCoS-RELCOMEX 2020. AISC, vol. 1173, pp. 493–502. Springer, Cham (2020). https://doi.org/10.1007/978-3-030-48256-5_48
17. Rajba, P., Orzechowski, N., Rzepka, K., Szary, P., Nastaj, D., Cabaj, K.: Identity and access management architecture in the silvanus project. In: Proceedings of the 19th International Conference on Availability, Reliability and Security, ARES '24, pp. 1–9. Association for Computing Machinery, New York (2024). https://doi.org/10.1145/3664476.3670935
18. Sandhu, R.S.: Role-based access control. In: Advances in Computers, vol. 46, pp. 237–286. Elsevier (1998)
19. Soltani, R., Nguyen, U.T., An, A.: A survey of self-sovereign identity ecosystem. Secur. Commun. Netw. **2021**, 1–26 (2021). https://doi.org/10.1155/2021/8873429
20. Stafford, V.: Zero trust architecture. NIST Special Publ. **800**, 207 (2020)
21. Standard, O.: extensible access control markup language (xacml) version 3.0. A (2013). http://docs.oasis-open.org/xacml/3.0/xacml-3.0-core-spec-os-en.html

5G-Pentest-UE: A Penetration Testing Framework for Identifying 5G System Vulnerabilities

Richard Riedel[✉][ID] and Stefan Köpsell[ID]

Barkhausen Institut, Dresden, Germany
richard.riedel@barkhauseninstitut.org
stefan.koepsell@barkhauseninstitut.org
https://www.barkhauseninstitut.org/en/

Abstract. This paper presents and evaluates an open source penetration testing framework for finding vulnerabilities in 5G systems under the assumption of malicious end devices. This is achieved by enabling the creation of arbitrary (5G) messages to be transmitted over the air interface of a 5G system. Our framework is modular and scriptable, allowing the easy creation of test cases. It is based on the OpenAirInterface (OAI) open source 5G stack. We evaluated our framework by implementing several tests and running it against a well-known open source 5G system. We were able to identify several vulnerabilities.

Keywords: 5G · security · OpenAirInterface · user equipment · penetration testing · vulnerabilities · mobile networks

1 Introduction

In today's society, mobile communications already play an important role in many areas of life.

In the future, the importance of mobile communications will continue to grow due to its ever-increasing influence on various aspects of social coexistence. With the 5th generation (5G) of mobile communications and the associated technological innovations, for example, Internet of Things (IoT) applications are increasingly becoming part of mobile networks.

Today, most mobile networks are public networks. They are complex systems run by large operators. However, in the last few years, developments in the field of private networks have gained significant interest. Such private networks usually are smaller-sized 5G systems. They are often used as a more flexible and more performant alternative or complement to WLAN networks. With the concurrent rise of open architectures like O-RAN and the resulting multi-vendor deployments, the number of different implementations of the 5G specifications is also growing. Besides this, the feature set of 5G is extended continuously to match the large number of new use case ideas, which also leads to many new implementations.

© The Author(s), under exclusive license to Springer Nature Switzerland AG 2025
F. Skopik et al. (Eds.): ARES 2025 Workshops, LNCS 15999, pp. 326–339, 2025.
https://doi.org/10.1007/978-3-032-00644-8_20

These developments result in a high chance of implementation errors. Also, the specifications for new and old features may not be perfect, which also favours the emergence of vulnerabilities. One obvious attack vector to utilise those errors is the air interface over which the User Equipments (UEs), such as phones or IoT devices, communicate with the 5G network. By the nature of wireless communication, this air interface will always be accessible by attackers, at least to some extent. Therefore, attacks over this interface must be considered wherever a 5G network is deployed.

In summary, in the current situation, many deployments and implementations of different 5G software stacks combined with the ability to attack them over the air demand rigorous tests to identify potential vulnerabilities early on. Therefore, we created a framework to facilitate the pentesting of 5G systems to find vulnerabilities before they can cause problems in production systems. Our contributions can be summarised as follows:

1. We designed a framework that allows the easy creation and execution of vulnerability test cases.
2. We evaluated the framework by testing an existing 5G stack.
3. We provide our framework as open source. This includes extensive documentation.

The rest of the paper is organised as follows: Sect. 2 gives an overview of the goals and requirements for our framework, Sect. 3 presents related work, while Sect. 4 describes the design of our framework. We present the related evaluation results in Sect. 5 and conclude the paper in Sect. 6.

2   Development Goals and Requirements

As mentioned in the introduction, our goal is to develop a framework that allows us to test 5G systems with respect to vulnerabilities. Thereby, we concentrate on the case of a malicious user equipment trying to attack the 5G system. We decided on this scenario because it is more easily executable from an attacker's perspective compared to, e.g., manipulating the 5G system itself. This is supported by the fact that freely programmable UEs can be easily realised with the help of existing open source software stacks in combination with cheap software-defined radios.

To describe what the testing framework shall be capable of, we first need to precisely describe what an UE in a 5G system can do in theory and practice. From this knowledge, the capabilities of our framework can be derived.

UEs have at least one thing in common: they communicate with the 5G system through electromagnetic waves. Therefore, on the lowest level, they have two capabilities: one is sending radio signals, and the other is receiving them. The 5G specifications describe precisely how UEs send and receive radio signals and how they talk to the 5G system. Thereby, protocols and related protocol messages are defined at several layers.

Our goal, therefore, consists of providing easy means to send and receive (manipulated) protocol messages at all layers. In the following, we describe the attacker model we have in mind and derive related requirements regarding our framework.

2.1   Attacker Model

Our attacker model is based on the idea of a malicious UE. Therefore, the attacker is able to deviate from the 5G specifications when taking part in 5G communication. Note that following some parts of the specifications is necessary to be able to deviate from other parts. This might sound obvious, but emphasising this fact is important to understand the framework's value, which makes it possible to deviate on different layers and in different situations easily.

We can subdivide our attacker model into two scenarios: the attacker can be either a legitimate user of a given 5G system or not. In the latter case, the attacker is an outsider.

This translates to the question of whether the attacker has valid authentication information to properly register with the 5G system or not. To a certain extent, our framework will be agnostic to this since it allows manipulation of all messages at all layers. Therefore, both attacker models can be analysed using our framework.

Nevertheless, one limitation of our framework is that it works only on the digital layer. Therefore, no attacks at the physical layer (i.e., at the layer of the analogous radio signal) like jamming can be executed. Finally, attacks implemented with the help of the framework are always active attacks since the attacker needs to interact with the mobile network.

2.2   Framework Requirements

Considering the attacker model, we find the following requirements for our framework.

First. We want to be able to adhere to the specifications at any place needed. This means we first need software that can do everything a normal 5G UE can do. For example, basic functionality like finding base stations, connecting to a base station, or registering at the core network.

Second. We want to deviate wherever we want. This part then poses the requirement of being able to tell the framework where and how it should deviate from normal behaviour. To be more precise, there are two things we need to be able to control:

1. Message order: testing different states of the 5G system
2. Message content: testing the message processing in the different states

This is because different code is used to process the messages received in different connection states. Since we want to be able to test as much of the 5G system code as possible, we need to be able to send anything in any state.

To be able to send at any point, the attacker must adhere to the protocol for every step necessary to get to this point (first requirement) and then be able to send any message to test the implementation (second requirement).

Third. A straightforward way of implementing all of this would be to enable the sending of arbitrary messages (streams of bits) at the lowest digital protocol layer. This would certainly allow sending anything in any state and, by that, attacking, e.g., the authentication implementation, but also all other interfaces and protocol layers. The drawback is that to get to the wanted state, the attacker would basically need to implement many parts of the 5G protocols until they reach the point they want to attack. This leads us to the third and final requirement: the framework's usability. Usability here means it shall be relatively easy to understand the framework and implement vulnerability tests.

In summary, the primary goal of this work is to provide a holistic testing tool for mobile network security from the UE side that is easy to use.

Further requirements are:

- *Open Source*: the tool shall be made available to everyone who needs to enhance the security of a 5G system
- *Documentation*: to make the framework usable and understandable for everyone, it needs to be well documented
- *Update*: Since the 5G specifications are evolving permanently, maintaining the framework shall be easy.
- *Extendability*: extendability here means that it should be rather easy to add new testing functionality to the framework

The three primary and four soft goals constitute the requirements for the developed framework.

3 Related Work

In this section, we look at existing work in the field of security testing for 5G networks. There are quite a few papers that study 5G security and penetration testing. Some of them require direct access to the components that are to be tested or at least their interfaces. For example, some work tries to insert malicious messages between the base stations (gNB) and the core network [11,12,15].

Others only use simulation of the UE to test the gNB and core network [8]. This will allow for the testing of the necessary interfaces in most cases. However, there are scenarios where the pentester cannot directly access the interfaces of the system under test. For example, when opting for a private network solution from a vendor, the customer should be able to check the security of such a system. This is one of the scenarios in which our framework can help.

In addition, much work on fuzzing 5G systems already exists. Most of it uses the network interfaces directly, as described above. Although there are works that allow for testing a black box network, the focus is on finding the right fuzzing content here. Therefore, the question of how to bring the fuzzing content to the system is only a necessary step, often conquered with some hacky solution that is not very flexible. For example, "Berserker" [14] focuses on generating the fuzzing content with the help of the ASN.1 protocol descriptions given by the 4G/5G specifications. "5G RRC Protocol and Stack Vulnerabilities Detection via Listen-and-Learn" [18] uses machine learning to understand 5G traffic and then uses the gained knowledge to create messages for fuzzing.

Future 5G fuzzing research could massively benefit from a pentesting framework, as it is provided in our paper. Especially because the framework allows for testing many different endpoints and states of the 5G system. Therefore, researchers do not need to work on how to send the fuzzing messages to the relevant interfaces and can instead completely focus on creating good fuzzing messages.

Finally, there are some papers that provide somewhat similar functionality to the framework provided in our work. But those have some shortcomings or different focus points, which makes the creation of an extensive and easy-to-use framework necessary.

The following list provides an overview of all work we are aware of regarding utilising UEs for security testing of 5G systems.

- "An Automated Vulnerability Detection Method for the 5G RRC Protocol Based on Fuzzing" [17] is an OpenAirInterface [3] based framework. It focuses on the Radio Resource Control (RRC) layer, which might make it hard to test the core network with this tool, due to things like Non Access-Stratum (NAS) integrity checks and encryption. Also, the work is not open source, and we could not find any implementation.
- "An Experimental Testbed for 5G Network Security Assessment" [7] has a similar approach as we have in our paper, but uses srsRAN [5] as a basis for their UE implementation. Also, the source code is only available upon request, and it seems that altering the connection establishment messages is not directly possible (only injection in "already established communications between a UE and a base station" [7]).
- "Towards Automated Fuzzing of 4G/5G Protocol Implementations Over the Air" [10] seems to have a similar approach to ours. Here, the OpenAirInterface [3] UE code is modified to allow intercepting, modifying, and replaying packets. The problem is that the source code is only available upon request, and our requests were not answered. Another issue is that this work, similar to [17], might (based on the explanations given in the paper) have problems with sending correctly encrypted and integrity-protected NAS messages.
- "5G/O-RAN Security Automated Testing" [9] provides an OpenAirInterface [3] framework. The framework is also not open source, or at least not yet, or not for the general public ("This fuzzing tool being funded by the NTIA grant will be open sourced to the ORAN community" [9]). Again, from what

is written in the paper, it seems that NAS integrity checks and encryption could become a problem.

– "CovFUZZ: Coverage-based fuzzer for 4G&5G protocols" [16] provides an srsRAN [5] based framework and does fuzzing with it. The framework is not able to test 5G uplink (UE to network), only 4G downlink and uplink, and 5G downlink. Since investigating 5G uplink is our goal, this work can only be of conceptual help. In addition to that, we could not find the implementation online, although it is stated that the framework is open source.

– "A 5G and Beyond Testbed for Cybersecurity Research and Education" [6] also contains a security testing UE (most likely based on OAI [3]) as part of the work. But in this case, the framework is only a small section of the research done in the paper, and there are no concrete implementation descriptions or code.

– "Soft Tester UE: A Novel Approach for Open RAN Security Testing" [13] provides an srsRAN [5] based framework. Here, additional tools for white box testing are provided, and some practical fuzzing is carried out. We are not sure if the given framework can provide all the functionality we described in Subsect. 2.2, especially altering NAS messages could again be a problem. This work is the only one where we were able to find the code online as open source [4]. If one is more familiar with srsRAN than with OAI this framework could be an alternative to our OAI-based framework.

The presented collection of related work represents and discusses all relevant papers we found regarding our topic. Therefore, the research gap we try to close consists of a fully open source, well-documented, holistic framework for UE-based 5G pentesting.

4 Design of the Framework

This section briefly describes the design and implementation of our framework. Extensive documentation and detailed descriptions will be made available on GitHub [1].

4.1 Concept

Our framework is based on the UE software stack provided by OpenAirInterface (OAI). The basic idea of the framework is to add different interfaces to the OAI code, which allow influencing the behaviour of the UE. To match the requirements stated in Subsect. 2.2, we choose a three-layer architecture, as shown in Fig. 1.

First Layer. The first layer of our framework is the OAI code with the added interfaces. Layer one, therefore, provides the 5G UE capabilities, which allow our framework to interact with 5G networks and the control interfaces, which are to be used by the higher layers.

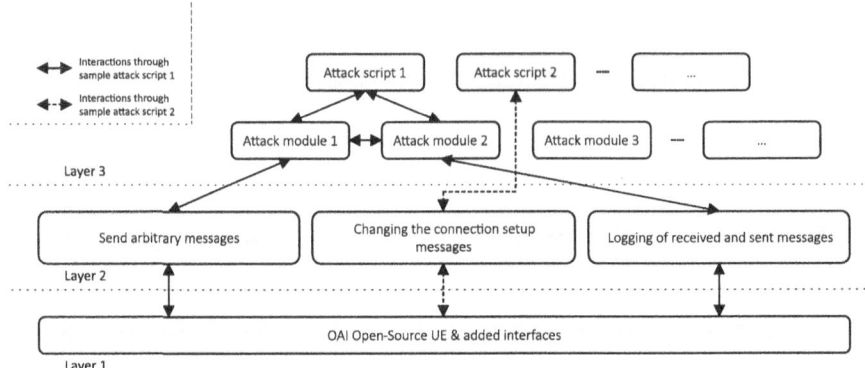

Fig. 1. Basic design of the 5G-Pentest-UE

To enhance maintainability, it is important on this layer to only add code and not change or remove anything. This will support easier upgrades to newer upstream versions of the OAI UE code. For the code added, there also has to be the possibility of disabling its execution to let our UE behave as a vanilla UE. Therefore, the execution of the added code is controlled by a configuration file. This means that if all framework functionalities are deactivated by this configuration file, the OAI UE will behave the same way as a normal, plain OAI UE would.

Second Layer. On the second layer, we now need to utilise the interfaces created on the first layer. To understand the three capabilities implemented on this layer, we need to recap what we want to accomplish.

Every 5G communication starts with establishing a connection. Here, the UE and the network negotiate different parameters and create the basis for practical use of the connection by exchanging control messages. This predefined message flow is time-critical, and being able to specify the messages sent on the fly is not helpful for us at the moment. Therefore, we implement a capability that allows us to predefine the connection establishment messages before starting the connection. This is done by creating the necessary fields in the configuration file. The control flow of the framework then works in a way that when the UE is executed, it checks if an alternative message is specified for a given connection establishment message and, if so, replaces the message that would usually be sent. By this, we are able to alter the connection establishment messages and test the involved message processing logic on the base station and the core network side.

In addition to being able to alter the connection establishment, we also want to be able to efficiently test all of the interfaces that are available on an existing connection. That means we want to be able to use the UE to send any data we want to the network after the connection is established. This is done by providing a REST-API inside the UE as shown in Fig. 2.

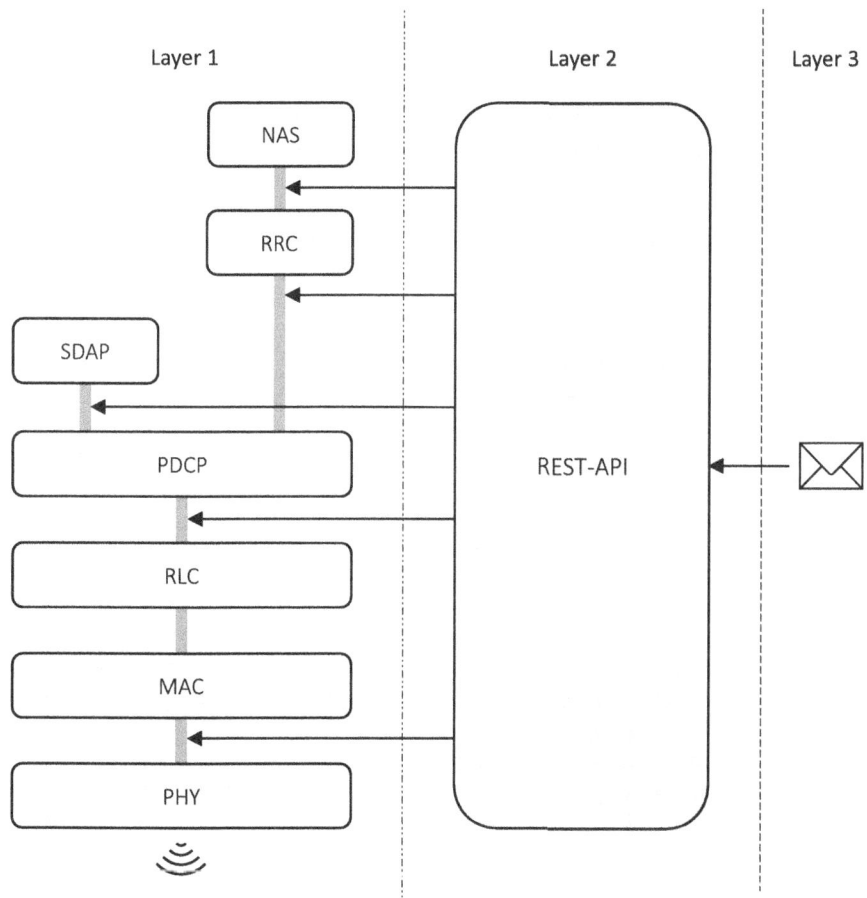

Fig. 2. Visualisation of the integration of the REST-Socket

Using the REST-API, one can let the UE insert a specific message on a given layer.

Besides adding means to influence what is sent by the UE, the framework also provides the capability to log everything sent or received by the UE. This enables the framework user to understand better what is happening and to react to specific messages sent by the network. The details of the log output (e.g., which messages at which layers should be logged) can be specified in the configuration file.

Third Layer. Although the two layers discussed so far already provide enough functionality to execute meaningful vulnerability testing, we added another logical layer to our design to make the framework easier and more efficient. Layer three contains generic and reusable modules that use and wrap the functionalities given on layer two. These modules combine common steps that happen in many attack paths. Separating these steps into modules makes the creation of new vulnerability tests easier.

For example, the framework user can automate the testing or create different attack scripts and analysis tools on this layer. An example for "Attack module 1" in Fig. 1 could be a module that takes inputs from the user, validates them, and sends them to the REST-API. Such a module could then be used by a proprietary fuzzing generator to eventually send the generated messages to the 5G network.

In summary, the attack modules on layer three implement common functionality shared among different attack scripts. The attack scripts themselves represent different vulnerability tests or attack ideas.

4.2   Implementation and Feature Set

This section describes some basic implementation details and the currently implemented features. A much more complete description will be provided in the GitHub repository [1].

Command Line Parameter. The first step of implementation was to add a command-line parameter to the OAI UE. This parameter allows us to specify a configuration file and, through that, activate the framework. If the parameter is not given when running the UE, it will behave like a vanilla OAI UE.

Configuration File. Inside the configuration file, which is in JSON format, we have three sections that allow us to control the three different capabilities at layer two. In the first section, we configure the REST-API. There, we have the option to activate or deactivate it and set the port number we want to use for the REST-API. In the second section, the connection establishment messages can be configured. Here, for every message of the connection establishment procedure, alternative message content can be specified by providing the message in hexadecimal format. The last part of the configuration file configures the logging capability. Here, we can independently activate/deactivate the output of sent and received messages at the MAC, RRC, NAS, and Data layer of the 5G protocol stack.

Code Structure. The configuration file and all other implementations except the interfaces added to the OAI code are located in a separate folder called "security_testing" inside the base directory of the OAI UE. The ability to exclude all of those additions is gained by including them inside IF-Statements, which only allows the execution if the command line parameter is specified and the corresponding configuration is active. For more information on why, where, and how the individual additions are included in the OAI code, please look at the documentation in the GitHub repository [1].

Feature Set. Regarding the current feature set, the framework provides the following capabilities:

- REST-API—the REST-API provides the ability to send any message content on the following layers:
  - NAS (Non Access-Stratum)
    * security protected as well as unprotected messages
  - RRC (Radio Resource Control)
    * SRB0 (Signaling Radio Bearer 0)
    * SRB1 (Signaling Radio Bearer 1)
    * SRB2 (Signaling Radio Bearer 2)
  - SDAP (Service Data Adaptation Protocol)
  - PDCP (Packet Data Convergence Protocol)
    * SRB1 (Signaling Radio Bearer 1)
    * SRB2 (Signaling Radio Bearer 2)
  - MAC (Medium Access Control)
- Connection establishment—for the connection establishment, the following messages can be adjusted
  - RRC Setup Request
  - RRC Setup Complete
  - NAS Registration Request
  - NAS Authentication Response
  - NAS Security Mode Complete
  - RRC Security Mode Complete
  - RRC Reconfiguration Complete
  - NAS Registration Complete
  - NAS Session Establishment Request
  - NAS Deregistration Request
- Message logging—the framework allows logging the received and transmitted messages on the following layers:
  - MAC
  - RRC
  - NAS
  - User data

5 Evaluation

In this section, we want to investigate if the proposed framework matches the requirements from Subsect. 2.2. We also want to discuss some practical tests we did with the framework and the results we gathered.

Requirements. In Subsect. 2.2, we set 3 main goals for the framework.

The **first goal** was to be able to adhere to the 5G specifications wherever needed. This goal is reached by allowing our framework to dynamically activate and deactivate all parts of added code and functionality.

The **second goal** was to be able to deviate wherever we want. Therefore, different interfaces were added to the OAI UE code. The possibilities given by those additions were sufficient for the investigations we did. However, some special attacks may require additional functionalities. The clear structure of the framework and the extensive documentation given in the GitHub repository will enable easy implementation of such possibly missing features.

The **third goal** was to enable the framework user to test different interfaces easily. We tried to reach this goal using a logical approach to the problem. With the connection establishment being time-critical, we allowed preconfiguring the involved messages inside the configuration file. For the fully connected state, after the connection establishment, we offer different interfaces to be able to create different attacks on different layers easily. Also, a logging feature was added to the framework to be able to output and, after that, process the received messages. This will enable the user to create adaptive attacks and, therefore, find complicated vulnerabilities in the network.

We want to evaluate the soft goals set in Subsect. 2.2 as follows. The first goal was to open source the whole framework and its documentation to be used as a basis for research and security testing of 5G networks. This is done via a GitHub repository [1]. With this repository, the second soft goal is also tackled. The repository contains the code we wrote and extensive documentation on the framework. In addition, there are examples of the usage of the framework, a tutorial on setting up a local testbed, and some documentation of the OAI UE. Also, a basic introduction to 5G and the protocol stack is available in the repository. The third and fourth soft goals were to make updates to the framework possible and allow easy extendability. We accomplish this by only making minimal additions to the OAI code and not changing anything. This has already proven to make it relatively easy to transfer the framework to a newer version of the OAI UE code, which is regularly updated, to add new features and stay up to date with the 5G specifications. Also, this, combined with the given documentation, should be very helpful for extending the framework's basic functionality. Besides that, extending also means implementing new test cases. Most of those test cases can already be realised with the available layer one and two functionality. Therefore, extending the framework may only mean adding some utility scripts to the third layer to be used by your test case.

Practical Evaluation. This paper is mainly about describing and publishing the framework we built. Nevertheless, we want to discuss some tests we did and what we learned. With the help of the framework, we discovered many different vulnerabilities in an existing open source implementation of the base station and the core network. Most of those vulnerabilities were crashes of the 5G stack (base station and core part) as well as other problems (e.g., deadlocks), leading to availability issues. For example, we found an infinite loop in the core network session management function (SMF). Here, a switch statement inside a loop was used to decrypt the message identifiers. Providing an identifier unknown to the switch statement caused the loop to run forever. This led to a situation where no UEs could register to the core network until the SMF was restarted.

Besides that, we also discovered an attack that allowed us to skip the authentication of the UE towards the core network. This vulnerability even allows for impersonating other UEs. This attack could be executed by rearranging and adjusting the connection establishment messages.

The issues found were reported to the developers of the 5G stack and are meanwhile mostly fixed.

In summary, we were able to make good use of our framework and improve some 5G implementations. In the future, we plan to extensively study different mobile network implementations to get an overall view of their security when assuming the malicious UE attacker model.

6   Conclusion

In this work, we present a framework for security testing of 5G networks. In the preceding sections, we described our requirements and goals, investigated related work and proposed and evaluated the framework. Our work closes the gap in open source, well-documented, and easy-to-use security testing software. This will allow future research to find and fix vulnerabilities in 5G protocol implementations faster.

Outlook. In the future, we want to use the framework extensively to test existing 5G implementations. Therefore, we want to combine the framework with existing fuzzing solutions, e.g., libfuzz [2]. In addition to that, we plan on creating specialised attacks and testing our assumptions in different networks. By that, we hope to gain a comprehensive overview of mobile network security investigated from the UE perspective.

Ethical Considerations. With regard to misuse of the framework for criminal activities, the large amount of existing work (partly also open source) on attacking mobile networks shows that attacks are possible in many different ways. For example, not much knowledge is necessary to implement an easy Fuzzer with the help of OAI or srsRAN UE. The difficulty is in implementing concrete attacks or finding the correct values to fuzz test. Our work does not provide help for those parts of the attack. Therefore, we believe that providing a framework that makes security testing easier will improve security in mobile networks rather than endanger it.

Acknowledgments. This work has been supported by the German Federal Office for Information Security (BSI) project 6G-ReS (grant no. 01MO23013D), the Federal

Ministry of Research, Technology and Space of Germany through the 6G-CampuSens project (grant no. 16KISK205) and by the Federal Ministry of Transport, Germany through the InnoDCon project (grant no. 19OI23013C). Additionally, the authors are also financed based on the budget passed by the Saxonian State Parliament in Germany.

Disclosure of Interests. The authors have no competing interests to declare that are relevant to the content of this article.

References

1. 5G-Pentest-UE GitHub Repository. https://github.com/Barkhausen-Institut/UE-based-5G-Pentesting-Framework. Accessed 12 June 2025
2. libFuzzer. https://llvm.org/docs/LibFuzzer.html. Accessed 30 Apr 2025
3. Open Air Interface GitLab. https://gitlab.eurecom.fr/oai/openairinterface5g. Accessed 17 Mar 2025
4. Soft Tester UE GitHub Repository. https://github.com/oran-testing/ran-tester-ue. Accessed 10 Apr 2025
5. srsRAN Project. https://www.srslte.com/. Accessed 09 Apr 2025
6. Almazyad, I., Elmadani, S., Hariri, S.: A 5G and Beyond Testbed for Cybersecurity Research and Education. In: 2024 IEEE/ACS 21st International Conference on Computer Systems and Applications (AICCSA), pp. 1–6 (2024). https://doi.org/10.1109/AICCSA63423.2024.10912627
7. Baccar, K., Lahmadi, A.: An Experimental Testbed for 5G Network Security Assessment. In: NOMS 2023-2023 IEEE/IFIP Network Operations and Management Symposium, pp. 1–6 (2023). https://doi.org/10.1109/NOMS56928.2023.10154283
8. Chianese, L., Granata, D., Palmiero, P., Rak, M.: Leveraging Threat Modelling for Effective Penetration Testing in 5G Systems. In: 2024 IEEE International Conference on Cyber Security and Resilience (CSR). pp. 180–185 (2024). https://doi.org/10.1109/CSR61664.2024.10679437
9. Dessources, D., Appiah-Mensah, S., Amato, C., Parikh, D., Bull, J.D., Burger, E.W.: 5G/O-RAN Security Automated Testing. In: MILCOM 2024 - 2024 IEEE Military Communications Conference (MILCOM), pp. 129–134 (2024). https://doi.org/10.1109/MILCOM61039.2024.10774015
10. Garbelini, M.E., Shang, Z., Chattopadhyay, S., Sun, S., Kurniawan, E.: Towards Automated Fuzzing of 4G/5G Protocol Implementations Over the Air. In: GLOBECOM 2022 - 2022 IEEE Global Communications Conference. pp. 86–92 (2022). https://doi.org/10.1109/GLOBECOM48099.2022.10001673
11. He, F., Yang, W., Cui, B., Cui, J.: Intelligent Fuzzing Algorithm for 5G NAS Protocol Based on Predefined Rules. In: 2022 International Conference on Computer Communications and Networks (ICCCN), pp. 1–7 (2022) https://doi.org/10.1109/ICCCN54977.2022.9868872
12. Mancini, F., Da Canal, S., Bianchi, G.: AMFuzz: Black-Box Fuzzing of 5G Core Networks. In: 2024 19th Wireless On-Demand Network Systems and Services Conference (WONS), pp. 17–24 (2024). https://doi.org/10.23919/WONS60642.2024.10449510
13. Moore, J., Abdalla, A.S., Ueltschey, C., Marojevic, V.: Soft Tester UE: A Novel Approach for Open RAN Security Testing. In: 2024 IEEE 100th Vehicular Technology Conference (VTC2024-Fall), pp. 1–5 (2024). https://doi.org/10.1109/VTC2024-Fall63153.2024.10757739

14. Potnuru, S., Nakarmi, P.K.: Berserker: ASN.1-based Fuzzing of Radio Resource Control Protocol for 4G and 5G. In: 2021 17th International Conference on Wireless and Mobile Computing, Networking and Communications (WiMob), pp. 295–300 (2021). https://doi.org/10.1109/WiMob52687.2021.9606317
15. Salazar, Z., Nguyen, H.N., Mallouli, W., Cavalli, A.R., Montes de Oca, E.: 5Greplay: a 5G Network Traffic Fuzzer - Application to Attack Injection. In: Proceedings of the 16th International Conference on Availability, Reliability and Security. ARES '21, Association for Computing Machinery, New York, NY, USA (2021). https://doi.org/10.1145/3465481.3470079,
16. Siroš, I., Singelée, D., Preneel, B.: CovFUZZ: Coverage-based fuzzer for 4G & 5G protocols (2024). https://arxiv.org/abs/2410.20958
17. Wang, H., Cui, B., Yang, W., Cui, J., Su, L., Sun, L.: An automated vulnerability detection method for the 5G RRC protocol based on fuzzing. In: 2022 4th International Conference on Advances in Computer Technology, Information Science and Communications (CTISC), pp. 1–7 (2022). https://doi.org/10.1109/CTISC54888.2022.9849690
18. Yang, J., Wang, Y., Tran, T.X., Pan, Y.: 5G RRC protocol and stack vulnerabilities detection via listen-and-learn. In: 2023 IEEE 20th Consumer Communications & Networking Conference (CCNC), pp. 236–241 (2023). https://doi.org/10.1109/CCNC51644.2023.10059624

Author Index

The manufacturer's authorised representative in the EU is Springer
Nature Customer Service Centre GmbH, Europaplatz 3, 69115 Heidelberg,
Germany. If you have any concerns regarding our products, please
contact ProductSafety@springernature.com

Printed and bound by CPI Group (UK) Ltd, Croydon, CR0 4YY

28/04/2026

02098527-0004